FORENSIC
APPLICATIONS
OF
THE
MMPI-2

Applied Psychology

Individual, Social, and Community Issues

Series Editor
Stevan E. Hobfoll, Kent State University

FORENSIC APPLICATIONS OF THE MMPI-2

YOSSEF S. BEN-PORATH
JOHN R. GRAHAM
GORDON C. N. HALL
RICHARD D. HIRSCHMAN
MARIA S. ZARAGOZA

EDITORS

APPLIED PSYCHOLOGY.   VOLUME 2
INDIVIDUAL, SOCIAL, AND COMMUNITY ISSUES

SAGE Publications
International Educational and Professional Publisher
Thousand Oaks   London   New Delhi

For information address:

Sage Publications, Inc.
2455 Teller Road
Thousand Oaks, California 91320
E-mail: order@sagepub.com

SAGE Publications Ltd.
6 Bonhill Street
London EC2A 4PU
United Kingdom

SAGE Publications India Pvt. Ltd.
M-32 Market
Greater Kailash I
New Delhi 110 048 India

Printed in the United States of America

Library of Congress Cataloging-in-Publication Data

Forensic applications of the MMPI-2 / edited by Yossef S. Ben-Porath, John R.
    Graham, Gordon C. N. Hall, Richard D. Hirschman, and Maria S. Zaragoza.
        p. cm.— (Applied psychology ; v. 2.)
        Papers presented at the 6th annual Kent Psychology Forum, 1994,
    and sponsored by Kent State's Psychology Department.
        Includes bibliographical references and index.
        ISBN 0-8039-7013-7 (cloth : alk. paper)
        1. Psychology, forensic. 2. Evidence, expert—United States.
    3. Psychological tests—Law and legislation—United States.
    4. Minnesota Multiphasic Personality Inventory. I. Ben-Porath,
    Yossef S. II. Kent State University. Dept. of Psychology.
    III. Kent Psychology Forum (6th: 1994: Kent, Ohio) IV. Series.
    KF8965.F67 1995   95-12873
    614'.1—dc20

This book is printed on acid-free paper.

95 96 97 98 99 10 9 8 7 6 5 4 3 2 1

Production Editor: Gillian Dickens

Contents

Preface

In April 1994, a small group of researchers and practitioners gathered in Ohio's Amish country at the Inn at Honey Run for the *Sixth Annual Kent Psychology Forum*. The Forum, sponsored by Kent State's Psychology Department through its Applied Psychology Center, convenes annually to provide a vehicle for generating scholarly discourse on issues pertaining to the application of psychological research.

The 1994 meeting was devoted to discussing Forensic Applications of the MMPI-2. Eleven researchers were invited to present papers in particular areas of expertise. Each of these papers is a chapter in the present volume. In addition to the researchers, seven clinical and legal practitioners from the community and eight graduate students participated in the Forum. Drafts of all of the chapters were distributed to all participants before the meeting. After each presentation the entire group discussed the paper just presented. Additionally, presenters received feedback from the group during informal meetings over the course of the conference. After the Forum, authors were asked to revise their chapters based on the feedback they received during the meeting and from the editors.

This volume is intended first and foremost for use by scholars in the area of forensic psychology. The authors of each chapter present a review of the psychological and legal literature pertaining to specific areas of forensic practice, and they discuss the empirical literature concerning relevant applications of the MMPI-2. The volume is therefore appropriate for use as a general reference to forensic applications of the MMPI-2. It could be assigned for use in graduate-level courses in forensic psychology and advanced psychological assessment seminars. Additionally, although not written specifically to address the practice of forensic psychological assessment, the book will be of interest to clinical and legal practitioners who wish to keep abreast of the state of the art in forensic psychological assessment.

The chapters included in this volume address major issues in forensic applications of the MMPI-2. Authors were asked to review the legal basis and the current empirical knowledge base pertaining to their topics. In addition, authors were asked to specify needs and directions for additional empirical research.

In the first chapter, Ben-Porath and Graham discuss the background of forensic uses of the test. They review the historical and scientific foundations of forensic applications of the MMPI-2. The potential strengths and weaknesses of the MMPI-2 as a tool for forensic psychological evaluations are discussed. In Chapter 2, Ogloff describes the legal community's perspective on forensic psychological assessment in general, and the use of objective tests such as the MMPI-2 in particular. The legal basis of forensic psychological assessment including relevant case law, the role of psychological testing in expert testimony, and a discussion of current positions within the legal community regarding the legal standing of psychological assessment data are presented. In Chapter 3, Weiner presents an overview of psychometric issues that should be considered when conducting forensic psychological evaluations. Psychometric issues that are relevant to using the MMPI-2 in forensic psychological evaluations are highlighted. In Chapter 4, Berry provides a review of the empirical literature on the detection of distortion with the MMPI-2 in forensic evaluations. After providing a general overview of this topic, the chapter focusses specifically on empirical findings regarding various MMPI-2 scales as indicators of response distortion.

Chapters 5 and 6 address issues related to the use of the MMPI-2 in criminal justice settings. Rogers and McKee discuss uses of the MMPI-2 in the assessment of criminal responsibility. The empirical literature on application of the MMPI-2 in such evaluations is reviewed. Questions about the ability of the MMPI-2 to address specific legal standards of criminal responsibility are discussed and some new data pertaining to this topic are presented. Next, Megargee and Carbonell review the empirical literature on uses of the MMPI-2 in correctional settings. The chapter provides an update on the revised Megargee

Classification System, and describes other ways in which the MMPI-2 can be used in correctional settings.

Chapters 7 through 10 address applications of the MMPI-2 in civil court proceedings. Heilbrun and Heilbrun review the empirical literature on use of the MMPI-2 in risk assessment. A general framework for risk assessment is presented and the utility of the MMPI-2 in evaluations of risk is discussed. Next, Butcher describes ways in which the MMPI-2 can be used in civil court proceedings involving personal injury claims. The research base and legal foundations for this application of the MMPI-2 are presented. Use of computer-generated interpretations in this area is highlighted. In the next chapter, Nelson provides an overview of uses of the MMPI-2 in forensic evaluations of individuals who are known or suspected of being neuropsychologically impaired. The empirical literature on the relation between neuropsychological impairment and scores on the MMPI-2 is reviewed. The potential roles and limitations of the MMPI-2 in a forensic neuropsychological test battery are discussed. In the final chapter of this section Otto and Collins provide an overview of the uses of the MMPI-2 in domestic court proceedings. The utility of the test in child custody evaluations is discussed and the empirical literature pertaining to this application of the MMPI-2 is reviewed.

In Chapter 11, Graham, Ben-Porath, and Stafford highlight the major themes that emerged at the *Sixth Annual Kent Psychology Forum* including topics in need of further research and suggestions for training in this area. The chapter also identifies the limits of scientifically grounded uses of the MMPI-2 in forensic psychological evaluations.

In addition to the authors who wrote chapters for this volume, we wish to acknowledge the important contributions of the practitioners who participated in the *Sixth Annual Kent Psychology Forum*. The practitioners were Daniel M. Davis, Clinical Director of the Buckeye Ranch in Grove City, Ohio; James J. Karpawich, a private practitioner in Akron, Ohio; John Kenny, a neuropsychologist with the Cleveland VA Medical Center; Steven M. Neuhaus, Director of the Cuyahoga County Juvenile Court Diagnostic Clinic; the Honorable Judith H. Nicely, Judge, Summit County Domestic Relations Court; and John Vuillemin, attorney with Mentzer, Vuillemin & Robinson. We are especially indebted to Kathleen P. Stafford, Director of the Court Psycho-Diagnostic Clinic in Akron, Ohio, for her assistance in helping to identify some of the scholars who participated in the forum, coordinating the efforts of the community practitioners, as well as her contributions during the Forum.

Eight graduate students in our clinical psychology training program also contributed to the discussions that shaped the chapters included in this volume. They are Stephanie C. Boerger, Heather A. Chapman, Andrea R. Fox-Boardman, Robert W. Gallagher, Brian K. McClinton, Devanand P. Somwaru, Lynda A. Stein, and Rodney E. Timbrook. We also wish to acknowledge the assistance of Stevan E. Hobfoll, director of the Applied Psychology Center in coordinating events at the *Sixth Annual Kent Psychology Forum.* Our coeditors, Gordon C. Nagayama Hall, Richard Hirschman, and Maria S. Zaragoza, provided very helpful assistance in reviewing chapters for this volume.

The chapters of this volume identify a number of areas where the MMPI-2 can contribute substantially to forensic psychological evaluations. They also point to a number of areas that require additional empirical research. It is our hope that this volume will help to stimulate and guide this research.

YOSSEF S. BEN-PORATH
JOHN R. GRAHAM

Scientific Bases of Forensic
Applications of the MMPI-2

YOSSEF S. BEN-PORATH

JOHN R. GRAHAM

The MMPI was developed in a medical setting during the late 1930s and early 1940s to serve as a screening instrument for the differential diagnosis of psychopathology. Although soon after its publication the test's diagnostic classification abilities were found to be limited, researchers were able to develop alternative, clinically useful applications of the MMPI (for examples of these early studies, see Welsh & Dahlstrom, 1956). Common to these and subsequent efforts was the conviction that empirical research must guide clinical uses of the MMPI. With its body of empirical literature now encompassing well over 7,500 publications, we can state with confidence that no psychological test rests on stronger scientific foundations than the MMPI and its updated version, the MMPI-2.[1]

Nowhere is the importance of the scientific bases of the MMPI-2 more essential and indispensable, than when the inventory is used in forensic settings. Forensic uses of psychological tests are subject to strict legal oversight

1

and scrutiny.[2] In Chapter 2 of this volume, Ogloff details the basis for admissibility of MMPI-2 findings in legal proceedings. A primary and necessary (although not always sufficient) condition for the admissibility of MMPI-2 data is that they be scientifically valid. Thus, the MMPI-2's solid empirical scientific foundations allow forensic psychologists to rely on the test in a variety of evaluations. Pope, Butcher, and Seelen (1993) provide a comprehensive practical guide to forensic applications of the MMPI-2. In this volume, we focus primarily on the research on which these applications are based.

Even critics of forensic psychology acknowledge that the MMPI can provide useful information in legal settings, although they challenge the ways in which some psychologists rely on MMPI/MMPI-2 data when serving as expert witnesses (Faust & Ziskin, 1988; Ziskin, 1981a). We concur with Faust and Ziskin's (1988) assertion that expert opinion in forensic matters must be scientifically grounded. However, we disagree with their conclusion that psychologists have little scientifically based information to offer the legal system. Our major goal in assembling this volume was to invite a diverse group of scholars to review and assess the scientific merit of various forensic applications of the MMPI-2.

A common theme throughout this book is that forensic psychologists labor on firm scientific footing in some applications of the MMPI-2, and on unsatisfactorily shaky foundations in others. It is our hope that this volume will help make forensic practitioners aware of the limits of scientifically supported applications of the MMPI-2. We also seek to encourage researchers to expand these boundaries. Thus we asked the authors of each chapter in this book to identify areas that are in need of additional research.

Before turning to the specific topics covered in this book, we present in this chapter a general overview of the scientific foundations of forensic applications of the MMPI/MMPI-2. The authors of each of the subsequent chapters address in greater detail the specific research base that pertains to the topics of their chapters. In this chapter, we also briefly address the implications for forensic assessment of the release of the updated version of the test, the MMPI-2.

Scientific Foundations

Over the years, several lines of research have evolved that are directly relevant to forensic applications of the MMPI-2. The first of these includes studies using the MMPI to predict behaviors or class membership that would be relevant to the criminal justice system. Common to these studies is the use of the MMPI as an independent variable and evaluation of its capacity to predict various dependent variables (e.g., criminal behavior).

A second set of studies has used the MMPI as a dependent variable to characterize the personalities of various classes of criminals. Dahlstrom, Welsh, and Dahlstrom (1975) refer to these as studies of the "Dynamics of Criminal Behavior." Investigators who conducted these studies were interested in unearthing personality characteristics that predispose an individual to criminal behavior. Both lines of research (i.e., studies of criminal behavior in which the MMPI serves as either a dependent or independent variable) rely on correlational analyses that can be used to identify the statistical association between MMPI scale scores and criminal behavior.

A broader line of research with direct relevance to forensic applications of the MMPI-2 includes studies of the test's ability to measure various symptoms of psychopathology. Many forensic psychological evaluations are conducted to answer referral questions that require information regarding the presence or absence of psychological disorder. These include, but are not limited to, evaluations of competence to stand trial, criminal responsibility, civil competence, parental fitness, and the emotional sequelae of physical and psychological trauma.

Finally, an important task of the forensic examiner is to evaluate the likelihood that the individual being assessed is disingenuous in her or his self-presentation. The stakes involved in many forensic examinations are high, ranging from one's life or freedom, custody over one's children, and may include potentially large sums of money. Consequently, significant motivation to distort one's self-presentation may exist. The MMPI-2's ability to detect and quantify such attempts makes it potentially an invaluable tool in forensic assessment.

We turn now to a brief review of the historical roots of each of these important lines of research: (a) the MMPI-2 as a predictor of criminal behavior, (b) the MMPI-2 as a measure of psychopathology, and (c) the MMPI-2 as a measure of self-presentation.

THE MMPI-2 AS A PREDICTOR OF CRIMINAL BEHAVIOR

The use of the MMPI-2 to study criminal populations dates back to its development. One of the original clinical scales was labeled Psychopathic

Deviate (later abbreviated Pd, and also referred to as Scale 4). In describing their development of this scale, McKinley and Hathaway (1944) explained that they were interested in identifying people who could be classified into the asocial or amoral types of psychopathic personality. Their initial derivation sample consisted of psychiatric inpatients diagnosed with this condition at the University of Minnesota Hospital. These patients were of both genders (although there were more women than men) and ranged in age from 17 to 22 years. Characteristic complaints included stealing, lying, truancy, alcohol abuse, forgery, and similar delinquencies.

McKinley and Hathaway were interested in developing a scale that would predict membership in a psychiatric class defined, among other important features, by criminal behavior. Thus it is not surprising that one of their initial cross-validation samples consisted of 100 men incarcerated at a federal reformatory. McKinley and Hathaway (1944) reported that the final version of Scale 4 was in fact highly elevated in this incarcerated sample in comparison to the "normal" sample.

As noted at the outset of this chapter, the original clinical scales, including Scale 4, proved largely unsuccessful at the narrow task of diagnostic classification. This failure had as much to do with the shortcomings of the then-prevalent nosology and the inherent unreliability of psychodiagnosis as it did with the scales themselves. Nevertheless, countless studies have shown that Scale 4 is predictive of the *characteristics* of people who were described in the 1940s as psychopathic deviates and today would be labeled psychopaths, sociopaths, or antisocial personalities. Thus, the existence of Scale 4 on the clinical profile made the MMPI a potentially useful tool for research with various forensic populations.

Dahlstrom, Welsh, and Dahlstrom (1975) noted that one of the earliest applications of the MMPI was in the study of juvenile delinquents. Capwell (1945) investigated the personality characteristics of delinquent girls by comparing their MMPI scores to those of nondelinquent girls. Not surprisingly, Scale 4 was the best predictor of membership in the delinquent sample.

Hathaway and Monachesi (1951, 1957) carried out one of the most extensive and comprehensive longitudinal investigations of the precursors of juvenile delinquency ever conducted. They administered the MMPI to large samples of ninth grade students, first in Minneapolis and then throughout the state of Minnesota, and investigated the test's ability to predict future juvenile delinquency as documented by police and public records. They identified several MMPI clinical scales that were predictive of subsequent juvenile delinquency. Specifically, they found that youngsters with elevated scores on Scales 4, 8, and 9 were more likely to be classified subsequently as juvenile delinquents whereas elevations on Scales 2, 5, and 0 predicted a lesser likelihood of this classification.

These early studies of juvenile delinquency represent an important line of MMPI research that has continued since the publication of the test. In addition to juvenile delinquents, researchers have studied the MMPI profiles of numerous other classes and subclasses of criminal offenders, including murderers (e.g., Kalischman, 1988), other violent offenders (e.g., Hale, Zimostrad, Duckworth, & Nichols, 1988), sex offenders (e.g., Hall, Graham, & Shepherd, 1991), and substance abusers (e.g., Craig & Dres, 1989). The specifics of these studies and an evaluation of their methodology and findings exceed the scope of this chapter. Of relevance, however, is the existence of this extensive body of literature to which forensic examiners may turn if it is relevant to a specific evaluation.

THE MMPI-2 AS A MEASURE OF PSYCHOPATHOLOGY

Earlier in this chapter, we observed that the original intent of Hathaway and McKinley was to develop a test that could identify, in an individual, the presence of various forms of psychopathology. In addition to psychopathic deviance, Hathaway and McKinley developed scales to predict the presence of hypochondriasis, depression, hysteria, paranoia, psychasthenia, schizophrenia, and hypomania. It is sometimes mistakenly stated that the MMPI was developed from a blind empirical (i.e., entirely atheoretical) perspective. This depiction of the MMPI's development is inaccurate because the test's authors labored under the influence of the then-prevalent Kraepelinian nosology. Their selection of potential items for the MMPI was based on the findings of previous investigators and the authors' own clinical experience. This approach yielded a broad, diverse, and, as it turned out, exceptionally fruitful set of items.

Hathaway and McKinley's attempts to develop differentially diagnostic scales were largely unsuccessful. Nevertheless, early users and investigators of the MMPI found that scores on individual scales, and particularly various combinations of scale elevations, were reliably predictive of various symptoms of psychopathology. Following Meehl's (1954, 1956) advocacy for reliance on statistical prediction in assessment, researchers conducted comprehensive empirical investigations of the statistical correlates of MMPI scale scores and code types, culminating in the publication of comprehensive codebooks for MMPI interpretation (e.g., Gilberstadt & Duker, 1965; Marks & Seeman, 1963). Many of the MMPI's empirical correlates identified in this research involved symptoms of various forms of psychopathology.

Several significant trends have occurred in MMPI research since the publication of the test's initial codebooks. First, researchers have continued to study the empirical correlates of the test's clinical scales and the code types they form. The results of these efforts are summarized in current guides to MMPI-2 interpretation (e.g., Butcher & Williams, 1992; Graham, 1993; Greene, 1991). Additionally, many new scales were developed for the test, some very directly related to various symptoms or syndromes of psychopathology (e.g., the MacAndrew Alcoholism Scale [MacAndrew, 1965]; the Post-Traumatic Stress Disorder Scale [PTSD; Keane, Malloy, & Fairbank, 1984]).

Common to many later scale development efforts was a move away from the method of scale construction—empirically contrasted groups—used in the development of the original clinical scales. An alternative approach that has received increasing acceptance among constructors of MMPI scales has been the development of content-based scales. In contrast to the original method, in which item-content played no role in the assignment of items to scales, the content-based approach emphasizes item content as a primary criterion for scale construction. Statistical analyses are also vital to ensure that content-based item selection yields statistically homogeneous scales. A set of content scales developed by Wiggins (1966) represented the most comprehensive attempt to employ a combined content-based/statistical approach to the construction of MMPI scales. Most of the Wiggins content scales measured various symptoms or syndromes of psychopathology.

An important advantage of content-based scales is that, by virtue of their method of construction, they are considerably more homogeneous in content and more internally consistent statistically than are scales constructed according to the method of empirical keying. Consequently, in contrast to empirically based scales, scores on content-based scales are much more directly interpreted as reflecting individual differences along a continuum of symptomatic severity. For example, a T-score score on the Wiggins Depression content scale could be interpreted as reflecting the individual's level of expressed depression more directly than a T-score score on clinical Scale 2.

There are two reasons for this discrepancy. First, like all of the clinical scales, Scale 2 is plagued by so-called subtle items, items bearing no conceptual relevance to the assessment of depression. These items were assigned to Scale 2, in part because Hathaway and McKinley did not have sufficient resources to cross-validate item selections using large samples. Consequently, items were assigned to the clinical scales based on undetected Type I errors. As a result, the ratio of signal to noise on the clinical scales is lower than on content-homogeneous scales such as the Wiggins content scales.

A second reason why content-based scales are more directly interpretable than the clinical scales is the inherent heterogeneity of the latter. Hathaway and McKinley were well aware of this feature of the clinical scales and viewed it positively, as a necessary and accurate reflection of the heterogeneous nature of the syndromes themselves. However, with movement away from heterogeneous syndromes to homogeneous symptoms (i.e., from the diagnostic group of people suffering from major depression to the dimensional construct of depression), the heterogeneous nature of the clinical scales became a hindrance to their interpretation. This problem was overcome by reliance on code types that allowed for classification of individuals into potentially homogeneous classes based on their MMPI profile configuration.[3] The Harris and Lingoes subscales, which allowed for the dissection of a heterogeneously generated score on a full clinical scale into more homogeneous content-based scores on its subscales, were also useful. The significant psychometric and interpretive benefits of content-based scales were acknowledged in the prominent role played by the MMPI-2 Content Scales (Butcher, Graham, Williams, & Ben-Porath, 1990) in the revision of the test. This issue is discussed further in a subsequent part of this chapter.

In conclusion, much of the empirical MMPI/MMPI-2 literature involves the identification of test-correlates reflecting symptoms or syndromes of psychopathology. Based on this literature, the MMPI-2 can be used to generate statements about the likely presence in an individual of various symptoms of psychopathology; many of these may be pertinent to forensic evaluations. Although it is important to recognize that the MMPI-2 cannot be used to generate specific diagnoses, the empirical literature supports the test's utility in symptomatic detection as well as personality description.

THE MMPI-2 AS A MEASURE OF SELF-PRESENTATION

The original MMPI was published at a time when clinicians were expressing great skepticism about the utility of self-report measures of psychopathology and personality. Ellis (1946)· published a highly critical review of self-report measures citing their susceptibility to distortion as a particularly worrisome weakness. Meehl (1945), responding to criticism that MMPI scores may be affected by how the test taker interprets the meaning of test items, suggested that, although pertinent to most other then-contemporary self-report instruments, concerns about item content were far less relevant to the MMPI. Meehl further asserted that it is not the content of an individual's response to a given item that is interpreted with the MMPI, but rather the empirical correlates of this response. Meehl's argument applied as well to concerns regarding intentional distortion, because interpretation of MMPI scores is based on empirical correlates, rather than inferences about what a test taker may have meant to say.

The developers of the MMPI believed that their method of scale construction and reliance on empirical data for test interpretation made their instrument less susceptible to the effects of distortion. Nonetheless, they concluded that it would be advantageous to develop scales allowing the test interpreter to detect any irregularities in the test taker's approach to the inventory. The first two scales developed for the MMPI, labeled *validity scales,* were L and F.

The L scale was designed to identify an overt, overly positive self-presentation that is referred to generally as "faking good." The F scale was developed to identify deviant test protocols. Initially, Hathaway and McKinley were interested in developing a measure that would detect unusual test patterns that result from scoring errors or reading and comprehension difficulties. However, it soon became evident that the F scale was sensitive to intentional efforts to generate an overly negative self-presentation, referred to generically as "faking bad."

Meehl and Hathaway (1946) described one of the first MMPI "faking" studies in which subjects were tested twice, once under standard instructions and a second time under instructions to "fake" their test results in either a positive or negative direction. Results of this study supported the use of scales L and F as indicators of intentional distortion. Additionally, Meehl and Hathaway (1946) developed the K scale as a measure of unconscious, defensive, positive distortion and the K-Correction as a tool for overcoming the effects of "K-like" responding.

Inclusion of these validity scales on the original MMPI reflected the test developers' opinion that intentional as well as unintentional distortion of one's self-presentation could attenuate the validity of the clinical scales. Use of validity scales became a standard component of MMPI interpretation and one of the hallmarks of the original MMPI. These scales proved to be of particular relevance in assessment situations in which individuals may be motivated to generate a positively or negatively distorted self-presentation.

The availability of a wide variety of empirically supported validity scales on the MMPI-2 makes the instrument particularly useful in forensic psychological evaluations. These scales often are the only scientific source of information regarding positive or negative malingering. As stated at the outset of this chapter, forensic psychologists are required to base their expert opinions on scientifically grounded data and observations. The examiner's *impression* that an individual is faking a psychotic condition will carry considerably greater weight if it is supported by a similar indication on the MMPI-2. In Chapter 4 of this volume, Berry presents a detailed review of current approaches to detecting distortion with the MMPI-2.

EVALUATION OF THE SCIENTIFIC FOUNDATIONS OF FORENSIC APPLICATIONS OF THE MMPI

We reviewed three areas of MMPI research that are of particular relevance to forensic assessment. Of the three areas reviewed, the use of the MMPI as a predictor of criminal behavior has been the least fruitful. Although it is possible to generate valid interpretive statements regarding the general likelihood that an individual has in the past engaged in illegal behavior, or that he or she may in the future engage in such behavior, there is currently little scientific support for the use of the test as a predictor of specific forms of criminal conduct (e.g., sex offending, violent offending, crimes against property).

Attempts to develop taxonomies or subclassifications of offenders have also met with equivocal success. A notable exception in this area is the system for classifying criminal offenders with the MMPI developed by Megargee and his colleagues (Megargee, Bohn, Meyer, & Sink, 1979). This system, now updated for the MMPI-2, is supported by an exceptionally solid body of scientific evidence. Megargee and Carbonell review this research and present up-to-date information on the system in Chapter 6 of this volume.

Forensic psychologists who use the MMPI-2 to identify the presence and level of severity of symptoms of psychopathology can rely on a generally well-founded body of scientific evidence that is summarized in several MMPI-2 interpretive guides (e.g., Butcher & Williams, 1992; Graham, 1993; Greene, 1991). There exist, however, some MMPI interpretive practices that are not supported by scientific evidence.

Most noteworthy of these scientifically questionable practices is reliance on the so-called "subtle" and "obvious" scales of the MMPI. These scales, rationally developed by Wiener and Harmon (1946) without any empirical verification, are subscales of the MMPI clinical scales. The subtle scales are made up of some items that bear little or no intuitive association with the constructs measured by the scales on which they are scored, and other items that appear to be scored in a counterintuitive direction. The obvious scales are comprised of items deemed by Wiener and Harmon to be related directly to, and scored in accordance with, the construct of interest.

Wiener and Harmon constructed these scales by conducting a rational review of each clinical scale's items and classifying them as subtle or obvious based on the criteria just mentioned. They believed that these scales would allow the test interpreter to detect intentional attempts to display a distorted self-presentation and to measure more subtle individual personality differences that occur within a normal, nondeviant population. Greene (1991) advocates use of the MMPI subtle scales in the assessment of personality and psychopathology. However, scientific research indicates that they are invalid for this purpose. For example, Weed, Ben-Porath, and Butcher (1990) suggested that the subtle scales are made up primarily of random noise. They provided support for this assertion by constructing pseudosubtle scales through a process of random item selection. Weed et al. (1990) found that their pseudosubtle scales performed similarly to the Wiener-Harmon Subtle scales. Both the subtle and pseudosubtle scales were essentially uncorrelated with extratest validity data.

Greene (1991) also advocates the use of an index comprised of the difference between the sum of the subtle scale T-scores and the sum of the obvious scale T-scores. He reasons that a significant discrepancy between these two sums could indicate either over- or underreporting of psychopathology. The rationale for this approach is that individuals will be far less able to intentionally distort their scores on the subtle scales and considerably more able to distort their scores on the obvious scales. Thus, any attempt to fake good or bad will be registered as a significant discrepancy between the two sets of scales.

However, this strategy is predicated on the assumption that both sets of scales, subtle and obvious, are equally valid measures of the same constructs. As already noted, there exists scientific evidence to refute this assumption. Thus, it is not surprising that scientific evidence also refutes the utility of the Subtle-Obvious index as an incrementally useful measure of profile validity

(Berry, Baer, & Harris, 1991; Timbrook, Graham, Keiller, & Watts, 1993; Weed et al., 1990). Although the Subtle-Obvious index is sensitive to intentional distortion, research suggests that this is entirely a function of the effect of distortion on the obvious scales and that this index does not add to the ability of the MMPI-2 to detect distortion beyond what is accomplished with the standard validity scales.

With the exception of the questionable practice of using the subtle-obvious index in assessing protocol validity, of the three areas of research reviewed in this section, use of the MMPI-2 as a measure of self-presentation is the most strongly supported by empirical research. It is also one application of the MMPI-2 that is relevant to virtually any forensic assessment. In Chapter 4 of this volume, Berry describes and discusses the current scientific literature in assessing profile validity with the MMPI-2 and its implication for forensic assessment.

Implications of the MMPI's
Revision for Forensic Assessment

With the revision of the MMPI and publication of the MMPI-2 in 1989 (Butcher, Dahlstrom, Graham, Tellegen, & Kaemmer, 1989), forensic psychologists are presented with challenges and opportunities. Although met initially with resistance from some quarters, the revised version of the MMPI-2 is now accepted as an improvement over the original. A recent survey of members of the Society for Personality Assessment indicated that the vast majority of those sampled now use the MMPI-2 (Webb, Levitt, & Rajdev, 1993). The authors projected that within the next few years, all but a small proportion of psychologists will have adopted the MMPI-2 in their practice. In this section, we discuss issues pertaining to the transition from the MMPI to the MMPI-2 in forensic assessment and some of the advantages offered by the MMPI-2 to forensic psychology.

TRANSITION TO THE MMPI-2

At least some of the resistance to the MMPI-2 stemmed from concerns about the comparability of MMPI and MMPI-2 findings. If, as suspected by some authors, the two versions of the test were to yield discrepant scores, which scores should be interpreted? After all, nearly all of the empirical foundations of the test were established with the original version of the inventory. Because the empirical, scientific bases of MMPI-2 interpretation are particularly vital to, and most likely to be scrutinized in forensic assessment, the issue of MMPI/MMPI-2 comparability is of particular importance to forensic psychologists.

Data published in the MMPI-2 manual and other places fueled some of the concerns about MMPI/MMPI-2 comparability. These data suggested the possibility that at least one third of all cases scored with the two sets of norms (original and revised) yielded discrepant code types. Such a level of incongruence could raise significant questions about forensic applications of the MMPI-2. Because, as stated earlier, a test's scientific foundation is vital to its admissibility in forensic settings, and because the empirical foundation of most MMPI applications was established with the original version of the test, it was vital that research be conducted to explore further the question of comparability across the two versions of the inventory.

Ben-Porath and Butcher (1989a) demonstrated that minor editorial changes in a small number of MMPI-2 items did not change these items' psychometric functioning. In a second study, Ben-Porath and Butcher (1989b) demonstrated that subjects in a nonclinical sample who took the MMPI once and the experimental form that yielded the MMPI-2 a second time were as likely to produce comparable scores as were subjects who took the original MMPI twice. Several subsequent studies that sought to examine the comparability of MMPI/MMPI-2 scores were methodologically flawed in that, unlike Ben-Porath and Butcher (1989b), they did not include a sample of subjects who took the MMPI twice to measure the baseline of temporal instability of MMPI scores (e.g., Duckworth, 1991).

Recent empirical analyses by Graham, Timbrook, Ben-Porath, and Butcher (1991) and conceptual analyses by Tellegen and Ben-Porath (1993) indicate substantial congruence for single scale scores and code types based on MMPI and MMPI-2. However, it is vital that code types be well-defined if we are to expect any level of stability across or within different versions and administrations of the test. Adequate code-type definition requires that the lowest scale in the code type be at least five T-scores points higher than the next highest scale on the profile. Such well-defined code types are highly congruent across the two sets of norms, and they are far more likely to be replicated on retest. Although Dahlstrom (1992) has questioned the use of well-defined code types, Tellegen and Ben-Porath (1993), in response to Dahlstrom's assertions, articulated a compelling psychometric rationale for reliance on well-defined code types.

ADVANTAGES OF THE MMPI-2
IN FORENSIC ASSESSMENT

With the issue of continuity between the two versions of the test resolved to most scholars' satisfaction, it is appropriate to discuss some of the important psychometric advantages of the MMPI-2 in terms of forensic psychological assessment. These include both the collection of new norms for the test and the introduction of new scales.

First and foremost among the advantages offered by the MMPI-2 is the availability of new normative data. Standard scores are now based on an up-to-date sample of individuals who well represent the general population of the United States with regard to several demographic variables including race, age, and place of residence. Unlike the original normative sample—whose subjects resided primarily in rural areas, were Caucasian, and had a low education level—the MMPI-2 normative sample is larger and considerably more diverse. Thus the forensic psychologist plotting MMPI-2 T-scores is using a significantly more appropriate standard than that of the original MMPI.

In addition to being more contemporary than norms collected over 50 years ago, the new norms were collected using current practices of MMPI administration. Subjects in the original normative sample completed the MMPI by sorting randomly administered items printed on individual index cards into three categories: "true," "false," and "cannot say." In contrast, contemporary test takers are most likely to take the booklet form of the inventory, in which the instructions discourage the "cannot say" response option.

Another advantage of the MMPI-2 norms is that, unlike the original sample, the new normative sample is ethnically diverse. Although proportional sampling is not sufficient to ensure nonbiased testing of minorities, it is more likely to eliminate biases than nonrepresentative sampling. A recent study by Ben-Porath, Shondrick, and Stafford (1995) indicates that the MMPI-2 does not generate substantially different scores for Caucasians and African Americans sampled at a forensic diagnostic center. Timbrook and Graham (1994) have found similarly that there are few clinically meaningful differences between nonclinical Caucasian and African American samples. Moreover, they found the MMPI-2 clinical scales to be comparably valid in the two groups.

In addition to current and more appropriately collected norms, the MMPI-2 offers several new scales that are likely to be useful in forensic assessment. Of particular relevance is the introduction of new validity scales. These scales, Fb, VRIN, and TRIN, add substantially to the examiner's ability to identify and quantify various invalidating test-taking approaches. As discussed earlier in this chapter, the availability of empirically grounded validity scales on the original MMPI makes the test particularly well suited for use in forensic evaluations. In Chapter 4 of this volume, Berry reviews the results of studies that show that the MMPI validity scales function on the MMPI-2 as effectively as they did on the original version of the test. He also evaluates some of the new validity scales introduced with the MMPI-2.

Another set of scales introduced with the MMPI-2 are the MMPI-2 Content Scales (Butcher et al., 1990). These scales were the main vehicle for introducing new item content to the MMPI-2. The volume just cited (Butcher et al., 1990) provides extensive information on the construction and psychometric functioning of these scales. Data presented by Butcher et al. (1990) indicate that the MMPI-2 Content Scales are reliable and have promising initial validity data.

As discussed earlier in this chapter, statistically internally consistent and conceptually homogeneous content scales have the potential to make significant contributions to the assessment of symptoms of psychopathology. Although they are still new to the test, and thus have considerably less scientific backing than the clinical scales, initial evaluations of the MMPI-2 Content Scales are generally positive (e.g., Ben-Porath, Butcher, & Graham, 1991; Ben-Porath, McCully, & Almagor, 1993). Furthermore, it is likely that as we learn more about their empirical qualities these scales will take on an increasing role in forensic assessment. For now, they must be relegated to a secondary role because of their relative novelty in comparison to the MMPI-2 clinical scales. Nonetheless, initial research with these scales in a forensic setting has yielded promising results (Ben-Porath & Stafford, 1993).

Conclusions

In a recent survey of forensic psychologists, Lees-Haley (1992) found that the MMPI/MMPI-2 is the psychological test most frequently used in forensic evaluations. The research reviewed in this chapter indicates that psychologists who use the MMPI-2 in forensic evaluations can base their interpretations on sound scientific findings. The following chapters in this volume review in greater detail the legal, psychometric, and empirical bases of forensic applications of the MMPI-2 in a variety of forensic settings and contexts. Common to all of these reviews is the conclusion that forensic psychologists may indeed rely on convincing scientific evidence in their use of the MMPI-2 but must avoid exceeding the boundaries of this evidence. In the concluding chapter of this volume we will summarize what the authors of the various chapters have identified as the boundaries of scientifically based MMPI-2 interpretation in forensic assessment and we will identify areas in need of additional research.

Notes

1. Throughout this chapter we refer primarily to the MMPI-2 unless we are describing a specific study that was conducted with the original version of the test, the MMPI. This reflects our view, supported by empirical evidence cited later in this chapter, that the scientific bases of the MMPI carry over to the MMPI-2.

2. This is not to suggest that nonforensic applications of the MMPI-2 do not need to rely on equally valid empirical foundations. Nonetheless, forensic assessment is, by virtue of its application in the legal domain, likely to be subjected to particular scrutiny.

3. However, as discussed later in this chapter and reviewed by Tellegen and Ben-Porath (1993), not all code-type classification systems yield homogeneous groups of subjects.

References

Ben-Porath, Y. S., & Butcher, J. N. (1989a). The psychometric stability of rewritten MMPI items. *Journal of Personality Assessment, 53,* 645-653.

Ben-Porath, Y. S., & Butcher, J. N. (1989b). The comparability of MMPI and MMPI-2 scales and profiles. *Psychological Assessment: A Journal of Consulting and Clinical Psychology, 1,* 345-347.

Ben-Porath, Y. S., Butcher, J. N., & Graham, J. R. (1991). Contribution of the MMPI-2 content scales to the differential diagnosis of psychopathology. *Psychological Assessment: A Journal of Consulting and Clinical Psychology, 3,* 634-640.

Ben-Porath, Y. S., McCully, E., & Almagor, M. (1993). Incremental validity of the MMPI-2 content scales in the assessment of personality and psychopathology by self-report. *Journal of Personality Assessment, 61,* 557-575.

Ben-Porath, Y. S., Shondrick, D. D., & Stafford, K. P. (1995). MMPI-2 and race in a forensic diagnostic center. *Criminal Justice and Behavior, 22,* 19-32.

Ben-Porath, Y. S., & Stafford, K. P. (1993, August). *Empirical correlates of MMPI-2 scales in a forensic diagnostic center: A preliminary report.* Paper presented at the meeting of the American Psychological Association, Toronto, Ontario, Canada.

Berry, D., Baer, R. A., & Harris, M. J. (1991). Detection of malingering on the MMPI: A meta-analysis. *Clinical Psychology Review, 11,* 585-598.

Butcher, J. N., Dahlstrom, W. G., Graham, J. R., Tellegen, A., & Koemmer, B. (1989). *The Minnesota Multiphasic Personality Inventory-2 (MMPI-2): Manual for administration and scoring.* Minneapolis: University of Minnesota Press.

Butcher, J. N., Graham, J. R., Williams, C. L., & Ben-Porath, Y. S. (1990). *Development and use of the MMPI-2 Content Scales.* Minneapolis: University of Minnesota Press.

Butcher, J. N., & Williams, C. L. (1992). *Essentials of MMPI-2 and MMPI-A interpretation.* Minneapolis: University of Minnesota Press.

Capwell, D. F. (1945). Personality patterns of adolescent girls: II. Delinquents and nondelinquents. *Journal of Applied Psychology, 29,* 289-297.

Craig, R. J., & Dres, D. (1989). Predicting DUI recidivism with the MMPI. *Alcohol Treatment Quarterly, 6,* 97-103.

Dahlstrom, W. G. (1992). Comparability of two-point high-point code patterns from the original MMPI norms to MMPI-2 norms for the restandardization sample. *Journal of Personality Assessment, 59,* 153-164.

Dahlstrom, W., Welsh, G., & Dahlstrom, L. (1975). *An MMPI handbook: Volume 1: Clinical interpretation, 1.* Minneapolis: University of Minnesota Press.

Duckworth, J. C. (1991). The Minnesota Multiphasic Personality Inventory-2: A review. *Journal of Counseling and Development, 69,* 564-567.

Ellis, A. (1946). The validity of personality questionnaires. *Psychological Bulletin, 43,* 385-440.

Faust, D., & Ziskin, J. (1988). The expert witness in psychology and psychiatry. *Science, 241,* 31-35.

Gilberstadt, H., & Duker, J. (1965). *A handbook for clinical and actuarial interpretation.* Philadelphia: W. B. Saunders.

Graham, J. R. (1987). *The MMPI: A practical guide* (2nd ed.). New York: Oxford University Press.

Graham, J. R., Timbrook, R. E., Ben-Porath, Y. S., & Butcher, J. N. (1991). Congruence between MMPI and MMPI-2: Separating fact from artifact. *Journal of Personality Assessment, 57,* 205-215.

Greene, R. L. (1991). *The MMPI-2/MMPI: An interpretive manual.* Needham Heights, MA: Allyn & Bacon.

Hale, G., Zimostrad, S., Duckworth, J., & Nichols, D. (1988). Abusive partners: MMPI profiles of male batterers. *Journal of Mental Health Counseling, 10,* 214-224.

Hall, G. C. N., Graham, J. R., & Shepherd, J. B. (1991) Three methods for developing MMPI taxonomies of sex offenders. *Journal of Personality Assessment, 56,* 2-13.

Hathaway, S. R., & Monachesi, E. D. (1951). The prediction of juvenile delinquency using the Minnesota Multiphasic Personality Inventory. *American Journal of Psychiatry, 108,* 469-473.

Hathaway, S. R., & Monachesi, E. D. (1957). The personalities of pre-delinquent boys. *Journal of Criminal Law, Criminology, and Police Science, 48,* 149-163.

Kalischman, S. C. (1988). MMPI profiles of women and men convicted of domestic homicide. *Journal of Clinical Psychology, 44,* 847-853.

Keane, T. M., Malloy, P. F., & Fairbank, J. A. (1984). Empirical development of an MMPI subscale for the assessment of combat-related post traumatic stress disorder. *Journal of Consulting and Clinical Psychology, 52,* 888-891.

Lees-Haley, P. (1991). MMPI-2 F and F – K scores of personal injury malingerers in vocational neuropsychological and emotional distress claims. *American Journal of Forensic Psychology, 9,* 5-14.

MacAndrew, C. (1965). The differentiation of male alcoholic outpatients from non-alcoholic psychiatric patients by means of the MMPI. *Quarterly Journal of Studies on Alcohol, 26,* 238-246.

Marks, P. A., & Seeman, W. (1963). *The actuarial prediction of personality: An atlas for use with the MMPI.* Baltimore: Williams and Wilkins.

McKinley, J. C., & Hathaway, S. R. (1944). The MMPI: V. Hysteria, hypomania, and psychopathic deviate. *Journal of Psychology, 28,* 153-174.

Meehl, P. E. (1945). The dynamics of "structured" personality tests. *Journal of Clinical Psychology, 1,* 296-303.

Meehl, P. E. (1954). *Clinical versus statistical prediction: A theoretical analysis and a review of the evidence.* Minneapolis: University of Minnesota Press.

Meehl, P. E. (1956). Wanted—A good cookbook. *American Psychologist, 11,* 263-272.

Meehl, P. E., & Hathaway, S. R. (1946). The K factor as a suppressor variable in the MMPI. *Journal of Applied Psychology, 30,* 525-564.

Megargee, E. I., & Bohn, M. J., Jr. (with Meyer, J., Jr., & Sink, F.). (1979). *Classifying criminal offenders: A new system based on the MMPI.* Beverly Hills, CA: Sage.

Pope, K. S., Butcher, J. N., & Seelen, J. (1993). *The MMPI, MMPI-2, & MMPI-A in court.* Washington, DC: American Psychological Association.

Tellegen, A., & Ben-Porath, Y. S. (1993). Code-type comparability of the MMPI and MMPI-2: Analysis of recent findings and criticisms. *Journal of Personality Assessment, 61,* 489-500.

Timbrook, R. E., & Graham, J. R. (1994). Ethnic differences on the MMPI-2 *Psychological Assessment, 6,* 212-217.

Timbrook, R. E., Graham, J. R., Keiller, S. S. W., & Watts, D. (1993). Comparison of the Wiener-Harmon Subtle-Obvious scales and the standard validity scales in detecting valid and invalid MMPI-2 profiles. *Psychological Assessment, 5,* 53-61.

Webb, J. T., Levitt, E. E., & Rajdev, R. (1993, March). *After three years: A comparison of the clinical use of the MMPI and MMPI-2.* Paper presented at the 53rd Annual Meeting of the Society for Personality Assessment, San Francisco, CA.

Weed, N. C., Ben-Porath, Y. S., & Butcher, J. N. (1990). Failure of the Wiener and Harmon Minnesota Multiphasic Personality Inventory (MMPI) scales as personality descriptors and as validity indicators. *Psychological Assessment: A Journal of Consulting and Clinical Psychology, 2,* 281-285.

Welsh, G. S., & Dahlstrom, W. G. (1956). *Basic readings on the MMPI in psychology and medicine.* Minneapolis: University of Minnesota Press.

Wiener, D. N., & Harmon, L. R. (1946). *Subtle and obvious keys for the MMPI: Their development* (Minneapolis V.A. Advisement Bulletin, No. 16). Minneapolis, MN: Minneapolis Veterans Administration.

Wiggins, J. (1966). Substantive dimensions of self-report in the MMPI item pool. *Psychological Monographs, 80*(22, Whole No. 630).

Ziskin, J. (1981). *Coping with psychiatric and psychological testimony.* Marina del Rey, CA: Law and Psychology Press.

2

The Legal Basis of Forensic Applications of the MMPI-2

JAMES R. P. OGLOFF

Throughout this book, the authors discuss the psychological basis of foren-sic psychological assessment and, in particular, the use of the MMPI-2, across a range of civil and criminal legal matters. Given the scope of this book, it is not difficult to imagine how widely accepted the MMPI-2,[1] and its predecessor the MMPI, have been in the legal system. Indeed, a computerized search of a legal database revealed 279 cases at the state level in which the MMPI or MMPI-2 was employed for some purpose (see Table 2.1). Similarly, 183 cases were obtained in a search of federal cases (see Table 2.2). As Tables 2.1 and 2.2 reveal, the MMPI has been relied on in court in a range of civil and criminal cases for a variety of purposes. It should be emphasized here that not all trial court decisions are reported and cataloged on the database. The

AUTHOR'S NOTE: The author gratefully acknowledges the assistance of Kevin Douglas, David Lyon, and Kathleen Ogloff, who assisted with the legal research. Correspondence may be addressed to James R. P. Ogloff, Department of Psychology, Simon Fraser University, Burnaby, British Columbia, Canada V5A 1S6.

Table 2.1 The Use of the MMPI in State Cases in the United States

Case Issues/Causes of Actions	Number of Cases[a]
Custody/access/parenting	67
Worker's compensation/employment disability	47
Criminal responsibility/insanity defense	36
Sexual offenses	36
Murder/death penalty	31
Automobile accident	14
Child abuse	12
Malingering	11
Competency to stand trial	11
Sentencing/treatability	9
Personal injury/negligence	9
Employment screening/discrimination	8
Juvenile delinquency/transfer to adult court	8
Substance abuse	5
Dangerousness	4
Medical malpractice	3
Police brutality/fitness of officers	3
Revocation/suspension of attorney licenses	3
Civil commitment	2
Post-traumatic stress disorder	2

a. Because some cases presented more than one issue concerning the MMPI, the number of cases totals more than the 279 cases identified. In addition to the above cases, several issues arose in only one case: assault, battered wife syndrome, denial of parole, divorce, driving under the influence, school screening, suspension of a psychologist's license to practice, and suspension of a teacher's license.

cases presented in Tables 2.1 and 2.2 are primarily appellate-level cases. Probably, the MMPI has been used in several times the number of cases identified in the tables. Furthermore, the vast majority of the cases presented in the tables did not explicitly address either the admissibility of the MMPI or the extent to which the courts relied—or failed to rely—on the information provided from the MMPI. Instead, the courts most often mentioned that the MMPI had been administered and presented in an expert's report or in the expert's *viva voce* testimony. Nonetheless, the tables provide useful information about the nature of cases in which the MMPI has been employed.

To fully consider the forensic applications of the MMPI-2, it is important to focus on the reception that psychological assessments and the MMPI-2 have received in the legal arena. Consideration of the use of the MMPI-2 in the legal system requires a two-step process. The first issue is a threshold matter

Table 2.2 The Use of the MMPI in Federal Cases in the United States

Case Issues/Causes of Actions	Number of Cases [a]
Worker's compensation/employment disability	106
Employment screening/discrimination	16
Criminal responsibility/insanity defense	15
Competency to stand trial	8
Murder	8
Cruel and unusual jail/prison confinement	6
Malingering	4
Personal injury	4
Court martial	3
Competency to be executed	2
Motor vehicle accident	2
Transfer of juvenile to adult court	2
Wrongful death	2

a. Because some cases presented more than one issue concerning the MMPI, the number of cases totals more than the 183 cases identified. In addition to the above cases, several issues arose in only one case: challenging attorney's fees, civil rights action against police, competency to waive rights, competency of witness, counterfeiter profile, defamation/pain and suffering, denial of aviation certificate, discrimination on grounds of mental disorder, mail fraud, negligence, negligent treatment, rape/sodomy, tax evasion, and threatening the president of the United States.

requiring a consideration of the admissibility of the MMPI-2 in court. If the judge decides to permit the psychologist to testify as an expert, the judge[2] must then decide the probative value of the testimony (i.e., the extent to which the testimony assists the judge, the jury, or both in deciding the case).

The questions concerning the admissibility of expert testimony based on the MMPI-2, and the extent to which the judge or jury finds that evidence compelling in arriving at a decision, form the basis of this chapter. Indeed, in studying how these questions have been answered, a great deal can be learned about the law's perspective on forensic psychological assessment in general, and the use of objective tests such as the MMPI-2 in particular. Therefore, the chapter begins with a general discussion of the legal basis for admitting expert psychological testimony, including the role of psychological testing in expert testimony. After reviewing the admissibility of expert psychological testimony, the discussion turns to an analysis of the extent to which judges and juries have, or have not, relied on the MMPI-2 results to address a variety of issues in the legal system. Throughout the chapter, information will be addressed regarding the legal standing of psychological assessment data in general, and the utility of the MMPI-2 in particular.

The Admissibility of Expert
Psychological Testimony

Before a psychologist will be permitted to testify as an expert, the judge must decide that the expert testimony meets the legal criteria to be held admissible. If the psychologist relies on test results to support his or her testimony, the judge also must make a determination concerning the admissibility of the test results. In the United States, questions of the admissibility of expert testimony fall within the jurisdiction of both state and federal courts. Therefore, there is some variability in the rules that govern the admissibility of expert testimony. In this chapter, the discussion will focus on the admissibility of expert testimony as governed by the Federal Rules of Evidence (FRE), 1976. Although the FRE is federal law, many states have incorporated at least some portion of the FRE into their evidentiary law. In interpreting the FRE, attention will be paid to a recent decision of the United States Supreme Court that considered the standard of acceptance for the admission of scientific evidence (*Daubert v. Merrell Dow Pharmaceuticals, Inc.*, 1993).

Prior to the adoption of the FRE, courts relied on the "*Frye* test" to determine whether the scientific evidence on which expert testimony is based should be admitted into evidence at trial. In *Frye v. United States* (1923), the defendant attempted to introduce results of a form of lie detector test. In rejecting the evidence, the court specified the standard for admitting scientific evidence:

> Just when a scientific principle or discovery crosses the line between the experimental and demonstrable stages is difficult to define. Somewhere in this twilight zone the evidential force of the principle must be recognized, and while courts will go a long way in admitting expert testimony deduced from a well-recognized scientific principle or discovery, the thing from which the deduction is made must be sufficiently established to have gained general acceptance in the particular field in which it belongs. (p. 1014)

Thus, the *Frye* test has been used to ensure that the scientific evidence on which expert testimony is based is "generally accepted" by the field in which it is offered. To satisfy the *Frye* test, an expert witness who offered an opinion based on a psychological test had to demonstrate not only that the test is generally accepted, but also that it is used in the relevant areas of psychology and that the techniques employed in conducting the evaluation comported with the state of the art in the field.

The *Frye* test enjoyed widespread use and endorsement by federal and state courts until Congress adopted the FRE in 1976. Since that time, considerable controversy arose regarding the extent to which *Frye* remained applicable, with different courts arriving at different conclusions (see *DeLuca v. Merrell Dow Pharmaceuticals,* 1990; *United States v. Shorter,* 1987). Finally, in 1993, the United States Supreme Court resolved the controversy by holding that the *Frye* test's general acceptance requirement "is not a necessary precondition to the admissibility of scientific evidence under the Federal Rules of Evidence" (*Daubert v. Merrell Dow Pharmaceuticals,* 1993, p. 2799).

In *Daubert,* two infants and their parents brought suit against a pharmaceutical company, arguing that the mothers' prenatal ingestion of the drug Bendectin had caused serious birth defects in the infants. During the trial, an expert testified that the corpus of scientific test results on the drug did not show that it was a risk factor for birth defects. As a result, the trial court decided in favor of the drug company. On appeal, the United States Court of Appeal for the Ninth Circuit relied on the *Frye* test and affirmed the lower court's decision. In overruling the decision, the Supreme Court held that nothing in the FRE incorporated *Frye*'s general acceptance rule, and that "a rigid 'general acceptance' requirement would be at odds with the 'liberal thrust' of the Federal Rules and their general approach of relaxing the traditional barriers to 'opinion' testimony" (*Daubert v. Merrell Dow Pharmaceuticals,* 1993, p. 2794).

In their decision in *Daubert,* the Court provided considerable commentary about the ways in which the FRE should be employed by courts when deciding whether to admit expert testimony based on scientific evidence. This commentary will be reviewed in the following discussion of the sections of the FRE pertaining to expert testimony. The evidentiary questions that courts address when deciding whether to admit expert testimony are outlined in Table 2.3. It may be useful to refer to the table while reviewing the following information.[3]

I. IS THE EXPERT TESTIMONY
ABOUT THE MMPI-2 RESULTS RELEVANT?

The first consideration to be made before any evidence, including expert testimony, is admitted, is whether the evidence is relevant (see FRE 402). Perhaps the most broadly defined rule of evidence is that of relevancy. Essentially all evidence that is relevant is admissible, providing that evidence comports to other legal requirements (e.g., constitutional and legislative

Table 2.3 Decision Model for Assessing the Admissibility of Expert Testimony About the MMPI-2

I. Is admission of MMPI-2 results relevant to the case?

    A. Will admission of the MMPI-2 results make some fact more probable or less probable than it would be without the evidence?
        If NO→STOP, testimony is INADMISSIBLE
        If YES→CONTINUE

    B. Is some matter related to mental state or personality at issue in the case?
        If NO→ STOP, testimony is INADMISSIBLE
        If YES→CONTINUE

II. Does the probative value of the expert testimony based on the MMPI-2 results outweigh the prejudicial impact?
    If NO→STOP, testimony is INADMISSIBLE
    If YES→CONTINUE

III. Will the proposed expert testimony based on MMPI-2 results assist the trier of fact in its determination?

    A. Is the MMPI-2 scientifically valid?
        If NO→STOP, testimony is INADMISSIBLE
        If YES→CONTINUE

    B. Are the MMPI-2 results relevant to the matters at issue in the case?
        If NO→STOP, testimony is INADMISSIBLE
        If YES→CONTINUE

IV. Does the witness qualify as an expert in administering and interpreting the MMPI-2?
    If NO→STOP, testimony is INADMISSIBLE
    If YES→CONTINUE

NOTE: In some states, the *Frye* test may be employed to determine whether the MMPI-2 has gained general acceptance in psychology or psychiatry for the purposes of addressing the question at issue in the case.

provisions).[4] Evidence is considered relevant when it has "any tendency to make the existence of any fact that is of consequence to the determination of the action more probable or less probable than it would be without the evidence" (FRE 401). The rule of relevancy is intentionally broad, leaving trial courts with considerable discretion to determine whether evidence is relevant (*Daubert v. Merrell Dow Pharmaceuticals,* 1993, p. 2794).

A. Will admission of the MMPI-2 results make some fact more probable or less probable than it would be without the evidence? To be considered relevant, an expert's testimony, therefore, must assist the decision maker to determine whether some important issue of the case is true. Any piece of evidence that makes the issue in question more or less likely to have occurred is generally considered to be relevant and admissible, provided the other conditions reviewed next and in Table 2.3 are met.

B. Is some matter related to mental state, personality, or character at issue in the case? With respect to the admissibility of expert testimony based on the MMPI-2, some issue about the mental state, personality, or character of a defendant in a criminal matter, or party in a civil matter, will have to be in question for the court to consider admitting such testimony. As Tables 2.1 and 2.2 make clear, there is a very broad range of cases in which the MMPI-2 has been considered relevant, and of information based, at least implicitly, on the test that has been admitted into evidence. In fact, as will become apparent in the second half of this chapter when individual cases addressing the admissibility of the MMPI-2 are discussed, the issue of relevance typically does not present a hurdle for admitting MMPI-2 results or interpretations into evidence. Rather, the question becomes the probative value of the MMPI-2 results.

II. IS THE PROBATIVE VALUE OF THE EXPERT TESTIMONY OUTWEIGHED BY ITS PREJUDICIAL AFFECT?

Once the court has determined that the proposed expert testimony based on the results of an MMPI-2 is relevant, the court must decide whether the expert testimony will be unduly prejudicial. FRE 403 provides that "evidence may be excluded if its probative value is substantially outweighed by the danger of unfair prejudice." This provision is of particular concern in those cases involving expert testimony where it is feared that the expert's qualifications and use of "scientific" instruments, such as the MMPI-2, may be so impressive that the jury (or judge) might give the expert's testimony undue weight, thus "prejudicing" the verdict.

To admit expert testimony, the court must be assured that the value of the expert's testimony will not be unduly outweighed by the expert's influence on the jury. This provision may be of some concern for the MMPI-2 because the trier of fact typically will not have any knowledge of psychological testing or, in particular, of the MMPI-2. As a result, the trier of fact may be particularly persuaded by an expert who uses an empirically based measure, such as the MMPI-2, to support his or her opinion. Because the judge or jury may put undue weight on the expert's testimony, the courts have concerns about the potential prejudicial nature of expert testimony based on the MMPI-2. However, if the jury learns about the specific empirical support for the MMPI-2 and whether it has been validated for the purpose for which it is intended to be used at trial, then the jury may not be unduly swayed by the expert's testimony.

Some cases are discussed later in this chapter in which judges have been reluctant to allow expert testimony based on the MMPI-2 for matters such as deciding whether a defendant meets the "profile" for a certain kind of offender (see *People v. Berrios*, 1991; *State v. Byrd*, 1992; *State v. Elbert*, 1992). In these cases, judges have expressed concern about providing the jury with information from the MMPI-2 because it may be highly prejudicial due to the "scientific" nature of the test and because it may not be particularly valid given the lack of evidence supporting such profiles. After the court has determined whether the expert testimony is relevant and that its probative weight outweighs its prejudicial value, then the court can turn to a direct review of the expert testimony itself.

III. WILL THE PROPOSED EXPERT TESTIMONY ASSIST THE TRIER OF FACT IN ITS DETERMINATION?

For expert testimony to be admissible under FRE 702, it must assist the trier of fact in making its decision. An expert may not testify unless the matter is beyond the ken (knowledge or understanding) of a layperson (*Dyas v. United States,* 1977). To be admissible, therefore, the MMPI-2 results may only be used in expert testimony if they provide the judge or jury with information that is beyond the understanding of laypersons. Also, it must assist them in reaching the legal decision.

Part of the decision of whether the expert testimony would assist the trier of fact has revolved around the scientific foundation of the information being considered. Where the *Frye* test[5] would have been used to resolve such concerns previously, the United States Supreme Court wrote in the *Daubert* (1993) case that

> "general acceptance" is not a necessary precondition to the admissibility of scientific evidence under the Federal Rules of Evidence, but the Rules of Evidence—especially Rule 702—do assign to the trial judge the task of ensuring that an expert's testimony both rests on a *reliable foundation* and *is relevant to the task at hand*. Pertinent evidence based on scientifically valid principles will satisfy those demands. (p. 2799, italics added)

Next, I discuss the need for deciding whether the MMPI-2 (a) has a reliable foundation and (b) is relevant to the matters at issue in the case, to ultimately decide whether its results will assist the trier of fact in deciding on a verdict.

A. Is the MMPI-2 scientifically valid? In Footnote 11 of their decision, the Supreme Court in Daubert (1993, p. 2796) provided further guidance about what they meant by terms such as "evidentiary reliability" and "scientific knowledge." There, the Court informed us that an assessment of scientific knowledge, as is mentioned in FRE 702, "entails a preliminary assessment of whether the reasoning or methodology underlying the testimony is scientifically valid" (p. 2796). In addition, the Court noted that scientific validity asks the question "does the principle support what it purports to show?" (p. 2795). Therefore, when determining whether the MMPI-2 may be admitted, courts will decide whether the test measures what it is intended to measure. On this general question, the answer will almost certainly be "yes." Indeed, as is made evident by the discussions throughout this chapter, the MMPI and MMPI-2 are empirically derived measures that have been extensively validated and tested. A more difficult question courts must address, and the one to which I now turn, is whether the MMPI-2 has been scientifically validated for the purpose of the questions raised at trial.

B. Are the MMPI-2 results relevant to the matters at issue in the case? As many of the cases that will be discussed show, it is particularly important to consider the specific purpose for which the MMPI was employed and for which it is intended to be used at trial (see State v. Elbert, 1992).[6] Thus it is important for clinicians who employ the MMPI-2 for a specific purpose to ensure that there is empirical support for that purpose. Furthermore, lawyers must be aware, taking into consideration relevant evidentiary issues, of the importance of establishing a foundation for admitting expert testimony based on the MMPI-2 in a particular case.

IV. DOES THE PROPOSED
WITNESS QUALIFY AS AN EXPERT IN
ADMINISTERING AND INTERPRETING THE MMPI-2?

Once the court determines that the techniques on which the proposed expert testimony are based are scientifically valid for the purposes raised at trial, the court must decide whether the proposed witness is qualified as an expert in administering and interpreting the MMPI-2 (FRE 702). As FRE 702 indicates, a witness may qualify as an expert based on his or her training or education, knowledge, skill, or experience.

Typically, it is not difficult for licensed mental health professionals to qualify as experts. For example, when faced with the question of whether a person with a master's degree who was licensed to practice in Virginia could be admitted as an expert witness, the Supreme Court of Virginia held that the test to determine whether the psychologist could be admitted as an expert "must depend upon the nature and extent of his knowledge" (*Rollins v. Commonwealth*, 1966, p. 750). In that case, the psychologist had several years of experience and, in fact, had testified as an expert in some 40 cases; and the court ruled that he should have been admitted as an expert. By contrast, in *Landis v. Commonwealth* (1978), a person with a master's degree in psychology with relatively little experience (e.g., a one year internship), was not permitted to testify as an expert psychologist in court. Thus duly trained and licensed psychologists (or other mental health professionals) will probably be admitted as experts in their profession.

Again, it is relatively easy for a duly qualified mental health professional to be qualified as an expert with respect to administering and interpreting the MMPI-2. This is particularly true of clinical psychologists who are typically trained to administer and interpret the test. As an example of the relative ease with which one may be qualified as an expert with respect to the MMPI, the Missouri Court of Appeals allowed a physician to testify about a defendant's mental state (*Bussell v. Leat*, 1989). During her examination, the physician, who was not trained in psychiatry, administered "several tests" to the defendant, including the MMPI. On appeal, the physician's qualifications to administer and interpret the MMPI were questioned. In holding that the physician's testimony was admissible, the appellate court noted that her medical training included "some psychiatry rotations," and that "she possesses a bachelor of arts degree in *clinical* psychology [and] . . . while in undergraduate school, she studied the administration and evaluation of the MMPI test" (p. 101, italics added).[7] By contrast, psychologists have been challenged regarding their testimony about mental illness based on the MMPI—although they typically are permitted to testify (see *State v. Gardner*, 1992).

In summary, to be admissible, expert testimony based on the MMPI-2 must be relevant to the issues in the case, and its probative value must outweigh its prejudicial impact. If these two general requirements are met, expert testimony about the MMPI-2 will be admissible in the form of opinion or otherwise (see FRE 701) if it can be demonstrated that (a) an issue at question is beyond the understanding of the trier of fact and the decision reached by the trier of fact would benefit as the result of special expertise regarding the MMPI-2, (b) the MMPI-2 is scientifically valid, and (c) the MMPI-2 is valid for the purposes of addressing an issue in dispute in the case. Finally, the proffered witness must have expertise in administering and interpreting the MMPI-2. Although the United States Supreme Court has held that the Frye test has been superseded by the FRE, it should be noted that because the FRE is federal legislation, and the Supreme Court only addressed that federal legislation, some state courts may still require satisfaction of the *Frye* test. A detailed analysis of the state-by-state consideration of *Frye* or "*Frye*-like" requirements is beyond the scope of this chapter. Practitioners should determine the extent to which the "general acceptance" rule is relied on in their own jurisdictions.

As mentioned at the outset, the question of the admissibility of expert testimony regarding the MMPI-2 may be considered as the "threshold" test. Indeed, if a judge decides that the testimony will not be admitted, the testimony will not be heard by the jury, and will not be entered into evidence at the trial. Once the judge decides to admit the evidence, the question becomes to what extent the judge and/or jury relied on the MMPI-2 evidence in reaching a verdict. In the second half of this chapter, several cases are presented in which courts specifically discussed the use of the MMPI in their decisions.

An Analysis of Cases Concerning the Use of the MMPI

Having reviewed the admissibility of expert psychological testimony concerning the MMPI-2, I now turn to an analysis of the extent to which judges and juries have—and have not—relied on MMPI-2 results to address a variety of issues in the legal system. It is important to note that the courts did not explicitly consider the probative effect of the MMPI in all of the cases mentioning the MMPI. The only use those cases serve here is to demonstrate (see Tables 2.1 and 2.2) that the use of the MMPI in reported cases in both state and federal courts has been quite extensive. The cases discussed next are organized into two broad categories: criminal law matters and civil law matters. Within those categories, the cases are grouped according to the specific nature of the case. To some extent, the organization is arbitrary. Some of the issues that arise in a particular section may be relevant between or across other sections.

CRIMINAL LAW MATTERS

Criminal responsibility/insanity defense. Not surprisingly, the MMPI has been used quite extensively in assessments of defendants' criminal responsibility (see Tables 2.1 and 2.2). Indeed, to the extent that mental illness or disorder is required for all insanity defense standards, a finding of mental illness is a necessary condition of the insanity defense. Given the MMPI's utility in identifying mental illness, it has been found useful in cases where the question of the existence of a mental disorder is at issue.

In a recent case, the Supreme Judicial Court of Massachusetts allowed the testimony of a psychologist who administered the MMPI-2 to the defendant to determine whether he was suffering from a mental illness (*Commonwealth v. Kappler,* 1993). The defendant, a 60-year-old retired anesthesiologist, drove his car onto a footpath adjacent to a highway, injuring one pedestrian and killing a second. At the trial, the defendant raised the insanity defense. Three experts testified for the defendant. One expert witnesses testified that the defendant suffered from a mental illness that resulted in his inability to conform his conduct to the law.

One of the prosecution's expert witnesses testified that the results of an MMPI-2 completed by the defendant were not consistent with the profile of an actively psychotic person. Instead, the expert argued that the protocol was quite consistent with a diagnosis of a personality or "character" disorder (i.e., antisocial personality disorder) and indicated that the defendant had a tendency toward overcontrolled hostility. The expert also reported that, during a clinical interview, the defendant was inconsistent concerning the number of voices that he had heard.

On weighing the evidence and the defendant's arguments on appeal, the court held that the expert testimony based on the MMPI-2 was admissible. The court mentioned the MMPI-2, relied on the expert's testimony regarding the MMPI-2 results, and even quoted the testimony of the psychologist who testified that the MMPI-2 was "probably the most widely used and most widely researched objective test of personality" (*Commonwealth v. Kappler,* 1993, p. 517). However, the court did not explicitly address the admissibility of the MMPI-2 for the purposes of determining whether a defendant has a mental illness.

In another case, the trial court judge refused to admit an expert's opinion regarding the defendant's mental state at the time of the offense (*State v. Gardner*, 1992). The judge reasoned that a psychologist[8] was not qualified to make a "retroactive diagnosis," that required linking a current diagnosis with the defendant's mental state at the time of the offense. The Supreme Court of Rhode Island reversed the trial judge's decision, holding that the psychologist's "experience with the issue of mental capacity qualified him to render an opinion to the jury concerning defendant's mental condition at the time of the offense" (p. 1128).

In addition to the general issue about the admissibility of the expert testimony, the Supreme Court of Rhode Island addressed the issue of whether the psychologist should have been permitted to give testimony at trial based on the results of the MMPI. At trial, the judge excluded expert testimony based on the MMPI, holding that it was equivocal and totally unreliable.[9] However, in reversing the trial court, the Supreme Court pointed out that the judge's decision was premised on an error concerning the interpretation of one of the MMPI items. Somehow, the trial court judge believed erroneously that the defendant had answered "true" to item number 137 ("I believe my home life is as pleasant as most people I know"), when, in fact, the defendant had responded "false" to the item. Based on his misunderstanding of the answer to the item, the judge wrote that he "could not conceive how a happy home life could result from alcoholism" (p. 1130). As a result of this confusion, the judge "concluded that the MMPI report was totally unreliable and excluded testimony regarding the report from evidence" (p. 1130).

In the cases discussed in this section, at least when the issue was addressed on appeal, the MMPI and MMPI-2 were admitted to help determine if the defendant had a mental illness or disorder for the purpose of the insanity defense. It should be mentioned that, at least in the cases where the MMPI explicitly was discussed, the MMPI was not employed to show that a defendant was not criminally responsible.

Competency to stand trial. The cases in which a defendant's competency to stand trial was at issue did not explicitly discuss the use of the MMPI-2 in competency evaluations. In such cases, however, there is little reason to believe that the MMPI-2 would be particularly useful. Indeed, the United States Supreme Court has held that the standard for competence to stand trial is whether the defendant has "sufficient present ability to consult with his lawyer with a reasonable degree of rational understanding" and has "a rational as well as factual understanding of the proceedings against him" (*Dusky v. United States*, 1960, p. 171; see also *Drope v. Missouri*, 1975; *Godinez v. Moran*, 1994). Given that the focus of a competency examination is not on the defendant's mental state or personality, the MMPI-2 results would have limited utility in such evaluations. Instead, competency evaluations are functional and present oriented, requiring the clinician to determine whether defendants understand the nature of the proceedings against them, and whether they are able to communicate with, and assist, counsel in their defense (see Melton, Petrila, Poythress, & Slobogin, 1987; Ogloff, Wallace, & Otto, 1991).

Criminal profile evidence. In some cases, lawyers have attempted—and sometimes have been successful—having psychologists testify that, in the expert's opinion, based at least in part on MMPI results, the defendant does or does not meet the "profile" of a particular type of offender. As the cases reviewed next show, when courts consider the matter carefully, they tend not to permit such testimony. However, in some cases, courts have not directly addressed the issue of the admissibility of MMPI results for the purpose of determining whether an individual meets the "profile," or demonstrates the "characteristics" of an offender who would commit a particular offense (e.g., murder, sexual offenses).

In *State v. Byrd* (1992), the defendant was convicted of murder and battery and sentenced to concurrent sentences of 40 years for the murder and 8 years for the battery. The defendant appealed to the Indiana Court of Appeals arguing that the trial court erred by not admitting the testimony of a psychiatrist who would have used the MMPI to testify that the defendant's personality was not consistent with the charge of murder. The defendant also argued that the court erred by not allowing the psychiatrist to testify that the defendant's memory loss was consistent with "retrograde amnesia," supporting the defendant's claim that he did not remember committing the crimes.

On appeal to the Supreme Court of Indiana, the state argued that the psychiatrist's testimony was properly excluded by the trial court judge. The Supreme Court overturned the decision by the Court of Appeals, and held that the trial court had properly excluded the psychiatrist's testimony because the results of the MMPI are not admissible for the purpose of proving that a defendant's character is inconsistent with committing intentional murder. Furthermore, in deciding not to allow the expert witness to testify about the defendant's character "based on his opinions on Byrd's behavior after the offense and on MMPI test performance" the court suggested that "this type of testimony comes cloaked with an aura of scientific reliability that certain individuals are or are not predisposed to commit a particular crime" (*State v. Byrd*, 1992, p. 1185).

The Missouri Court of Appeals also has directly addressed the issue of whether results from the MMPI could be admitted to "prove" that a defendant did not fit the profile of a particular type of offender (*State v. Elbert*, 1992). In *Elbert*, the appellant was convicted of sexual abuse and sodomy of a child. At trial, the appellant attempted to have a psychologist testify that "appellant's [MMPI] test scores did not fit the profile of a sex offender" (p. 647). The trial court judge did not permit the admission of the testimony, and the defendant raised this issue on appeal.

Applying an analysis based on the *Frye* case, the Missouri Court of Appeals wrote that "there is a world of difference between whether a psychological test is generally accepted for the purpose of diagnosis and treatment, and whether the test is generally accepted for the purpose of determining whether a criminal defendant fits the psychological profile of a sex offender" (p. 648). After reviewing the case law, and considering a law review article, the court affirmed the trial court's decision to exclude the psychologist's testimony.

It is interesting to mention that the court in *Byrd* noted that other courts have admitted similar expert testimony by psychologists, but that in those cases the courts typically did not directly address the admissibility of the testimony (see *Bond v. State*, 1980; *Robertson v. State*, 1974; *Storey v. State*, 1990). This highlights the point made at the outset of this chapter that the MMPI often is mentioned by courts, almost in passing, without explicitly addressing the admissibility or propriety of the use of the MMPI. This is problematic because judges most often will lack the understanding of the MMPI-2—or of psychological procedures in general—necessary to determine whether the proposed use of the MMPI-2 results is supported by the psychological literature. If such a question is not addressed directly, courts may place too heavy a reliance on the expert's professional integrity as well as the expert's knowledge of the test.

In *People v. Stoll* (1989), the Supreme Court of California decided whether a defendant who was charged with committing "lewd and lascivious" acts to a child could introduce expert testimony by a psychologist who would testify that the defendant displayed no signs of "deviance" or "abnormality," and, therefore, was falsely charged. In *Stoll*, four defendants were charged with a number of sexual crimes against children. The defendant in question here was interviewed by the psychologist for 2 hours, and completed an MMPI and Millon Clinical Multiaxial Inventory (MCMI). Based on this information, the psychologist's opinion was that the defendant

> has a normal personality function, likely has had throughout her lifetime, and . . . is falsely charged in this matter. . . . Especially in light of a low indication for antisocial or aggressive behavior, I must conclude that it is unlikely . . . she would be involved in the events she's been charged with. (p. 118)

In deciding whether such testimony should be admissible at trial, the court distinguished expert testimony using tests, such as the MMPI and MCMI, that were reasonably relied on by psychologists, from expert testimony based on new or novel scientific evidence:

> No precise legal rules dictate the proper basis for an expert's journey into a patient's mind to make judgments about his behavior. In effect, however, California courts have deferred to a qualified expert's decision to rely on "standardized" psychological tests such as the MMPI to reach an opinion on mental state at the time acts were committed. . . . Such deference is not less appropriate here. Indeed, voir dire testimony indicated that qualified professionals routinely use raw material from the MMPI . . . as a basis for assessing personality, and drawing behavioral conclusions therefrom. (p. 122)

By deciding that the expert testimony in question fell into the category of tests on which experts reasonably rely, the court avoided the need to apply the *Frye* test to the MMPI, and held that the testimony should have been admitted at trial. With respect to the issue of the testimony's potentially prejudicial impact, the court held that the psychologist could have been cross-examined, and that other experts could have been called to testify. Interestingly, the court in *Stoll* also avoided characterizing the proffered testimony as "profile" testimony.

Unfortunately, the psychologist in *Stoll* placed the MMPI in a more favorable light than empirical research—and clinical experience—might warrant. First, the psychologist testified that "the MMPI is always used by psychiatrists and psychologists to diagnose patients at various stages of clinical treatment" (p. 117). This simply is not true, the MMPI is not used in *all* cases by both psychologists and psychiatrists. Second, the psychologist "indicated that the test probably has a competence level of .9 for 'normal' persons, whereas the 'usual' standard in psychological tests is .7 and above" (p. 118). Without knowing exactly what he meant, this statement is difficult to evaluate. Third, the psychologist testified that the "psychopathic deviant" [sic] scale was "commonly elevated in criminal populations and in sexual deviancy cases and problems" (p. 119). Apart from the expert's apparent mistake in calling the scale the "psychopathic deviant," instead of the "psychopathic deviate," the expert was unable to support his statement with empirical data. For example, when asked on cross-examination, about studies that supported his position, the psychologist was unable to name studies that "had identified certain general characteristics in convicted child molesters" (p. 119, footnote 14).

One year after deciding the *Stoll* case, a California District Court of Appeal relied on the *Stoll* decision to permit a psychologist to testify that, based on the MMPI, the defendant "was not a sexual deviant, or was not a pedophile, or was not likely to have committed the charged acts" (*People v. Ruiz,* 1990, p. 1245). In *Ruiz,* the court emphasized that it was important to consider whether proper foundation could be laid for its use in the specific case (i.e., whether the test was being used for the purposes for which it was designed).

An important and directly related concern discussed in *Elbert* is why "profile" or "character-type" expert testimony has been almost universally rejected in jurisdictions where the issue has been raised (e.g., see *People v. Berrios,* 1991). One main reason has been the fear courts have of having a "battle of experts" erupt during the trial. This concern is illustrated in the following quote from the New Jersey Supreme Court in *State v. Cavallo* (1982):

> If defendants are permitted to introduce psychiatric testimony on their character, the State will not stand idly by without producing psychiatrists favorable to its cause. . . . The results must necessarily be a "battle of experts" concerning the validity of the expert evidence. This would consume substantial court time and cost both parties much time and expense. Much of the trial would focus on the tangential issue of the reliability of the expert evidence rather than the central issue of what the defendants did or did not do. (p. 1025)

Byrd, Elbert, and *Stoll* all raise very important issues regarding the propriety of using the MMPI to show that a defendant does or does not meet the "profile" or "characteristics" of a specific type of offender. As the judges in *Elbert* noted, this issue has been addressed in the literature. Indeed, Myers et al. (1989) wrote that, although the MMPI may be useful for such things as psychological diagnosis or treatment, "there is *no* psychological test or combination of tests that can determine whether a person has engaged or will engage in deviant sexual activity" (p. 135). Psychologists need to be particularly concerned about whether the purpose for which they intend to use the MMPI-2 is supported by the literature. Not to do so is not only unprofessional, but it serves to place the reputation of psychologists in further jeopardy within the legal system.

A matter related to criminal profiles is whether the MMPI may be used to establish that a defendant did, or did not, have the capacity to form the specific intent necessary for the crime charged. In one case that directly addressed this matter, the Seventh Circuit Court of Appeals held that barring psychological or psychiatric testimony used to establish a defendant's specific intent did not violate the defendant's right to due process (*Haas v. Abrahamson,* 1990). Thus many courts have not allowed expert testimony based on the MMPI—or otherwise—claiming that a defendant either does or does not meet the profile of a particular type of offender. Courts have also been reluctant to admit similar evidence arguing that the defendant did or did not have the specific intent necessary for a particular crime.

Death penalty. The defendant's mental state may arise as an important legal issue at several junctures within the death penalty process. Most often, the MMPI is used to determine current mental state, or mental state at the time of the offense, for criminal responsiblity adjudication or sentencing purposes. However, in *Ford v. Wainwright* (1986), the United States Supreme Court held that the execution of insane prisoners is barred by the eighth amendment, which prohibits cruel and unusual punishment (the so-called competency to be executed requirement) (see Ogloff et al., 1991). Therefore, the MMPI also has been used to determine whether a defendant is "insane" for the purposes of the competency to be executed requirement.

In one such case, *Lowenfield v. Butler* (1988), the condemned man attempted to have the Fifth Circuit Court of Appeals stay his execution by arguing that a clinical psychologist's affidavit proved that he was "insane." In the affidavit, the clinical psychologist stated that

> on the basis of the interview and the MMPI, I have reached a preliminary conclusion . . . that it is highly probably that Mr. Lowenfield is suffering from paranoid schizophrenia . . . as a paranoid schizophrenic Mr. Lowenfield's capacity to understand the death penalty would be impaired. Indeed, my clinical

interview with Mr. Lowenfield indicated that he is currently unable to understand the death penalty. (p. 187)

The Court of Appeals denied the condemned man's petition, holding that the
affidavit did not meet the threshold necessary to show that the man falls within
the class of "mentally deranged prisoners" for whom execution would be
unconstitutional. This is not to say that the MMPI was not held admissible,
rather that, based on the psychologist's affidavit, the evidence of the defendant's mental illness was not sufficient to trigger the issue of the defendant's
competence to be executed.

Transfer of juvenile offenders to adult court. As Tables 2.1 and 2.2 show, the
MMPI has occasionally been used in assessing whether a juvenile offender
should be transferred to ordinary court to be prosecuted as an adult. In *United
States v. Doe* (1989), an adolescent appealed his transfer to adult court by arguing,
among other things, that the court should not have accepted as evidence
results from an MMPI that he completed. The test results were interpreted to
indicate that Doe exhibited psychopathic traits and had a high risk of violence
and aggression. In upholding the decision of the trial court judge to accept
the MMPI testimony, the Fifth Circuit Court of Appeals did not anlayze
explicitly the validity of the MMPI for the purpose for which it was used.
Instead, the court simply stated that it was in the judge's discretion to accept
the MMPI results, and to evaluate it as evidence in relation to other testimony.
Therefore, the case was remanded for another hearing in which the MMPI
testimony would be admitted.

Sexual abuse victims. As discussed previously, lawyers have attempted to call
psychologists to testify that a defendant's MMPI results indicated that the
defendant did (or did not) match MMPI profiles of known offenders. Lawyers
too have attempted to introduce expert testimony based on the MMPI to
argue that sexual abuse victims' MMPI profiles matched profiles of known
sexual abuse victims (described later in text).

In *State v. Randle* (1992), the defendant was convicted of sexually abusing
a fellow employee. The defendant argued that, although they had sexual
relations, those relations were consensual. At trial, the judge prohibited a
psychologist from testifying about the results of the MMPI completed by the
alleged victim 5 days following the sexual incident. The trial court judge held
that to admit the testimony would be a violation of the physician-patient

privilege and that the fact that the alleged victim signed a waiver authorizing the doctor to release the MMPI information to the department of criminal investigation did not mean that she intended to have the information shared in court. On this issue, the Court of Appeals of Iowa held that the alleged victim's waiver of the MMPI information to the department of criminal investigation "destroys the confidential nature of the disclosures and renders them admissible" (p. 221).

After deciding that the MMPI information should have been admitted into evidence at trial, the court turned to a review of the admissibility of the MMPI information. The court held that although there were several witnesses who testified at trial that the alleged victim's demeanor was calm, the proposed testimony of a psychologist reviewing the MMPI would have been the "most probative evidence of Haglund's lack of anxiety following the abuse" (*State v. Randle*, 1992, p. 222). Further deciding that the exclusion of this testimony was prejudicial to the defendant, the Court of Appeals ordered a new trial.

Criminal matters summary. In summary, the MMPI has been employed across a range of issues raised in criminal cases. The extent to which the MMPI was held admissible, or employed as an important factor in the decision making, has varied across cases. Although used relatively frequently for criminal responsibility purposes, there have been relatively few cases explicitly evaluating the extent to which the MMPI would be admissible, and useful, for determining whether a defendant was mentally ill for the purposes of the insanity defense. Generally, those cases that have considered the MMPI have found it to be admissible and useful for identifying mental illness but not for deciding whether the defendant was criminally responsible. Although the MMPI-2 has been employed in evaluations for competency to stand trial, courts have not explicitly addressed its admissibility for those purposes. Furthermore, because of the functional and present-oriented competency to stand trial criteria, the MMPI-2 has limited utility for such evaluations. It is safe to say that courts have not admitted MMPI based testimony for the purposes of arguing that a defendant meets a "criminal profile" or displays the characteristics of specific types of offenders. The MMPI has been used as evidence to argue that a person convicted of murder should have his or her sentence mitigated or that the accused murderer meets some of the requirements for the insanity defense. Attempts also have been made to use the MMPI to identify a condemned inmate's potential mental illness that might result in a stay of execution based on the competency to be executed standard. The cases discussed show that attempts were made to employ the MMPI for purposes of deciding whether a juvenile should be transferred to adult court for trial and sentencing. Finally, the MMPI has been employed in cases to argue that a person was, or was not, actually assaulted sexually.

CIVIL LAW MATTERS

In this book attention is focused on both criminal and civil law matters in which the MMPI has been employed. As in criminal matters, the use of the MMPI has been most successful in civil matter situations involving the identification of a mental illness, rather than as a basis for legal conclusions. It is interesting that the range of cases in which the MMPI has been used in the civil context is more limited than it is in the criminal context. Furthermore, there has been less explicit consideration of the MMPI by courts with regard to the civil matters.

Custody and access. Given the acrimonious nature of divorce, and the difficult questions that arise when courts attempt to make decisions regarding custody and access, it is not difficult to imagine that experts are frequently called to offer an opinion about the suitability of the parents. There is considerable room for misuse of the MMPI-2 here, especially if clinicians intend on using it to make statements that are not supported by research.

In a recent case, a trial court in Indiana terminated the parental rights of two men who were the fathers of two children born of the same mother (*Tipton v. Marion County Department of Public Welfare, 1994*). The court based its decision in part on results of MMPIs that were administered to the men. On appeal, the Court of Appeals of Indiana reviewed the MMPI results in passing. For one of the fathers (Tipton), the court held that the MMPI results indicated that he was less than an optimal parent, but that his continued relationship with the child would pose no threat to the child. For the other father (Boster), however, the court agreed with the trial court in holding that Boster was unable to function adequately as a parent. At trial, the judge apparently echoed the opinion of the expert witness:

> Results of Mr. Boster's depression, anxiety, poor judgment and impulse control, and resentment of external demands all suggest an inability to function adequately as a parent. His emotional problems are such that he is only marginally capable of managing his life; and would not be able to care for a child. His

suspiciousness and tendency to externalize responsibility for problems suggest that he may be resistive to therapy, but he needs to resolve his own problems before parenting issues can be addressed. (p. 14)

Based on their interpretation of the expert's review of the MMPI results, the court held that Tipton would not have his parental rights terminated, but that Boster would.

The *Tipton* case raises serious questions about the extent to which the MMPI has been found to be a valid instrument for determining whether an individual's personality characteristics are conducive to the person's ability to care for a child. Without directly addressing this matter, both the trial and appellate courts merely took the expert testimony based on the MMPI at face value, and used that information to help determine whether the fathers' parental rights should have been terminated. Given the gravity of the matter, it is indeed unfortunate that the court—and the expert—did not consider more carefully the application of the MMPI.

In another recent case, the Court of Appeals of Washington was asked to reverse a lower court's decision granting a father unsupervised visits with his 11-year-old son (*In re Marriage of Luckey,* 1994). At trial, some evidence was admitted suggesting that the father may have abused his son. The evidence was presented by a psychologist who testified that one of the father's former stepdaughters reported having been sexually abused by the father when she was young. In addition, the psychologist administered an MMPI to the father, and stated that the father's "scaled scores matched the profiles of known child molesters" (p. 4). The Court of Appeals upheld the trial court's decision to permit unsupervised visits, holding that the use of the MMPI to determine whether the father, in fact, was a child molester was questionable.

Again, one must ask whether the MMPI is a valid instrument for determining whether a father may have abused his son. As a result of the enmity that exists in custody battles, psychologists need to be particularly cautious about the techniques they employ and the conclusions they draw. Indeed, in recent work, Ogloff, Beck, and Olley (1994) have found that next to allegations of inappropriate sexual behavior, the most frequent cause for ethics complaints against psychologists—at least in some jurisdictions—stem from child custody evaluations.

Personal injury lawsuits. Results of MMPIs have been used quite extensively in personal injury lawsuits to help prove either that an individual has been caused psychological harm or distress, or that a defendant had the requisite level of intentionality to be found liable in a tort action. It indeed is unfortunate that, given the extensive use of the MMPI in this area (see Tables 2.1 and 2.2), so few courts have explicitly considered the applicability of the MMPI. Indeed, the cases reviewed next focus rather exclusively on the narrow issue of whether specific questions and responses from the MMPI may be used to cross-examine a party or expert witness.

In *Fisher v. Johnson* (1993), the Supreme Court of North Dakota addressed two issues concerning the use of the MMPI. The victim of a beating (Todd Fisher) brought suit against his attackers (Rodger and Dale Johnson) for compensatory and exemplary damages. A jury found in favor of Fisher, awarding him approximately $52,000 for damages. Among the issues raised on appeal, Rodger Johnson argued that the trial court erred in not providing him an opportunity to cross-examine Fisher about three statements in the MMPI that Fisher completed.

Following the attack, Fisher met with a clinical psychologist who conducted two interviews with him and administered the MMPI. Based on the interview and the MMPI results, the psychologist diagnosed Fisher as suffering from post-traumatic stress disorder (PTSD). At trial, the psychologist testified that her "opinion is based primarily upon my clinical interview. The MMPI I used to substantiate what I found in the clinical interview" (*Fisher v. Johnson,* 1993, p. 354). During his cross-examination of the psychologist, Rodger Johnson's lawyer wanted to have the psychologist read Fisher's responses to three questions on the MMPI.[10] Again, on cross-examination of Fisher, Rodger Johnson's lawyer tried to ask Fisher about his responses to the questions and, again, the judge did not allow the questions. The lawyer intended to use the responses to the questions to challenge Fisher's credibility and to discredit the psychologist's opinion. The trial court judge refused to allow the questions to be asked. Johnson's lawyer made a motion for a new trial based on these matters. In denying the motion, the judge "balanced the different interests and concluded that the questions and answers were not of sufficient probative value as to Plaintiff's motives and truthfulness to offset the undue prejudice to the Plaintiff which would occur if deemed admissible" (p. 355).

In affirming the lower court's decision, the Supreme Court of North Dakota held that although an expert may be required to disclose the facts underlying her or his opinion, the psychologist in this case did not rely on the specific individual responses on the MMPI in forming her opinions. Although Fisher's responses to the items could be considered "prior inconsistent statements" that could be used to impeach the testimony of a witness, the responses were not allowed because their probative value would have been far outweighed by their prejudicial effect against Fisher.

Two other recent cases addressed the issue of whether specific MMPI responses could be presented at trial. Like the court in *Fisher v. Johnson,* (1993), the Supreme Court of Montana held, in *Mason v. Ditzel* (1992), that presentation of MMPI testimony that was disputed during the trial "tended to confuse the issues and may have misled the jury" (p. 714). However, the Supreme Court of New Jersey upheld a prosecutor's use of individual MMPI responses when the defendant's expert witness initially stated that the defendant was "faking bad" but later changed his mind and opined that the defendant was neither "faking good or bad" (*State v. Martini,* 1993, p. 1251).

Medical malpractice. In *DeHaven v. Gant* (1986), a patient who alleged that the nerves in her arm were damaged during a skin graft procedure brought suit against the surgeon. Medical examination procedures did not reveal any nerve damage that could have been attributed to the surgery. Following her referral to a pain clinic, the plaintiff completed an MMPI. At trial, a physician, Dr. Wyler, testified that, based on the MMPI results, he believed that the plaintiff was suffering from a hysterical conversion reaction. The plaintiff objected to the admission of the MMPI results on the basis that they were hearsay and prejudicial. Over these objections, the trial court admitted the testimony, and the court found for the defendant surgeon.

On appeal to the Court of Appeals of Washington, the appellant argued, among other things, that the MMPI results were hearsay and should not have been admitted into evidence at trial. The court denied the argument, and affirmed the trial court's decision to admit the testimony. In so deciding, the court held that the MMPI was "reasonably relied upon by physicians in the diagnosis and treatment of patients" (p. 153) and that because the results formed the basis of an expert's opinion, the admissibility of the test results was not an issue.

As with the criminal cases discussed previously (in which psychologists attempted to testify that a defendant had an MMPI profile that matched that of an offender), courts also have been reluctant to accept such testimony in civil suits. In the *Luckey* case discussed in the earlier "Custody and Access" section, the court relied on a decision holding that profile testimony had little probative value, but had the potential for a considerable level of unfair prejudice (see *State v. Braham,* 1992).

Civil matters summary. As in criminal matters, the MMPI-2 has been more successful for civil matters that involve identifying a mental illness than it has been for basing legal conclusions. The extents of civil cases in which the MMPI has been used is more limited than in the criminal context, and there has been less consideration of the MMPI in civil matters. The MMPI-2 may be useful for evaluating parents' mental states and personality traits in custody evaluations. Of course, the MMPI-2 is not useful for determining whether, in fact, a parent has abused a child or is likely to be abusive. Although more explicit analysis is required, the MMPI-2 may be useful in personal injury lawsuits for helping determine the nature or extent of an individual's psychological harm or distress. Finally, depending on the nature of the specific claim, the MMPI-2 may be useful in medical malpractice claims for evaluating issues of psychological harm. In tort suits, the MMPI-2 has no utility for determining whether an individual has the requisite level of intentionality to be found liable in a tort action.

Conclusions

The fact that the United States Supreme Court has ruled that the *Frye* test has been superseded by the more liberal FRE standards for admitting scientifc evidence may mean that the courts' rather limited analysis of the admissibility and utility of the MMPI-2 may be reduced even more in future cases. This is particularly problematic given the range of issues for which the MMPI has been employed and the extent to which some psychologists and medical professionals have gone beyond the empirical research to employ the MMPI for a variety of highly questionable purposes. Indeed, in those cases where the MMPI has been employed for the purposes for which it has been validated (e.g., to help determine a defendant's mental state), results from the MMPI-2 have been found to be admissible in court and to have considerable utility for such forensic applications.

The MMPI has been employed widely across a range of issues in criminal cases. In many cases, the MMPI-2 has been used appropriately in situations for which its use has been clearly demonstrated. In the case of criminal responsibility evaluations, the MMPI has generally been found to be admissible and useful for identifying mental illness. Given the utility of the MMPI-2 in identifying symptoms of mental illness, the MMPI has been used to identify a condemned inmate's potential mental illness that might result in a stay of execution based on the competency to be executed standard.

In other cases, though, the utility of the MMPI-2 for the purposes for which it was employed is questionable. For example, the MMPI-2 may not be admissible, and is not useful, for deciding whether the defendant is (or is not) criminally responsible. Similarly, the MMPI-2 has been employed in competency to stand trial evaluations. Because the competency to stand trial criteria do not focus on the defendant's mental state or character, but are functional and present oriented, the MMPI-2 has limited utility for such evaluations. Appropriately, courts have refused to admit MMPI-based testimony for the purposes of arguing whether a defendant meets a "criminal profile." Although employed less frequently, the MMPI unfortunately has been used to argue that a person convicted of murder should have his or her sentence mitigated. Similarly, some attempt has been made to admit expert testimony based on the MMPI-2 to show that a juvenile should be transferred to adult court for trial and sentencing. Finally, it is unfortunate that the MMPI has been used to argue that a person was (or was not) actually assaulted sexually.

Although the MMPI has been used fairly extensively in civil cases, few courts have taken the time to review carefully the extent to which the MMPI is valid for the purposes for which it was used. As the review of the few civil cases cited earlier shows, the MMPI has met with mixed success in cases involving custody and access determinations, personal injury and medical malpractice lawsuits.

Some of the cases reviewed in this chapter raise questions about the validity of the MMPI-2 for a variety of forensic applications. As the chapters in this book indicate, the MMPI-2 has considerable utility for some forensic applications, although its use for some forensic purposes may be questionable. Psychologists and others who use the MMPI-2 in court for purposes for which it has not been validated run the risk of jeopardizing both their professional standing and the very reputation of their profession.

It is disconcerting that so many courts, as outlined in Tables 2.1 and 2.2, have readily admitted and considered expert testimony based on the MMPI without any formal analysis of the validity of the MMPI. More alarming, perhaps, is the fact that so many psychologists, and other clincians, have based their testimony in court on highly questionable uses of the MMPI. Indeed, one need only consider *some* of the American Psychological Association (APA) ethical standards to realize how problematic it is to use assessment techniques for purposes for which the tests have not been validated. Ethical standards including the need to maintain expertise,[11] the requirement for making scientific and professional judgments,[12] and, perhaps more importantly, the need to substantiate clinical findings,[13] the requirement to use psychological assessment techniques,[14] and interpreting assessment results[15] all raise concerns about the improper use of MMPI-2 test results. In addition to the general standards, psychologists also need to pay careful attention to APA's ethical standard that governs forensic assessments:

> Psychologists' forensic assessments, recommendations, and reports are based on information and techniques . . . sufficient to provide appropriate sustantiation for their findings. (APA, 1992, Ethical Standard 7.02)

On a brighter note, in those cases in which courts have considered the use of the MMPI and MMPI-2 more carefully, the courts have tended to make reasonable decisions. For example, many courts have been reluctant to allow expert testimony based on MMPI results in cases in which lawyers are trying to argue that the defendant's MMPI profile is not consistent with that of a specific class of offenders. Yet, courts generally have held the MMPI to be admissible in cases in which it is being offered to help determine whether a person has a mental illness.

Given the widespread use of the MMPI-2, and the extent to which it has been researched and validated for a wide variety of purposes, there is little doubt that the MMPI-2 can be a valuable tool in forensic assessments. To maximize the utility of the instrument, however, clinicians must be cautious about employing the MMPI-2 for purposes for which it was not intended, or has not been validated. Furthermore, there is a need for increased research regarding the MMPI-2 to determine the extent to which it may be useful for forensic applications.

Notes

1. Due to the relative recency of the MMPI-2, and the length of time it takes for a case to make its way to court and to appeal, this chapter necessarily relies on cases that dealt specifically with the MMPI. Indeed, only 12 reported cases were found to mention the MMPI-2. Similarly, only one reported case was retrieved that mentioned the MMPI-A. For most legal purposes, the distinctions among the MMPI, MMPI-2, and MMPI-A are irrelevant.

2. In cases tried by a judge and jury, the jury decides on the probative value of all of the evidence presented at trial.

3. I have relied on variations of Table 2.3, and the information that accompanies it, previously (see Ogloff, 1990; Ogloff & Otto, 1993). However, as a result of the Court's decision in *Daubert,* the information in Table 2.3 has been considerably altered.

4. "All relevant evidence is admissible, except as otherwise provided by the Constitution of the United States" (FRE 402).

5. It is important to note that FRE 702 is considered to be less demanding than the *Frye* test. Whereas *Frye* limits the admissibility of scientific evidence to that which is generally accepted by the scientific community, FRE 702 permits experts to rely on scientific facts or data as long as they are "reasonably relied upon by experts in [the] particular field" (FRE 702).

6. For example, in *Elbert,* the Missouri Court of Appeals wrote that "there is a world of difference between whether a psychological test is generally accepted for the purpose of diagnosis and treatment, and whether the test is generally accepted for the purpose of determining whether a criminal defendant fits the psychological profile of a sex offender" (p. 648).

7. In *Hagen v. Swenson* (1975), the Supreme Court of Minnesota held that a neurologist and psychiatrist, who was not a licensed psychologist, was qualified as an expert in interpreting the MMPI. Indeed, the physician in question trained at the University of Minnesota, had worked with the developers of the MMPI, and reported having read between 10,000 and 15,000 MMPIs.

8. On appeal, the Supreme Court of Rhode Island commented that

the fact that Dr. Seghorn was a psychologist and not a psychiatrist is not dispositive on the issue of his qualifications as an expert. There is a growing trend among courts to allow a psychologist to testify about mental capacity in situations in which the psychologist has extensive training and experience with people suffering from mental defects . . . Dr. Seghorn's experience, education, and training rendered him qualified to offer his testimony to the jury. (*State v. Gardner,* 1992, p. 1128)

9. Interestingly, the trial court judge readily admitted the results of a Rorschach (ink blot) Test and the Thematic Aptitude Test (TAT) without mention.

10. The questions were as follows: Number 41 "I do not always tell the truth"; Number 134 "At times I feel like picking a fist fight with someone else"; and Number 150 "Sometimes I feel as if I must either injure myself or someone else." Fisher answered "true" to all three questions.

11. "Psychologists . . . maintain a reasonable level of awareness of current scientific and professional information in their fields of activity" (American Psychological Association [APA], 1992, Ethical Standard 1.05).

12. "Psychologists rely on scientifically and professionally derived knowledge when making scientific or professional judgments or when engaging in scholarly or professional endeavors" (APA, 1992, Ethical Standard 1.06).

13. "Psychologists' assessments, recommendations, reports, and psychological diagnostic or evaluative statements are based on information and techniques . . . sufficient to provide appropriate substantiation for their findings" (APA, 1992, Ethical Standard 2.01).

14. "Psychologists who develop, administer, score, interpret, or use psychological assessment techniques, interviews, tests, or instruments do so in a manner and for purposes that are appropriate in light of the research on or evidence of the usefulness and proper application of the technique" (APA, 1992, Ethical Standard 2.02).

15. "When interpreting assessment results . . . psychologists take into account the various test factors and characteristics of the person being assessed that might affect psychologists' judgments or reduce the accuracy of their interpretations. They indicate any significant reservations they have about the accuracy or limitations of their interpretation" (APA, 1992, Ethical Standard 2.05).

References

American Psychological Association. (1992). *Ethical principles of psychologists and code of conduct.* Washington DC: Author.

Bond v. State, 273 Ind. 233, 403 N.E.2d 812 (1980).

Bussell v. Leat, 781 S.W.2d 97 (Mo. Ct. App. 1989).

Commonwealth v. Kappler, 416 Mass. 574, 625 N.E.2d 513 (1993).

Daubert v. Merrell Dow Pharmaceuticals, 727 F. Supp. 570 (S.D. Cal. 1989), *aff'd,* 951 F.2d 1128 (9th Cir. 1990), *vacated,* 113 S. Ct. 2786 (1993).

DeHaven v. Gant, 713 P.2d 149 (Wash. Ct. App. 1986).

DeLuca v. Merrell Dow Pharmaceuticals, 911 F.2d 941 (3d Cir. 1990).

Drope v. Missouri, 420 U.S. 162 (1975).

Dusky v. United States, 362 U.S. 402 (1960).

Dyas v. United States, 376 A.2d 827 (1977).

Federal Rules of Evidence (1976). 28 United States Code 101-1103.

Fisher v. Johnson, 508 N.W.2d 352 (N.D. 1993).

Ford v. Wainwright, 477 U.S. 399 (1986).

Frye v. United States, 293 F. 1013 (D.C. Cir. 1923).

Godinez v. Moran, 113 S. Ct. 2680 (1994).

Haas v. Abrahamson, 910 F.2d 384 (7th Cir. 1990).

Hagen v. Swenson, 236 N.W.2d 161 (Minn. 1975).

In Re Marriage of Luckey, WL 58252 (Wash. Ct. App. March 1, 1994).

Landis v. Commonwealth, 241 S.E.2d 749 (Va. 1978).

Lowenfield v. Butler, 843 F.2d 183 (5th Cir. 1988).

Mason v. Ditzel, 255 Mont. 364, 842 P.2d 707 (1992).

Melton, G. B., Petrila, J., Poythress, N., & Slobogin, C. (1987). *Psychological evaulations for the courts: A handbook for mental health professional and lawyers.* New York: Guilford.

Myers, J. E., Bays, J., Becker, J., Berliner, L., Corwin, D. L., & Saywitz, K. J. (1989). Expert testimony in child sexual abuse litigation. *Nebraska Law Review, 68,* 1-145 .

Ogloff, J. R. P. (1990). The admissibility of expert testimony regarding malingering and deception. *Behavioral Sciences and the Law, 8,* 27-43.

Ogloff, J. R. P., Beck, K. A., & Olley, M. C. (1994, July). *A survey of ethical complaints against mental health professionals in Canada.* Paper presented at the Annual Meeting of the Canadian Psychological Association Convention, Penticton, British Columbia.

Ogloff, J. R. P., & Otto, R. K. (1993). Psychological autopsy: Clinical and legal perspectives. *Saint Louis University Law Journal, 37,* 607-646.

Ogloff, J. R. P., Wallace, D. H., & Otto, R. K. (1991). Competencies in the criminal process. In D. K. Kagehiro & W. S. Laufer (Eds.), *Handbook of psychology and law* (pp. 343-360). New York: Springer-Verlag.

People v. Berrios, 150 Misc.2d 229, 568 N.Y.S.2d 512 (N.Y. Sup. Ct. 1991).

People v. Ruiz, 222 Cal. App.3d 1241, 272 Ca.Rptr. 368 (Cal. Ct. App. 1990).

People v. Stoll, 265 Cal.Rptr. 111, 783 P.2d 698 (1989).

Robertson v. State, 262 Ind. 562, 319 N.E.2d 833 (1974).

Rollins v. Commonwealth, 207 Va. 575, 151 S.E.2d 622 (1966).

State v. Braham, 67 Wash. App. 930, 841 P.2d 785 (Wash. App. Ct. 1992).

State v. Byrd, 593 N.E.2d 1183 (Ind. 1992).

State v. Cavallo, 88 N.J. 508, 443 A.2d 1020 (1982).

State v. Elbert, 831 S.W.2d 646 (Mo. Ct. App. 1992).

State v. Gardner, 616 A.2d 1124 (R.I. 1992).

State v. Martini, 131 N.J. 176, 619 A.2d 1208 (1993).

State v. Randle, 484 N.W.2d 220 (Iowa Ct. App. 1992).

Storey v. State, 552 N.E.2d 477 (1990).

Tipton v. Marion County Department of Public Welfare, WL 59326 (Ind. App. Ct. March 2, 1994).

United States v. Doe, 871 F.2d 1248 (5th Cir. 1989).

United States v. Shorter, 809 F.2d 54 (D.C. Cir. 1987), *cert. denied,* 484 U.S. 817 (1987).

3

Psychometric Issues in Forensic Applications of the MMPI-2

IRVING B. WEINER

The MMPI-2 is generally regarded as a psychometrically sound instrument for assessing personality functioning (Archer, 1992; Nichols, 1992). This positive regard for the instrument is based on (a) extensive research over the past 50 years attesting the psychometric soundness of the original MMPI; (b) the expectation as delineated by Graham (1993, chap. 8) that MMPI research findings are largely applicable to the MMPI-2; and (c) certain psychometric enhancements in the MMPI-2 compared to the original MMPI, particularly with respect to its normative database. Accordingly, although psychometric evaluation of the MMPI-2 in its own right is still in its early stages, psychologists who use the instrument in research studies or clinical assessments have good reason to believe that they are employing a reliable, valid, and adequately standardized measure of personality.

However, because of the typically adversarial nature of legal procedures, clinicians trained as helping professionals face some special challenges in communicating the forensic implications of their assessment data (see Weiner, 1987; Weiner, 1995). The kinds of psychometric information that are most critical from a scientific perspective may at times differ from the kinds of information that are most pertinent to reaching judgment in a court of law, and some of the information sought in the courtroom may not be available for instruments of proven clinical utility.

In this chapter the basic concepts of normative data, reliability, validity, and utility are reviewed briefly with respect to their clinical requirements and their specific applicability in forensic practice. Some observations are then offered concerning how well the MMPI-2 presently meets forensic psychometric needs and what kinds of research are needed to address current gaps in knowledge. The chapter closes with a discussion of the potential clinical and forensic benefits of integrating MMPI-2 findings with other sources of information.

Normative Data

Adequate normative data to support clinical applications of psychological tests consist of (a) sufficiently extensive sampling of performance on the test by persons who are broadly representative of groups to which individual subjects belong and (b) sufficiently detailed description of normative test performance to provide relevant points of comparison between expectation and the performance of individual subjects. Considering first the importance of having a broadly representative normative database, sophisticated test construction in contemporary times commonly involves examining diverse samples that include males and females of different ages drawn from various geographic, socioeconomic, and racial/ethnic backgrounds. The assumption is then made that the test performance of individual subjects who happen to be male or female, rural or urban, rich or poor, or Anglo, African American, Hispanic, Asian American, or Native American can be compared with normative expectation because each of these groups is represented in the standardization sample.

Although reasonable and widely used in personality assessment, this assumption embodies some shortcomings that not infrequently come to light in forensic proceedings. Knowing that economically disadvantaged or minority group persons are included in a normative sample does not indicate whether and how middle-class and working-class people differ in their responses to the test, or whether African Americans differ from Anglo Americans, or city-dwellers from farmers, and so forth. Clearly there are limits to the number of subgroups that can or should be identified in developing normative standards for an assessment instrument. Specific norms for rural, midwestern males who are well-to-do and Protestant, if extrapolated nationwide in terms of locale, gender, social class, and religion, would create an unmanageable number of cells in a normative database and foster meaningless hair splitting: Is there any reason, for example, why Protestants should differ from Catholics on the particular test?

On the other hand, for such broad demographic characteristics as gender, socioeconomic status, and sociocultural background, there may be good reason to expect differences in personality test responses, or at least to question in the courtroom whether such differences exist. If a subject is Hispanic or African American, for example, a cross-examining attorney may with good effect inquire whether a subject's responses resemble or differ from the responses generally given by Hispanic or African American subjects. To respond that a particular test is applicable to these minority groups because they were represented in the normative or standardization sample does not answer this question very well.

A satisfactory answer to this question requires sufficient normative data concerning demographic subgroups to demonstrate either (a) that the particular subgroup does not differ significantly from the total normative sample in its typical test performance, or (b) that whatever differences may exist between the subgroup and the total normative sample do not have any clinically significant behavioral correlates, or (c) that a particular subject's test responses do or do not differ significantly from normative expectation among his or her own demographic subgroup.

Implicit in these alternatives is the sometimes overlooked fact that group differences on a test do not necessarily signify bias for or against one group or another. The potential for bias arises only when consistent test score differences between demographic subgroups are associated with different behavioral correlates, lead to different clinical conclusions, or both. Thus, a mean difference between subgroups on a particular scale may reach statistical significance using a null hypothesis approach to the data but be so slight as to have little bearing on how an individual subject's scale scores would be interpreted. Moreover, there may be instances in which subgroup differences on some particular scale of a multidimensional instrument are large enough to lead to different conclusions, but in which these particular conclusions have little bearing on the assessment question at issue. Being a relatively reflective or relatively expressive person is independent of general adjustment level, for example, and any subgroup differences in scales measuring such aspects of personality style would accordingly not bias an assessment of possible adjustment difficulties; only demonstrated subgroup differences in indexes of adjustment would be likely to introduce bias into the assessment of adjustment difficulties.

Turning next to available descriptions of normative test findings, psychometric data reports tend most commonly to identify means, standard deviations, and product-moment correlations. Methodologists generally value these parametric descriptive statistics over nonparametric descriptors, because they provide the basis for calculating relatively powerful inferential statistics. In clinical work in general, however, and in forensic personality assessment in particular, nonparametric descriptions frequently carry considerable weight. Psychologists seeking to support their testimony effectively often find that means, standard deviations, and correlation coefficients are no match in a court of law for medians, modes, percentages, and percentiles.

There are two reasons for this greater influence of nonparametric than parametric data in the courtroom. First, nonparametric descriptive statistics are easier to explain and understand than are parametric descriptions. Second, the critical element in forensic testimony about personality characteristics as assessed by psychological tests is not how *scores* are distributed, but how *people* are distributed.

The importance of people rather than scores in supporting forensic testimony derives from the fact that forensic psychological issues typically hinge on the extent to which a person being evaluated is similar to or different from other people. The more that a person being examined in a forensic case can be demonstrated to resemble most other people, the less likely he or she is to be considered as incompetent, as not responsible for a criminal act, as suffering from psychic trauma or neuropsychological impairment, or as unfit to be a parent or custodian. Conversely, being demonstrably different from most people increases the likelihood that a litigant or defendant will be found incompetent, not guilty by reason of insanity, personally injured, or unfit to fill some role.

Accordingly, to convey the import of test findings to a psychometrically unsophisticated audience and to satisfy legalistic concerns with reasonable certainty, psychological examiners benefit from being able to present basic nonparametric data, in the following way: For any test index or configuration to which interpretive significance is being attached, how commonly or infrequently does it occur? What percentage of people in general are likely to show this same index or configuration? And, in relation to the demographic considerations already noted, how typical or unusual is this index or configuration in persons comparable to the subject in age, gender, place of residence, and social, cultural, and economic background? Being able to say that a particular test finding of considerable interpretive significance ordinarily occurs in fewer than 5% of persons demographically similar to a subject has a far more telling effect in a court of law than does citing means and standard deviations.

FORENSIC STATUS
OF MMPI-2 NORMATIVE DATA

With respect to forensic requirements for normative data, the MMPI-2 is presently better developed and more adequate than most if not all other omnibus measures of personality. As reviewed by Butcher and Williams (1992, chap. 1), Graham (1993, chap. 1), Greene (1991, chap. 1), and Pope, Butcher, and Seelen (1993, Appendix H), the normative sample on which the MMPI-2 was standardized comprised 1,462 women and 1,138 men, age 18 through the adult years, drawn from seven different regions of the United States, coming from diverse socioeconomic backgrounds, and resembling the 1980 census in representation of African American (approximately 12%), Native American (3%), Hispanic (3%), and Asian American (1%) persons. One could argue that the percentage of minority group subjects in this normative sample is a bit light given the composition of the United States population in the mid-1990s. Nevertheless, in contrast to the narrow sampling on which the original MMPI was based, the importance of diversity and broad representation has clearly been recognized in the standardization of the MMPI-2.

In addition, the published MMPI-2 normative data include specific comparisons among ethnic groups. Butcher and Williams (1992, p. 189) reported mean values and standard deviations for the validity and clinical scales separately for both male and female Anglo Americans, African Americans, Native Americans, Hispanic Americans, and Asian Americans, and they concluded from the general similarity among these values that "the MMPI-2 norms apply equally well, regardless of ethnic group background, and . . . no special interpretive considerations need to be made with regard to race" (p. 188). Greene (1987; 1991, chap. 8) draws a similar conclusion regarding broad use of the original MMPI: "It appears that moderator variables, such as socioeconomic status, education, and intelligence . . . are more important determinants of MMPI performance than ethnic status" (1991, p. 254).

Emerging research, although not yet plentiful, appears to confirm the broad applicability of the MMPI-2 normative data to groups differing not merely in ethnicity but in socioeconomic status as well. Using the MMPI-2 standardization sample, Timbrook and Graham (1994) compared the mean validity and clinical scale scores of 116 African American men with those of 116 Caucasian men matched for age, years of education, and total family income. Scale score comparisons were also made between similarly matched groups of 176 African American and 176 Caucasian women. The African American men scored significantly higher than their Caucasian counterparts only on Scale 8 (Sc), and the African American women scored significantly higher than the Caucasian women on Scales 4 (Pd), 5 (Mf), and 9 (Ma). However, the magnitude of each of these statistically significant differences was less than 5 T-score points, which means that they are unlikely to have any interpretive significance.

Pursuing further the implications of the differences they found, Timbrook and Graham (1994) examined how well the MMPI-2 validity and clinical scales predicted behavioral and personality ratings made by the spouses of a subset of matched African American and Caucasian subjects (72 males and 64 females in each group). No significant differences were found between the ethnic groups in the accuracy with which the MMPI-2 predicted these extratest criteria, except for a tendency of Scale 7 (Pt) to underpredict ratings of anxiety for the African American women. The authors conclude that "differences between African American and Caucasian persons are minimal when the effects of age, years of education, and total family income are taken into account" (p. 214).

Ben-Porath, Shondrick, and Stafford (1995) collected new samples of 137 Caucasian and 47 African American males receiving court-ordered forensic evaluations and compared their mean scores on the validity, clinical, content, and substance abuse scales of the MMPI-2. The two groups produced very similar profiles, with the only significant difference consisting of higher scores among the African American subjects on the content scales for Cynicism and Antisocial Practices. Noting that their groups were similar in socioeconomic status, Ben-Porath et al. suggest that some previously reported ethnic differences on the original MMPI may have been artifacts of social class differences between subject groups.

With respect to socioeconomic status, Long, Graham, and Timbrook (in press) examined the relationship of mean validity and clinical scale scores to educational and family income levels in the 1,138 men and 1,462 women in the MMPI-2 standardization sample. They were also able to examine ratings of symptoms and problems provided by the spouses of 841 of these subjects. Across five income levels, none of the clinical scales showed a T-score difference of more than 5 points among either men or women. Across five educational levels, only Scale 5 (Mf) for men, but not for women, showed a T-score difference greater than 5 points, with higher scores associated with higher levels of education. The authors concluded that, "The effects of educational level and family income on MMPI-2 clinical scale scores are minimal and probably not clinically meaningful" (p. 166).

With respect to the validity scales, Long et al. (in press) found significant mean differences involving more than 5 T-score points between socioeconomic status and Scales F and K. For both men and women, and for both income and educational level, higher status was associated with a lower F Scale and a higher K Scale. The authors postulated that these differences probably do not influence conclusions about test validity, but they did not have relevant extratest measures available from which to determine whether these differences have different clinical correlates.

In an overview of the applicability of the MMPI-2 to diverse subject groups, Graham (1993, chap. 8) has noted that the initial analyses of the MMPI-2 normative data did not appear to call for separate norms for subjects of different ages, geographic areas, or ethnicity. Commenting on the available research, Graham (1993, chap. 9) pointed out further that neither African American, Hispanic, or Native American subjects have thus far shown many substantial scale score differences from Caucasian subjects similar in socioeconomic status.

At the same time, however, Graham (1993, chap. 9) observed that relatively little is yet known about extratest correlates of whatever ethnic-related scale score differences may exist. In Graham's opinion, one cannot yet be certain to what extent MMPI-2 scores of African Americans, Hispanics, and Native Americans should be interpreted similarly to those of Caucasians (pp. 196-200). As for Asian Americans, Graham noted, the limited sampling available to date is insufficient to warrant conclusions about MMPI-2 scale score similarities to Caucasians (pp. 202-203).

Hence, for the forensic examiner testifying about the MMPI-2 protocol of a minority group subject, the ground may not yet provide solid footing. Being cross-examined about the appropriateness of applying customary interpretive guidelines to the MMPI-2 protocol of a minority individual, expert witnesses may be able to fall back safely on the assurances of Butcher and Williams (1992) that no special interpretive considerations are necessary, or they may be effectively challenged by reference to Graham's (1993) observations that knowledge is still limited concerning the interpretive significance of MMPI-2 differences between ethnic minority and Caucasian subjects.

Expert witnesses must also be prepared for challenges based on the small numbers of minority subjects who were in the MMPI-2 standardization sample and on whom the normative descriptive statistics are based: for females, 39 Native Americans, 38 Hispanics, and 13 Asian Americans; for males, 38 Native Americans, 35 Hispanics, and 6 Asian Americans (Pope et al., 1993, pp. 22-23). Imagine the plight of a colleague attempting to explain how an MMPI-2 protocol obtained from an Asian American man compares with normative expectation for his ethnic group, when the cross-examining attorney is poised to inquire just how many Asian American males make up the normal comparison group in this supposedly well-standardized instrument that the psychologist wants the court to believe is appropriate for drawing conclusions about the personality of an Asian American man.

Forensic examiners are also limited in the types of MMPI-2 normative data on which they can draw. Expert witnesses do benefit from the T-score transformations that were employed in designing the instrument, because percentile ranks are now the same for a given T-score elevation on all of the clinical scales except Scales 5 (Mf) and 0 (Si) and on all of the content scales. Accordingly, by drawing on the published tables of percentile ranks for T-scores, examiners can indicate the percentage of people in general who are likely to show particular scores on individual scales.

However, many clinicians have traditionally based their MMPI inferences less on individual scale scores than on code types and configurations. Moreover, it is generally recognized that the certainty of a clinical inference depends not only on a particular high-point or two- or three-point code, but on the extent to which these points are elevated above the remaining scale scores. Nonparametric data concerning MMPI-2 high points and code types are not readily available. What percentage of people in general show a high point on Scale 2, for example, and of these, for how many does Scale 2 exceed the next highest scale by 5 points or more? What percentage of people in general show a 49/94 or a 278 variant? Being able to speak to such questions with authority would greatly enhance the ability of expert witnesses to present their MMPI-2 findings clearly and convincingly, especially with respect to the issue of reasonable certainty.

To be sure, Greene (1991, pp. 241-243) does provide some tables indicating the frequency of MMPI-2 code types in samples of psychiatric and medical patients. However, aside from lacking a normative nonpatient sample, these data are based on rescoring of original MMPI protocols to approximate the MMPI-2, and not on any actual administration of the MMPI-2. As an additional source of information, the revised Minnesota Report, an automated MMPI-2 analysis available from National Computer Systems, now includes a section called "Profile Frequency" that indicates the frequency with which a subject's high point, code type, and any scale spikes occur among persons seen in various settings. This information is not presently available to nonusers of the revised Minnesota Report, however.

RESEARCH DIRECTIONS
CONCERNING NORMATIVE DATA

As implied by the preceding discussion, future research with the MMPI-2 should address, in further detail, possible normative differences among demographic groups that bear on guidelines for interpretation. In particular, additional normative data are needed on patient as well as nonpatient groups who differ in sociocultural and socioeconomic background; on women as well as men examined in forensic settings; and on Asian Americans of all kinds. Considerable additional data are likewise needed concerning extratest correlates of subgroup differences to determine whether they call for different types of interpretation.

The need for additional data of these kinds does not mean that investigators pursuing such research should anticipate finding group differences in scale scores that will necessitate the formulation and use of separate norms for these groups. Whereas consistent and substantial gender differences have been found and acknowledged with separate norms for males and females on both the original MMPI and the MMPI-2, the differences among socioeconomic and sociocultural groups that have emerged in the limited research to date have, as already noted, been few in number and for the most part small in size. Even if future studies were to demonstrate some consistently significant scale score differences related to demography, moreover, separate norms might still not be necessary, for three reasons.

First, as implied in the previous discussion, the keys to effective MMPI interpretation are the empirical correlates of the test, not its scale scores. Scale score differences between groups are meaningful only if they point to dissimilar correlates. Hence, consistent demographic differences in the inferences drawn from MMPI-2 data would be necessary to call for separate norms, not just group differences in the mean values of scale scores.

Second, because clinical interpretation is based largely on code types and configurations and not individual scale scores, any identified demographic group differences in mean scale values may wash out in the process of identifying high-point or two- or three-point codes. Only consistently significant demographic differences in the frequency of code types and configurations, together with evidence that these code types and configurations have different extratest correlates for different demographic groups, would require separate norms. These separate norms would then be norms for code types and configurations, not scale scores.

Third, there is good reason to believe that core aspects of personality functioning are basic to the human condition and manifest among all groups of people. Everywhere in the world, for example, there will be some people who are relatively passive and others who are relatively assertive; some who are relatively self-serving and exploitative in their interpersonal relationships and some who are relatively caring and nurturant; some who are emotionally expansive and others who are emotionally inhibited; some who are relatively contemplative and methodical in their problem-solving style and others who are relatively intuitive and undisciplined; and so on.

These differences among people can be measured by the MMPI-2 and other personality assessment techniques wherever people are and however they identify themselves; why else have the MMPI and MMPI-2 been translated into dozens of languages and used to apparently good effect around the world? Hence, MMPI-2 findings that indicate personality styles in one group of people are likely to do so in another, independently of how common or frequent those styles happen to be in a particular group.

With respect to future research, however, what is still needed for forensic purposes is substantially expanded information concerning how code types and configurations are distributed among groups differing in demography. Whether a given code type generally indicative of psychopathology should be considered more or less pathologic in relation to how commonly or infrequently it occurs in a subject's demographic group is a complex question that touches on the broad issue of whether normality is an absolute or relative concept. Without tackling this thorny issue, forensic psychologists would still be better off than they presently are if they could at least (a) report the incidence of critical MMPI-2 findings among specific subgroups to which subjects belong and (b) indicate the extent to which MMPI-2 findings mean the same thing in various subgroups.

Reliability

As defined in classical test theory, reliability consists of the extent to which an obtained score corresponds to the "true" score. The "true" score is an abstraction that can never be known for sure, and the obtained score is a combination of this unknowable true score and some error variance. Reducing the error variance in a particular measurement increases the likelihood that an obtained score will approximate the true score, and reduced error variance justifies increased confidence that the obtained score provides reliable information concerning the true extent of the phenomenon it is intended to measure (Anastasi, 1988, chap. 5).

Traditionally, reliability has been estimated by parallel form, split-half, test-retest, and internal consistency methods. Psychologists frequently speak of reliability as if it were synonymous with these methods, as when they refer to the split-half reliability of Test A or the retest reliability of Test B. In fact, however, such statements are only shorthand ways of identifying reliability as estimated by different methods. Moreover, for multidimensional tests with numerous scores and scales, test reliability exists only as an averaging or general impression based on the estimated reliability of its individual components, and omnibus measures often comprise some mix of highly reliable, moderately reliable, and not so reliable component scores or scales.

As one further qualification, the various methods of estimating reliability may not be equally relevant in assessing the psychometric adequacy of different scales. A scale may yield consistent scores over time but lack internal consistency, because it is multifactorial, for example, and another scale may show consistently high split-half correlations but an inconsistent total score over time, because it is measuring a state rather than a trait variable.

These distinctions between ways of estimating whether a personality test is reliable—that is, whether it yields scores on which one can rely as providing a true picture of the subject's personality characteristics—have important implications for forensic testimony. When psychologists are working with broad-band, multidimensional personality instruments, parallel forms are typically unavailable, equivalent split-halfs are difficult or impossible to identify, and factorial purity may be elusive. Efforts to surmount these problems by constructing parallel forms for long and complex measures may not be feasible; forced equivalences among items to achieve a split-half may disrupt the integrity of the measure; and extracted factors may lack the interpretive richness of identified subscale diversity within individual scales or scores. As a consequence, test-retest findings typically constitute the touchstone of reliability for omnibus personality tests.

The temporal stability of test findings also turns out to be the aspect of reliability that most frequently comes into consideration in the courtroom. A majority of the judgments sought in forensic psychology cases rest on extrapolations from the present status of plaintiffs or defendants to their psychological functioning at some past or future time. To be sure, in cases of civil competency or competency to stand trial, the entire judgment of the court may depend on a present status evaluation alone—for example, when test data clearly indicate the presence of dementia or psychosis. In most other kinds of forensic cases, however, judgment is likely to rest with comparisons between presently observed characteristics of the individual and the likely nature of those characteristics in the past or future.

Thus, in cases of personal injury, especially those involving allegations of psychic trauma, the court is typically interested in whether any presently observed psychological difficulties constitute a change from the plaintiff's psychological condition prior to the allegedly traumatic event. In cases concerning criminal responsibility, the central question concerns not so much the defendant's present mental state as his or her probable mental state at the time when the offense was committed. When forensic testimony addresses whether a convicted offender should be imprisoned or placed on probation, or whether an incarcerated offender should be paroled, or whether a mother or father is likely to meet the best needs of a child, the court would mainly like to know what can be predicted from present test data about the future personality functioning of the individual being judged.

These concerns of the court focus on issues of temporal stability—what can be said with reasonable certainty, on the basis of present test findings, about what this person was like at some past moment or will be like at some future time? Even when forensic questions are framed in terms of a person's mental *state* at some past moment, the challenge for assessors is to draw conclusions from presently available data concerning (a) what kind of person the subject is and (b) how this kind of person might have been likely to respond to the circumstances of the past moment.

To answer questions concerning past and future likelihoods, forensic assessors need to be able to draw on temporally stable test indexes. In the case of an alleged felon, for example, a spike 4 (Pd) profile might have some implications for how or why the alleged offense happened to be committed; in the case of a convicted felon, a spike 4 (Pd) profile might have some implications for recommending incarceration or probation. To formulate any such implications with reasonable certainty, an examiner needs to be reasonably certain that a subject showing a spike 4 profile today was likely to have shown it in the past, will do so in the future, or both.

On the other hand, psychologists attempting to answer questions about the past and future need to keep in mind that temporal stability is not synonymous with reliability. Test-retest correlations provide estimates of reliability only for phenomena that are expected to be stable over the time interval of the retest. In the measurement of personality characteristics that are known to change substantially over time or have for whatever reason changed in a particular subject or group of subjects, retest correlations do not adequately reflect the intrinsic reliability of a scale—and less so the longer is the retest interval.

Accordingly, although temporal stability speaks to reliability in the assessment of *trait* dimensions of personality, retest correlations say nothing about the reliability with which a *state* dimension is being measured. Conversely, high split-half or internal consistency indexes of reliability provide no assurance that a test finding will be temporally stable. At any rate, in the courtroom, where attention is focused on trait dimensions of what people were like in the past or will be like in the future, or on whether what people are like now resembles or differs from past or future expectation, the strength of forensic psychological testimony will often depend on the extent of temporal stability that has been demonstrated for the measures from which inferences are being drawn.

FORENSIC STATUS OF
MMPI-2 RELIABILITY DATA

Little information is presently available concerning the temporal stability of the MMPI-2. If retest findings with the original MMPI are considered applicable to the MMPI-2, then some preliminary conclusions about the stability of the newer instrument can be drawn. With respect to the forensic implications of temporal stability, these conclusions are both reassuring and troubling. The MMPI has generally been regarded as a reliable instrument, and with good reason. The results of a meta-analytic study led Parker, Hanson, and Hunsley (1988) to conclude that the MMPI is equivalent in reliability to the Wechsler Adult Intelligence Scale (WAIS)—a conclusion that would support strong positive statements about MMPI reliability. On the other hand, given the specific nature of the temporal stability data that are available, it is surprising that the forensic relevance of MMPI findings has not more often been challenged in the courtroom than seems to be the case.

Regarding these stability data, what is known and what has yet to be learned parallel the distinction between scale scores and code types on one hand and between short-term and long-term stability on the other. As reviewed in the texts by Graham (1993, chap. 8) and Pope et al. (1993, Appendix H), the short-term stability of the validity and clinical scales of the MMPI is quite satisfactory. In various studies of nonpatient subjects retested after intervals ranging from 1 day to 2 weeks, the original MMPI scales have typically shown stability coefficients between .70 and .80. For the MMPI-2, a first study involving retesting of 82 males and 111 females after 1 week yielded comparable results, with stability coefficients ranging from .67 (Mf) to .92 (Si) for males and from .58 (Mf) to .91 (Si) for females. Although this MMPI-2 study suggests the possibility of some scale differences in stability, the original MMPI research has not identified any scales as being consistently more stable than any other scales.

In contrast to these substantial short-term stability coefficients, readministrations of the original MMPI after an interval of 1 year or more have yielded scale correlations ranging typically from .35 to .45. Correlations of this or even lesser magnitude are quite acceptable for scales measuring variable phenomena, such as state dimensions of anxiety or depression, but they fall below usual standards for demonstrating reliable measurement of presumably stable phenomena such as trait dimensions of antisocial attitudes and social introversion. In the absence of MMPI retest studies at various intervals between 2 weeks and 1 year, moreover, the point in time at which score stabilities begin to decline from .70 to .80 after 2 weeks to .35 to .45 after one year or more is unknown.

As for the MMPI-2, there are (with one exception) no retest data available for intervals greater than 1 week. This exception is notable, however, for it not only suggests potential for greater long-term stability than has previously been demonstrated, but also provides nonparametric as well as parametric analyses of the data. In this study, Spiro, Bosse, Butcher, Levenson, and Aldwin (1993) were able to compare the MMPI-2 profiles of a community sample of 1,072 men age 45 to 93 with responses they had given 5 years previously on an experimental form of the MMPI-2 used in its development (Form AX). Across the validity, clinical, content, and seven supplementary scales of the instrument, the mean scale scores rarely changed by more than 1 T-score point, and the 5-year stability coefficients ranged from .55 (on Scale 6) to .85 (on Scale 0). Retest correlations of .70 or more were found on one of the validity scales (K Scale), two of the clinical scales (Scale 2 and Scale 6), all of the content scales except Bizarre Mentation, and all of the seven supplementary scales examined except Overcontrolled Hostility.

Turning to the Spiro et al. (1993) nonparametric data, the men in this study generally maintained the same relative rank order over time on the scales, even though there were some who changed dramatically on one scale or another. The investigators analyzed such change by comparing each individual's placement in three clinically significant portions of the T-score distribution for each scale: < 36, 36-64, and > 64. Over the 5-year interval of the study, the percentage of subjects who changed their placement in these three categories ranged from just 20% for the most changeable scale down to only 4% for the least changeable scale.

Further research involving diverse subject groups and retest intervals is necessary to document the long-term temporal stability suggested by the Spiro et al. (1993) data. In the meantime, forensic assessors need to be aware that they are limited in what they can say with confidence about similarities between a subject's current MMPI-2 scale scores and what these scale scores would have been more than a few weeks ago or will be more than a few weeks hence. Whatever the temporal stability of individual MMPI-2 scales, moreover, a more important forensic consideration may, as already noted, be the stability of its code types. The stability of original MMPI code types has been examined in only a small number of studies, and most of these studies have involved retesting intervals of one week or less. No information has yet become available concerning the retest correlations of MMPI-2 configurations over any interval of time.

Generally speaking, as summarized by Graham (1993, chap. 8), retest studies with the original MMPI indicate that about one half of subjects have the same high-point code on short-term retesting, one fourth to one third have the same two-point code, and about one fourth have the same three-point code; no high-point or two-point code appears to be more stable than other codes. To the extent that a code type is expected to measure a personality trait or style, these modest stability data do not provide much support for forensic testimony. Expert witnesses speculating about past or future adaptation or mental state on the basis of a two-point code will not fare well in the hands of informed attorneys who are prepared to elicit from them the information that 50% of subjects are likely to show a different two-point code a few weeks later.

Although caution in this and other regards will typically serve forensic examiners well, the code type stability data are not in truth as shaky as has just been suggested. As Graham (1993, chap. 8) has also pointed out, certain characteristics of a profile can bolster the confidence one can have in the stability of MMPI code types. The more that high-point codes are elevated initially, and the more that two- and three-point codes are clearly defined and extreme, the more likely they are to be stable over time. Moreover, among subjects whose code types change over short retest intervals, from one half to two thirds are likely to show code types in the same general diagnostic grouping of neurotic, psychotic, and characterological code types.

Even so, many questions about MMPI stability, let alone stability on the MMPI-2, remain unanswered. Just how much elevation in codes and how much clear definition of code types are necessary to promote just how much temporal stability? Among the one third to one half of subjects retested thus far who show changes among groups of code types, how many are likely to show these changes because their condition has in fact changed, or instead because the MMPI has not provided a reliable measurement of the unchanged nature of their condition? Graham suggests that dramatic changes in code types are likely to be accompanied by equally dramatic behavioral changes. However, except for some preliminary evidence in this regard reported for the MMPI by Graham, Smith, and Schwartz (1986), parallels between changes in code types and changes in behavior have not yet been examined.

Because of the still uncertain parameters of original MMPI stability and the largely uncharted waters of MMPI-2 stability, expert witnesses may be hard pressed to justify basing inferences about past or future behavior on current test findings. What can an MMPI-2 say about the likely mental state or even the general personality orientation of a defendant at the time he or she committed a crime several months earlier? What can MMPI-2 data tell us about the psychological condition or personality style that an individual will bring to bear on life problems as a parent or probationer several months in the future?

Going beyond the stability of MMPI-2 data in this way to consider their implications for past and future behavior shifts the focus of the present discussion from issues of reliability to issues of validity. The discussion returns to these validity issues following some observations on future directions in reliability research.

RESEARCH DIRECTIONS
CONCERNING RELIABILITY DATA

The preceding questions call attention to some MMPI-2 research directions sorely in need of pursuit. As a prelude to specifying these research needs, personality assessors need to squarely face some discomfiting characteristics of MMPI research in general. The MMPI has been the most widely studied of all personality assessment instruments. However, it can be fairly said (a) that a preponderance of MMPI research has been narrowly focused on current corollaries and (b) that a preponderance of this MMPI research on current corollaries has been pedestrian.

Regarding the narrow focus of MMPI research, much of the available literature addresses relationships between test responses and other characteristics subjects display at approximately the same time they take the MMPI. Current corollaries are advantageous to pursue, because, when identified, they help to establish the concurrent validity of an assessment instrument and support inferences concerning the present functioning of individual subjects. The search for current corollaries has the further advantage of lending itself to relatively undemanding research designs. All of the necessary data can be collected more or less concurrently, with a one-time administration of measures, and the results become quickly available to submit for publication or to satisfy dissertation or research grant requirements.

By contrast, longitudinal studies and research designed to measure personality characteristics prior or subsequent to particular events that occur only occasionally in people's lives, rather than at the convenience of the researcher, are difficult to mount and time consuming to complete. Repeated measures, prolonged subject finding and tracking, and delayed results typify this kind of research. The abundance of relatively easy to manage concurrent research studies and the dearth of relatively difficult to implement prospective and retrospective studies is the reason why we know so little about the long-term stability of MMPI profiles and their implications for past and future personality functioning.

As for the pedestrian quality of MMPI research on current corollaries, the attractive efficiency of collecting all of one's data at one fell swoop has, as is well-known, often been compounded by the use of convenience samples and nonbehavioral dependent variables. To take a hypothetical example involving validity, consider the contrast between (a) a potentially valuable concurrent validity study of the sensitivity and specificity of a broad range of MMPI variables in discriminating among psychiatric patients with different patterns of manifest symptomatology and (b) an almost meaningless examination of congruence between Scale 0 (Si) and some paper-and-pencil measure of sociability among college sophomores. Perhaps an accumulation of the latter kind of studies is in some way helpful in demonstrating the convergent validity of Scale 0 and building a nomological net for sociability. However, the absence of observable, extratest correlates in such MMPI studies and the limited generalizability of the results they yield do little to advance knowledge of the instrument or serve the purposes of forensic psychologists who base testimony on it.

Turning to the implications of these considerations for reliability research, investigators should focus future studies of MMPI-2 reliability on the temporal stability of its indexes and should address (a) long-term changes over time as assessed by repeated measures, (b) consistency and change over time in code types and configurations as well as scale scores, and (c) persistence of code types and configurations in relation to critical events. Regarding the first of these, retesting over extended intervals will reveal much more than is currently known about the stability of MMPI-2 findings over periods longer than a few weeks and provide critical information for forensic psychologists attempting to extrapolate from present data to past or future likelihoods. In addition to identifying the extent of long-term stability, repeated measurements will also reveal at what point in time extrapolations from present findings to likely findings in the past and future become unreliable.

As for attention to code types and configurations in retest findings, repeated measurement research will provide the temporal stability information currently lacking about these interpretively significant features of MMPI-2 protocols. Finally, collecting MMPI-2 data prior to, following critical events in persons' lives, or both will considerably extend present knowledge concerning which scale elevations and profile patterns measure personality traits that persist independently of such events as developing or recovering from psychological disturbance, being injured or traumatized, or experiencing disruptions in family and interpersonal relationships; and which code types and configurations measure state characteristics of people that vary in response to such events.

Adequate study of persistence and change subsequent to critical events requires an investment in case finding that, as noted, has too infrequently characterized MMPI research. Subjects who have experienced a critical real-world event of interest to a forensic investigator, such as committing a particular kind of crime under certain kinds of circumstances or suffering a particular kind of accident, are unlikely to be available in undergraduate classrooms, and they may also not be present in the individual investigator's clinical or practice setting in sufficient numbers to support a powerful research design. Especially when test reliability is to be inferred from scores that change when people have changed, as well as from unchanged test scores in the absence of personal change, appropriate subjects will often have to be painstakingly found rather than easily stumbled on.

Hence, advances in MMPI-2 reliability research are likely to require collaborative networks of researchers and effective means of searching out study participants who satisfy specific and clearly defined requirements—such as having been a victim of physical or sexual assault. In this same vein, searching for MMPI-2 protocols that happened to have been obtained shortly before some critical event occurred, such as committing a crime, can generate revealing comparisons with a retest conducted after the event. Developing networks and procedures for collecting records taken just prior to critical events also has obvious implications for examining the predictive validity of the MMPI-2, to which the discussion now turns.

Validity and Utility

Validity as classically defined consists of the extent to which it is known what a test measures (Anastasi, 1988, chap. 6). Various approaches to identifying what a particular test measures are reflected in several types of validity that have traditionally been grouped in the categories of *content validity, criterion-related validity,* and *construct validity.* A test is considered to have face validity if its items have some clear and obvious relationship to the purpose of the test and appear broadly representative of the kinds of items that should be included in it. If a test is intended to serve as a measure of depression, for example, the item "Are you feeling depressed?" is highly content (or face) valid, and the absence of any items concerned with dysphoric mood, negative cognitions, or diminished energy will detract from the apparent content validity of the test.

Criterion-related validity consists of the relationship between a test or test score and some other measured variable. Substantial correlations between test findings and current events, conditions, and behaviors (including how subjects perform on other tests), demonstrate *concurrent validity* for these test findings. Substantial correlations between test findings and future events, conditions, and behaviors provide evidence of their *predictive validity*. Finally, construct validity consists of the extent to which observed relationships between test findings and present or future corollaries can be conceptualized in terms of a theoretical rationale that accounts both for the test findings and the extratest corollaries.

Just as speaking of test reliability is a shorthand notation, it is simplistic to speak of "test validity" or to ask such questions as whether Test A and Test B are valid and which is more valid. First of all, tests may differ in the kinds of validity they demonstrate. A test that because of its subtlety and indirect approach has little apparent content validity may nevertheless be a good predictive instrument; a test that measures state variables may show good concurrent validity but little predictive validity; and a test that has been empirically rather than theoretically derived may demonstrate good concurrent and predictive validity in the absence of very much construct validity.

Second, speaking to the validity of a test is meaningless without adequate attention to the purpose for which its validity is in question. One test may be valid for identifying schizophrenia but invalid as a measure of neuropsychological impairment, another test may be a good predictor of school learning difficulties but a poor predictor of conduct problems, and so on.

Third, for any test that generates multiple scores, and particularly for an omnibus test of personality, validity inheres not in the test itself but in the individual scores that it yields. To be sure, an overall sense of whether a test is valid can be formed from some mathematical or impressionistic averaging of various validity coefficients for its component parts. With few exceptions, however, the various scales of an omnibus or multifactorial instrument will yield scores that differ in their correlates and vary in their validity for different purposes.

In forensic applications of psychological tests, each of the three broad categories of validity can lead to specific kinds of questions from attorneys who are challenging expert testimony. Attention to content validity is reflected in questions about whether a test was appropriate to use. Thus, an attorney might inquire whether the general nature of the test and the specific content of its items give any reason to expect that it will identify relevant characteristics of the subject's personality or help resolve a forensic question at issue. A challenge to content validity typically involves an effort to discredit a test on commonsense grounds and make its use in such important matters as civil and criminal proceedings seem foolish. Thus, an expert witness may be asked, "Do you want us to believe that whether a man would like to be a singer or sometimes feels like swearing indicates what kind of person he is and whether he is legally sane?" Or the witness may be asked, "Isn't it true that these ink splotches you call a test really come from a parlor game?"

When attorneys address criterion-related validity, their focus shifts from the seeming appropriateness of a test to whether the test in fact works; that is, has it been demonstrated that the test measures the psychological conditions or makes the behavioral predictions that are critical to the case being tried? Accordingly, a focus on criterion validity poses a challenge to the available research literature concerning the empirically established correlates of the instruments on which expert witnesses are basing their testimony.

Should attorneys choose to pursue the construct validity of a test, then their questions typically call for an explanation of why a test works the way that it does. Despite the psychometric significance of this question, it usually does not constitute a serious challenge to forensic testimony. The court is concerned primarily with determining fact, not expanding knowledge, and a proven relationship between events carries weight even if the reasons for this relationship are not fully understood. Usually, then, an attorney who asks for explanations of why a test works, especially after the criterion validity of its relevant correlates has already been delineated, is attempting to cast doubt not on the test but on the expert knowledge of the witness (e.g., "Do you really understand the procedures on which your testimony is based?"). Experts who do understand their procedures and can account for their conclusions in clear terms will usually acquit themselves more effectively on the witness stand than those who lack this capability, but the difference in such instances is a function of the caliber of the psychologist, not the quality of the research data.

Although it is clearly important in clinical practice and forensic testimony to know if a test is appropriate, whether it works, and why it works, these aspects of a test's validity do not fully address whether it is useful. The *utility* of a test, which can also be referred to as its *incremental validity,* consists of how much useful information it provides beyond what is already known or can be learned in simpler ways than administering the test. Thus, for example, an alcoholism scale may yield a statistically significant mean value difference between alcoholic and nonalcoholic subjects and thereby demonstrate concurrent validity, but a simpler, more accurate, and hence more useful way to find out if people have a drinking problem is to ask them.

Psychometric attention to test utility, as distinct from test validity, began with identification of the *base rate problem* (Meehl & Rosen, 1955). Simply put, the base rate problem involves the potential inefficiency of criterion-valid test indexes in assessing highly frequent or infrequent events. For example, in a clinical setting in which 10% of the patients are suicidal, a valid test of suicidality that has a hit rate of 60% (i.e., is correct 60% of the time in identifying subjects as suicidal or nonsuicidal) is technically less efficient than simply calling all of the patients nonsuicidal, which would be correct 90% of the time. Likewise, if aggressiveness characterizes 90% of a prison population, a test for aggressiveness with a 60% hit rate is technically less efficient than considering all prisoners potentially aggressive.

Technical efficiency from a psychometric perspective does not always satisfy clinical priorities, however. Consider a scale that is inefficient in assessing suicidality, given its low base rate even in most patient populations, but is nevertheless able to identify a subgroup of patients in whom suicidal behavior is relatively likely to occur. Then efforts at suicide prevention could beneficially be concentrated on this subgroup, rather than on the total patient population—which is a much more attractive clinical option than overlooking the needs of the high-risk group by exercising the technically efficient option of calling all of the patients nonsuicidal.

With such considerations in mind, concern with test utility has shifted in contemporary practice from attention to base rates to attention to the rate of *false positive* and *false negative* findings yielded by test indexes and to the *sensitivity* and *specificity* of tests in identifying various conditions and characteristics of the individual. Depending on the nature of the condition or characteristic being assessed, the frequency of false positives and false negatives is often more important clinically than the overall hit rate of a test. A low rate of false positives means that subjects who elevate on an index are very likely to have the condition or characteristic measured by that index; even when a high rate of false negatives means that the condition cannot be ruled out among subjects who do not elevate on the index, infrequent false positives support firm clinical judgments and reasonably certain forensic testimony based on a positive finding.

As the rate of false negatives declines, the sensitivity of a test index to some condition or characteristic increases. Coupled with a low rate of false positives, such demonstrable sensitivity makes it increasingly unlikely that cases have been missed or wrongly classified. This is the point at which specificity also needs to be questioned, however. Granted that the test findings are associated with the particular conditions or characteristics that the clinician has inferred from them, how likely are they to be associated with certain other conditions or characteristics as well? From a forensic perspective, this specificity question concerning the utility of a valid measure may be the most critical of all. Concerning these test findings that are said to indicate psychotic functioning, an attorney may ask, how likely are they to occur as well in people with a serious personality disorder?

Like aspects of standardization and reliability, the various aspects of test validity identify the kinds of validity data that are likely to prove critical in forensic purposes. In terms of validity, these will be the data that bear meaningfully not only on present personality and behavioral correlates of test findings, but also on their likely past and future corollaries. Additionally, these will be data that indicate not only statistically significant associations between test findings and their corollaries, but also indicate the frequency or degree of certainty with which particular test findings are likely to be associated with particular corollaries and unlikely to be associated with other corollaries. In a case of alleged psychic injury, for example, how certain is it that a particular test finding demonstrates the presence of post-traumatic stress disorder that could not have arisen for other reasons independent of this condition?

FORENSIC STATUS OF
MMPI-2 VALIDITY DATA

As the most widely researched of all personality assessment instruments, the MMPI has been extensively validated by significant correlations of its various scales and configurations with a broad range of criterion variables. If substantial comparability of the MMPI-2 to the original MMPI can be stipulated, without waiting for all of the MMPI validity research to be repeated with the MMPI-2, and if the favorable endorsement of MMPI validity in the Parker,

Hanson, and Hunsley (1988) meta-analysis can be given credence without presenting a further literature review here, there can be little question that the MMPI-2 is on balance a valid assessment instrument.

However, with respect to the different types of validity, the four major questions addressed in forensic psychology—competence, criminal responsibility and disposition, psychic injury, and suitability as a parent—call for different kinds of information. Incompetence is measured largely in terms of present status, as is impairment of psychological or neurological functioning, although often the latter may involve comparisons with estimates of previous functioning and future potential. By contrast psychodiagnostic assessment of criminal responsibility, as previously noted, requires clinicians to infer past status from present behavior; recommendations concerning probation and parole derive from present estimates of subsequent conduct; and evaluating parental suitability calls for predicting future interactions between parents and their children.

Because personality factors do in interaction with environmental events predict behavior, and because the MMPI-2 is a good measure of personality, there is every reason to expect that it can assist in looking backward or forward in time. As already discussed, however, most MMPI research has examined primarily concurrent correlates and thereby left the predictive validity of the instrument largely untouched. Parallel to the limited information concerning the long-term stability of MMPI profiles, then, relationships between present profiles and past or future behavior are substantially undocumented.

There have been two noteworthy exceptions to the dearth of longitudinal research with the MMPI, both of which address forensic predictions. Many years ago, Hathaway and Monachesi (1953) administered the MMPI to several thousand ninth-grade students in Minneapolis and other Minnesota communities and then examined the profiles of those who became known to law enforcement agencies for delinquent behavior during the next 4 years. They found that initial elevations on Scales 4 (Pd), 8 (Sc), and 9 (Ma) predicted a delinquency rate considerably higher than the overall population rate among both boys and girls. As noted by Megargee and Carbonell (see chap. 6, this volume), subsequent research has consistently confirmed elevations of Scales 4, 8, and 9 in youthful offenders.

The other predictive effort of note has been the work of Megargee and his colleagues in developing an MMPI typology for classifying criminal offenders and predicting aspects of their behavior in correctional settings. This research has yielded evidence, for example, that MMPI profiles on admission to a correctional institution can predict use of sick call and adequacy of adjustment to prison life (Carbonell, Megargee, & Moorhead, 1984; Megargee & Carbonell, 1991). However, although the correlations obtained in this research between the MMPI and subsequent behavior were significant with sufficient frequency to establish predictive validity, they rarely exceeded a magnitude of .20. Accordingly, Carbonell et al. (1984) concluded that their scales "might, at best, be of some help in differentiating large groups that might differ somewhat in prison adjustment" (p. 292) but were not adequate for any decision making in the individual case.

In light of the extremely limited data available on predictive validity, especially with respect to predictions about individuals, expert witnesses may be hard-pressed to justify MMPI-based inferences that bear on past or future events and have to rely on indirect ways of supporting their testimony. For example, in a case of contested custody, the psychological expert may be looking at an MMPI-2 from one parent that suggests considerable self-centeredness and lack of responsibility (e.g., an elevated 49/94 profile) and at an MMPI-2 from the other parent that is entirely within normal limits. The expert may testify that people who are highly self-centered and lack a sense of responsibility are generally less effective as parents than people who do not show these characteristics, and that therefore the high 49/94 parent will probably be less suitable as the custodian. However, asked to produce data demonstrating that 49/94 people actually perform poorly as parents or that the children of 49/94 parents turn out bad, the witness will have to state that there are no data to this effect.

Before turning to future directions in MMPI-2 validity research, some comments are in order concerning the *convergent* and *discriminant* validity of the instrument. The convergent and discriminant validity of a test consists of the correspondence between its scores and the scores on other tests or procedures assumed to measure similar or different characteristics. Conventional expectation is that congruence between tests or procedures assumed to measure similar constructs is a good sign with respect to their validity, whereas divergence is a bad sign; for example, significant positive correlations between MMPI-2 indexes of adjustment level and the adjustment level shown on some other tests affirm the convergent validity of the MMPI-2 as a measure of adjustment. Likewise, when dissimilar or contrary constructs are being measured by different tests, divergence is good and congruence is bad for their validity; for example, significant negative correlations between MMPI-2 indexes of depressed mood and indications from other tests of elevated mood affirm the discriminant validity of the MMPI-2 as a measure of depression.

Like the notion of incremental validity, however, convergent and discriminant validity considerations can easily lend themselves to faulty psychometric inferences. In the actual practice of multifaceted personality assessment, the failure of different assessment instruments to demonstrate expected congruence and divergence may well reflect inadequate conceptualization rather than insufficient validity. Tests containing scales that are intended or presumed to measure some similar or identical constructs may measure them quite differently. Specifically, by virtue of differences in their format, item content, and instructions to subjects, different tests may measure dimensions of personality at different levels of conscious awareness or at different levels of subjective or objective decision making in the response process, and they may sample different or even nonoverlapping facets of these dimensions. Less likely but still possible, tests containing scales designed or intended to measure dissimilar constructs may, by virtue of differences between them, measure some similar dimensions of personality.

For this reason, congruent and divergent findings between tests speak to their convergent and discriminant validity only when there is good reason to believe that they are proceeding in very similar ways to identify similar or dissimilar features of personality. In the practice of forensic psychology, examiners are unlikely to be using multiple instruments aimed at identifying the same psychological characteristics in the same way. Instead, a test battery is usually selected purposefully to include tests that measure different characteristics or measure similar characteristics in different ways.

The contemporary watchword in conjoint use of tests in clinical assessment is accordingly changing from attention to their convergent or discriminant validity to their *complementarity* in identifying dimensions of personality functioning. Concern with complementarity introduces the topic of integrating the MMPI-2 with other tests in conducting forensic assessments, which will constitute the final section of this discussion following some comments on future directions in validity research.

RESEARCH DIRECTIONS
CONCERNING VALIDITY DATA

The current status of MMPI-2 validity data leaves little doubt concerning needs for the future. The strength of the instrument resides in its amply demonstrated concurrent validity, whereas, even if the entire body of relevant research with the original MMPI is considered applicable to the MMPI-2, skimpy data on predictive validity remain an Achilles heel. Parallel to the need for long-term temporal stability studies of the instrument, an investment needs to be made in the kinds of problematic, expensive, time-consuming long-term retrospective and especially prospective validity studies that can provide an adequate basis for positing relationships between presently obtained MMPI-2 data and the past and future likelihood of persons thinking, feeling, or acting in certain ways.

With specific reference to MMPI-2 forensic assessment, efforts to mount predictive validity studies are likely to be complicated by difficulties in assembling appropriate subject groups. Clinics and hospitals pass hundreds of people through their doors each year, allowing investigators who work in these settings to study a broad range of health problems, and college students provide a constant flow of subjects for research on personality processes within the normal range. By contrast, subjects involved in specific forensic issues, civil or criminal, are neither numerous in the practice of individual assessors and clinics nor easily obtainable in institutional settings, at least not on a voluntary basis.

As already mentioned with respect to future work on the temporal stability of the MMPI-2, further validation of the instrument for forensic purposes will accordingly require research networks through which relatively small numbers of individual cases can be systematically assembled into large samples. Large groups of persons definitely known to have demonstrated civil or criminal competence or incompetence subsequent to an MMPI-2 evaluation, for example, fed into a research database as they occur in the individual experience of a network of clinicians, will undergird more effective validation of test indexes of competence than has thus far been possible to achieve. The same can be said for personal injury plaintiffs who turn out definitely to be impaired or to have been malingering, probationers who honor their treatment contracts or commit further crimes instead, and parents who perform well or poorly in their child-rearing responsibilities. Large-scale data collection on case outcome would considerably enhance present prospects for demonstrating the validity of MMPI-2 indexes in addressing forensic issues.

Integrating the MMPI-2
With Other Data Sources

Psychologists testifying in forensic cases may be asked to address the adequacy of the MMPI-2 as an assessment instrument or to comment on the implications of a particular MMPI-2 protocol. In this circumstance the expert knowledge on which the expert witness draws will concern the MMPI-2 alone and will not extend to additional information about the subject. Expert testimony on a particular instrument or protocol may be sought to challenge or defend the use to which the test has been put, or to affirm or take issue with conclusions that have been based on it. Testimony of this kind does not require integrating MMPI-2 findings with the results of other tests or even with the circumstances that brought the subject into the courtroom.

In other forensic cases psychological assessors are asked to serve as diagnosticians rather than test specialists. As diagnosticians, expert witnesses are expected to use many different sources of information as a basis for describing an individual's psychological characteristics and relating these characteristics to the issues in the case. Accordingly, forensic assessors are typically encouraged to enter the courtroom thoroughly familiar with all reports, depositions, and allegations relevant to the case; acquainted from first-hand observation with what subjects say and how they conduct themselves in interview and test-taking situations; and armed with data from a carefully selected but adequately comprehensive battery of tests (Blau, 1984; Maloney, 1985; Shapiro, 1991; Weiner, 1995).

To elaborate on the clinical and forensic utility of employing test batteries in psychological evaluations, rather than relying on any single instrument, the conjoint use of various measures can enhance assessment results in three respects:

1. First, using instruments that measure different aspects of psychological functioning helps assessors describe a subject's characteristics *broadly* by drawing on the obtained data in an *additive* fashion. Thus, administering a WAIS-R as well as an MMPI-2 makes it possible to draw inferences about subject's intellectual functioning as well as his or her personality functioning.

2. Second, using instruments that measure similar aspects of psychological functioning helps assessors describe a subject's characteristics *conclusively* by drawing on the obtained data in a *confirmatory* fashion when they happen to converge. Thus, a spike Scale 8 (Sc) and an elevated Bizarre Mentation Scale on the MMPI-2, an elevated Schizophrenia Index on the Rorschach, and disjointed or illogical discourse on the verbal subtests of the WAIS-R make it more likely that a subject has a schizophrenic disorder than any one of these findings by itself.

3. Third, using instruments that measure similar aspects of psychological functioning helps assessors describe a subject's characteristics *in depth* by drawing on the obtained data in *complementary* fashion when they happen to diverge. Thus, the combination of an MMPI-2 with a defensive pattern on the validity scales and noticeably low clinical and content scales with a Rorschach containing numerous indexes of psychological distress and personality disarray (which is not unusual in evaluation of parents seeking custody or felons seeking parole) provides valuable information beyond what could be learned from either test alone. In similar fashion, the combination of a bland Rorschach with an MMPI-2 showing a large F-K difference and many scale elevations (which is not unusual in the evaluation of personal injury plaintiffs) is highly informative because of the divergence between the two measures, which provides useful complementary information.

Of these three potential advantages of a test battery, the least appreciated over time has been the diagnostic value of divergence among measures of similar aspects of psychological functioning. Failure to find expected congruence, such as indications of psychological disturbance on one measure of adjustment being matched by indications of psychological disturbance on another measure of adjustment, has often been viewed with dismay as an impediment to understanding the subject and a challenge to the validity of one or both measures. Presently, however, personality assessors are coming increasingly to recognize the extent to which tests measuring similar functions may measure them in different ways.

Specifically, mention has already been made of the fact that differences in the way tests are structured can result in their assessing personality characteristics at various levels of subject awareness, with differing degrees of objectivity and subjectivity, and with dissimilar susceptibility to influence by test-taking attitudes. Moreover, because of subtle differences in their item content, even structurally similar scales intended to measure the same personality construct may be measuring different aspects or distinct factorial components of this construct.

A research review by Archer and Krishnamurthy (1993) confirms, for example, that the variables scored on the relatively structured MMPI and the relatively unstructured Rorschach are only minimally related to each other, even though both measures are valid in their own right. Going beyond the differences in their structure, Archer and Krishnamurthy noted that there are scales on these instruments carrying similar construct names, such as the Schizophrenic Scale (Sc) on the MMPI and the Schizophrenia Index (SCZI) on the Rorschach, but addressing theoretically or behaviorally dissimilar dimensions of these constructs.

Regarding such dimensional differences even between similarly structured tests, McCann (1991, 1992) reported poor convergent validity between the Compulsive (CPS) scale on the MMPI and the Obsessive-Compulsive (Scale 7) scale on the Millon Clinical Multiaxial Inventory-II (MCMI-II). However, after examining the factor structure of these scales, McCann pointed out that they sample different aspects of obsessive-compulsive behavior. The MMPI scale emphasizes obsessive preoccupation, indecisiveness, and worry, whereas the MCMI-II scale focuses on a high level of behavioral restraint and low levels of instability and sensation seeking.

It is because of such differences that seemingly divergent results on different tests and apparent disagreement between separate indexes of the same personality construct may be as informative as congruence and agreement. Personality assessors are in particular likely in this regard to enhance their results by including in their test batteries at least one relatively structured instrument (such as the MMPI-2) and one relatively unstructured instrument (such as the Rorschach). Differences between these two types of measures in what they suggest about general adjustment level and what they imply about a broad range of problems, complaints, and psychological characteristics provide valuable insights into how people are likely to feel and function in real-life situations.

Knowing whether particular problems, complaints, and characteristics are more likely to be manifest in structured or in unstructured situations can facilitate differential diagnosis among various types of psychological disorder and shed light on how chronic or acute the subject's condition is likely to be. Such information also has significant implications for the type of living arrangements in which individuals are most likely to be comfortable and for the forms of treatment they are most likely to find beneficial. With recognition of how such purposes can be served by a test battery, conjoint use of the

MMPI-2 and the Rorschach has begun to receive attention in the literature and in continuing education programs (Acklin, 1993; Butcher & Weiner, 1994; Exner & Ben-Porath, 1993; Lovitt, 1993; Weiner, 1993).

As a final note concerning the advantages of using the MMPI-2 within the context of a test battery, research findings indicate that neither MMPI nor MMPI-2 code types bear a strong relationship to formal diagnostic categories. The MMPI-2 works best as a measure of personality characteristics and of the nature and severity of psychological symptom formation. With respect to clinical psychiatric diagnosis, agreement with MMPI and MMPI-2 code types has been found to range from 35% to 40%, and diagnoses based exclusively on either instrument are more likely to differ from than agree with an established clinical diagnosis (Morrison, Edwards, & Weissman, 1994; Pancoast, Archer, & Gordon, 1988).

For this reason, appropriate cautions have been raised in the literature against relying on the MMPI alone as the basis for suggesting a psychiatric diagnosis (Brems, 1991; Libb, Murray, Thurstin, & Alacron, 1992). Forensic assessors who infer diagnoses from the MMPI are accordingly at risk both for making frequent errors and for being criticized on the witness stand for acting contrary to reported data and recommended practice. The preferable alternative in arriving at a diagnostic formulation is to integrate MMPI-2 findings with other test findings and sources of clinical data.

Conclusions

This chapter has discussed the psychometric status of the MMPI-2, with particular respect to its applications in forensic assessment. Three conclusions have emerged in the course of this presentation:

1. The MMPI-2 is a basically sound instrument that can readily be defended in the courtroom with respect to its standardization, reliability, and validity.
2. Despite its demonstrably good psychometric qualities, the MMPI-2 has not yet been examined sufficiently with respect to demographic subgroup norms, long-term temporal stability, and predictive validity, and the instrument is vulnerable to cross-examination in these respects.
3. The MMPI-2 can be used most effectively in forensic as well as clinical assessment when combined with other sound instruments to provide opportunities to compare and contrast indications of problems, complaints, and characteristics as manifest on both relatively structured and relatively unstructured

assessment instruments. The issues considered in arriving at these conclusions are by no means unique to the MMPI-2; rather, they are applicable to all psychological assessment procedures, each of which has its own particular blend of strengths, applications, limitations, and aspects in need of further study.

Regarding future research on the psychometric foundations of the MMPI-2, the chapter has suggested several directions that need taking. With respect to available normative data, additional detail should be sought concerning demographic subgroup differences, with particular attention to learning more about typical responses of patient groups differing in socioeconomic status, females examined in forensic settings, and Asian Americans in various circumstances. Increasing attention should also be paid to expressing normative data in nonparametric as well as parametric terms and in code type as well as individual scale expectations. Finally, considerable work remains to be done to explore the extratest correlates of any demographic subgroup differences as may emerge with consistency, to determine with reasonable certainty whether these differences have any clinical interpretive significance.

With respect to reliability, additional work should be done on the long-term stability of MMPI-2 findings. These studies should address (a) long-term changes over time as assessed by repeated measures, (b) consistency and change over time in code types and configurations as well as scale scores, and (c) persistence of code types and configurations in relation to critical events in persons' lives. Adequate study of persistence and change subsequent to critical events will require increased investment in case finding, and the kinds of longitudinal data collection that are needed will call for collaborative networks of researchers and effective means of searching out study participants who satisfy specific and clearly defined requirements with respect to their demographic characteristics and experienced life events.

As for validity, future research with the MMPI-2 should focus on further identification of its predictive strengths and limitations. An investment is needed in long-term retrospective and especially prospective validity studies that can provide an adequate basis for positing relationships between presently obtained data and the past or future likelihood of persons thinking, feeling, or acting in certain ways. Like further work on the temporal stability of the instrument, longitudinal investigations of the predictive validity of the MMPI-2 will require research networks through which relatively small numbers of cases of particular kinds available to individual investigators can be combined into large samples.

References

Acklin, M. R. (1993). Integrating the Rorschach and the MMPI in clinical assessment: Conceptual and methodological issues. *Journal of Personality Assessment, 60,* 132-140.

Anastasi, A. (1988). *Psychological testing* (6th ed.). New York: Macmillan.

Archer, R. P. (1992). Minnesota Multiphasic Personality Inventory-2. In J. J. Kramer & J. C. Conoley (Eds.), *Eleventh mental measurements yearbook* (pp. 558-562). Lincoln, NE: Buros Institute of Mental Measurements.

Archer, R. P., & Krishnamurthy, R. (1993). A review of MMPI and Rorschach interrelationships in adult samples. *Journal of Personality Assessment, 61,* 277-293.

Ben-Porath, Y. S., Schondrick, D. D., & Stafford, K. P. (1995). MMPI-2 and race in a forensic diagnostic center. *Criminal Justice and Behavior, 22,* 19-32.

Blau, T. H. (1984). *The psychologist as expert witness.* New York: John Wiley.

Brems, C. (1991). Depression and personality disorder: Differential diagnosis with the MMPI. *Journal of Clinical Psychology, 47,* 669-675.

Butcher, J. N., & Weiner, I. B. (1994, March). *Clinical assessment using the MMPI-2 and Rorschach.* Workshop presented at Conference on Clinical Assessment: Contemporary Applications, Kona, HI.

Butcher, J. N., Williams, C. L. (1992). *Essentials of MMPI-2 and MMPI-A interpretation.* Minneapolis: University of Minnesota Press.

Carbonell, J. L., Megargee, E. I., & Moorhead, K. M. (1984). Predicting prison adjustment with structured personality inventories. *Journal of Consulting and Clinical Psychology, 52,* 280-294.

Exner, J. E., & Ben-Porath, Y. (1993, March). *Clinical assessment using the MMPI-2 and the Rorschach.* Workshop presented at Society of Personality Assessment Annual Meeting, San Francisco, CA.

Graham, J. R. (1993). *MMPI-2: Assessing personality and psychopathology* (2nd ed.). New York: Oxford University Press.

Graham, J. R., Smith, R. L., & Schwartz, G. (1986). Stability of MMPI configurations for psychiatric inpatients. *Journal of Consulting and Clinical Psychology, 54,* 375-380.

Greene, R. L. (1987). Ethnicity and MMPI performance: A review. *Journal of Consulting and Clinical Psychology, 55,* 497-512.

Greene, R. L. (1991). *The MMPI-2/MMPI: An interpretive manual.* Needham Heights, MA: Allyn & Bacon.

Hathaway, S. R., & Monachesi, E. D. (1951). The prediction of juvenile delinquency using the Minnesota Multiphasic Personality Inventory. *American Journal of Psychiatry, 108,* 469-473.

Libb, J. W., Murray, J., Thurstin, H., & Alacron, R. D. (1992). Concordance of the MCMI-II, the MMPI, and Axis I discharge diagnosis in psychiatric inpatients. *Journal of Personality Assessment, 58,* 580-590.

Long, K. A., Graham, J. R., & Timbrook, R. E. (in press). Socioeconomic status and MMPI-2 interpretation. *Measurement and Evaluation in Counseling and Development.*

Lovitt, R. (1993). A strategy for integrating a normal MMPI-2 and dysfunctional Rorschach in a severely compromised patient. *Journal of Personality Assessment, 60,* 141-147.

Maloney, M. P. (1985). *A clinician's guide to forensic psychological assessment.* New York: Free Press.

McCann, J. T. (1991). Convergent and discriminant validity of the MCMI-II and MMPI personality disorder scales. *Psychological Assessment, 3,* 9-18.

McCann, J. T. (1992). A comparison of two measures for obsessive-compulsive personality disorder. *Journal of Personality Disorders, 6,* 18-23.

Meehl, P. E., & Rosen, A. (1955). Antecedent probability and the efficiency of psychometric signs, patterns, or cutting scores. *Psychological Bulletin, 52,* 194-216.

Megargee, E. I., & Carbonell, J. L. (1991). Personality factors associated with frequent sick call utilization in a federal correctional institution. *Journal of Prison & Jail Health, 10,* 19-42.

Morrison, T. L., Edwards, D. W., & Weissman, H. N. (1994). The MMPI and MMPI-2 as predictors of psychiatric diagnosis in an outpatient sample. *Journal of Personality Assessment, 62,* 17-30.

Nichols, D. S. (1992). Minnesota Multiphasic Personality Inventory-2. In J. J. Kramer & S. C. Conoley (Eds.), *Eleventh mental measurements yearbook* (pp. 562-565). Lincoln, NE: Buros Mental Measurement Institute.

Parker, K. D. H., Hanson, R. K., & Hunsley, J. (1988). MMPI, Rorschach, and WAIS: A meta-analytic comparison of reliability, stability, and validity. *Psychological Bulletin, 103,* 367-373.

Pancoast, D. L., Archer, R. P., & Gordon, R. A. (1988). The MMPI and clinical diagnosis: A comparison of classification system outcomes with discharge diagnoses. *Journal of Personality Assessment, 52,* 81-90.

Pope, K. S., Butcher, J. N., & Seelen, J. (1993). *The MMPI, MMPI-2, & MMPI-A in court.* Washington, DC: American Psychological Association.

Shapiro, D. L. (1991). *Forensic psychological assessment: An integrative approach.* Boston: Allyn & Bacon.

Spiro, A., Bosse, R., Butcher, J. N., Levenson, M. R., & Aldwin, C. M. (1993, August). *Personality change over five years: The MMPI-2 in older men.* Paper presented at the 101st Annual Convention of the American Psychological Association, Toronto, Ontario, Canada.

Timbrook, R. E., & Graham, J. R. (1994). Ethnic differences on the MMPI-2. *Psychological Assessment, 6,* 212-217.

Weiner, I. B. (1987). Writing forensic reports. In I. B. Weiner & A. K. Hess (Eds.), *Handbook of forensic psychology* (pp. 511-528). New York: John Wiley.

Weiner, I. B. (1993). Clinical considerations in the conjoint use of the Rorschach and the MMPI. *Journal of Personality Assessment, 60,* 142-148.

Weiner, I. B. (1995). How to anticipate ethical and legal challenges in personality assessments. In J. N. Butcher (Ed.), *Clinical personality assessment* (pp. 95-103). New York: Oxford University Press.

4

Detecting Distortion in Forensic
Evaluations With the MMPI-2

DAVID T. R. BERRY

Psychological evaluations conducted in forensic settings differ from inpatient psychodiagnostic testing or outpatient personality assessment because the stakes are usually much higher in the forensic arena. Conclusions drawn from forensic psychological evaluations may affect criminal proceedings, potentially resulting in extended prison terms or civil actions involving millions of dollars. The powerful reinforcements and punishments present in legal settings raise the possibility that forensic clients may consciously or unconsciously distort their presentation during an evaluation. The objective evaluation offered by psychological testing, as well as the presence of scales intended to detect response bias, have contributed to the growing use of formal psychopathology inventories in legal settings. The MMPI/MMPI-2 (Butcher, Dahlstrom, Graham, Tellegen, & Kaemmer, 1989) is currently the

AUTHOR'S NOTE: The contributions of Ruth Baer, Martha Wetter, and Robert Gallen to the preparation of this chapter are gratefully acknowledged. Correspondence should be addressed to David T. R. Berry, Department of Psychology, Kastle Hall, University of Kentucky, Lexington, KY 40506-0044.

most commonly used psychopathology instrument in legal settings (Lees-Haley, 1992b).

Nichols, Greene, and Schmolck (1989) offered a useful conceptualization of response distortions on the MMPI/MMPI-2. They divided nonveridical approaches to the test into two major categories, content nonresponsiveness (CNR) and content responsive faking (CRF). CNR involves a failure to respond to the content of questions in a meaningful way, such as occurs with random responding (e.g., marking the answer sheet without reference to the questions). CRF involves responding to test questions with the goal of misrepresenting oneself, as occurs with overreporting or underreporting of symptoms. Greene (1991) recommends a sequential approach to evaluating test data in which CNR must be ruled out prior to addressing CRF, which in turn must be ruled out before interpreting test results. Both the MMPI and the MMPI-2 include a number of validity scales designed to detect CRF and CNR. As reviewed below, the validity scales of the MMPI/MMPI-2 are among the best-documented tools currently available for identifying distorted approaches to testing, with a half century of research exploring their characteristics. However, before we turn to a review of these scales, a number of important methodological issues must be considered.

Methodological Issues

An initial point that must be addressed involves whether response distortions should be a major concern to clinicians using the MMPI/MMPI-2. Considering CNR, Berry et al. (1992) reported that substantial percentages (29% to 60%) of college students, young adults from the general population, and applicants for police training admitted to responding randomly to at least part of an MMPI-2 completed under standard instruction sets. Although the vast majority of these subjects indicated small numbers of random responses, the widespread acknowledgement of CNR indicates that it should not be dismissed as an unlikely problem in any test administration. Considering CRF, Wasyliw, Grossman, Haywood, and Cavanaugh (1988) found substantial numbers of insanity evaluation defendants to overreport symptoms on the MMPI (14% to 37%), and Grossman, Haywood, Ostrov, Wasyliw, and Cavanaugh (1990) found evidence for minimization of psychopathology on the MMPI in police officers motivated to return to work who were undergoing mandatory psychological evaluations for fitness to regain active duty status. These objective data reinforce the commonsense concern that some individuals undergoing forensic evaluation may attempt to distort their presentation in a direction favorable to their goals.

Another important issue involves the definition of the response distortion in question. For example, in the report by Berry et al. (1992), many subjects administered the MMPI-2 under standard instructions admitted on a post-testing feedback questionnaire to giving random responses to some test questions. The vast majority of these subjects indicated small numbers of random responses (12 to 36). At what level should these "partially random" protocols be considered "too" random and thus discarded?

An even more complex problem exists in the case of overreporting of symptoms, commonly known as "malingering." *DSM-IV* (American Psychiatric Association [APA], 1994) defines malingering as the presence of false or greatly exaggerated reports of problems given with the goal of achieving external goals such as avoiding prison or receiving monetary compensation. Although this may seem clear-cut at first glance, two alternative diagnoses— somatoform disorders and factitious disorders—must also be considered in the *DSM* diagnostic scheme. Somatoform disorders involve unconsciously motivated false symptoms manifested for intrapsychic goals (e.g., conversion disorder), whereas factitious disorders involve consciously false reports given for intrapsychic goals such as receiving medical attention. In the absence of an independent indicator of volition, the distinction among these categories rests on extremely challenging clinical judgments of uncertain validity. Rogers, Bagby, and Rector (1989) have explored these ambiguities in greater depth.

Regarding minimization of psychopathology, Paulhus (1984) postulated two types of influences in underreporting of symptoms, self-deception and other-deception. Thus, precise definition of the response set in question must be carefully considered in any investigation of the phenomenon.

Another important issue in use of MMPI/MMPI-2 validity scales involves the research base supporting the validity of these indexes. In evaluating the literature on detection of malingering in analog designs, Rogers (1988) notes problems such as small and nonrandom samples, failure to give explicit instructions with emphasis on a believable presentation, failure to give time for preparation of strategies, lack of powerful contingent reinforcers, and failure to check on subject compliance with instructions. Additionally, as Berry, Baer, and Harris (1991) noted, analog investigations of malingering represent an important initial step in validating indexes, but subsequent exploration of more ecologically representative groups is necessary for com-

plete validation of any "fake bad" index. Ideally, groups of identified malingerers would be used in this second stage of research. However, because
identified malingerers are so rare, use of groups with various inferred levels
of motivation to distort responses, such as Gallucci's (1984) study of VA
disability applicants (discussed later), fills a critical need in this area.

Another interesting and underexplored area involves the strategies employed by individuals approaching psychological testing with the goal of
misrepresenting themselves. At least three potential strategies can be generated rationally. The first approach involves frank fabrication of problems. The
fabricator endorses symptoms that he or she does not actually experience, and
thus must base his or her report on second-hand information about psychopathology. Fabricators may become familiar with psychiatric symptoms through
personal acquaintances, perusal of volumes such as the *DSM-IV* (APA, 1994),
textbooks in psychiatry, or even through exposure to lay sources such as
magazine articles and movies about individuals with mental disorders. A
second strategy involves exaggeration of actually experienced psychopathology,
such as magnification of depression or anxiety. In this approach, the malingerer simply "turns up the volume" on psychological problems experienced
to a lesser degree. A third strategy might be taken by the malingerer who has
previously suffered mental illness but recovered and relies on memory to
guide responses to psychopathology inventories. Combinations of these approaches are obviously possible as well. Given that most "fake bad" indexes
are sensitive to endorsement of an improbably wide range of symptoms or
complaints that mentally ill individuals do not actually make, it seems likely
that frank fabrication of symptoms would be most easily detected, followed
by exaggeration of current problems, and finally by reports based on past
symptoms that are no longer experienced. However, this proposition has not
yet been empirically tested. Development of an adequate theory of malingering strategies would be of great assistance in guiding future research efforts.

Another interesting issue involves whether overreporting of symptoms, underreporting of symptoms, or both occurring in forensic contexts is intrinsically
different from that found in everyday life. For example, most individuals would
acknowledge having misrepresented their health to avoid unpleasant social,
academic, or work obligations. Is "begging off" a dreaded dinner party because
of a "headache" *qualitatively* different from seeking to avoid responsibility for
a crime due to mental illness? Similarly, most job applicants strive to present
themselves in the best possible light, and deny minor peccadilloes or neurotic
symptoms. Is this qualitatively different from the child custody litigant who

denies all psychopathology in a court-ordered evaluation? If over/underre-porting of problems is conceptualized as an operantly maintained behavior (Rogers, 1990), perhaps these examples differ only in the extent of formal social sanctions apportioned to them and the power of stimuli, reinforcers, or both eliciting and/or maintaining them.

Research Findings

RANDOM RESPONDING

Inconsistent or random responding (CNR), as noted above, involves giving answers without reference to the questions. On the MMPI/MMPI-2, this may occur for a variety of reasons, such as inadequate reading skills, inability to sustain attention, visual deficits, language comprehension problems, or un-cooperativeness. On the original MMPI, this problem was detected primarily by reference to the F scale, which consisted of 64 items chosen simply for their skewed distributions of endorsement ($< 10\%$ in the scored direction) in the normative sample (Dahlstrom, Welsh, & Dahlstrom, 1975). Thus, elevation of the F scale indicated endorsement of an unusual number of rare symptoms or complaints. Although the F scale remains one of the best indicators of random responding as discussed below, interpretation of a high F score is complicated by the fact that high levels of genuine psychopathology (Gynther, 1961) as well as overreporting of symptoms elevate this scale (Gough, 1947). The obvious importance of distinguishing random responding from over-reporting of symptoms led to the development of scales designed to be sensitive only to inconsistent responding. Buechley and Ball (1952) intro-duced the TR index, which consisted of 16 questions that were repeated to facilitate processing in an early machine scoreable form of the MMPI. Incon-sistent answers to these repeated questions raise the TR score and the prob-ability of a random approach to the test. Greene (1978) developed the CLS scale, which consists of 12 pairs of items with similar or opposite content, with discordant answers suggestive of inconsistent responding. Nichols et al. (1989) compared psychiatric patient protocols with computer-generated ran-dom protocols and found adequate hit rates using a combination of TR and CLS indexes (85% to 92% across three samples). Gallucci (1985) compared four groups of VA disability applicants whose F scales linearly increased as their inferred motivation to overreport symptoms rose, and found that the TR and CLS indexes did not increase across groups. Overall, these results indicated that the TR and CLS indexes were sensitive to random responding but not to overreporting of problems, implying that reference to these indexes could help to clarify whether an elevated F scale was due to inconsistent responding.

With the MMPI-2 came the introduction of standard validity scales intended to detect inconsistent responding. The Variable Response Inconsistency scale (VRIN) consists of 49 item pairs with similar or opposite content that are scored as inconsistent when any of 67 pairs of answers occur (18 items are scored for either of two combinations and 31 items are scored for only one combination of answers). The True Response Inconsistency scale (TRIN) contains 14 item pairs for which answering true to both questions is inconsistent, and 9 item pairs for which answering false to both questions is inconsistent. VRIN is intended to be sensitive to a generic inconsistency in answering questions, whereas TRIN is intended to be sensitive to a tendency to answer "true" or "false" without reference to item content. Thus, TRIN indicates a "yea-saying" or a "nay-saying" bias.

Berry, Wetter et al. (1991) examined the utility of MMPI-2 validity indexes in detecting fully and partially random protocols in several hundred college students. The VRIN scale had the highest overall hit rate (97%) in classifying protocols as random versus nonrandom. However, the F scale and the similarly derived Fb scale were also quite sensitive to random responding (F: 96%; Fb: 96%). Berry et al. (1992) correlated self-estimates of numbers of random responses given by subjects completing the MMPI-2 under standard instructions with validity scale scores and found modest but reliable correlations (rs = .25 to .56). Paolo and Ryan (1992) compared 200 completely random MMPI-2 protocols with MMPI-2 protocols from 200 male VA psychological patients. In addition to the F, Fb, & VRIN scales, Paolo and Ryan (1992) evaluated two supplementary scales proposed by Greene (1991): (a) the absolute value of the raw F score minus the raw Fb score {F(raw) − Fb(raw)} and (b) the sum of the F and Fb raw scores added to the absolute value of the raw F score minus the raw Fb score {[F(raw) + Fb(raw)] + F(raw) − Fb(raw)}. All the indexes reliably differentiated the patient from random protocols. However, a stepwise discriminant analysis incorporated only the standard validity indexes, with order of entry as follows: VRIN, F, and Fb. The supplementary indexes did not add significantly to the accuracy of the discriminant function, which correctly classified 96.5% of the protocols. Using the cutoff of VRIN ≥ 13 recommended in the MMPI-2 manual, an overall hit rate of 92% was achieved. Currently available evidence supports the use of VRIN as the main indicator of random responding.

Wetter, Baer, Berry, Smith, and Larsen (1992) examined MMPI-2 validity indexes under several instruction sets: standard, fake moderate mental illness, fake severe mental illness, and random responding. The F and Fb indexes were elevated in the presence of overreporting as well as random responding, whereas the VRIN scale was elevated only for the random responding group. Taken together, these studies suggest that VRIN is sensitive to random responding but not to overreporting of symptoms, indicating that it can be used to help identify the source of an elevated F.

Although the research base supporting the MMPI-2 random responding indexes is strong at this time, several important questions remain to be addressed. First, tables incorporating positive predictive power, negative predictive power, and overall classification accuracy at various cutting scores are needed for various base rates (Widiger, Hurt, Frances, Clarkin, & Gilmore, 1984). Second, additional alternative random responding indexes have been proposed by Greene (1991). The efficacy of these indicators relative to the standard indexes should be determined. A third area requiring further exploration springs from the report by Berry et al. (1992) that the majority of those subjects who indicated random responding admitted to only partially random protocols, with the onset of random responding toward the end of the test. Given that the MMPI-2 basic clinical scales all occur in the first 370 items, it is possible that a subject who begins randomly responding toward the end of the MMPI-2 might nevertheless produce interpretable clinical scales. Exploration of validity configurations such as the number of F and Fb items endorsed by blocks of 100 items might generate rules for identifying interpretable clinical scales in the face of partially random protocols. A fourth area that merits attention is further study of the discrimination of random and malingered MMPI-2 protocols. Obviously, the forensic clinician would not want to attribute elevated validity indexes to malingering when random responding was the actual cause. Finally, little is known about the correlates and utility of the TRIN scale in detecting biased responding.

OVERREPORTING OF SYMPTOMS

Although malingering is the term most commonly used to refer to false or exaggerated psychological complaints, overreporting of symptoms is preferred here because MMPI scales in isolation do not definitively document malingering. As noted in *DSM-IV* (APA, 1994), identification of malingering requires gross overreporting of symptoms as well as apparent pursuit of external goals. Although the MMPI may provide data on the former, additional data are required to document the latter.

Overreporting of symptoms occurs when a test taker falsely reports problems or significantly exaggerates those that are actually present. Berry, Baer et al. (1991) meta-analytically reviewed 28 studies published from 1947 to 1989 that investigated the utility of MMPI validity scales for the detection of overreporting of symptoms. Differences between overreporting and honestly responding groups were reported as *d* scores, or effect sizes, which represent the difference between groups in terms of pooled standard deviation units. The mean across all comparisons and all indexes was 2.07, indicating an average difference of about 2 pooled standard deviation units between dissimulating and honest groups. The most effective indicator was the F scale with a mean *d* of 2.3, followed by the Ds scale (Gough, 1954) with a mean of 2.2 and the F – K index (Gough, 1950) with a mean *d* of 1.9. Other approaches such as the Ds-r scale (Gough, 1957) and Subtle/Obvious scales (Wiener, 1948) had much weaker effects in the meta-analysis. These results were interpreted as supporting continued use of the F, Ds, and F – K scales for the detection of overreporting of symptoms, with caution recommended regarding remaining indexes.

Several relevant methodological points emerged from the review as well. First, the effect size depended to a large extent on the type of groups being compared. Thus, comparing normals answering honestly to normals faking psychopathology generated the highest mean *d* (2.7), followed by the comparison of normals faking psychopathology versus genuine psychiatric patients (*d* = 1.9), and psychiatric patients answering honestly versus patients exaggerating their problems (*d* = 1.5). The effect size declined as the ecological validity of the comparison increased, although differences were still respectable in the patient honest versus patient exaggerate contrast. A final comparison type, between individuals presumed to be answering honestly versus individuals presumed to be likely to overreport problems, generated the weakest effect size (*d* = .8). The weakness of the last contrast in which response set was inferred is probably due to the heterogeneity of the groups (even samples of individuals with strong motivation to overreport symptoms probably include some accurately reporting psychopathology as well as others fabricating or exaggerating problems).

A second relevant point is that effect sizes indicate group differences, not accuracy in individual cases. A review of published cutting scores for these MMPI scales indicated a fairly wide range of values. For example, proposed cutting scores for the F scale raw score ranged from 9 to 34, although the highest classification rates were found across studies using cutting scores between 12 and 16. The wide range of cutting scores was interpreted as requiring development of normative data based on specific groups such as forensic samples, psychiatric inpatients, and psychiatric outpatients. Cutting scores specifically tailored to those groups could then be investigated. Only five studies examined in the meta-analysis dealt specifically with forensic populations, and three of these employed groups whose motivational status was inferred. As mentioned previously, the resulting heterogeneity of groups probably contributed to the relatively low mean d score of 1.0 across these five studies. However, the limited number of studies and the modest effect sizes observed suggest the need for additional research and caution in applying available data.

The major points emerging from the meta-analytic review included the following: (a) The MMPI validity scales are fairly good at discriminating malingering and honest groups, with F, $F - K$, and Ds performing the best; (b) cutting scores specific to particular groups need to be developed and validated; and (c) regarding forensic samples, more data, particularly including groups with known motivational status, are needed.

The MMPI-2 introduced one new validity scale, back F (Fb), intended to be sensitive to overreporting of symptoms, and modified the existing scales to varying extents. The Fb scale was constructed after the fashion of the F scale, with items chosen for their low endorsement rates in the normative sample. The 40 Fb items appear in the latter part of the MMPI-2, whereas the F scale items appear before question 370. Theoretically, the diverse content and low endorsement rate of Fb items should render it sensitive to overreporting of symptoms, just as the F scale is, although this is an empirical question. Regarding changes to the original scales, F lost 4 items, bringing the scale item total down to 60, and minor wording changes were introduced to a number of items. The Ds scale lost 16 items, bringing its total down to 58. Finally, changes in the demographic characteristics of the normative sample for the

MMPI-2 may have resulted in changes in expected F and K values, and hence affected the F – K scale. The relatively minor changes to the F, Ds, and F – K scales suggest the need for no more than confirmatory studies of these scales within the context of the MMPI-2, although revised cutting scores may well be needed. In contrast, the Fb scale requires validation before it can be accepted as fully comparable to the F scale.

As of this writing, a number of papers have appeared investigating the utility of various MMPI-2 validity scales in detecting overreporting of symptoms. Wetzler and Marlowe (1990) reported F – K indexes for 35 psychiatric inpatients who took the MMPI-2 and 134 who took the MMPI. The mean F – K score was lower for the MMPI-2 than for the MMPI (MMPI-2: –8.7; MMPI: –3.5). Lees-Haley (1991a) compared MMPI-2 data from personal injury litigants divided into a malingering and nonmalingering group. Cutting scores on the F and the F – K index that classified subjects accurately were much lower than proposed in past work with the MMPI. In similar studies, Lees-Haley (1991b, 1992a) suggested that the Es scale as well as the F and F – K scales had some utility for identifying malingering of post-traumatic stress disorder (PTSD). Lees-Haley, English, and Glenn (1991) presented a rationally derived "Fake Bad Scale" (FBS) that discriminated malingering personal injury litigators from a variety of other groups. Lees-Haley et al. (1991) emphasized that personal injury "malingerers" often mixed "fake bad" and "fake good" approaches to the MMPI-2, depending on the relationship of the item to their claims. Thus, FBS contains both types of questions and is therefore quite heterogeneous.

Graham, Watts, and Timbrook (1991) contrasted normal college students asked to simulate a psychiatric disorder with actual psychiatric inpatients tested within one week following admission to a psychiatric facility. Although the two groups were fairly accurately discriminated using the F and F – K scales, optimal cutting scores were much higher than reported in the past and different for males and females. Clearly, the higher F scores of acute psychiatric inpatients contributed to the differences in cutting scores, and Graham et al. (1991) recommended developing cutting scores in groups matched on level of psychopathology. Also of note was the performance of the Fb scale, which was comparable to that of the F scale and provided support for its use in detecting overreporting of problems.

Wetter et al. (1992) studied college students asked to adopt one of four response sets: standard, random, fake moderate psychological disturbance, or fake severe psychological disturbance. The F, Fb, and Ds scales were elevated by overreporting as well as random responding, whereas the VRIN scale was elevated only by random responding. Also of interest was the fact that subjects were able to "titrate" the level of disturbance they demonstrated on the MMPI-2, as the "fake severe" group was significantly higher on most clinical scales than the "fake moderate" group, although the F scale was comparable for both faking groups. Cassisi and Workman (1992) found that the extracted L, F, and K items performed like those embedded within the entire MMPI-2 in an analog design. Timbrook, Graham, Keiller, and Watts (1993) found the F scale superior to the Subtle-Obvious scales in detecting overreporting of symptoms. Austin (1992) compared a college student group instructed to "fake bad" on the MMPI-2 with another receiving standard instructions. The F, F – K, and O – S scales reliably discriminated the two groups, with the best overall hit rate achieved by the F and F – K scales.

Arbisi and Ben-Porath (1993) developed an F(p) scale through identification of 27 items that were endorsed infrequently by both inpatients and nonpatients. These items were thought to be less sensitive to severe psychopathology and thus potentially useful in identifying individuals elevating F through overreporting of symptoms. Rothke et al. (1994) present normative data for the F – K index derived from a variety of groups, including the standardization sample, psychiatric patients, head-injured patients, disability applicants, job applicants, candidates for a police force, candidates for the priesthood, and substance abusers. Mean F – K values were more negative on the MMPI-2 than on the MMPI, suggesting a need to modify cutting scores. Group membership, as well as gender, had a significant impact on F – K scores.

In summary, presently available data suggest that MMPI-2 overreporting scales have functional characteristics very similar to the MMPI parent scales, and, at least provisionally, that the Fb scale functions comparably to the F scale. Several studies note the need to develop cutting scores for appropriate group contrasts (e.g., normals faking disorder versus psychiatric patients answering honestly). Cutting scores should also be generated for specific groups such as disability applicants, civil litigants, and criminal defendants contrasted with control groups having appropriate levels of psychopathology. Taking into consideration the dimensions of inpatient versus outpatient status as well as gender seems important as well. Finally, exploration of possible subsets of F, Fb, and Ds items that might outperform the parent scales seems potentially useful, although the incremental validity of any such subsets relative to standard scales should be demonstrated as part of their development. Nichols

(1993) has explored the development of content subscales for the MMPI-2 Fb scale, although validation of these subscales is not yet available.

An emerging trend in this area of research has involved exploration of the impact of "coaching" on the success of analog malingerers. Some authors have raised concern about the possibility of specific, targeted information about psychopathology or evaluation procedures being delivered overtly or covertly to potential malingerers (Faust, Ziskin, & Hiers, 1991; Lees-Haley, 1992a). Several recent studies have addressed the effect of coaching on success in malingering. Wetter, Baer, Berry, Robison, and Sumpter (1993) found that normals simulating specific psychological disorders on the MMPI-2 were detected at high rates (73% to 95%) by the F, Fb, & Ds scales despite having received detailed information about a target disorder as well as potential monetary incentives. As with the Graham, Timbrook, Ben-Porath, and Butcher (1991) study, optimal cutting scores were higher than for past studies. Rogers, Bagby, and Chakraborty (1993) investigated the effect on simulators of information on paranoid schizophrenia, information on MMPI-2 validity scales, or both. Although knowledge about the disorder did not dramatically raise the success rate of simulators, information on MMPI-2 validity scales allowed substantial numbers to escape detection. In a similar design, Lamb, Berry, Wetter, and Baer (1994) compared information on closed-head injury symptoms with information on MMPI-2 validity scales and found that information on the disorder decreased the success of head injury simulators, whereas information on MMPI-2 validity scales increased successful malingering.

Ben-Porath (1994) has pointed out that this type of research, at least potentially, offers the possibility of compromising the integrity of the MMPI-2, as results could be used to guide coaching efforts toward more successful strategies. Berry, Lamb, Wetter, Baer, and Widiger (1994) agree with this concern and outline several potential approaches to limiting the negative impact of these types of studies. Clearly, investigators pursuing this line of research should carefully consider these issues in designing and publishing their work. At the same time, coaching does appear likely to have a significant effect on the success of dissimulators, and thus warrants continued investigation, albeit mindful of the ethical issues involved.

UNDERREPORTING OF SYMPTOMS

Denial or minimization of psychopathology is of concern in a number of forensic situations, such as child custody determinations and parole evaluations. The MMPI includes a number of standard and supplementary scales intended to be sensitive to underreporting of symptoms. Baer, Wetter, and Berry (1992) meta-analytically reviewed 25 studies from the literature on detection of "faking good" using MMPI scales published from 1948 to 1989. Using the d statistic described earlier, the overall effect size for detection of underreporting of symptoms was about 1.0, indicating mean group differences of about 1 pooled standard deviation between underreporting and accurately responding groups. Although the standard L and K scales had effect sizes of about 1, the positive malingering scale (Mp) of Cofer, Chance, and Judson (1949) and the social desirability scale (Sd) of Wiggins (1959) had larger effect sizes of about 1.5. However, optimal cutting scores on all of these scales varied widely across studies. The authors concluded that detection of underreporting of problems on the MMPI was not as successful as detection of overreporting, and that cutting scores specific to particular groups needed to be derived. Further research on Mp and Sd was recommended.

The MMPI-2 included no changes in composition of the L and K scales, although the Mp scale lost 7 of 34 items and the Sd scale lost 7 of 40 items. Much less research on the detection of underreporting of symptoms with the MMPI-2 has appeared than for detection of overreporting of symptoms. Graham et al. (1991) included both faking good and faking bad student groups in their study, and found that detection of faking good was only modestly successful using the L and K scales. Interestingly, Graham et al. (1991) found that the L scale was more elevated than the K scale by underreporting of symptoms, which was the reverse of the pattern usually found with the MMPI. (This probably occurred because of changes for the T-scale distributions for the L and K scales on the MMPI-2 relative to the MMPI.) Additionally, gender differences in optimal cutting scores and even in the most effective index were found. Data on Mp and Sd were not reported in this study. Austin's (1992) study included a "fake good" group in addition to the "fake bad" and "honest" groups previously discussed. As with the Graham et al. (1991) study, Austin's data suggest that MMPI-2 validity scales were less successful at identifying underreporting than overreporting of symptoms. The L scale appeared to be the best indicator of underreporting of symptoms in this study. At the time of this writing, no other full-length articles on the detection of underreporting of symptoms with the MMPI-2 were available. However, Butcher and Han (1993) presented data on the Superlative, or S scale, which was developed on airline pilot applicants to detect the tendency to present oneself as a superior individual.

Baer, Wetter, Berry, Nichols, and Greene (1993) evaluated a variety of MMPI-2 underreporting scales and found the L, K, Sd, Mp, and S scales to have relatively high d values when normals answering under standard instructions were contrasted with normals instructed to "fake good." However, optimal cutting scores again varied widely. Clearly, substantial additional research is necessary to explore the utility of various MMPI-2 underreporting scales.

Implications for Clinical Practice

MMPI

The literature reviewed above suggests that the MMPI validity scales are probably the best-documented tools available for detecting response bias within the context of a psychopathology inventory. MMPI validity indexes appear to be sensitive to random responding as well as overreporting of symptoms. However, underreporting of symptoms is not as efficiently identified. The TR and CLS indexes should be used to identify random responding, and the F, F – K, and Ds scales can be used to index overreporting of problems. Although the Mp and Sd scales appeared promising for the detection of underreporting, the indexes do not have the weight of accumulated evidence supporting the random responding and overreporting scales. Although a great deal of data are available supporting the sensitivity of MMPI validity scales to random responding and overreporting of problems on a group basis, it appears that consensus on appropriate cutting scores for each scale has not yet emerged. In general then, the higher the score on a given index, the more concern there should be about the presence of response bias. However, the clinician should probably not rely solely on an MMPI validity index to make a determination of overreporting or underreporting of symptoms. In light of the rapidly growing database for the MMPI-2 as well as improvements such as standardized validity scales and an updated normative sample, it appears to offer significant advantages over the MMPI for forensic purposes.

MMPI-2

Currently available data support the comparability of MMPI-2 indexes with their "parent" scales on the MMPI. The VRIN scale now has strong support

Table 4.1 Diagnostic Utility of MMPI-2 Content Nonresponsiveness (CNR) Indexes at Three Base Rates of Random Responding

						Base Rate						
		5%					10%				20%	
	CS	PPP	NPP	HR[a]	CS	PPP	NPP	HR[a]	CS	PPP	NPP	HR[a]
VRIN	13	100	97	97	12	93	95	95	10	85	93	92
Fb	18	85	98	97	18	92	95	95	15	87	93	92
F	21	77	97	96	21	88	93	93	16	76	88	86

NOTE: CS = cutting score, PPP = positive predictive power, NPP = negative predictive power, HR = overall hit rate. All hit rates given are optimal for that index and base rate of random responding. Data from Gallen (1993).
a. Percentage correct classification.

as an index of random responding, and can be used with some confidence for this purpose. Table 4.1 presents data on hit rates for detecting random responding from the VRIN, Fb, and F scales derived from a study by Gallen (1993) replicating the Berry, Wetter et al. (1991) report. However, rather than detailing sensitivity and specificity, this table provides positive and negative predictive power estimates at the overall optimal cutting score for each scale. VRIN is clearly superior to F in every instance, although Fb is closer to VRIN. However, given VRIN's insensitivity to overreporting of symptoms as documented by Wetter et al. (1992), VRIN should probably be the index of choice in a forensic setting where symptom magnification is of primary concern. It should also be noted that a VRIN cutting score of 13 provided 100% positive predictive power (PPP) for detecting random responding at all three base rates in the Gallen (1993) study, supporting this value as a good "rule of thumb" cutting score for identifying CNR.

The F, F – K, and Ds scales on the MMPI-2 have good construct validity supporting their sensitivity to overreporting of problems, based on the Austin (1992), Graham et al. (1991), Lees-Haley (1991b), and Wetter et al. (1992) studies. Table 4.2 provides a summary of research comparing F scale scores for a group instructed or assumed to have simulated a psychiatric disorder with a patient group presumed to be answering honestly. As can be readily appreciated, cutting scores vary widely, as do sensitivity and specificity values. It seems possible that some of this variability is attributable to the nature of the patient contrast group, with the 100% outpatients used by Lees-Haley

Table 4.2 Detection of Overreporting of Symptoms on the MMPI-2

Citation	Percentage Inpatients	Mean F	Raw F Cut Score Percentage Correctly Classified	
Lees-Haley (1991a)			m: > 9; f: > 7	
Normals faking		79.2	81	Sensitivity
Patients honest	0	47.4	100	Specificity
Wetter, Baer, Berry, Robison, and Sumpter (1993)			m: > 19; f: > 16	
Normals faking		111.3	85	Sensitivity
Patients with post-traumatic stress disorder	50	79.8	70	Specificity
Normals faking		119.4	100	Sensitivity
Patients with paranoid schizophrenia	50	80.8	90	Specificity
Graham, Watts, and Timbrook (1991)			m:> 26; f: > 28	
Normals faking		117.6	m: 93; f: 95	Sensitivity
Patients honest	100	79.7	m: 90; f: 90	Specificity
Rogers, Bagby, and Chakraborty (1993)			> 28	
Coached symptoms		120+	73	Sensitivity
Coached strategies		93?	21	Sensitivity
Coached symptoms and strategies		118?	47	Sensitivity
Uncoached		120+	60	Sensitivity
Patients honest	100	89?	97	Specificity
Bagby, Rogers, and Buis (1994)			m: > 22; f: > 20	
Normals faking		115	88	Sensitivity
Patients honest	100	75	81	Specificity
Bagby, Rogers, Buis, and Kalemba (1994)			m: > 17; f: > 15	
Normals faking		115	92	Sensitivity
Patients honest	100	72	81	Specificity

NOTE: ? = Estimated from data presented in article.

Table 4.3   Mean MMPI-2 F and Fb Scores From Three Groups of Subjects

Group	F Scale Mean T Score		Fb Scale Mean T Score	
	Males	Females	Males	Females
Normals faking psychiatric disturbance (N = 447)	120	120	120	120
Psychiatric inpatients (N = 402)	67	75	75	81
Psychiatric outpatients (N = 409)	61	65	63	62

NOTE: One-way ANOVAs within each column indicate that all means are significantly different from each other at $p < .05$ for both F and Fb scales.

(1992a) and the 50% outpatients studied by Wetter et al. (1993) producing lower-cutting scores than the entirely inpatient samples by the other researchers. This variability suggests that separate normative data must be gathered for inpatients and outpatients to adjust cutting scores appropriately, although this idea should be tested empirically. As an initial attempt to explore this issue, Table 4.3 presents mean F and Fb scores for analog malingerers, psychiatric inpatients, and psychiatric outpatients. It can be seen that F and Fb scale scores are significantly higher for inpatients than for outpatients, suggesting that cutting scores for the discrimination of overreporting of symptoms from patient protocols may need to be adjusted depending on whether the setting is an inpatient or outpatient clinic.

Overall, considering available data conservatively, unlike detection of CNR, detection of overreporting of symptoms with these MMPI-2 scales is not yet fully developed, with the effect of setting base rates, PPP, and negative predictive power (NPP) not yet documented for these indexes. Thus, the clinician may regard the F, Fb, F – K, and Ds scales as sensitive to overreporting, but should keep in mind the lack of firm cutting scores for identifying overreporting. Elevation of these scales in the absence of an elevation of VRIN signals the likelihood of overreporting, but this should be confirmed by convergent data from other domains, as reviewed later in this chapter.

Data on the detection of underreporting of symptoms on the MMPI-2 are not yet adequate to engender confidence in their accuracy. Just as with the

MMPI, a consensus about which scales should be used for the detection of underreporting of problems has not yet emerged, nor have ecologically valid studies been published to date. Clinically, an elevated L score on the MMPI-2 has the best support as an indicator of "faking good," although again, firm cutting scores have not yet been documented.

A CLINICAL STRATEGY

The present state of the art in forensic psychology is such that there are no "perfect" tests or procedures for detecting nonveridical responding in evaluations. Therefore, the most defensible approach to addressing this issue is probably to use all available sources of information, including historical data, medical/psychological records, behavioral observations, specific procedures for detecting malingering such as the SIRS (Rogers, Bagby, & Dickens, 1992) and validity scales from the MMPI-2. The more evidence suggesting the presence of nonveridical responding in a forensic evaluation, the more confident the clinician can be in his or her conclusions. MMPI-2 validity scales provide very useful information about the presence of response distortions in forensic evaluations, but as with any indicator, they should not be used in isolation for these critical decisions.

Future Research

The MMPI-2 has now been available for more than 5 years, and substantial evidence regarding its characteristics relative to the MMPI has been published. Thus, it is recommended that future research focus on the MMPI-2, rather than the original MMPI. Additionally, in light of the limited data currently available on forensic samples tested with the MMPI-2, further work in this area should be a high priority.

Of the three response sets considered in this chapter, random responding appears to be the most readily detected by MMPI-2 validity scales. However, research designed to establish validity configurations that would allow "salvaging" of basic clinical scales from a partially random MMPI-2 would be valuable. Documentation of the characteristics and interpretation of the TRIN scale is needed. Finally, demonstration of the reliable discrimination of random from overreported protocols using validity scale configurations should be a high priority.

In addition, although a number of articles have been published on over-reporting of symptoms on the MMPI-2, surprisingly few have dealt with the critical comparison of normals "faking bad" and psychiatric patients answering honestly. Further studies contrasting these groups are needed, particularly in forensic samples. The effect of gender and level of psychopathology in the patient control groups should be explored further. Methodological safeguards noted by Rogers (1988) should be employed. Finally, use of large samples that allow the development of detailed information on the effect of various cutting scores and base rates is needed, so that clinically useful tables presenting PPP and NPP can be made available.

The final response set considered here, underreporting of symptoms, is the least developed in the MMPI-2 literature. Virtually any methodologically sound work would be helpful in this area, although exploration of the promising Mp, Sd, and S scales is particularly recommended. Data based on clinically relevant contrasts would also be especially welcome.

References

American Psychiatric Association. (1994). *Diagnostic and statistical manual of mental disorders* (4th ed.). Washington, DC: Author.

Arbisi, P., & Ben-Porath, Y. (1993, March). *Interpretation of F scales for inpatients: Moving from art to science.* Paper presented at 28th Annual Symposium on Recent Developments in MMPI/MMPI-2/MMPI-A Research, St. Petersburg, FL.

Austin, S. (1992). The detection of fake good and fake bad on the MMPI-2. *Educational and Psychological Measurement, 52,* 669-674.

Baer, R., Wetter, M., & Berry, D. (1992). Detection of underreporting of psychopathology on the MMPI: A meta-analysis. *Clinical Psychology Review, 12,* 509-525.

Baer, R., Wetter, M., Berry, D., Nichols, D., & Greene, R. (1993, August). *Sensitivity of MMPI-2 scales to underreporting of symptoms.* Paper presented at the Annual Meeting of the American Psychological Association, Toronto, Canada.

Bagby, R., Rogers, R. & Buis, T. (1994). Detecting malingered and defensive responding on the MMPI-2 in a forensic inpatient sample. *Journal of Personality Assessment, 62,* 191-203.

Bagby, R., Rogers, R., Buis, T. & Kalemba, V. (1994). Malingered and defensive response styles on the MMPI-2: An examination of validity scales. *Assessment, 1,* 31-38.

Ben-Porath, Y. (1994). The ethical dilemma of coached malingering research. *Psychological Assessment, 6,* 14-15.

Berry, D., Baer, R. A., & Harris, M. J. (1991). Detection of malingering on the MMPI: A meta-analysis. *Clinical Psychology Review, 11,* 585-598.

Berry, D., Lamb, D., Wetter, M., Baer, R., & Widiger, T. (1994). Ethical considerations in research on coached malingering. *Psychological Assessment, 6,* 16-17.

Berry, D., Wetter, M., Baer, R., Larsen, L., Clark, C., & Monroe, K. (1992). MMPI-2 random responding indices: Validation using a self-report methodology. *Psychological Assessment, 4,* 340-345.

Berry, D., Wetter, M., Baer, R., Widiger, T., Sumpter, J., Reynolds, S., & Hallam, R. (1991). Detection of random responding on the MMPI-2: Utility of F, back F, & VRIN scales. *Psychological Assessment, 3,* 418-423.

Buechley, R., & Ball, H. (1952). A new test of validity for the group MMPI. *Journal of Consulting Psychology, 16,* 299-301.

Butcher, J. N., & Han, K. (1993, March). *Development of an MMPI-2 scale to assess the presentation of self in a superlative manner: The S scale.* Paper presented at the 28th Annual Symposium of Recent Developments in the Use of the MMPI/MMPI-2/MMPI-A, St. Petersburg, FL.

Cassisi, J., & Workman, D. (1992). The detection of malingering and deception with a short form of the MMPI-2 based on the L, F, and K scales. *Journal of Clinical Psychology, 48,* 54-58.

Cofer, C., Chance, J., & Judson, A. (1949). A study of malingering on the MMPI. *Journal of Psychology, 27,* 491-499.

Dahlstrom, W., Welsh, G., & Dahlstrom, L. (1975). *An MMPI handbook: Volume 1: Clinical interpretation, 1.* Minneapolis: University of Minnesota Press.

Faust, D., Ziskin, J., & Hiers, J. (1991). *Brain damage claims: Coping with neuropsychological evidence.* Los Angeles, CA: Law & Psychology Press.

Gallen, R. (1993). *VRIN, Back F, and blocked data as indicators of valid and clinically interpretable MMPI-2 protocols.* Unpublished master's thesis, University of Kentucky, Lexington.

Gallucci, N. (1984). Prediction of dissimulation on the MMPI in a clinical field setting. *Journal of Consulting and Clinical Psychology, 52,* 917-918.

Gallucci, N. (1985). Influence of dissimulation on indexes of response consistency for the MMPI. *Psychological Reports, 57,* 1013-1014.

Gough, H. (1947). Simulated patterns on the MMPI. *Journal of Abnormal and Social Psychology, 42,* 215-225.

Gough, H. (1950). The F minus K dissimulation index for the MMPI. *Journal of Consulting Psychology, 14,* 408-413.

Gough, H. (1954). Some common misconceptions about neuroticism. *Journal of Consulting Psychology, 18,* 287-292.

Gough, H. (1957). *California Psychological Inventory manual.* Palo Alto, CA: Consulting Psychologists Press.

Graham, J. R., Timbrook, R. E., Ben-Porath, Y. S., & Butcher, J. N. (1991). Congruence between MMPI and MMPI-2: Separating fact from artifact. *Journal of Personality Assessment, 57,* 205-215.

Graham, J., Watts, D., & Timbrook, R. (1991). Detecting fake good and fake bad MMPI-2 profiles. *Journal of Personality Assessment, 57,* 264-277.

Greene, R. (1978). An empirically derived MMPI consistency scale. *Journal of Clinical Psychology, 34,* 407-410.

Greene, R. L. (1987). Ethnicity and MMPI performance: A review. *Journal of Consulting and Clinical Psychology, 55,* 497-512.

Grossman, L., Haywood, T., Ostrov, E., Wasyliw, O., & Cavanaugh, J. (1990). Sensitivity of MMPI validity scales to motivational factors in psychological evaluations of police officers. *Journal of Personality Assessment, 55,* 549-561.

Gynther, M. (1961). The clinical utility of invalid MMPI F scores. *Journal of Consulting Psychology, 25,* 540-542.

Lamb, D., Berry, D., Wetter, M., & Baer, R. (1994). Effects of two types of information on malingering of closed-head injury on the MMPI-2: An analog investigation. *Psychological Assessment, 6,* 8-13.

Lees-Haley, P. (1991a). Ego strength denial on the MMPI-2 as a clue to simulation of personal injury in vocational neuropsychological and emotional distress evaluations. *Perceptual and Motor Skills, 72,* 815-819.

Lees-Haley, P. (1991b). MMPI-2 F and F – K scores of personal injury malingerers in vocational neuropsychological and emotional distress claims. *American Journal of Forensic Psychology, 9,* 5-14.

Lees-Haley, P. (1992a). Efficacy of MMPI-2 validity scales and MCMI-II modifier scales for detecting spurious PTSD claims: F, F – K, Fake Bad Scale, Ego Strength, Subtle-Obvious subscales, DIS, and DEB. *Journal of Clinical Psychology, 48,* 681-689.

Lees-Haley, P. (1992b). Psychodiagnostic test usage by forensic psychologists. *American Journal of Forensic Psychology, 10,* 25-30.

Lees-Haley, P., English, L., & Glenn, W. (1991). A fake bad scale on the MMPI-2 for personal injury claimants. *Psychological Reports, 68,* 203-210.

Nichols, D. (1993). *Subscales for the Minnesota Multiphasic Personality Inventory: Augmented and revised for the MMPI-2 environment.* Unpublished manuscript.

Nichols, D., Greene, R., & Schmolck, P. (1989). Criteria for assessing inconsistent patterns of item endorsement on the MMPI: Rationale, development, and empirical trials. *Journal of Clinical Psychology, 45,* 239-250.

Paolo, A., & Ryan, J. (1992). Detection of random response sets on the MMPI-2. *Psychotherapy in Private Practice, 11,* 1-8.

Paulhus, D. (1984). Two-component models of socially desirable responding. *Journal of Personality and Social Psychology, 46,* 598-609.

Rogers, R. (1988). Researching dissimulation. In R. Rogers (Ed.), *Clinical assessment of malingering and deception* (pp 309-327). New York: Guilford.

Rogers, R. (1990). Models of feigned illness. *Professional Psychology: Research and Practice, 21,* 182-188.

Rogers, R., Bagby, R., & Chakraborty, D. (1993). Feigning schizophrenic disorders on the MMPI-2: Detection of coached simulators. *Journal of Personality Assessment, 60,* 215-226.

Rogers, R., Bagby, R., & Dickens, S. (1992). *Structured Interview of Reported Symptoms: Professional manual.* Odessa, FL: Psychological Assessment Resources.

Rogers, R., Bagby, R., & Rector, N. (1989). Diagnostic legitimacy of factitious disorder with psychological symptoms. *American Journal of Psychiatry, 146,* 1312-1314.

Rothke, S., Friedman, A., Dahlstrom, W., Greene, R., Arredondo, R., & Mann, A. (1994). MMPI-2 normative data for the F – K index: Implications for clinical, neuropsychological, and forensic practice. *Assessment, 1,* 1-15.

Timbrook, R. E., Graham, J. R., Keiller, S. S. W., & Watts, D. (1993). Comparison of the Wiener-Harmon Subtle-Obvious scales and the standard validity scales in detecting valid and invalid MMPI-2 profiles. *Psychological Assessment, 5,* 53-61.

Wasyliw, O. E., Grossman, L. S., Haywood, T. W., & Cavanaugh, J. L. (1988). The detection of malingering in criminal forensic groups: MMPI validity scales. *Journal of Personality Assessment, 52,* 321-333.

Wetter, M., Baer, R., Berry, D., Robison, L., & Sumpter, J. (1993). MMPI-2 profiles of motivated fakers given specific symptom information: A comparison to matched patients. *Psychological Assessment, 5,* 317-323.

Wetter, M., Baer, R., Berry, D., Smith, G., & Larsen, L. (1992). Sensitivity of MMPI-2 validity scales to random responding and malingering. *Psychological Assessment, 4,* 369-374.

Wetzler, S., & Marlowe, D. (1990). Faking bad on the MMPI, MMPI-2, and MCMI-II. *Psychological Reports, 67,* 117-118.

Widiger, T., Hurt, S., Frances, A., Clarkin, J., & Gilmore, M. (1984). Diagnostic efficiency and the DSM-III. *Archives of General Psychiatry, 41,* 1005-1012.

Wiener, D. (1948). Subtle and obvious keys for the MMPI. *Journal of Consulting Psychology, 12,* 164-170.

Wiggins, J. (1959). Interrelationships among MMPI measures of dissimulation under standard and social desirability instructions. *Journal of Consulting Psychology, 23,* 419-427.

Use of the MMPI-2 in the
Assessment of Criminal Responsibility

RICHARD ROGERS

GEOFFREY R. McKEE

E valuations of insanity and other forms of criminal responsibility constitute one of the greatest challenges in forensic evaluations. These evaluations are complicated by both their retrospective nature and the application
of unwieldy psycholegal standards. Because of the extended time framework
in which the alleged crime often occurred months to years in the past,
psychologists must develop a comprehensive multimethod database. This
database is used to assess (a) self/others' reports of the defendant at the time
of the offense, (b) self/others' retrospective accounts of the defendant at the
time of the offense, and (c) self/others' reports of the defendant at the present
time.

This chapter is organized into four major components. First, we provide a
brief overview on the nature of insanity evaluations. Second, we address the
available MMPI/MMPI-2 research on insanity and pretrial criminal evaluations. In this section, we present MMPI-2 data from 245 insanity evaluatees

from the William S. Hall Psychiatric Institute. Third, we offer guidelines for the use and interpretation of the MMPI-2 in insanity evaluations. Fourth, we outline research recommendations on the MMPI-2 and insanity evaluations. As an important caveat, there are no substitutions (including this chapter) to close supervision by senior colleagues and postdoctoral training for developing the required competence in conducting insanity evaluations.[1]

Overview of Insanity Evaluations

Insanity is a legal term used to describe the acquittal (i.e., most commonly, "not guilty by reason of insanity") of a criminal defendant because of a severe mental disorder on the basis of specified legal criteria. The very nature of the insanity defense appears to be a paradox. How can a defendant be acquitted from an act that he or she perpetrated? The answer (whether entirely satisfactory or not) lies in a basic premise of Anglo-Saxon law—namely, that an individual should not be held culpable for a crime unless he or she is aware of its criminality and chooses to do it (Golding & Roesch, 1987).

The history of the insanity defense is rich in celebrated, if sometimes grisly, cases of murder and mayhem that both excited and revolted the public (Quen, 1981, 1985). Standards of insanity bow to public outrage and legislative indignation, particularly in attacks on public figures. As examples, the 1843 M'Naghten standard was a direct outgrowth of Daniel M'Naghten's attempt to kill the Prime Minister, and the Federal Insanity Act of 1984 as well as many concomitant changes in state statutes resulted from John W. Hinckley, Jr.'s assassination attempt of former-President Ronald Reagan. Insanity standards and associated practices do not remain static but fluctuate in response to pressures from both the public (e.g., see Hans & Slater, 1983) and professionals (American Bar Association, 1989; American Psychiatric Association [APA], 1983) and are also shaped by appellate decisions (e.g., United States v. Lyons, 1984). For psychologists involved in insanity evaluations, the first task is to develop a working knowledge of the insanity standard in his or her jurisdiction and the procedures for its implementation.

Weiner (1985), as part of a large-scale project by the American Bar Foundation, summarized the different standards that prevailed at that time. As noted by Weiner, even a general summary of insanity standards is likely to be misleading, because many have adopted slightly different language and are interpreted in light of specific state case law. The four commonly employed standards of insanity are the M'Naghten (1843); M'Naghten-Irresistible Impulse (original case was *State v. Thompson,* 1842, with further refinements, e.g., *Smith v. United States,* 1929); American Law Institute or ALI (*United States v. Brawner,* 1972); and the Federal Insanity Defense Act of 1984. In addition, several states have adopted their own standards (American Bar Association, 1989) or have eliminated the insanity defense entirely in favor of a *mens rea* approach.

Key language of the four prevailing standards is presented in the following outline:

1. *M'Naghten:* The M'Naghten case held that "The party accused was laboring under such a defect of reason, from disease of the mind, as not to know the nature and quality of the act he was doing; or if he did know, that he did not know what he was doing was wrong" (p. 722).
2. *M'Naghten and Irresistible Impulse:* Following *Smith v. United States,* "The accused must be capable, not only of distinguishing right from wrong, but that he was not impelled to do the act by an irresistible impulse, which means before it will justify a verdict of acquittal that his reasoning powers were so far dethroned by his diseased mental condition as to deprive him of the will power to resist the insane impulse to perpetrate the deed, though knowing it to be wrong" (p. 549).
3. *American Law Institute (ALI):* As articulated in the Model Penal Code (American Law Institute, 1962) "As a result of mental disease or defect he lacks substantial capacity either to appreciate the criminality [wrongfulness] of his conduct or to conform his conduct to the requirements of law. As used in the Article, the terms 'mental disease or defect' do not include an abnormality manifested only by repeated criminal or otherwise antisocial conduct" (pp. 490-491).
4. *Federal Insanity Defense Act of 1984:* "The defendant, as a result of a severe mental disease or defect, was unable to appreciate the nature and quality or the wrongfulness of his acts" (p. 201).

Components of the insanity standard vary, of course, by jurisdiction. As outlined by Rogers (1986), the first two components (mental disease or defect, and cognitive incapacity) are consistent across jurisdictions, whereas inclusion of the remaining two (volitional incapacity and exclusion of antisocial behavior) varies with each state's insanity standard:

1. *Mental disease or defect.* All jurisdictions require some form of mental disorder or mental retardation as a necessary precondition to the finding of insanity. As with all components, the standard of what constitutes a "disease of the mind" or a "mental disease or defect" is defined by relevant case law.

For example, some jurisdictions continue to follow *McDonald v. United States* (1962) in defining mental disease or defect as "Any abnormal condition of the mind which substantially affects mental or emotional processes and substantially impairs behavior controls" (p. 851). Interestingly, this definition comes close to the definition of psychosis employed in *DSM-II* (American Psychiatric Association, 1968).

2. *Cognitive incapacity.* Definitions of cognitive incapacity vary considerably across jurisdictions both in form and severity. The M'Naghten standard emphasizes the inability of the accused to comprehend. In contrast, the ALI standard emphasizes a lack of substantial ability to appreciate that is less than the total incapacity implied by *M'Naghten.* The term "appreciate" was intended to broaden the concept of comprehension to include not only a basic awareness by the accused of his or her actions but also a cognizance of their magnitude (Rogers, 1986). The Federal Insanity Defense Reform Act of 1984 amalgamated elements of both standards by reintroducing the "unable" language of M'Naghten with the "appreciate" wording of ALI.

Three of the four prevailing standards focus on the accused's awareness of the "nature and quality" of his or her actions. This element is generally defined as knowing one's physical actions and their immediate consequences. As an example reported by Rogers (1986), when a delusional woman zealously attempted to baptize the devil out of her child through total immersion, she appeared to have no awareness of the fatal consequences of her actions.

Most insanity evaluations hinge on the defendant's awareness of the wrongfulness of his or her actions. Individuals found not guilty by reason of insanity (NGRI) often suffer from delusional beliefs in which criminal acts were perpetrated in "self-defense" (e.g., the defendant defends himself or herself against a perceived threat) or as part of "official duties" (e.g., the defendant carries out his or her supposed duties as a Central Intelligence Agency [CIA] operative). The *M'Naghten* case also included moral wrongfulness (i.e., against the laws of God) in its definition of wrongfulness; states are divided on whether they include moral wrongfulness within this element for either the *M'Naghten* or ALI standards (see American Bar Association, 1989). *United States v. Sullivan* (1976) provided a clear definition of moral wrongfulness when the accused "commits a criminal act under a false belief, the result of mental disease or defect, that the act is morally justified, does indeed lack substantial capacity to appreciate the wrongfulness of his conduct, irrespective of whether he can be correctly diagnosed, medically, as 'delusional.'"

3. *Volitional incapacity.* Both the "irresistible impulse" of the *M'Naghten* and Irresistible Impulse standard and "conform his conduct" of the ALI standard indicate an inability to choose other noncriminal options and to refrain from the criminal behavior in question. As noted by Rogers (1987), this lack of volitional capacity typically involves severe mood disorders (e.g., a severely depressed person poignantly aware of his or her immoral and criminal actions kills one or more of his or her children to save them from suffering) and severe obsessive-compulsive disorders. Controversy surrounds creative but often less-substantiated attempts to use the volitional prong for impulse control disorders (e.g., pathological gambling) or reactivation of previous trauma (post-traumatic stress disorder with flashbacks for Vietnam War veterans).

4. *Exclusion of abnormalities of antisocial behavior.* The intent of this prohibition in the ALI standard was to eliminate defendants whose only abnormality was psychopathy. However, it could be argued that even defendants with antisocial personality disorders (APD) have symptoms that extend beyond simply antisocial and criminal behavior (see American Psychiatric Association, 1987). Moreover, criminality is not a necessary component of APD.

Research on the MMPI/
MMPI-2 in Insanity Evaluations

MMPI INSANITY STUDIES

Five studies have investigated directly the usefulness of the MMPI in assessments of criminal responsibility. The first three studies (Boehnert, 1987; Kurlychek & Jordan, 1980; Rogers & Seman, 1983) examined differences in MMPI profiles through comparisons of validity and clinical scales. The fourth study (Daniel, Beck, Herath, Schmitz, & Menninger, 1984) examined MMPI correlates with psychiatric recommendations of sanity/insanity. The fifth and final study (Arnold, Quinsey, & Velner, 1977) considered the clinical utility of the overcontrolled hostility (O – H) scale in differentiating sane and insane defendants.

Kurlychek and Jordan (1980) conducted the first study of the MMPI with pretrial defendants evaluated for insanity. They compared 20 insane and 30 sane criminal defendants as classified by clinicians. Interestingly, they found no significant differences in single scale elevations between the two groups.

Although they attempted a chi-square analysis of two-point codes, insufficient sample size constrained interpretation of these findings.

Rogers and Seman (1983) combined MMPI data from two forensic centers and examined data on three groups: (a) defendants clinically evaluated as insane ($n = 12$), (b) defendants clinically evaluated as sane ($n = 40$), and (c) patients previously adjudged insane by the courts and currently involved in outpatient treatment ($n = 25$). Insane and sane defendants tended to have remarkably similar profiles with elevations on F (insane, $M = 74.00$; sane, $M = 70.58$), 4 (insane, $M = 77.17$; sane, $M = 78.08$), 7 (insane, $M = 76.92$; sane, $M = 74.93$), and 8 (insane, $M = 81.00$; sane, $M = 83.00$). As expected, patients with extensive treatment histories, after being found NGRI, tended to have lower elevations on clinical scales (all $Ms < 70$).

Boehnert (1987) compared 30 patients found NGRI with 45 patients evaluated but not found NGRI, 30 psychiatric inpatients, and 30 correctional subjects. Although statistical comparisons of her data were not provided, the NGRI group tended to have lower clinical profiles than the other groups, including the nonclinical correctional sample. She did not report the length of time that had transpired since the NGRI sample was adjudicated insane and tested.

Daniel et al. (1984) performed a series of zero-order correlations on MMPI clinical scales and psychiatric judgments for 48 defendants determined to be insane and 72 defendants found to be sane. They found virtually no relationship between scales and psychiatric conclusions regarding sanity. The nonsignificant correlations ranged from $-.09$ to $.14$ with a median of $-.05$.

Arnold et al. (1977) examined the usefulness of the O – H scale with patients found NGRI. They excluded patients with low IQ, poor reading comprehension, omitted items, and elevated F scales (i.e., > 22). They found that NGRI patients did not have elevated O – H scale scores ($M = 54.6$) and did not differ from other forensic patients. Two important limitations occur in the generalizability of these findings: (a) Several years had transpired from the finding of insanity to their data collection and (b) the Canadian standard of insanity used at the time of the study permitted an unusually high number of personality-disordered persons (41% of the sample) to be found NGRI.

NORMATIVE DATA ON PRETRIAL DEFENDANTS

Available studies offer a paucity of clinical data on the usefulness of the MMPI in insanity evaluations. The next logical step is to investigate the use

of the MMPI in the slightly broader context of pretrial forensic evaluations
that often include determinations of criminal responsibility. This broader
context allows psychologists to examine differences among pretrial and post-
trial defendants as comparison points in conducting their assessments of
insanity. In this brief review of normative studies, we will focus on three facets
of the MMPI: (a) fake bad profiles as determined by F scale elevations, (b)
evidence of psychopathy on Scale 4 and O – H, and (c) scales associated with
psychotic symptoms (6, 7, and 8). Data from the five major studies are
summarized in Table 5.1.

Quinsey, Arnold, and Pruesse (1980) examined MMPI profiles for 150
pretrial defendants who were categorized by offenses. Remarkably, no differences in scale elevations were found across six groups that spanned murders,
child molestations, and property offenses. As noted in Table 5.1, the defendants, as a group, had clinical elevations on Scales 4, 7, and 8.

Hawk and Cornell (1989) investigated MMPI profiles of 17 psychotic and
36 nonpsychotic patients referred for evaluations of competency to stand trial,
insanity, or both. These patients had been screened prior to the study exclud-
ing any patients with evidence of malingering. One important finding was
that psychotic nonmalingering defendants tended to have marked elevations
on F ($M = 85$). In addition, both psychotic and nonpsychotic defendants had
moderate elevation of the scales associated with psychotic symptoms, although Scale 8 for psychotic defendants was extremely elevated ($M = 93$).

Several investigators have studied MMPI profiles from pretrial evaluations
of defendants charged specifically with homicide. For example, Langevin,
Paitich, Orchard, Handy, and Russon (1982) compared MMPI data for 53
defendants charged with homicide to 21 nonviolent defendants and 54 community controls. They found very high elevations for Scales 7 and 8 for both
groups of defendants, despite the fact that few had psychotic diagnoses
(approximately 13%). Rather unexpectedly, a verdict of NGRI correlated at
only .23 with a psychotic diagnosis.

Holcomb and his colleagues (Anderson & Holcomb, 1983; Holcomb &
Adams, 1982; Holcomb, Adams, & Ponder, 1985) conducted a series of closely
related studies on male defendants charged with homicide and referred for
pretrial inpatient evaluations. Samples ranged from 110 to 137 defendants,
most of whom were used in all three studies. Anderson and Holcomb (1983)
performed a cluster analysis that yielded five clusters. Of these, one cluster (26
defendants) would appear to be associated with overreporting or malingering,
given the extreme elevation of F ($T = 120$), markedly elevated clinical profiles

Table 5.1 Normative Data on Forensic Patients and Offenders for Selected MMPI Scales

Study	Fake Bad F	Antisocial 4	O – H	Psychotic 6	7	8
Pretrial evaluations of forensic patients						
Quinsey et al. (1980) (150 males)	70	78	55	68	71	78
Langevin et al. (1982) (128 n.a.)[a]	74	73	n.a.	68	71	75
Holcomb et al. (1985) (160 males)	70	79	n.a.	83	74	106
Valliant et al. (1984) (35 males)[a]	80	74	n.a.	73	81	82
Hawk and Cornell (1989)						
17 psychotics	85[b]	77	n.a.	79	76	93
36 nonpsychotics	72[b]	75	n.a.	71	71	77
Forensic patients in treatment						
Rice et al. (1983) (25 males)	60[c]	75	59	56	58	65
Postsentencing evaluations of convicted offenders						
McCreary (1976) (450 males/females)	62	71	n.a.	62	62	65
Gendreau et al. (1979) (646 n.a.)	70	71	n.a.	65	64	73
MacAndrew (1979) (91 males)	68	69	n.a.	65	60	71
Edinger (1979) (3,518 males/females)[a]	62	73	n.a.	63	62	66
Holland and Levi (1980) (250 males)	57	70	n.a.	58	60	60

NOTE: O – H = Overcontrolled Hostility scale; n.a. = not available.
a. These studies do not specify whether scale elevations are K-corrected.
b. This sample was screened to remove any cases where malingering was suspected.
c. The M of F is an underestimate, because any forensic patients with highly elevated Fs were precluded from the study.

(six scales ≥ 90), and the general absence of psychotic diagnoses (only 7.7%). Three clusters included multiple elevations on clinical scales, which were sometimes associated with moderately elevated F scales. The final cluster had no *M* elevations in the clinical range, although Scale 4 was marginally elevated ($T = 67$). Other studies (Holcomb & Adams, 1982; Holcomb et al., 1985) addressed racial differences that will be summarized in a later section on minorities.

Valliant, Asu, Cooper, and Mammola (1984) conducted a small study of 18 dangerous and 17 nondangerous defendants referred for a pretrial assessment. They found substantially high elevations[2] for the scales associated with psychotic symptoms and also elevations on Scales F and 4.

Rice, Arnold, and Tate (1983) examined MMPI profiles of 25 forensic patients including 13 persons found NGRI after extensive inpatient treatment. As might be expected, their scores are substantially lower than those in studies of pretrial defendants. Perhaps because of treatment, their mean scores are more similar to the norms of convicted offenders, described later, than pretrial defendants. An alternative explanation is that the defendants minimized their psychological problems in an effort to be discharged from a maximum security hospital.

Our understanding of MMPI normative data on pretrial defendants can be enhanced by comparisons to offenders who were adjudged guilty at trial. We have compiled representative studies (Daniel et al., 1984; Edinger, 1979; Gendreau, Grant, Leipciger, & Collins, 1979; Holland & Levi, 1980; MacAndrew, 1979; McCreary, 1976) on nearly 5,000 convicted offenders (see Table 5.1). Convicted offenders have appreciably lower elevations, particularly on Scales 7 and 8, than do those referred for pretrial psychological assessments. In spite of this, Scales 7 and 8, which are associated with psychotic symptoms, were consistently although slightly elevated across studies ($> 60T$). Furthermore, both pretrial defendants and convicted offenders appear to have moderate elevations on Scale 4.

What is the clinical relevance of these normative data on pretrial evaluations? These data, combined with three studies of insanity evaluations (Boehnert, 1987; Kurlychek & Jordan, 1980; Rogers & Seman, 1983), suggest strongly that many defendants in pretrial evaluations are likely to have evidence of atypical reporting (F), antisocial characteristics (4), and psychotic symptoms (6, 7, and 8). Moreover, all offenders, even those convicted and serving time, appear to have moderate elevations of Scale 4 and slight to moderate elevations of Scales 6, 7, and 8. Therefore, we cannot draw any firm conclusions from MMPI data that elevations on Scale F (atypical responding), Scale 4 (antisocial characteristics), or both, provide any specific evidence of "sanity." By the same token, elevations of Scales 6, 7, and 8 (associated with psychotic symptoms) should not be construed as providing any specific evidence of "insanity."

MALINGERING BY PRETRIAL DEFENDANTS

A major concern of insanity evaluations is whether patients are attempting to simulate a severe mental disorder to avoid a guilty verdict. Although Chapter 4 addresses research on malingering and dissimulation more generally, several studies have examined feigning on the MMPI and MMPI-2 as it applies to pretrial forensic evaluations. As noted earlier in this chapter, the retrospective nature of insanity adds an important time dimension. In other words, a defendant could feign a past episode of a mental disorder for the time of the offense while responding honestly about current symptomatology. Whether such feigning of prior impairment is detectable by the MMPI or MMPI-2 remains to be investigated.

Studies of the MMPI suggest its potential efficacy in the detection of malingering among pretrial defendants referred for psychological assessments. These assessments typically address either competency to stand trial or insanity. For example, Heilbrun, Bennet, White, and Kelly (1990) reported a convergence between MMPI and additional clinical data in distinguishing malingering and other response styles in a factor analytic study of 159 criminal defendants awaiting trial in a maximum security hospital. Several descriptive studies (Grossman & Wasyliw, 1988; Wasyliw, Grossman, Haywood, & Cavanaugh, 1988) compared MMPI profiles for 35 defendants evaluated for insanity to 39 patients who had previously been acquitted as NGRI. Elevated validity scores in the fake bad direction varied by specific scale/index from 14% to 37% of those evaluated for insanity and from 3% to 18% for those already acquitted with no apparent motivation to feign. Finally, Schretlen and Arkowitz (1990) asked 20 prison inmates to fake insanity, incompetency to stand trial, or both on the MMPI, Bender-Gestalt, and other tests. Although these inmates feigning insanity had high F scales and F − K indexes, these indicators did not appear to be markedly elevated.[3]

Rice et al. (1983) conducted a study, using a within-subjects design that asked 25 forensic patients (13 of whom had been adjudicated NGRI) to fake more severe impairment. These protocols were compared to earlier administrations of the MMPI under standard instructions and yielded highly significant differences in the predicted directions. Highly significant differences have also been observed in two studies of pretrial evaluations (Hawk & Cornell, 1989; Roman, Tuley, Villanueva, & Mitchell, 1990) that employed known-groups design (i.e., comparison of actual malingerers with bona fide patients). As noted by Berry in Chapter 4, the enduring problem is establishing consistent cutting scores between feigners and bona fide patients.

Bagby, Rogers, and Buis (in press) assessed the usefulness of the MMPI-2 in detection of malingering. They asked 32 simulators feigning mental illness to adopt one of several scenarios that included simulated insanity, unwarranted disability benefits, and unneeded rehabilitation services. These simulators were compared to 66 pretrial defendants who were referred for inpatient psychiatric evaluations. They found highly significant differences on the MMPI-2 with cutting rules that exceeded 80% accuracy. Linblad (1993) also found the MMPI-2 to be highly effective, especially together with the Structured Interview of Reported Symptoms (SIRS; Rogers, Bagby, & Dickens, 1992) in assessment of malingering in forensic and correctional samples.

SCALE 4 AS A MEASURE OF REPETITIVE ANTISOCIAL BEHAVIOR

Many jurisdictions, which employ the ALI standard, exclude from their insanity standard disorders or conditions manifested only by repetitive antisocial behavior. The relevant question is the following: To what extent can Scale 4 or related indexes be employed as a measure of repetitive antisocial behavior? Studies have examined differences between the chronicity of offenders through comparison of first-time and multiple offenses or incarcerations. Of course, the difference between the two groups may be more apparent than it is real, because a large proportion of criminal behavior does not result in arrests and convictions. Moreover, Scale 4 cannot be equated with an antisocial personality disorder (APD) diagnosis (see, e.g., Cooney, Kadden, & Litt, 1990).

Studies (Adams, 1976; Bauer & Clark, 1976; Flanagan & Lewis, 1974) have reported small but statistically significant differences between persons first incarcerated and those with multiple incarcerations. More specifically, M elevations on Scale 4 for first incarcerations range from 65 to 75 and for multiple incarcerations from 72 to 78. Research is mixed on whether high Scale 4 scores reflect violence (Ingram, Marchioni, Hill, Caraveo-Ramos, & McNeil, 1985) or repetitive property offenses (Holland & Levi, 1980).[4]

Morey, Waugh, and Blashfield (1985) constructed personality disorder scales for the MMPI, including the Antisocial (ANT) scale. The initial validation of this scale appeared to be promising (Morey, Blashfield, Webb, & Jewell, 1988) with group differences between persons diagnosed with APD and others. More recently, Rogers and Bagby (in press) found small, albeit significant, differences on the ANT between pretrial forensic patients and general inpatients.

The MMPI-2 has a newly developed 22-item content scale that is labeled Antisocial Practices (ASP). This scale has significant overlap with the Cynicism content scale and purports to measure a combination of attitudes about criminality and self-acknowledged antisocial acts (Butcher & Williams, 1992). To date, only Ben-Porath, Shondrick, and Stafford (1995) have reported descriptive data on the ASP scale with forensic patients. They found that mentally disordered offenders tended not to report elevations on this scale and they also observed racial differences (Whites, $M = 53.70$; African Americans, $M = 61.09$; $F = 13.02$, $p < .001$). Therefore, we caution psychologists to consider the ASP scale only as ancillary information in their evaluations of criminal responsibility.

In summary, Scales 4 and ANT may offer corroborative data about antisocial characteristics. However, neither scale should be employed to diagnose APD or to make statements regarding repetitive criminal behavior or violence potential.

GENERALIZABILITY OF MMPI
FORENSIC STUDIES TO MINORITIES

Psychologists are sensitized to differences in MMPI/MMPI-2 profiles that may be due to race and ethnicity. Studies of offenders, grouped by race (i.e., Anglo American, African American, and Hispanic), have yielded mixed results that range from few differences (e.g., McCreary & Padilla, 1977) to significant differences on the majority of clinical scales (Holland, 1979). With reference to pretrial evaluations, Holcomb et al. (1985) found differences between 49 African American and 111 Anglo American offenders on Scales F and 9. Interestingly, attempts to control for intelligence through ANCOVAs yielded new differences on Scales K and 0 but no differences on F and 9. A particular concern, because validity scales are interpreted without covariates, is the extreme elevations on F ($M = 22r$ or $92\,T$) for African American offenders. Although finding a higher elevation for F among recidivating African American offenders than for their Anglo American counterparts, Ingram et al. (1985) reported only moderate elevations ($M = 71$). In contrast, Cook-Culley, Shea,

McKee, and Rush (1993) found no differences between Anglo Americans and African Americans on MMPI-2 validity indices in a study of 108 male pretrial defendants.

Elion and Megargee (1975) explored differences on the MMPI Scale 4 for African American and Anglo American males. They found that the scale discriminated between offenders and nonoffenders for each race but had consistently higher scores for African Americans. Although they opined that Scale 4 was a valid measure of social deviance, they concluded that the norms for the scale appeared to be racially biased. Because other studies (e.g., Holcomb & Adams, 1982; Ingram et al., 1985; McCreary & Padilla, 1985) have consistently failed to corroborate these differences on Scale 4, we do not believe that racial bias has been demonstrated.[5] However, the key issue is the examination of external validity (*DSM-IV* diagnosis or Psychopathy Checklist—Revised; Hare, 1991) with race and ethnicity.

Indicators of malingering on the MMPI and MMPI-2 have not been validated with specific reference to race. The previously described results of Holcomb are difficult to interpret, particularly because some persons with extreme elevations on F (see Anderson & Holcomb, 1983) appeared to be feigning. The two nonmutually exclusive explanations for Holcomb et al. (1985) findings are (a) Scale F is biased against African Americans, (b) more African Americans in this particular study were feigning or responding inconsistently, or both.[6] Research by Smith and Graham (1981) does not support a third possible explanation for the Anderson and Holcomb finding, namely that elevated F scales are indicative of psychopathology in African Americans.[7] Because of these studies, we would recommend that clinicians use conservative cutting scores for African American referrals and corroborate their findings. With respect to the latter, research data (Connell, 1991; Gothard, 1993) provide strong evidence of the SIRS's usefulness with African Americans in pretrial and correctional settings.

NEW DATA ON THE MMPI-2
AND INSANITY EVALUATIONS

The foregoing review of empirical studies has focused almost exclusively on the MMPI rather than the MMPI-2, because of the dearth of MMPI-2 research on insanity and pretrial evaluations. As a partial remedy, we conducted a descriptive study of MMPI-2 protocols for four criterion groups:

1. Sane—No major mental illness (Sane-NMI). This group ($n = 149$) was composed of defendants with no diagnoses, adjustment disorders, substance abuse, and/or personality disorders.

2. Sane—Major mental illness (Sane-MI). This group ($n = 50$) comprised defendants with severe psychotic, mood disorders, or both that were evaluated by the assessment team (PhD forensic or clinical psychologist and a Board eligible/certified psychiatrist) as legally sane.

3. Guilty but mentally ill (GBMI). This group ($n = 25$) consisted of defendants that met the South Carolina GBMI standard. For purposes of comparison, the language of the GBMI standard parallels the American Law Institute standard of insanity: "A defendant is guilty but mentally ill if . . . he had the capacity to distinguish right from wrong or to recognize his act as being wrong . . . but because of a mental disease or defect, he lacked sufficient capacity to conform his conduct to the requirements of the law" (South Carolina Code of Laws Ann., 1976, p. 164).

4. Not guilty by reason of insanity (Insane). This group ($n = 21$) was comprised of defendants that were clinically evaluated as meeting the South Carolina insanity standard that excludes antisocial behavior and is generally consistent with the *M'Naghten* rule: ". . . the defendant, as a result of mental disease or defect lacked the capacity to distinguish moral or legal right from moral or legal wrong or to recognize the particular act charged as morally or legally wrong" (South Carolina Code of Laws Ann., 1976, p. 164).

Assessment site. All subjects were evaluated at the William S. Hall Psychiatric Institute in Columbia, South Carolina. This forensic center is a university-based clinic that performs pretrial competency to stand trial and insanity assessments for the criminal courts. To maintain its objectivity, all evaluations are conducted under a judge's order with full disclosure of results to both the defense and prosecution. All defendants in the present study were individually evaluated by a multidisciplinary team (forensic psychologist, Board eligible/certified psychiatrist, and psychiatric social worker). In all, four psychologists, eight psychiatrists, and five social workers in various combinations conducted assessments of the defendants.

Procedure. Patients were carefully screened for reading comprehension with a 15-item multiple-choice test of reading comprehension that was calibrated for a seventh grade reading level (Fry, 1968). In addition, their overall capacity and willingness to complete self-report measures were assessed by the team's forensic psychologist. As a result of this screening, the MMPI-2 was administered to 46.2% of 530 consecutively registered pretrial defendants. All MMPI-2s were administered under standard instructions and with direct supervision by clinical staff.

Sample. The complete sample was composed of 217 (88.6%) male and 28 (11.5%) female defendants with an average age of 31.5 (*SD* = 10.9). The racial composition of the sample was 55.5% Anglo American, 44.1% African American, and 0.4% other. With respect to educational attainment, the average years of school completed were 11.7 (*SD* = 1.9).

Subjects were also categorized by their most severe charges. The charges ranged from murder (61.2%) to felony assault (16.7%), rape and sexual assault (4.9%), other felonies (15.8%), and misdemeanors (1.4%). Female defendants had no sexual charges and a smaller proportion of homicides when compared to their male counterparts.

Results. Data analyses were limited to male defendants, given the very small representation of female defendants. Differences among the four groups were examined through ANOVAs with Duncan multiple range tests (alpha = .05). Table 5.2 summarizes the K-corrected *M* elevations and the *F* ratios for the validity and clinical scales.

One important finding is that the F scale is elevated across criterion groups with moderate mean scale elevations for the Sane-NMI, GBMI, and Insane groups and an extreme *M* elevation (*T* = 89) for the Sane-MI group. Review of psychological reports to the court revealed that very few defendants, despite having access to MMPI-2 profiles, were deemed to be malingering or overreporting their symptomatology. As a descriptive study, we believe that these data are best interpreted as a general caution to review additional indexes and sources of clinical data before concluding that a defendant is malingering. This result for the MMPI-2 is consistent with previous studies of pretrial defendants on the original MMPI.

A general observation from reviewing the mean clinical elevations in Table 5.2 is the general lack of differentiation among the criterion groups. Interest-

Table 5.2   Differences on the MMPI-2 Among Male Defendants Referred for Insanity
Evaluations Organized by Clinical Judgment

| | Criterion Groups | | | | |
| | Sane | | | | |
MMPI Scale	No Major Mental Illness ($n = 136$)	Major Mental Illness ($n = 42$)	Guilty but Mentally Ill ($n = 21$)	Insane ($n = 18$)	F
L	55$_a$	57$_a$	54$_a$	61$_a$	1.59
F	74$_a$	89$_b$	79$_{ab}$	79$_{ab}$	2.34
K	46$_a$	43$_a$	47$_a$	48$_a$	1.40
1	63$_a$	74$_b$	57$_a$	69$_{ab}$	6.82**
2	65$_a$	78$_b$	71$_{ab}$	67$_a$	7.04**
3	59$_a$	70$_b$	63$_{ab}$	64$_{ab}$	4.60*
4	70$_{ab}$	72$_a$	70$_{ab}$	62$_b$	2.18
5	47$_a$	51$_b$	50$_{ab}$	48$_{ab}$	2.11
6	72$_a$	86$_b$	75$_{ab}$	77$_{ab}$	3.66
7	67$_a$	82$_b$	70$_a$	63$_a$	6.24**
8	74$_a$	89$_b$	82$_{ab}$	77$_a$	4.80*
9	57$_a$	57$_a$	55$_a$	54$_a$	.47
0	58$_a$	67$_b$	61$_{ab}$	57$_b$	5.53*

NOTE: All means are reported as K-corrected T scores. Because the table is restricted to male defendants, the numbers are slightly lower than those reported in the text. The probabilities for F ratios are corrected for family-wise error (.05/13 = .0038). Probabilities are * for .0038 and ** for < .001. Groups with common subscripts are not significantly different at the .05 level.

ingly, the Sane-MI group tended to have comparable, if not higher, clinical scales than the other three groups. Moreover, the Sane-NMI group cannot be differentiated from either the GBMI or the NGRI groups on the basis of single scale elevations. We think that a safe conclusion is that clinical scale elevations, by themselves, are not indicative of sanity/insanity but rather of the type of psychopathology. In other words, these results do not question the validity of the MMPI-2 but strongly caution against overinterpretations of its results in relationship to determinations of criminal responsibility.

An interesting, although nonsignificant, trend was observed with Scale 4. The NGRI group was the only group not elevated on this scale. In reviewing the content scales (see discussion later), the ANG scale also tended to be lower for the NGRI group than for the other three criterion groups. These trends for Scale 4 and the ANG scale would suggest the possible use of the MMPI-2 to examine affective and antisocial characteristics that may be useful data in insanity determinations.

The NGRI group had its highest elevations on Scales 6 and 8 with only slight to moderate elevations on other clinical scales. In contrast, the Sane-MI group had many more elevations and presented a much more diffuse clinical picture that included seven scales with moderate to marked elevations.

Analysis of content scales would appear to be only indirectly related to insanity evaluations, in the absence of forensic research establishing their external validation. Interestingly, most scales with significant differences manifested higher elevations for Sane-MI than for other groups. As previously noted a nonsignificant trend was observed for the ANG scale being lower for the Insane group; however, none of the mean scale elevations reached the clinically interpretable range.

Clinical Applications of the MMPI-2

The MMPI-2 serves three important functions in insanity evaluations. It assists forensic psychologists in addressing matter of response style, antisocial characteristics, and patterns of psychopathology. Each function will be described separately.

The MMPI-2 offers information about defendants' response styles. Besides the issue of malingering, the MMPI-2 offers valuable information about the underreporting of symptoms (defensiveness) as well as random, careless, or inconsistent responding. With a range of standard and specialized validity indicators, the MMPI-2 is an effective measure to examine a defendant's approach to the evaluation.

The MMPI-2 provides useful corroborative data about antisocial characteristics of defendants.[8] Although this information may be imprecise with respect to repetitiveness and APD diagnosis, it nevertheless adds an important dimension to the forensic assessment.

The MMPI-2 enhances the overall assessment by presenting often well-validated information on two-point codes and individual scale elevations. Although this information cannot be directly translated into judgments of criminal responsibility, it provides a benchmark for the evaluation of a particular defendant and his or her psychopathology. In other words, the best use of the MMPI-2 is for intraindividual comparisons rather than for between-group comparisons.

SPECIFIC RECOMMENDATIONS
FOR THE USE OF THE MMPI-2

1. The MMPI or MMPI-2 should be a standard assessment measure in most evaluations of insanity and related psycholegal issues. Exceptions may be based on clinical status (e.g., too psychotically confused), comprehension and limited intellect (e.g., unable to read sufficiently), and cultural (e.g., no available normative data on Native Americans). One method of integrating data from the MMPI-2 and other clinical sources is the employment of the Rogers Criminal Responsibility Assessment Scales (R-CRAS; Rogers, 1984).

2. Any evidence of malingering on the MMPI-2 should be thoroughly investigated both by the use of multiple MMPI-2 fake bad indexes and other measures, such as the SIRS. Psychologists must be cognizant of the fact that defendants as a whole often have elevated scores, whether or not feigning has occurred (see also Shea, Cook-Culley, McKee, & Rush, 1993). Extreme elevations supported by interview and collateral data may help to safeguard against misclassifications.

3. High scores on Scale 4 deserve a fuller investigation that may be accomplished by clinical interviewing, the administration of the Psychopathy Checklist—Revised (PCL-R; Hare, 1991), or both. Psychologists are cautioned against overinterpretation of the Harris and Lingoes subscales for Scale 4, given their psychometric limitations (unpublished data from Harris and Lingoes, cited in Graham, 1987) and lack of external validation (Bayer, Bonta, & Motiuk, 1985).

4. Review of clinical elevations, particularly on scales associated with psychotic symptoms, is very helpful to insanity evaluations. In some cases, an item analysis yields important information that confirms or disconfirms other data. Psychologists must be cautioned that inconsistencies can sometimes be explained simply as a time factor, because the MMPI-2 is administered for the current time and the psychological functioning at the time of the offense may be months to years in the past.

Research Recommendations

Research on the usefulness of the MMPI/MMPI-2 in insanity evaluations is very circumscribed. Even when the scope is broadened to include other pretrial evaluations only a dozen or so studies have emerged. Moreover, the great majority of these studies occurred prior to the latest revisions in statutes and case law pertaining to the insanity defense. Researchers should have no difficulty in identifying basic but important issues to investigate.

An important priority is the need for programmatic research on insanity evaluations that uses convergent validity. For example, the R-CRAS has been employed with large samples of insanity evaluatees and appears to have substantial evidence of construct validity (see Rogers, 1984, 1986; Rogers, Dolmetsch, & Cavanaugh, 1981; Rogers & Ewing, 1992; Rogers, Seman, & Clark, 1986; Rogers, Seman, & Wasyliw, 1983; Rogers, Wasyliw, & Cavanaugh, 1984). In addition, preliminary research (Rogers & Cavanaugh, 1981; Rogers, Thatcher, & Cavanaugh, 1984) has suggested the importance of structured interviews, particularly the Schedule of Affective Disorders and Schizophrenia (SADS; Spitzer and Endicott, 1978) in determinations of criminal responsibility. Studies of the MMPI-2 could be combined with the R-CRAS and the SADS in a comprehensive evaluation of insanity. In particular, MMPI correlates for the R-CRAS decision model would be useful in furthering our understanding of specific elevations and their relevance to criminal responsibility.

A second priority is the establishment of clinical correlates for the MMPI-2 that are specific to forensic populations and based on the best-validated clinical measures. For example, forensic clinicians have commonly noted that markedly elevated F scales are common among mentally disordered offenders who do not appear to be feigning psychopathology. Different cutting scores are likely to be needed in facilitating accurate interpretation of clinical data among pretrial defendants. For clinical scales, the emergence of well-validated diagnostic interviews (see Rogers, 1995) provides an important avenue to reliably assess specific symptoms and syndromes. Cross-validated clinical descriptions based on reliable diagnostic measures would enhance the interpretation of the MMPI-2 both in forensic and general populations.

Other priorities for MMPI-2 research have been noted in earlier portions of this chapter. These priorities include the following:

1. Further validation of the MMPI-2 employing minority and female offenders with particular attention paid to external validation (see Rogers, Flores, Ustad, & Sewell, in press)
2. Systematic examination of MMPI-2 patterns in large samples of pretrial defendants evaluated as sane and insane
3. Further assessment of malingering with the MMPI-2 specifically among pretrial defendants

4. Evaluation of Pd and APS scales in relation to *DSM-IV* antisocial personality disorder and psychopathy as measured by the PCL-R

Notes

1. We would recommend ABPP in forensic psychology and nonprofit advanced workshops through the American Academy of Forensic Psychology.

2. The Valliant et al. (1984) study does not specify whether clinical elevations are K-corrected.

3. Scale 4 has also been questioned with respect to gender; Sutker, Allain, and Geyer (1978) found that violent female offenders had *lower* scores than their nonviolent female offenders.

4. Schretlen and Arkowitz (1990) combined two samples of simulators (the other feigning retardation), thereby obscuring differences among experimental groups. Still, the F score of 8.5 (63 *T*) appears to be very low for malingering research (see Berry, Baer, & Harris, 1991).

5. See Bayer et al. (1985) regarding the usefulness of Harris and Lingoes's subscales of Scale 4 in offender populations.

6. A greater proportion of African Americans could have responded inconsistently, which would have resulted in higher elevations of Scale F. It is interesting to observe that racial differences on F disappeared when samples are controlled for IQ estimates.

7. On the contrary, Smith and Graham (1981) found the small but significant correlations between F and the ratings of psychopathology on the BPRS were underrepresented by African Americans (i.e., only one versus seven significant correlations for Whites).

8. The utility of the MMPI-2 to identify antisocial patterns is also suggested in the nearly significant finding ($p = .053$) that insane-NMI group members have the highest ASP *M* elevations of the four groups.

References

Adams, T. C. (1976). Some MMPI differences between first and multiple admissions within a state prison population. *Journal of Clinical Psychology, 32,* 555-558.

American Bar Association. (1989). *ABA criminal justice mental health standards.* Washington, DC: Author.

American Law Institute. (1962). *Model penal code, proposed official draft.* Philadelphia: Author.

American Psychiatric Association. (1968). *Diagnostic and statistical manual of mental disorders* (2nd ed.). Washington, DC: Author.

American Psychiatric Association. (1983). American Psychiatric Association statement of the insanity defense. *American Journal of Psychiatry, 140,* 681-688.

American Psychiatric Association. (1987). *Diagnostic and statistical manual of mental disorders* (3rd ed. rev.). Washington, DC: Author.

Anderson, W. P., & Holcomb, W. R. (1983). Accused murderers: Five MMPI personality types. *Journal of Clinical Psychology, 39,* 761-768.

Arnold, L. S., Quinsey, V. L., & Velner, I. (1977). Overcontrolled hostility among men found not guilty by reason of insanity. *Canadian Journal of Behavioral Science, 9,* 332-340.

Bagby, R., Rogers, R., & Buis, T. (in press). Malingered and defensive response styles on the MMPI-2: An examination of validity scales in a forensic population. *Journal of Personality Assessment.*

Bauer, G. E., & Clark, J. A. (1976). Personality deviancy and prison incarceration. *Journal of Clinical Psychology, 32,* 279-283.

Bayer, B. M., Bonta, J. L., & Motiuk, L. L. (1985). The Pd subscales: An empirical validation. *Journal of Clinical Psychology, 41,* 780-788.

Ben-Porath, Y. S., Shondrick, D. D., & Stafford, K. P. (1995). MMPI-2 and race in a forensic diagnostic center. *Criminal Justice and Behavior, 22,* 19-32.

Berry, D., Baer, R. A., & Harris, M. J. (1991). Detection of malingering on the MMPI: A meta-analysis. *Clinical Psychology Review, 11,* 585-598.

Boehnert, C. E. (1987). Characteristics of those evaluated for insanity. *Journal of Psychiatry and Law, 15,* 229-246.

Butcher, J. N., & Williams, C. L. (1992). *Essentials of MMPI-2 and MMPI-A interpretation.* Minneapolis: University of Minnesota Press.

Connell, D. K. (1991). *The SIRS and the M test: The differential validity and utility of two instruments designed to detect malingered psychosis in a correctional sample.* Unpublished doctoral dissertation, University of Louisville, Louisville, KY.

Cook-Culley, D., Shea, S., McKee, G. R., & Rush, C. (1993, August). *Racial differences in MMPI-2 profiles of male pretrial defendants.* Paper presented at the meeting of the American Psychological Association, Toronto, Ontario, Canada.

Cooney, N. L., Kadden, R. M., & Litt, M. D. (1990). A comparison of methods for assessing sociopathy in male and female alcoholics. *Journal of Studies on Alcohol, 51,* 42-48.

Daniel, A. E., Beck, N. C., Herath, A., Schmitz, M., & Menninger, K. (1984). Factors correlated with psychiatric recommendations of incompetency and insanity. *Journal of Psychiatry and Law, 12,* 527-544.

Edinger, J. D. (1979). Cross-validation of the Megargee MMPI typology for prisoners. *Journal of Consulting and Clinical Psychology, 47,* 234-242.

Elion, V. H., & Megargee, E. I. (1975). The validity of the MMPI Pd scale among black males. *Journal of Consulting and Clinical Psychology, 43,* 166-172.

Federal Insanity Defense Act of 1984, 18 U.S.C.A. 20a (Supp. 1986).

Flanagan, J. J., & Lewis, G. R. (1974). First prison admissions with juvenile histories and absolute first offenders: Frequencies and MMPI profiles. *Journal of Clinical Psychology, 30,* 358-360.

Fry, E. (1968). A readability formula that saves time. *Journal of Reading, 11,* 513-516.

Gendreau, P., Grant, B. A., Leipciger, M., & Collins, S. (1979). Norms and recidivism rates for the MMPI and selected experimental scales on a Canadian delinquent sample. *Canadian Journal of Behavioral Science, 11,* 21-31.

Golding, S. L., & Roesch, R. (1987). Assessment of criminal responsibility: A historical approach to a current controversy. *Handbook of forensic psychology* (pp. 395-436). New York: John Wiley.

Gothard, S. (1993). *Detection of malingering in mental competency evaluations.* Unpublished doctoral dissertation, California School of Professional Psychology, San Diego, CA.

Graham, J. R. (1987). *The MMPI: A practical guide* (2nd ed.). New York: Oxford University Press.

Grossman, L. S., & Wasyliw, O. E. (1988). A psychometric study of stereotypes: Assessment of malingering in a criminal forensic group. *Journal of Personality Assessment, 52,* 549-563.

Hans, V. P., & Slater, D. (1983). John Hinckley, Jr. and the insanity defense: The public's verdict. *Public Opinion Quarterly, 47,* 202-212.

Hare, R. D. (1991). *Manual for the revised psychopathy checklist.* Toronto, Canada: Multi-Health Systems.

Hawk, G. L., & Cornell, D. G. (1989). MMPI profiles of malingeres diagnosed in pretrail forensic evaulations. *Journal of Clinical Psychology, 45,* 673-678.

Heilbrun, K., Bennett, W. S., White, A. J., & Kelly, J. (1990). An MMPI-based empirical model of malingering and deception. *Behavioral Sciences and the Law, 8,* 45-53.

Holcomb, W. R., & Adams, N. A. (1982). Racial influences on intelligence and personality measures of people who commit murder. *Journal of Clinical Psychology, 38,* 793-796.

Holcomb, W. R., Adams, N. A., & Ponder, H. M. (1985). Are separate Black and White MMPI norms needed?: An IQ-controlled comparison of accused murderers. *Journal of Clinical Psychology, 40,* 189-193.

Holland, T. R. (1979). Ethnic group differences in MMPI profile pattern and factorial structure among adult offenders. *Journal of Personality Assessment, 43,* 72-77.

Holland, T. R., & Levi, M. (1980). Canonical versus factor analytic perspectives on the structure of associations between the MMPI and the Buss-Durkee Hostility Inventory. *Journal of Personality Assessment, 44,* 479-483.

Ingram, J. C., Marchioni, P., Hill, G., Caraveo-Ramos, E., & McNeil, B. (1985). Recidivism, perceived problem-solving abilities, MMPI characteristics, and violence: A study of Black and White incarcerated male adult offenders. *Journal of Clinical Psychology, 41,* 425-432.

Kurlychek, R. T., & Jordan, L. (1980). MMPI profiles and code types of responsible and nonresponsible criminal defendants. *Journal of Clinical Psychology, 36,* 590-593.

Langevin, R., Paitich, D., Orchard, B., Handy, L., & Russon, A. (1982). Diagnosis of killers seen for psychiatric assessment. *Acta Psychiatrica Scandanavia, 66,* 216-228.

Linblad, A. D. (1993). *Detection of malingered mental illness with a forensic population: An analogue study.* Unpublished doctoral dissertation, University of Saskatchewan, Sakatoon.

MacAndrew, C. (1979). On the possibility of the psychometric detection of persons who are prone to the abuse of alcohol and other substances. *Addictive Behaviors, 4,* 11-20.

McCreary, C. P. (1976). Trait and type differences among male and female assaultive offenders and nonassaultive offenders. *Journal of Personality Assessment, 40,* 617-621.

McCreary, C. P., & Padilla, E. (1977). MMPI differences among Black, Mexican-American, and White male offenders. *Journal of Clinical Psychology, 33,* 171-177.

McCreary, C. P., & Padilla, E. (1985). MMPI differences among Black, Mexican-American, and White male offenders. *Journal of Clinical Psychology, 33,* 171-177.

McDonald v. United States, 312 F.2d 847 (D.C. Cir. 1962).

Morey, L. C., Blashfield, R. K., Webb, W. W., & Jewell, J. (1988). MMPI scales for DSM-III personality disorders: A preliminary study. *Journal of Clinical Psychology, 44,* 47-50.

Morey, L. C., Waugh, M. H., & Blashfield, R. K. (1985). MMPI scales for DSM-III personality disorders: Their derivation and correlates. *Journal of Personality Assessment, 49,* 245-256.

M'Naghten, 10 Cl. & F. 200, 8 Eng. Rep. 718 (1843).

Quen, J. M. (1981). Anglo American concepts of criminal responsibility. In S. J. Hucker, C. D. Webster, & M. H. Ben-Aron (Eds.), *Mental disorder and criminal responsibility* (pp. 1-10). Toronto, Canada: Butterworths.

Quen, J. M. (1985). Violence, psychiatry, and the law: A historical perspective. In R. Rosner (Ed.), *Critical issues in American psychiatry and the law* (Vol. 2, pp. 43-55). New York: Plenum.

Quinsey, V. L., Arnold, L. S., & Pruesse, M. G. (1980). MMPI profiles of men referred for a pretrial psychiatric assessment as a function of offense type. *Journal of Clinical Psychology, 36,* 410-417.

Rice, M. E., Arnold, L. S., & Tate, D. L. (1983). Faking good and bad adjustment on the MMPI and overcontrolled hostility in maximum security psychiatric patients. *Canadian Journal of Behavioral Science, 15,* 44-51.

Rogers, R. (1984). *Rogers criminal responsibility assessment scales (RCRAS) and test manual.* Odessa, FL: Psychological Assessment Resources.

Rogers, R. (1986). *Conducting insanity evaluations.* New York: Van Nostrand Reinhold.

Rogers, R. (1987). The APA position on the insanity defense: Empiricism versus emotionalism. *American Psychologist, 42,* 840-848.

Rogers, R. (1995). *Diagnostic and structured interviewing: A handbook for psychologists.* Odessa, FL: Psychological Assessment Resources.

Rogers, R., & Bagby, R. M. (in press). Dimensions of psychopathy: A factor analytic study of the MMPI antisocial personality disorder scale. *International Journal of Offender Therapy and Comparative Criminology.*

Rogers, R., Bagby, R., & Dickens, S. (1992). *Structured Interview of Reported Symptoms: Professional manual.* Odessa, FL: Psychological Assessment Resources.

Rogers, R., & Cavanaugh, J. L. (1981). Application of the SADS diagnostic interview to forensic psychiatry. *Journal of Psychiatry and Law, 9,* 329-344.

Rogers, R., Dolmetsch, R., & Cavanaugh, J. L. (1981). An empirical approach to insanity evaluations. *Journal of Clinical Psychology, 37,* 683-687.

Rogers, R., & Ewing, C. P. (1992). The measurement of insanity: Debating the merits of the R-CRAS and its alternatives. *International Journal of Law and Psychiatry, 15,* 113-123.

Rogers, R., Flores, J., Ustad, K., & Sewell, K. W. (in press). Initial validation of the personality assessment inventory—Spanish version with clients from Mexican American communities: A brief report. *Journal of Personality Assessment.*

Rogers, R., & Seman, W. (1983). Murder and criminal responsibility: An examination of MMPI profiles. *Behavioral Sciences and the Law, 1,* 89-95.

Rogers, R., Seman, W., & Clark, C. C. (1986). Assessment of criminal responsibility: Initial validation of the R-CRAS with the M'Naghten and GBMI standards. *International Journal of Law and Psychiatry, 9,* 67-75.

Rogers, R., Seman, W., & Wasyliw, O. E. (1983). The RCRAS and legal insanity: A cross validation study. *Journal of Clinical Psychology, 39,* 554-559.

Rogers, R., Thatcher, A. A., & Cavanaugh, J. L. (1984). Use of the SADS diagnostic interview in evaluating legal insanity. *Journal of Clinical Psychology, 40,* 1538-1541.

Rogers, R., Wasyliw, O. E., & Cavanaugh, J. L. (1984). Evaluating insanity: A study of construct validity. *Law and Human Behavior, 8,* 293-303.

Roman, D. D., Tuley, M. R., Villanueva, M. R., & Mitchell, W. E. (1990). Evaluating MMPI validity in a forensic psychiatric population: Distinguishing between malingering and genuine psychopathology. *Criminal Justice and Behavior, 17,* 186-198.

Schretlen, D. J., & Arkowitz, A. (1990). A psychological test battery to detect prison inmates who fake insanity or mental retardation. *Behavioral Sciences and the Law, 8,* 75-84.

Shea, S., Cook-Culley, D., McKee, G. R., & Rush, C. (1993, August). *MMPI-2 profiles of male pretrial defendants.* Paper presented at the meeting of the American Psychological Association, Toronto, Ontario, Canada.

Smith, C. P., & Graham, J. R. (1981). Behavioral correlates for the MMPI standard F scale and for a modified F scale for Black and White patients. *Journal of Consulting and Clinical Psychology, 49,* 455-459.

Smith v. United States, 36 F.2d 548, 549 (D.C. Cir. 1929).

Spitzer, R. L., & Endicott, J. (1978). *Schedule of affective disorders and schizophrenia* (3rd ed.). New York: Biometrics Research.

South Carolina Code of Laws Ann. (1976). Title 17, Chapter 24, sections, 10(A), 20(A).

State v. Thompson, Wright's Ohio Rep. 483 (1842).

Stephen, D. J., & Arkowitz, H. (1990). A psychological test battery to detect prison inmates who fake insanity or mental retardation. *Behavioral Sciences and The Law, 8,* 75-84.

Sutker, P. B., Allain, A. N., & Geyer, S. (1978). Female criminal violence and differential MMPI characteristics. *Journal of Consulting and Clinical Psychology, 46,* 1141-1143.

United States v. Brawner, 471 F.2d 969 (D.C. Cir. 1972).

United States v. Lyons, 731 F.2d 243 (1984).

United States v. Sullivan, 544 F.2d 1052 (1976).

Vaillant, P. M., Asu, M. E., Cooper, D., & Mammola, D. (1984). Profile of dangerous and non-dangerous offenders referred for pretrail psychiatric assessment. *Psychological Reports, 54,* 411-418.

Wasyliw, O. E., Grossman, L. S., Haywood, T. W., & Cavanaugh, J. L. (1988). The detection of malingering in criminal forensic groups: MMPI validity scales. *Journal of Personality Assessment, 52,* 321-333.

Weiner, B. A. (1985). Mental disability and the criminal law. In S. J. Brakel, J. Parry, & B. A. Weiner (Eds.), *The mentally disabled and the law* (3rd ed., pp. 693-801). Chicago: American Bar Foundation.

Use of the MMPI-2 in Correctional Settings

EDWIN I. MEGARGEE

JOYCE L. CARBONELL

In the past 20 years the number of men and women incarcerated in the United States has more than quadrupled and the *rate* of incarceration per 100,000 citizens has tripled. From 1986 to 1993, as legislators jostled each other in their haste to file bills calling for ever increasing mandatory prison

AUTHORS' NOTE: The original research reported in this chapter was supported by the following sources: USPHS Research Grants No. MH 18468, NIMH (Center for Studies of Crime and Delinquency) to E. I. Megargee, J. E. Hokanson and C. D. Spielberger. National Institute of Justice Grant No. 83-IJ-CX-0001, "The early prediction of future career criminals," to J. L Carbonell and E. I. Megargee. National Institute of Justice Grant No. 88-IJ-CX-0006, "A longitudinal study of violent criminal behavior," to E. I. Megargee and J. L. Carbonell. National Institute of Justice Grant No. 89-IJ-CX-0028, "Impact of the revised MMPI ('MMPI-2') on the Megargee MMPI-based offender classification system" to E. I. Megargee. National Computer Systems Professional Assessment Services provided testing materials, scoring services, and specialized data analyses for the research on adapting the MMPI-based classification system to MMPI-2. All opinions expressed are the authors' and do not reflect positions of the National Institute of Mental Health, the U.S. Department of Justice, or National Computer Systems, Inc.

terms, the number of Federal prisons increased from 29 to 77 and the number of state prisons grew from 556 to 770 (American Correctional Association, 1987, 1994). Meanwhile, the numbers of beds in existing institutions were greatly increased. Moreover, those actually in prison on June 30, the day appointed for the annual prison census, are only a fraction of the overall number of offenders dealt with by the criminal justice system at all levels in the course of a year.

At every stage of the criminal justice system, crucial decisions must be made regarding each alleged offender. When people are first arrested, it must be decided whether they should be released or detained, diverted or prosecuted. For those who are charged and convicted of criminal offenses, judges must decide whether they should be admonished, fined, placed on probation, enrolled in an appropriate rehabilitation program, or sentenced to a term of confinement. For those incarcerated in jails and prisons, correctional authorities must determine the facilities and programs best suited to their particular needs. In jurisdictions in which parole is an option, it must be determined when, and under what conditions, prisoners should be released.

Accurate, cost-effective assessment and classification are essential if the criminal justice system is to make such decisions in the face of burgeoning increases in the number of offenders. In 1973, the National Advisory Commission on Criminal Justice Standards and Goals'(NACJSAG) *Report on Corrections* stated, "a good classification system . . . enables a correctional agency to utilize its limited manpower to maximize its impact on offenders" (p. 209). Increasingly, the courts are holding that prisoners have a right to rational, meaningful classification (Clements, 1982, 1985, 1987). As Clements (1982, p. 44) reported, "Inadequacies in the classification process have been major contributing factors to the finding of unconstitutional prison conditions."

Although the National Commission argued over two decades ago that "current knowledge dictates that offense is not a suitable index of an offender's character, dangerousness or needs" (NACJSAG, 1973, p. 198), through statutes and policies, the criminal offense, along with age and gender, remain the most important determinants of correctional placement and programming. Psychology has much to contribute to criminal justice decision making. Ever since Lightner Witmer founded the world's first psychological clinic at the University of Pennsylvania in 1896, 4 years after he received his PhD from Wilhelm Wundt, clinical psychologists have dedicated their skills to serving the criminal justice system. Among Witmer's first clients were "unruly and disruptive children" with "moral defects" who would be called "juvenile delinquents" today (Reisman, 1966, p. 41f). In 1909, psychologist Grace Fernald and psychiatrist William Healey founded the world's first court clinic, the Juvenile Psychopathic Clinic, on the ground floor of Chicago's juvenile detention facility.

Even before the original Minnesota Multiphasic Psychological Inventory (MMPI) was published in 1943, correctional psychologists began examining its usefulness in criminal justice settings (Archer, 1992). In the late 1940s and early 1950s, many studies investigated the MMPI scores of juvenile delinquents and adult offenders as a function of age, race, gender, and setting. From the 1950s through the 1970s, a number of special scales and regression equations specifically designed to assess such criteria as propensity for violence, institutional adjustment, and recidivism were devised, and their validity and usefulness investigated. In 1977, an empirically derived MMPI-based system for classifying adult criminal offenders was introduced (Megargee, 1977; Megargee & Bohn, 1979).

However, by the 1980s, the original MMPI's norms and psychometric properties had become increasingly inappropriate for use in criminal justice settings, especially those serving juveniles and members of minority groups. The MMPI-2, restandardized, renormed, and psychometrically improved, retains the original MMPI's empirically derived clinical scales virtually intact and adds several new validity scales (Butcher, Dahlstrom, Graham, Tellegen, & Kaemmer, 1989). It is better suited for use with minorities than the original MMPI (Timbrook & Graham, 1994), and is available in a number of languages (Butcher & Sloore, 1993). For juveniles, the new adolescent form, MMPI-A, has replaced the original MMPI (Butcher et al., 1992). Recently, the MMPI-based classification system, which had generated considerable research (Sliger, 1992; Zager, 1988), was adapted for use with MMPI-2 (Megargee, 1992, in press).

This chapter will provide a broad overview of research on the use and applications of the original MMPI and MMPI-2 in corrections, concentrating on their use in assessment and classification. Because the item composition of the original MMPI's basic validity and clinical scales has remained relatively unchanged in MMPI-2 and MMPI-A, much of the research on the original MMPI is still relevant. However, readers should be cognizant of the fact that the new norms based on more representative national samples using current administration procedures that encourage respondents to answer all the items, as well as the adoption of uniform T-scores for Scales 1, 2, 3, 4, 6, 7, 8, and 9, have generally lowered the elevations and to some extent altered the configurations of offenders' MMPI-2 and, especially, MMPI-A profiles (Megargee, in press; Peña & Megargee, 1994).

For the analysis of the literature from 1945 through 1977, we will rely heavily on previous reviews by Carbonell, Megargee, and Moorhead (1984), Dahlstrom and Welsh (1960), Dahlstrom, Welsh, and Dahlstrom (1975), Gearing (1979), and Haven (1970). The discussion of the more recent literature will include findings from the our longitudinal investigations on the prediction of criminal behavior with the original MMPI (Carbonell & Megargee, 1984; Carbonell et al., 1984; Megargee & Carbonell, 1985, 1993) as well as a description of the development and validation of the MMPI-based classification system for criminal offenders (Megargee & Bohn, 1979) and the subsequent research on the system.

Descriptive Studies

Most of the early investigations of the MMPI in corrections focused on determining the typical MMPI profiles to be found among various samples of criminal offenders. Some compared these profiles with those of "normals," but many did not. This section will present an overview of these early, essentially exploratory, studies, some of which are now being repeated with MMPI-2 and, especially, MMPI-A.

JUVENILE DELINQUENTS

Although we now regard the original MMPI and its successor, MMPI-2, as adult instruments, many early studies in correctional settings examined teenagers and adolescents, perhaps because clinical psychology, with its emphasis on assessment and treatment, was more firmly established in juvenile than in adult agencies and institutions.

One of the earliest studies was also one of the best and most ambitious investigations in the history of the MMPI. Beginning in 1947, Starke Hathaway, coauthor of the MMPI, and Elio Monachesi, a sociologist, collaborated on an extensive longitudinal study on the prediction of juvenile delinquency with the newly devised test (Hathaway & Monachesi, 1953, 1957; Monachesi, 1948, 1950; Monachesi & Hathaway, 1969). During the 1947-1948 school year, the MMPI was administered to 3,971 ninth graders in Minneapolis, and, in a state-wide assessment in 1954, another 11,329 ninth graders in 86 Minnesota communities were tested. The investigators also obtained school records and teachers' nominations of the students they felt were most likely to run afoul of the law or develop mental health problems.

In subsequent follow-ups after 2 and 4 years, those students known to law enforcement agencies were identified and their records rated on the extent and the seriousness of their delinquent behavior. Although Hathaway and Monachesi have been criticized for their liberal definition of "delinquency," which produced apparent delinquency rates of 21.1% in the first sample and 35.5% in the second (Haven, 1970), their basic findings have stood the test of time. For both boys and girls, Scales 4, 8, and 9 were identified as "excitatory" scales. When these scales were elevated, singly or in combination, delinquency rates were considerably higher than the overall population's rates. Scales 0, 2, and 5 were identified as "suppressor" or inhibitory scales because they were associated with below-average rates of delinquency. Scales 1, 3, 6, and 7 had little relation to subsequent delinquency.

In a unique follow-up, Wirt and Briggs (1959) demonstrated how personality and environmental factors interact by selecting 71 boys from each of four groups: delinquents with the 489 code type, nondelinquents with the 489 code type, delinquents with the 025 code type, and nondelinquents with the 025 code type. They then examined the boys' home environments. The nondelinquent boys with the 489 profiles came from the very best homes; presumably their superior environment offset the delinquency proneness associated with the excitatory scales. Conversely, the delinquent boys with the 025 (inhibitory) profiles came from the worst, most socially deviant home environments whose adverse influence overrode their benign personality traits.

Hathaway and Monachesi obtained their MMPIs in ordinary school settings using subjects who had nothing to gain or lose as a result of the test. In contrast, most research on the MMPIs of juvenile delinquents has been conducted in criminal justice settings using subjects who have every reason to believe that the staff will use the results in some fashion.

Haven (1970) and Gearing (1979), among others, have noted serious deficiencies in many of these studies, including inadequate descriptions of the samples regarding their racial composition, IQ, socioeconomic status, educational level, and even age, information on how the subjects to be tested were selected, whether the MMPI was administered on intake or later in the course of confinement, the nature of the contrast group (if, indeed, one was used), whether the subjects' reading level was assessed, how the tests were administered, whether the standard MMPI or a short form was used, whether the profiles were screened for validity, and which MMPI scales were scored.

Despite the diversity among these studies and the drawbacks that have been noted, the results have been quite consistent. Confirming the pattern discovered by Hathaway and Monachesi (1969), Scales 4, 8, and 9 are typically elevated among male juvenile delinquents and youthful offenders (Caditz, 1959; Richardson & Roebuck, 1965; Wheeler & Megargee, 1970). The evidence with respect to the so-called inhibitory scales is less supportive; indeed, one of the supposed inhibitory scales, Scale 2, is often elevated among offenders tested on intake, perhaps reflecting depression resulting from being incarcerated (Wheeler & Megargee, 1970).

On the mean profiles of delinquent girls, Scales 4, 8, and 9 are also elevated, along with Scale 6 (Capwell, 1945; Jurjevich, 1963; Stone & Rowley, 1963). However, Dahlstrom et al. (1975, p. 61) noted that Paul Meehl, who had examined Capwell's individual profiles, reported that few resembled the average pattern. According to Dahlstrom et al. (1975, p. 61), Meehl, "found they fell into three rather distinct subpatterns: the largest subgroup of girls showed primarily spikes on Scale 4 with submerged profiles on the remaining scales; a smaller group had profiles with elevations on scales making up the psychotic tetrad; and a very small group produced patterns showing elevations on the neurotic triad." Each of these configurations resembles a type delineated in Megargee's MMPI-based classification system.

Because the subjects used in deriving Scale 4 ranged in age from 17 to 22, some of the Scale 4 elevations noted among delinquents could be attributed to their youth. Using a cross-sectional design, Levy, Southcombe, Cranor, and Freeman (1952) compared samples of state prisoners ranging in age from 16 to over 50. They reported that mean scores on Scale 4 became progressively higher in each sample through the 26- to 30-year-old group; in the older samples, the means declined with the mean obtained by the 45-year-old sample being normal. Panton (1959), too, found lower scores on Scale 4 among older offenders. However, as Haven (1970) noted, in cross-sectional studies of prison inmates, age is likely to be confounded with a number of other variables.

Although the MMPI's clinical scales have received the most attention, Scale F, a validity scale, is also typically elevated among juvenile (and adult) offenders. Only Scale 4 is more reliably associated with criminal behavior. After examining the F Scale's item content and comparing it with the events many delinquents experience, McKegney (1965) argued that one should expect Scale F to often be elevated if juvenile offenders respond truthfully.

ADULT OFFENDERS

Reviewing studies of adult offenders, Haven (1970) reported elevations on Scale 2 as well as Scales 4, 8, and 9 in the mean profiles of male state and military prisoners. Among women, Scales 4, 6, 8, and 9 were the most prominent. It should be pointed out that most of the studies reviewed by Haven (1970) and by Dahlstrom et al. (1975) described mean profiles and, as Meehl noted earlier, individual profiles may not resemble the mean, any more than any one of the eight vegetable juices blended into "V-8®" tastes like the final mixture.

MINORITIES

Minorities are overrepresented in many, probably most, American correctional systems. A number of studies showed that presumably normal African Americans obtained elevated scores on the original MMPI (Gynther, 1972; Gynther, Fowler, & Erdberg, 1971), which had few, if any, Blacks in its derivation or standardization samples (Elion & Megargee, 1975). Black offenders tested in criminal justice settings also tend to get more elevated MMPI scores than their White counterparts (Dahlstrom et al., 1975; Gearing, 1979; Haven, 1970). This raises the question of whether the original MMPI may be used with members of minority groups in correctional settings.

Elion and Megargee (1975, p. 166f.) argued, "The critical question . . . is not whether blacks and whites have different mean MMPI scores . . . [but] whether the various MMPI scales are *valid* when applied to blacks." They addressed this question by testing the validity of Scale 4 among young Black men differing in social deviance. Using samples of young Black prison inmates and culturally deprived Black students of the same age, they found that the inmates had significantly higher scores than the students. Moreover, among the inmates, recidivists had significantly higher Pd scale scores than first offenders, whereas among the students, the groups with more self-reported delinquency were significantly higher than those with the least. They concluded that Scale 4 scores validly differentiate levels of social deviance among young Black men, but noted that the original MMPI's norms appeared to be biased. Fortunately, Black, Hispanic, Native American, and Asian American subjects were included in the MMPI-2 and MMPI-A standardization samples, and recent studies have begun to investigate the actual validity of these instruments among ethnic minorities (Timbrook & Graham, 1994).

Applications of the MMPI and MMPI-2

Although the profile patterns of different inmate groups have intrinsic interest, most correctional users of the MMPI are more interested in applications, that is, how the MMPI can assist them in managing and treating criminal offenders.

RETROSPECTIVE VERSUS PROSPECTIVE ASSESSMENTS

In the criminal justice system, most referral questions fall into two broad categories, "retrospective" and "prospective." Retrospective questions are posed when psychologists know what offenders have done and are asked to explain why they did it or to evaluate their mental condition when the offense occurred. In retrospective assessments, clinicians typically have the advantage of being able to use relatively detailed information derived from a number of sources, such as an interview and case history as well as tests.

Prospective questions require psychologists to forecast future behavior, such as recidivism, or the probable response to some intervention such as an anger control program. In these assessments, psychologists are often at a disadvantage because they typically have limited information about the situational circumstances their clients will encounter, even though such factors, interacting with personality variables, will determine much of their clients' future behavior. This makes it difficult for psychologists making prospective evaluations to avoid what social psychologists term "the fundamental attribution error" (Ross, 1977), ascribing greater weight to personality factors than to situational determinants. Whereas retrospective evaluations are typically idiographic, prospective assessments are more apt to be nomothetic, with the psychologist having limited information about large numbers of people.

Some MMPI measures are better suited to retrospective questions, others to prospective. For example, because of the low base rates for violence, Megargee, Cook, and Mendelsohn's (1967) Overcontrolled Hostility (O – H) scale is not very practical for predicting assaultive behavior. However, when used with people who have already been assaultive, it can be very helpful in determining whether or not their violence stemmed from overcontrolled hostility. On the other hand, although Megargee and Bohn's (1979) MMPI-based classification system is not very helpful in retrospective evaluations of offenders' mental states at the time of their offenses, it has proven itself useful in suggesting what sorts of facilities are best suited to the needs of different groups of prisoners and in guiding management and treatment programming.

The retrospective use of the MMPI-2 in criminal justice settings does not differ greatly from individual psychological evaluations elsewhere. True, certain forensic questions, such as determining competency to stand trial, require specialized knowledge and training, and the clientele does pose some special challenges.[1] Nevertheless, clinicians who are skilled in using MMPI-2 in individual assessments in more traditional settings should not experience great difficulty adapting to retrospective assessment in corrections.

Prospective assessments are another matter. When we try to predict future behavior, knowing how to assess personality is only part of the task. We also need to understand the situational factors offenders are likely to encounter and the sorts of behaviors these interactions may elicit (Holt, 1958; Megargee, 1976a). Rare or "low base rate" events are especially difficult to forecast accurately (Meehl & Rosen, 1955).

Escaping from custody is a case in point. Unless one is dealing with someone who has a well-established pattern of attempting to escape, it is risky to attempt to try to predict escaping solely on the basis of personality test patterns, especially if one has not already studied the characteristics of people who have tried to abscond. A trustee who slips away from an outside detail probably differs from the inmate of a secure facility who "hits the fence." Unpredictable situational factors may play a major role; a temporarily unguarded exit or a letter from home reporting that one's sweetheart is seeing someone else may precipitate escape attempts. Conversely, a well-planned escape attempt may be foiled by a random shakedown or a transfer to another facility. Finally, low base rates are likely to result in an inordinate number of false positives (Meehl & Rosen, 1955).

Many behaviors of interest to correctional personnel stem from scenarios with more than one actor. Violence requires a victim as well as a perpetrator. Predicting whether an offender will be reported for disciplinary violations in prison or have his or her parole revoked on the street requires us to forecast not only how the offender will behave, but also how correctional or parole officers are likely to respond to that behavior. Other things being equal, it should be easier to predict behavior occurring in an institutional setting, if only because there is less environmental variability.

The next three subsections will discuss prospective research using the MMPI to predict criteria of interest in correctional settings. The first will describe studies using the regular MMPI and MMPI-2 scales, the next will focus on special MMPI scales, and the third will discuss studies using multiple regression and discriminant function analyses.

STUDIES USING THE STANDARD MMPI AND MMPI-2 SCALES

Assaultive behavior and violence. The prediction of violence has long been a concern of correctional psychologists (Megargee, 1976b). In a postdictive investigation, Megargee and Mendelsohn (1962) compared the MMPI scores of extremely assaultive ($N = 14$), moderately assaultive ($N = 25$), and nonviolent ($N = 25$) adult male applicants for probation, as well as a comparable sample of noncriminals ($N = 46$). The results were disappointing. Although Scales 2, 4, and 8 could significantly differentiate some of the criminal groups from the noncriminals, none of the regular MMPI validity or clinical scales could distinguish either of the assaultive samples from the nonviolent offenders.

Instead of examining individual scales, three investigations focused on MMPI two-point codes. Davis and Sines (1971) and Persons and Marks (1971) both reported the "43" code type was associated with significantly higher rates of criminal violence among men and Davis (1971) found a similar pattern among female offenders. Examining male inmates with "42," "48," and "49" profile types, Persons and Marks (1971) reported only average rates of violence, using the commitment offense as the criterion.

The present writers recently completed a predictive study of the MMPI and criminal violence (Megargee & Carbonell, 1993, 1994). The data for this study were collected as part of a broader longitudinal investigation at the Federal Correctional Institution ("FCI") in Tallahassee, Florida. Because a number of findings from this "FCI Study" will be cited in this chapter, the overall project will be briefly described.

From November 3, 1970 through November 2, 1972, every inmate admitted to the FCI, a medium security facility for male youthful offenders aged 18 to 27, was a subject in a broad-scale longitudinal study. Most of the 1,345 subjects, 64% of whom were White and 35% of whom were Black, were serving indeterminate zero- to 6-year ("zip six") sentences under the Youth Corrections Act in which their release date was based on evaluations of their behavior and progress in the institution. Typical offenses were interstate transportation of a stolen motor vehicle, larceny, and fraud. During the initial 30 day Admissions and Orientation period, the subjects were administered an extensive array of ability, achievement, interest, and personality tests, including the original MMPI. Staff psychologists interviewed each and recorded their observations using Q-sorts and Gough-Heilbrun Adjective Checklists (Gough & Heilbrun, 1965). Audio tapes of these interviews and the Bureau of Prisons' Presentence Investigation reports were coded by teams of trained raters on a wide variety of scales. The subjects were monitored throughout the course of their FCI stay, with data on their adjustment, health, behavior, and progress collected at regular intervals until they left the institution or until the end of data collection in July 1974. Before leaving the FCI, most were reexamined and reinterviewed (Megargee & Hokanson, 1975; Megargee, Hokanson, & Spielberger, 1971). In 1983, when most of the subjects were in their middle 30s, a follow-up was carried out. Complete FBI arrest records ("RAP sheets") were obtained on 971 of the former inmates, and their subsequent criminal careers examined (Carbonell & Megargee, 1984).

To evaluate the MMPI's relation to subsequent violent criminal behavior, the subjects' records were classified according to whether they had ever been arrested for a violent criminal offense; 346 had never been arrested for any crime of violence, but 625 had one or more such arrests. In the first set of analyses, the mean MMPI scores of the violent offenders were compared with those of the nonviolent subjects (Megargee & Carbonell, 1993). Just as Megargee and Mendelsohn (1962) had found 30 years earlier, there were no significant differences on any of the clinical scales nor on the average elevation of the MMPI. The nonviolent offenders were significantly higher on the L Scale, whereas the violent offenders were higher on the K Scale, but the magnitude of the mean differences was quite small and the results were attributed to chance.

A different picture emerged when we compared the violent offenders who had but a single arrest for a violent crime with those who had two or more. The repetitively violent group was significantly higher than the single violent offense group on Scales K, 1, 2, 4, 7, 8, and 9, and on the mean overall clinical scale elevation, despite the fact that the single violent offense group also had noteworthy elevations (Megargee & Carbonell, 1993, 1994).

Institutional adjustment. After an exhaustive review of the literature on predicting prison adjustment with the MMPI and other structured personality inventories, Carbonell et al. (1984) identified 22 such studies from 1938 through 1981, 15 of which used the MMPI. They noted a number of deficiencies in this literature: (a) a proliferation of unreplicated "one-shot" studies; (b) test data often collected after the criterion data so that their usefulness in prediction could not be determined; (c) failure to report base rates of criterion behaviors such as rule violations; (d) comparison of extreme groups, thereby inflating significance levels and limiting generality; (e) failure to report the actual magnitude of "statistically significant" mean differences or correlations; (f) use of atypical test administration procedures, such as assuring inmates test responses would be kept confidential; and (g) failure to cross-validate multiple significance tests.

In addition to these problems, the literature also suffered from many of the shortcomings noted by Gearing (1979). Investigators reporting their results often failed to describe how they administered their tests, screened profiles for validity, or ensured representative sampling (Carbonell et al., 1984, pp. 283-284).

The results of the 15 MMPI studies were inconsistent. Most reported no differences. Those that did tended to compare extreme groups such as "ideal prisoners" with "persistent rule violators" (Truxal & Sabatino, 1972), and the results were rarely cross-validated.

Using data from the FCI study, Carbonell et al. (1984) assigned two thirds of the 1,213 subjects who had taken the MMPI to a derivation sample and one third to a cross-validation sample. They then correlated the MMPI validity and clinical scales with six criteria of adjustment. Three were derived from institutional records: (a) the number of reported disciplinary infractions, (b) the number of days spent in disciplinary segregation, and (c) the number of days on sick call per quarter. Three were based on ratings by (a) the custodial staff, (b) the work crew supervisors, and (c) the educational staff. Given the large sample sizes, it was stipulated that correlations had to be statistically significant ($p < .05$, two-tail) in *both* the derivation and cross-validation samples to be considered reliable.

Overall, 43% of the correlations were significant, with Scales 4, 8, and F having the most consistent relations to the criteria. However, the actual magnitude of most of the correlation coefficients was rather small. None exceeded .30 and few were over .20. It should be noted that characteristics of the criterion data were partly responsible. The institutional data were skewed because only a minority of the inmates were reported for disciplinary infractions, and a number of staff members tended to rate most men as "average," avoiding the extremes on the five-point Likert-type scales. Nevertheless, relatively little variance on the adjustment measures was reliably associated with the personality traits measured by the MMPI clinical scales.

Educational achievement. In most correctional institutions, especially those for juveniles and youthful offenders, academic and vocational training is available. Two studies investigated whether the MMPI could predict success in such programs. Levine (1969) reported significant negative correlations, ranging from –.22 to –.37 between MMPI Scales F, 6, 7, 8, and 9 and teachers' ratings of academic success in a sample of 90 youthful offenders enrolled in a high school equivalency (GED) program at the FCI.[2]

Steuber (1975) found somewhat lower, but still significant, negative correlations with Scales F (–.13) and 8 (–.15) in a sample of 245 youthful offenders. He also reported a significant positive correlation with Scale 5.

Levine (1969) also investigated vocational achievement as evaluated by work supervisors' ratings in a furniture refinishing program. None of the regular MMPI scales was related to successful performance.

Homosexual behavior. Although homosexuality is no longer regarded as a psychiatric disorder, an offender's sexual orientation is still a concern for classifications personnel who must assign inmates to living quarters. In some settings, for example, homosexual offenders may be exploited and victimized by other inmates. Gearing (1979) reported that a number of early correctional studies investigated whether the MMPI could differentiate male prisoners who had been identified as engaging in homosexual behavior from the rest of the inmate population. Although some scales were found to discriminate these groups, no consistent patterns were found when Gearing compared the results from different studies. Again, too many significance tests and too little cross-validation appear to be likely culprits.

Recidivism. Of all the variables correctional psychologists are asked to predict, recidivism is one of the most ubiquitous. It is also one of the most difficult to define operationally; Megargee (1976a) did a study comparing no less than 13 different operational definitions of recidivism.

In the earliest attempt to use the MMPI to predict recidivism, Clark (1948) compared the MMPIs of 55 soldiers who had been absent without leave

(AWOL) two or more times with those of 45 others who had been AWOL only once. He found only slight differences on Scales 4 and 9. Both Black (1967) and Mack (1969) reported that the regular MMPI scales failed to identify recidivists in nonmilitary settings.

Using California Youth Authority wards, Gough, Wenk, and Rozynko (1965) compared the MMPI scores of 183 parole violators with 261 non-violators and cross-validated their findings using 130 violators and 165 nonviolators. Significant differences between the two groups in both samples were obtained for only one MMPI scale, Scale 9, and the magnitudes of these mean differences were less than 1.5 raw score points. Smith and Lanyon's (1968) attempt to replicate Gough et al.'s (1965) findings using 287 New Jersey probationers was unsuccessful, and they reported, "The MMPI failed completely as a predictive device" (p. 57).

Carbonell and Megargee (1984) classified the first 947 FCI subjects[3] for whom they obtained FBI arrest records into three groups: "terminators" ($N = 370$) who had few if any subsequent arrests, none of which was for a serious offense, "persistent offenders" ($N = 261$) who continued to engage in frequent or serious criminal activity, and "occasional offenders" ($N = 316$) whose subsequent histories fell between these two extremes.

Based on the literature regarding career criminals, differences had been hypothesized on a number of variables including one of the standard MMPI scales, Scale 4. As predicted, the terminators were found to have the lowest mean T-score (71.9) and the persistent offenders had the highest (75.3), with the occasional offenders falling in the middle (73.5). This study is unusual because it used an entire population rather than extreme groups and because it tested predictions based on test scores obtained a number of years earlier. However, even though the mean differences were highly significant ($p = .001$), their absolute magnitudes were small.

STUDIES USING SPECIAL SCALES

When the original MMPI was published it provided psychologists with a new technology and a robust item pool for creating new scales. If behaviors of interest were not adequately assessed by the original scales, investigators could gather their own criterion groups and derive new scales. Or, if they preferred the rational-intuitive approach to test construction, they could read the items and decide which should be included. By 1960, when the first edition of the *MMPI Handbook* was published, it included an appendix listing 213 scales, indexes, and scoring procedures (Dahlstrom & Welsh, 1960). By the time the second edition was published, the number had grown to 455 (Dahlstrom et al., 1975). In this section we will survey some studies using these special scales to assess correctional constructs.[4]

Assaultive behavior and violence. In their postdictive study, Megargee and Mendelsohn (1962) compared their 14 extremely assaultive, 25 moderately assaultive, and 25 nonviolent offenders as well as 46 noncriminals on a dozen scales and indexes purporting to assess hostility, aggression, and control, including Panton's (1958) Adjustment to Prison scale, Schultz's (1954) Hostility Control and Overt Hostility scales, Cook and Medley's (1954) Hostility scale, Harris and Lingoes's (1968) Inhibition of Aggression subscale, Siegel's (1956) Judged Manifest Hostility, Gough's (1960) Impulsivity, and Block's (1955) Ego Overcontrol, Neurotic Undercontrol, and Bimodal Control scales as well as Welsh and Sullivan's Active Hostility Index (a combination of Scales 4 and 0) as cited in Dahlstrom and Welsh (1960), and Beall and Panton's (1957) Frustration Tolerance Index (the sum of Scales 4 + 9 divided by the sum of Scales 2 + 3).

Although several scales differentiated the criminals from the noncriminals, none discriminated the assaultive from the nonassaultive offenders significantly in the expected direction. Some actually worked in reverse, indicating that the extremely assaultive offenders were, paradoxically, more controlled and less aggressive than the other groups (Megargee & Mendelsohn, 1962). Megargee (1966, 1982) later hypothesized that there are several different types of violent offenders, and was able to demonstrate empirically the existence of two such syndromes, the increasingly prevalent "undercontrolled assaultive type" and the now rather rare "chronically overcontrolled assaultive type." He also discovered that an unsuccessful general "assaultiveness" scale he had derived from the four samples of MMPIs actually identified the chronically overcontrolled type. After additional construct validation, it was published as the Overcontrolled–Hostility (O – H) scale (Megargee et al., 1967). Although only high O – H scores have any meaning, the construct and the scale have stimulated considerable research in this country and England,[5] which is why O – H is included among MMPI-2's Supplementary Scales.

In our recent longitudinal investigation of the factors associated with violent criminal behavior (Megargee & Carbonell, 1993), a number of special

MMPI scales were used to test hypotheses suggested by the literature on criminal violence and by Megargee's (1993) theory of aggression. They included several of the measures described above, namely Cook and Medley's (1954) Hostility (Ho) scale, Megargee et al.'s (1967) Overcontrolled Hostility (O – H) scale, Panton's (1958) Adjustment to Prison (Ap,r) scale, and Welsh and Sullivan's Active Hostility Index (AHI) as cited in Dahlstrom and Welsh (1960), as well as McQuary and Truax's (1955) Underachievement scale (Un), Sines and Silver's (1963) Index of Psychopathology (Ip), Tydlaska and Mengel's (1953) Negative Work Attitudes (Wa) scale, and six of Wiggins's (1966) content scales: Authority Conflicts (AUT), Family Problems (FAM), Manifest Hostility (HOS), Poor Health (HEA), Psychoticism (PSY), and Social Maladjustment (SOC).

Whereas none of the regular clinical scales had differentiated the violent from the nonviolent offenders, significant differences were obtained on six of the special scales: AUT ($p < .007$), Ho ($p < .001$), HOS ($p < .022$), PSY ($p < .027$), and Wa ($p < .024$), as well as the AHI ($p < .025$), which combines Scales 4 and 9. O – H approached significance ($p < .075$). All tests were two tail, with the Violent offenders obtaining the more deviant scores (Megargee & Carbonell, 1993, 1994).

Three scales differentiated the Repetitively Violent offenders from those charged with but a single offense, HEA ($p < .046$), Wa ($p < .032$), and the AHI ($p < .006$) (all tests two tail). Approaching significance were Ip ($p < .066$) and PSY ($p < .102$). It thus appears that these selected special scales were better able to differentiate violent from nonviolent offenders, but the regular scales were more sensitive to the differences between the single and repetitively violent groups. Perhaps the latter distinction is more closely related to psychopathology, which the original clinical scales were designed to assess. In any event, it should be noted that the absolute magnitudes of all these mean differences were quite small, attaining significance only by virtue of the large sample sizes (Megargee & Carbonell, 1993, 1994). Thus, their theoretical significance outweighs their practical value.

Institutional adjustment. James H. Panton, of the North Carolina Department of Corrections, conducted one of the few systematic programs of research in corrections, devising a number of special scales and indexes to be used in correctional settings, including the following: "Adjustment to Prison, Revised, Ap,r" (Panton, 1958), "Escape, Ec" (Beall & Panton, 1956), the "Frustration

Tolerance Index, FTI" (Beall & Panton, 1957), "Habitual Criminalism, HC" (which combined the raw scores on his Ap,r scale with those on the regular MMPI Pd scale) (Panton, 1962a), "Homosexuality, HSX" (Panton, 1960), "Parole Violation, PaV" (Panton, 1962b), and "Religious Identification, RI" (Panton, 1979). Panton constructed a special "Prison Classification Inventory" (Panton, 1970), a profile that included some of these measures along with those regular MMPI scales Panton felt were most useful in correctional settings, using T-scores based on North Carolina prisoners' norms.

Evidence regarding the validity of Panton's various scales is mixed (Dahlstrom et al., 1975; Gearing, 1979; Megargee & Carbonell, 1985). Gearing (1979) noted that studies conducted in North Carolina were more likely to report positive results than those conducted elsewhere, which is not surprising because Panton's empirically derived scales used North Carolina prison inmates.

Wattron (1963) empirically derived a "Prison Maladjustment Scale, PMS," for the MMPI by contrasting the responses of 100 inmates in disciplinary segregation with those of 100 successful parolees, a procedure similar to that used by Panton who had compared 56 prisoners with two or more infractions with 72 prisoners having none when building his Ap,r scale. Despite their similar origins, PMS and Ap,r share only two items scored in the same direction. When Megargee and Carbonell's (1985) FCI data were scored for all these scales, they found that the correlation between PMS and Ap,r was low ($r = .10$, $p < .05$) and that they served to define two separate orthogonal factors.

Megargee and Carbonell (1985) correlated the scores on Panton's Ap,r, Ec, HC, HSX, RI, and PaV scales, as well as Wattron's PMS and Clark's AWOL Recidivism scale, Rc, with their six criteria of subsequent correctional adjustment. All of these scales had been used to assess prison adjustment in one or more prior studies. Some significant correlations with the criterion measures were obtained, but their magnitudes were low. None exceeded .29 and few were as high as .20. Wattron's PMS scale and Panton's HC performed best, but neither did better than the regular MMPI's Scales F and 4 (Megargee & Carbonell, 1985).

Educational achievement. Levine (1969) reported a significant negative correlation between Panton's Ap,r scale and teachers' ratings of youthful offenders' success in the academic program ($r = -.32$, $p < .01$), but Steuber (1975) failed to replicate Levine's finding ($r = .09$).

Homosexual behavior. Panton (1960) derived his HSX scale by comparing the responses of confirmed homosexual offenders with those of (presumably) nonhomosexual prisoners who were matched for age and IQ. Although HSX does not predict prison adjustment, several studies reviewed by Megargee and Carbonell (1985) indicate it can differentiate male homosexuals in various settings. Panton (1960) reported a cross validation in which the scale correctly identified 18 of 21 homosexuals (86%) and 15 of 21 (81%) of nonhomosexuals. He failed to discuss the implications of a 19% false positive rate in any institution with a low base rate of homosexuality, or the consequences that might ensue to offenders who might be mislabeled.

Recidivism. Four special measures have been designed to predict recidivism, Black's (1967) Recidivism-Rehabilitation (Rmn) scale, Clark's (1948) AWOL Recidivism (Rc) scale, Panton's Habitual Criminal (1962a) (HC) scale and his (1962b) Parole Violation (PaV) scales. Gearing (1979, p. 951) reported that Black, using his scale alone and with other scales, had obtained an overall hit rate of 90% with only 7.8% false positives, and that Frank (1971) had obtained an overall hit rate of 73.1% with 15.9% false positives using Rmn, but found Black's combination of scales was somewhat less successful. Clark (1953) reported his Rc scale successfully identified a new sample of AWOL recidivists, but Freeman and Mason (1952) were unable to validate Rc.

Gough et al. (1965) found both of their two samples of Youth Authority parole violators to be about half a point higher on Rc than the comparison groups of nonviolators; in the larger sample this difference was enough to attain significance, in the smaller it was not. PaV was not significant in either comparison.

Adams (1976) reported that HC successfully differentiated samples that differed in the extensiveness of their criminal record, and Carbonell and Megargee (1984) found that their terminators' mean HC score (68.8) was significantly lower than that of the occasional offenders (71.5), which in turn was significantly lower than that of the persistent offenders (74.7). Thus, adding Panton's Ap,r items to the non-K-corrected Pd scale to produce HC improved the discrimination possible with Scale 4 alone. Among the difficulties associated with interpreting these studies are their differing operational definitions and base rates of recidivism, whether they used predictive or postdictive designs, and whether they employed MMPIs administered on intake or before release.

STUDIES USING MULTIVARIATE ANALYSES

All the studies reviewed thus far examined the ability of individual MMPI scales, both regular and special, to assess correctional criteria. Another strategy is to determine whether weighted combinations of scales, identified by means of discriminant function or multiple regression analyses, can predict correctional criteria better than individual scales. Some investigators use only MMPI scales, whereas others have tried combining MMPI scales with other sources of information. Many derive several equations using different combinations of predictors and criteria. Gough et al. (1965) created six equations to predict parole outcomes, whereas Carbonell et al. (1984) derived 21 to predict prison adjustment. All such equations should be cross-validated on a new sample. The resulting reports are typically long and complex, so rather than providing detailed descriptions we will simply present their highlights.

Institutional adjustment and behavior. Jones, Beidleman, and Fowler (1981) used the MMPI scored on regular and special scales in conjunction with demographic variables to postdict violent behavior in prison. Their discriminant function correctly classified 73% of the violent and 81% of the nonviolent inmates in the derivation groups, but no base rates or cross-validation were reported.

Scott, Mount, and Duffy (1977) used regression analysis to differentiate between women prisoners who had and had not escaped from prison. Their MMPI-based equation yielded a multiple R of .50 on cross-validation. Sutker and Moan (1973) compared 21 male prisoners with six or more rule violations with 30 who had none to derive a discriminant function based on the regular MMPI plus three special scales. Their equation correctly classified 91% of a similar cross-validation sample. In both these studies, the *predictive* validity of the equations and the base rates for the criterion behavior would determine the equations' usefulness. Moreover, the ability of Sutker and Moan's equations to classify correctly less-extreme groups remains to be determined.

Carbonell et al. (1984) used regression analyses to derive a series of equations to predict ratings of adjustment made by the custodial staff, the work crew supervisors, and the educational staff. One set of equations used the regular MMPI scales and another used only MMPI Factors A and R. The scales' multiple Rs, ranging from .27 to .36, were higher than those based on Factors A and R (.13 to .15), although with large samples all were highly significant.

On cross-validation, the scales predicting the custodial officers' ratings ($R = .31$, $p < .001$) and the teachers' ratings ($R = .27$, $p < .001$) held up, but the one predicting work supervisors' ratings did not. The authors pointed out, however, that these multiple Rs were not much higher than the first-order correlations of Scale F with these criteria. The fact that Carbonell et al. (1984) used an entire prison population rather than selected extreme groups and cross-validated their findings probably accounts for the fact that the correlations they obtained were generally lower than those reported by other investigators.

Because their criteria of disciplinary reports, cell house time, and sick call use were highly skewed, Carbonell et al. (1984) performed discriminant function analyses in their derivation samples, using the actual base rates in the population. They reported 66% to 78% of the cross-validation sample were correctly classified by the various equations; this finding lost some of its luster when they further noted that base rate predictions would have yielded hit rates ranging from 61% to 72%.

Educational achievement. Levine (1969) derived a stepwise regression formula to predict youthful offenders' success in the academic program at the FCI. The optimal formula, combining Scale F with Panton's Ap,r scale, achieved a multiple R of .42 when applied to the derivation sample, but was not cross-validated. As part of a larger study, Steuber (1975) derived two multiple regression equations predicting grades in the FCI academic program, one using only the MMPI, scored on special as well as the regular scales, the second using the MMPI in conjunction with the Revised Beta, and a third using the MMPI along with the California Psychological Inventory (CPI). On cross-validation, all three of the equations predicted the criterion significantly, but with multiple Rs ranging from .19 to .29, Steuber concluded the magnitude of the correlations was too small for them to be used as predictors.

Recidivism. Gough et al. (1965) used the MMPI alone and in conjunction with the CPI and a demographic Base Expectancy (BE) table to predict parole outcomes. Applied to a cross-validation sample with a base rate for parole violations of 44%, all the equations derived were statistically significant. However, the MMPI contributed less than either the BE or CPI. On cross-validation, the equation based on the MMPI alone had a hit rate of 55%, slightly lower than the BE's 59% and the CPI's 60%. The MMPI and the BE together had a hit rate of 60%, no better than the BE or CPI alone. The MMPI combined with the BE and CPI correctly classified 63%, the same proportion correctly classified with the BE and CPI alone. Although ages were not reported, it appears that most of the subjects were below the optimal age for the original MMPI; it would be interesting to replicate this research with MMPI-A.

After testing hypotheses on the characteristics of career criminals, Carbonell and Megargee (1984) attempted to derive equations that would correctly classify their three groups: terminators, occasional offenders, and persistent offenders. Two sets of MMPIs, one administered on intake and the other prior to release, were among the data sets used. Different scale patterns characterized the White and non-White subjects. Among the White samples, Scales F, 1, 2, 4, 6, 7, 8, and 9 significantly differentiated the groups on the intake MMPIs, and Scales L, 4, 6, 7, and 9 significantly discriminated the prerelease MMPIs. Stepwise discriminant function analyses selected Scales F and 4 as the best predictors for the intake tests, and Scales 4, 6, and 9 for the prerelease tests. Although the equations that were derived were statistically significant, they only classified 42% to 55% of the subjects in the original derivation groups correctly, far below the hit rate required for any practical application. Among the non-White subjects, none of the individual MMPI scales attained significance, and the equations that were derived were even less accurate than those for the Whites. This pattern could reflect racial differences in the meaning of the MMPI scales for Black and White offenders, racial disparities in criminal history records, or both. Whatever the explanation, these data suggest that investigators should be cautious in generalizing from one racial group to the other, and instead conduct separate analyses for different ethnic or racial subgroups. Similarly, in correctional settings, one should not assume that test data collected at intake necessarily assess offenders who have been in the institution for a period of time or who are about to be released.

Taken as a whole, these multivariate studies indicate that occasionally a combination of MMPI scales can, on cross-validation, improve on the basic MMPI scales and, possibly, the best special scales in predicting correctional criteria, but not always and, even then, not by much. Using the MMPI in conjunction with other data may increase accuracy, but decrease practicality and cost-effectiveness. In applied correctional settings, few psychologists are likely to administer several tests to compute complex multivariate equations.

In all of the literature reviewed thus far, linear relationships have been examined, whether it is the correlation of single scales with criteria or multiple regression equations. However, the MMPI is essentially a configural instrument designed to be interpreted as a whole. No one scale can substitute for an

MMPI *profile.* In the remainder of this chapter a complex, empirically derived classification system for criminal offenders that uses the MMPI's configural properties will be described.

The MMPI-Based System of Offender Classification

All of the studies reviewed thus far investigated whether the MMPI could assess selected correctional criteria accurately. In devising an MMPI-based offender classification system, Megargee and his colleagues (Megargee, 1977; Megargee & Bohn, 1979) took the opposite approach, first creating a way to categorize criminal offenders' MMPI profiles and then ascertaining what, if anything, the categories assessed.

To be useful in applied criminal justice settings, a classification system must

1. be comprehensive, so that most clients can be classified;
2. have clear operational definitions of the various types;
3. have interrater reliability;
4. be valid, that is, display evidence that the proposed types actually exist and have the hypothesized attributes;
5. be dynamic, that is, have the potential to change over time;
6. have differential management and treatment implications for the various types;
7. be cost-effective so that large numbers of offenders can be classified quickly and inexpensively with minimum reliance on highly trained personnel (Clements, 1982, 1987; Megargee, 1977).

When work on the MMPI-based system began in 1970, no system for classifying adult offenders met all these criteria. We hoped that it would be possible to derive a system based on the MMPI that met these criteria and that would contribute useful data on personality functioning that would be useful in correctional planning.

DERIVATION OF THE MMPI-BASED SYSTEM

Hierarchical profile analyses were conducted on the MMPI profiles of three samples of male youthful offenders incarcerated at the FCI. The same basic profile types were found in each sample (Meyer & Megargee, 1972, 1977). Subsequent independent replications of these analyses using the MMPIs of state prisoners (Nichols, 1980) and halfway house clients (Mrad, Kabacoff, & Duckro, 1983) have yielded similar groups.

Meyer and Megargee (1972, 1977) next established that, working independently, they were able to assign individual offenders' profiles to the same group in 87% of the cases. Subsequently, Megargee and Dorhout (1976, 1977) formulated a set of classificatory rules that constituted operational definitions for each of the 10 MMPI-based groups. These configural rules considered elevation, slope, patterns of high and low scores, and the other aspects of an MMPI profile that most clinicians interpret. Primary rules determined eligibility for classification into a group; to be included, a given profile had to meet all of these requirements. Secondary rules helped clarify goodness of fit when a profile satisfied the primary rules for two or more types. A computer program was written embodying these rules that was able to classify the most clear-cut cases, constituting about two thirds of the profiles. The rest were to be classified by a clinician familiar with the MMPI and the system who could consult published guidelines that addressed the more difficult discriminations.

In keeping with MMPI tradition, whereby the scales are referred to by their numbers rather than by names to avoid the connotations associated with terms such as "Psychopathic Deviate," the 10 types were assigned neutral names based on the phonetic alphabet: Able, Baker, Charlie, Delta, Easy, Foxtrot, George, How, Item, and Jupiter.

CHARACTERIZING THE TYPES

The key question was whether the 10 groups differed on anything other than their MMPI profiles. To answer this question, the MMPI profiles of the 1,213 youthful offenders in the FCI project who had completed the MMPI on intake were classified according to this typology. Using Duncan multiple-range tests for continuous variables and chi-square analyses for categorical data, the 10 groups were compared on a broad array of variables reflecting early developmental history, social, demographic and attitudinal factors, childhood and adult adjustment and achievement, subsequent adjustment to the institution, and eventual recidivism some years later. Overall, 140 of the 164 comparisons proved to be statistically significant (Megargee, 1984b; Zager, 1988).

In addition, analyses of Gough and Heilbrun's (1965) Adjective Checklist (ACL), which had been completed by the offenders on intake, revealed that the members of the 10 groups differed in the adjectives they did and did not endorse as being self-descriptive; likewise, psychologists who used the ACL to characterize inmates immediately after having interviewed them described the 10 groups differently (Megargee, 1984a).

The differences in all of these measures were used to formulate modal descriptions of each type and suggest strategies for their optimal management and treatment, focusing on the best setting, the most suitable change agent, and the most appropriate treatment techniques (Megargee & Bohn, 1979). These descriptions have proven to be useful guides to the management and treatment of offenders. In one study the typology was used to assign inmates to living units so as to separate the most predatory offenders from those whose MMPI classifications suggested they were most likely to be victimized. As a result of this change, the rate of serious assaults, which had been steadily increasing, dropped 46% (Bohn, 1978), a gain that was maintained in subsequent years (Bohn, 1979).

Over the years since its initial publication (Megargee, 1977), a number of investigators have successfully applied the MMPI-based classification system to a variety of samples including prisoners confined in federal, state, and military prisons, halfway houses, community restitution centers, and local jails. Specialized populations include presidential threateners and prisoners confined in forensic mental health units and Death Row.

One advantage of an MMPI-based system is that, in contrast to offense-based systems, the MMPI profile can reflect changes over the course of the sentence. Several studies reviewed by Zager (1988) showed that many offenders' classifications change after several months or so of incarceration. Unfortunately these changes were often confounded with changes in set and motivation, because the retests were typically administered to volunteers for research rather than to everyone for classification. Zager (1983, 1988) concluded that the available evidence indicated that changes in type reflect changes in adjustment. Nevertheless, because most of the research to date has used intake MMPIs, users should be cautious in applying the system to MMPIs given later, and should base their midsentence evaluations on observed behavior and adjustment rather than on a personality test.

The MMPI-based system has been well received and widely investigated (Clements, 1987; Gearing, 1981; Sliger, 1992; Zager, 1988).[6] One reviewer wrote, "impressive in every way . . . this new MMPI system unquestionably defines the present state of the art in correctional classification" (Gearing, 1981, pp. 106-107). Although others are less enthusiastic, the preponderance of the evidence, as well as its widespread adoption, suggests that the MMPI-based typology met the basic requirements for a useful classification system and filled a need in correctional classification (Clements, 1987).

The advent of MMPI-2 raised the question of whether the rules devised for the original MMPI could be used to classify MMPI-2s and, if not, whether new rules for MMPI-2 could be devised. To answer this question, the original MMPIs of 1,213 subjects from the FCI project that had been previously classified when the characteristics of types were being determined were re-scored and reprofiled to yield estimated MMPI-2s. MMPI-2s administered to 422 male state and federal offenders were rescored to estimate original MMPIs. When all of the profiles were classified according to the original MMPI rules, identical classifications were obtained in only 60% to 67% of the cases, indicating the original rules should not be applied to MMPI-2s.

Accordingly, a new set of rules specifically devised for male MMPI-2s was devised. On cross-validation these rules yielded agreement with the original MMPI classification in 82% of the cases. These rules are considerably more complex than the original rules, but their use reduces the number of unclass-ifiable profiles (Megargee, in press). Research is currently in progress to determine whether the descriptors associated with the original MMPI types apply equally well when the types are defined on the basis of MMPI-2.

Research is also under way on the MMPI-2s of female offenders. Prelimi-nary results indicate that neither the original rules nor the new rules derived for male offenders are suitable for women's MMPI-2s. New rules specifically designed for female offenders are currently being tested.

DIRECTIONS FOR FUTURE RESEARCH

At the conclusion of a book surveying the past 50 years of personality assessment, the senior author endeavored to forecast the future of assessment in the next 50 years (Megargee & Spielberger, 1992). Some of the trends noted for the field in general also apply to the narrower area of MMPI-2 and corrections.

Several basic trends should be noted, some of which have already been alluded to. The first is the exponentially increasing need for assessment and classification in correctional settings. Prisoners are flooding the criminal justice system in record numbers, and as a number of authorities and court decisions have noted over the years, accurate, accountable classification pro-grams are not only desirable but essential (Clements, 1982, 1987; National Advisory Commission on Criminal Justice Standards and Goals, 1973).

A second basic principle is that technology, once introduced, cannot be undone. The technological advances that will influence the use of the MMPI in correctional settings are, first, the development of MMPI-2 and MMPI-A, and, second, computerized assessment technology, including administration, scoring, and interpretation.

A third trend is the decreasing emphasis on assessment in graduate training programs (J. N. Butcher, personal communication, August 20, 1994). As the sheer amount of knowledge in psychology has expanded, the proportion of time devoted to learning how to administer and interpret individual intelligence and personality tests has decreased for the typical graduate student. Although there will always be those whose primary interest is assessment, we can no longer expect the average graduate of a doctoral program to have the expertise and knowledge of assessment that were expected 20 years ago.

Putting these trends together, what is the likely future for the MMPI-2 and MMPI-A in corrections? First, given the fact that they are widely researched, objective, standardized instruments that are amenable to computerized scoring and interpretation, and given the fact that a classification system whose use can be defended in court is available, it seems likely that MMPI-2 and MMPI-A will continue to be the most widely used personality assessment instruments in correctional settings. This does not necessarily mean that MMPI-2 and MMPI-A will be used routinely in most correctional settings because costs will be a major consideration. The days when the Federal Bureau of Prisons could administer the MMPI to all 10,000 newly admitted inmates for a total cost, including materials and computerized scoring, profiling, and classification, of $15,000 or less are gone forever. In 1992, almost 33,000 offenders were admitted to federal prisons, and the cost of computerized MMPI-2 scoring was considerably higher. Handscoring 33,000 protocols is an onerous chore. As a result, the Bureau has long since abandoned routine administration of the MMPI-2 and bases its screening on less-expensive demographic data that are already available. If the courts should afford psychological assessment the same status as medical evaluations, so an MMPI-2 is deemed as necessary as a blood test or a chest X-ray, then funds may become available. Or, if prisoners were to retain their medical benefits while incarcerated, then more systems would be able to use MMPI-2 and MMPI-A. Otherwise, given the current cost patterns, budgetary considerations are likely to limit their use to offenders who are referred for psychological evaluations.

Turning to research, additional studies are needed on the comparability of MMPI-2 to the original MMPI in correctional settings. Such studies will determine the degree to which practitioners in the criminal justice system can generalize safely from the vast store of research on the original MMPI to MMPI-2 and MMPI-A. The correlates of the new MMPI-2 and MMPI-A validity and content scales among offenders also need to be determined, and the validity of MMPI-A among delinquents must be established. Given the large number of minorities in correctional populations, investigators should be especially concerned with possible racial and ethnic differences in reliability and validity.

Personality characteristics are, of course, only one factor in predicting behavior. Investigations of situational and environmental variables in correctional settings, and the results of their interactions with measurable personality dimensions would enhance psychologists' ability to make prospective assessments, as would more research on base rates.

One negative aspect of the computerization of psychology is that early studies that are not electronically retrievable are lost from our collective memory. Judging from manuscripts we are asked to review, many researchers are unwittingly duplicating studies done 10 or 20 years ago; At best they are rediscovering the wheel; at worst, flat tires. Correctional psychologists should be encouraged to collect, preserve, and pass on the knowledge that has already been painstakingly accumulated, not only regarding substantive findings but also methodological principles. Projects such as this one, gathering, analyzing, and communicating what we presently know about the forensic applications of MMPI-2, will do much to advance this process.

Notes

1. A recent advertisement for a staff psychologist's position at a correctional institution noted that the job was not for "the faint of heart."

2. Although these studies were conducted at the FCI, Tallahassee, they were not part of the large longitudinal investigation cited elsewhere.

3. Additional records were received from the FBI after this study was completed, which is why there were more subjects available for the study on violent criminal behavior (Megargee & Carbonell, 1993, 1994).

4. Aside from O – H, none of the special scales discussed in this section was marked for preservation in MMPI-2. Readers interested in scoring them can look up the item composition in the original article or in Appendix I of Dahlstrom et al.'s (1975) *MMPI Handbook.* By

consulting Pope, Butcher, and Seelen's (1993) Appendix F, they can determine which items from the original scale remain on MMPI-2. Our analyses indicate that both Panton's (1958) Ap,r and Wattron's (1963) PMS are still scoreable, Ap,r having lost three of its 36 items and PMS two of its 72 items.

5. For a recent review of approximately 100 published studies on overcontrolled hostility and the O – H scale see White (1987).

6. A September 1983 editorial in *Criminal Justice and Behavior,* noting that two thirds of the articles in that issue dealt with our system, advised authors that further articles on the subject would be "substantially delayed in publication unless they are of notably unusual importance" (p. 251).

References

Adams, T. C. (1976). Some MMPI differences between first and multiple admissions within a state prison population. *Journal of Clinical Psychology, 32,* 555-558.

American Correctional Association. (1987). *American Correctional Association 1987 directory.* Laurel, MD: Author.

American Correctional Association. (1994). *American Correctional Association 1994 directory.* Laurel, MD: Author.

Archer, R. P. (1992). *MMPI-A: Assessing adolescent psychopathology.* Hillsdale, NJ: Lawrence Erlbaum.

Beall, H. S., & Panton, J. H. (1956). Use of the MMPI as an index to "escapism." *Journal of Clinical Psychology, 12,* 392-394.

Beall, H. S., & Panton, J. H. (1957). *Development of a Prison Adjustment Scale for the MMPI.* Raleigh, NC: Central State Prison.

Black, W. G. (1967). The description and prediction of recidivism and rehabilitation among youthful offenders by the use of the MMPI (Doctoral dissertation, University of Oklahoma, 1967). *Dissertation Abstracts, 28,* 1691B.

Block, J. (1955). *The development of an MMPI based scale to measure ego control.* Unpublished manuscript, Psychology Department, University of California, Berkeley.

Bohn, M. J., Jr. (1978, July). *Classification of offenders in an institution for young adults.* Paper presented at the 19th International Congress of Applied Psychology, Munich, Germany.

Bohn, M. J., Jr. (1979). Inmate classification and the reduction of violence. In *Proceedings of the 109th Annual Congress of Correction* (pp. 63-69). College Park, MD: American Correctional Association.

Butcher, J. N., Dahlstrom, W. G., J. R., Tellegen, A., & Kaemmer, B. (1989). *Minnesota Multiphasic Personality Inventory-2 (MMPI-2): Manual for administration and scoring.* Minneapolis, MN: University of Minnesota Press.

Butcher, J. N., & Sloore, H. (1993, March). *Application of the MMPI-2 with diverse cultural and ethnic groups.* Symposium presented at the 28th annual symposium on recent developments in the use of the MMPI (MMPI-2 and MMPI-A). St. Petersburg, FL.

Butcher, J. N., Williams, C. L., Graham, J. R., Archer, R., Tellegen, A., Ben-Porath, Y. S., & Kaemmer, B. (1992). *Minnesota Multiphasic Personality Inventory-Adolescent (MMPI-A): Manual for administration, scoring and interpretation.* Minneapolis: University of Minnesota Press.

Caditz, S. (1959). Effect of a training school experience on the personality of delinquent boys. *Journal of Consulting Psychology, 23,* 501-509.

Capwell, D. F. (1945). Personality patterns of adolescent girls: II. Delinquents and nondelinquents. *Journal of Applied Psychology, 29,* 289-297.

Carbonell, J. L., & Megargee, E. I. (1984). *The early prediction of future career criminals* (Final report, N.I.J. Grant No. 83-IJ-CX-0001). Tallahassee: Florida State University, Department of Psychology.

Carbonell, J. L., Megargee, E. I., & Moorhead, K. M. (l984). Predicting prison adjustment with structured personality inventories. *Journal of Consulting and Clinical Psychology, 52,* 280-294.

Clark, J. H. (1948). Application of the MMPI in differentiating AWOL recidivists from non-recidivists. *Journal of Psychology, 26,* 229-234.

Clark, J. H. (1953). Additional applications of the AWOL recidivist scale. *Journal of Clinical Psychology, 9,* 62-64.

Clements, C. B. (1982). Psychological roles and issues in recent prison litigation. In J. Gunn & D. P. Farrington (Eds.), *Abnormal offenders, delinquency and the criminal justice system* (pp. 37-59). London: John Wiley.

Clements, C. B. (1985). Prison resource management: Working smarter, not harder. *Annals of the American Academy of Political and Social Science, 478*(March), 173-182.

Clements, C. B., (1987). Psychologists in adult correctional institutions: Getting off the treadmill. In E. K. Morris & C. J. Brankmann (Eds.), *Behavioral approaches to crime and delinquency* (pp. 521-541). New York: Plenum.

Cook, W. W., & Medley, D. M. (1954). Proposed hostility and pharisaic virtue scales for the MMPI. *Journal of Applied Psychology, 38,* 411-418.

Dahlstrom, W. G., & Welsh, G. S. (1960). *An MMPI handbook: A guide to use in clinical practice and research.* Minneapolis: University of Minnesota Press.

Dahlstrom, W. G., Welsh, G. S., & Dahlstrom, L. E. (1975). *An MMPI handbook, Volume 2: Research applications* (Rev. ed.). Minneapolis: University of Minnesota Press.

Davis, K. R. (1971). The actuarial development of a female 4'3 MMPI profile (Doctoral dissertation, St. Louis University, 1971). *Dissertation Abstracts International, 32,* 1207B. (Cited by Gearing, 1979, p. 943).

Davis, K. R., & Sines, J. (1971). An antisocial behavior pattern associated with a specific MMPI profile. *Journal of Consulting and Clinical Psychology, 36,* 229-234.

Frank, C. H. (1971). The prediction of recidivism among young adult offenders by the recidivism-rehabilitation scale and index (Doctoral dissertation, University of Oklahoma, 1970). *Dissertation Abstracts International, 32,* 557B.

Freeman, R. A., & Mason, H. M. (1952). Construction of a key to determine recidivists from non-recidivists using the MMPI. *Journal of Clinical Psychology, 9,* 207-208.

Gearing, M. L., II. (1979). The MMPI as a primary differentiator and predictor of behavior in prison: A methodological critique and review of the literature. *Psychological Bulletin, 86,* 929-963.

Gearing, M. L., II. (l981). The new MMPI typology for prisoners: The beginning of a new era in correctional research and (hopefully) practice. *Journal of Personality Assessment, 45,* 102-107.

Gough, H. G. (1960). *California Psychological Inventory manual.* Palo Alto, CA: Consulting Psychologists Press.

Gough, H. G., & Heilbrun, A. B. (1965). *Manual for the Adjective Checklist.* Palo Alto, CA: Consulting Psychologists Press.

Gough, H. G., Wenk, E. A., & Rozynko, V. V. (1965). Parole outcome as predicted from the CPI, the MMPI, and a base expectancy table. *Journal of Abnormal Psychology, 70,* 432-441.

Gynther, M. D. (1972). White norms and black MMPIs: A prescription for discrimination? *Psychological Bulletin, 78,* 386-402.

Gynther, M. D., Fowler, R. D., & Erdberg, P. (1971). False positives galore: The application of standard MMPI criteria to a rural, isolated, Negro sample. *Journal of Clinical Psychology, 27,* 234-237.

Harris, R. H., & Lingoes, J. C. (1968). *Subscales for the MMPI: An aid to profile interpretation* [Mimeographed materials]. San Francisco: Langley Porter Clinic, University of California Medical School.

Hathaway, S. R., & Monachesi, E. D. (1953). *Analyzing and predicting juvenile delinquency with the MMPI.* Minneapolis: University of Minnesota Press.

Hathaway, S. R., & Monachesi, E. D. (1957). The personalities of pre-delinquent boys. *Journal of Criminal Law, Criminology, and Police Science, 48,* 149-163.

Haven, H. J. (1970). The MMPI with incarcerated adult and delinquent offenders. *Federal Correctional Institution Technical and Treatment Notes, 1*(1), 1-46. Federal Correctional Institution, Tallahassee, FL.

Holt, R. R. (1958). Clinical and statistical prediction: A reformulation and some new data. *Journal of Abnormal and Social Psychology, 56,* 1-12.

Jones, T., Beidleman, W. R., & Fowler, R. D. (1981). Differentiating violent and nonviolent prison inmates by use of selected MMPI scales. *Journal of Clinical Psychology, 37,* 673-678.

Jurjevich, R. M. (1963). Normative data for the clinical and additional scales for a population of delinquent girls. *Journal of General Psychology, 69,* 143-146.

Levine, R. V. (1969). The MMPI and Revised Beta as predictors of academic and vocational success in a correctional institution. *FCI Research Reports, 1*(3), 1-52. Federal Correctional Institution, Tallahassee, FL.

Levy, S., Southcombe, R. H., Cranor, J. R., & Freeman, R. A. (1952). The outstanding personality factors among the population of a state penitentiary: A preliminary report. *Journal of Clinical and Experimental Psychopathology, 13,* 832-839.

Mack, J. L. (1969). The MMPI and recidivism. *Journal of Abnormal Psychology, 74,* 612-614.

McKegney, P. F. (1965). An item analysis of the MMPI F scale in juvenile delinquents. *Journal of Clinical Psychology, 21,* 201-205.

McQuary, J. P., & Truax, W. E. (1955), An underachievement scale. *Journal of Educational Research, 48,* 393-399.Meehl, P. E., & Rosen, A. (1955). Antecedent probability and the efficiency of psychometric signs, patterns or cutting scores. *Psychological Bulletin, 52,* 194-216.

Megargee, E. I. (1966). Undercontrolled and overcontrolled personality types in extreme antisocial aggression. *Psychological Monographs, 80,*(3, Whole No. 611).

Megargee, E. I. (1976a). *A comprehensive investigation of recidivism.* Report submitted to the Bureau of Criminal Justice Planning and Assistance. Tallahassee: Florida State University, Department of Psychology.

Megargee, E. I. (1976b). The prediction of dangerous behavior. *Criminal Justice and Behavior, 3,* 3-21.

Megargee, E. I. (Ed.). (1977). A new classification system for criminal offenders [Special issue]. *Criminal Justice and Behavior, 4,* 107-216.

Megargee, E. I. (1982). Psychological correlates and determinants of criminal violence. In M. Wolfgang & N. Wiener (Eds.), *Criminal violence* (pp. 81-170). Beverley Hills, CA: Sage.

Megargee, E. I. (1984a). A new classification system for criminal offenders, VI: Differences among the types on the Adjective Checklist. *Criminal Justice and Behavior, 11,* 348-376.

Megargee, E. I. (1984b). Derivation, validation and application of an MMPI-based system for classifying criminal offenders. *International Journal of Medicine and Law, 3,* 109-118.

Megargee, E. I. (1992). *Impact of the revised MMPI ("MMPI-2") on the Megargee MMPI-based offender classification system* (Final report, N.I.J. Grant No. 89-IJ-CX-0028). Tallahassee: Florida State University, Department of Psychology.

Megargee, E. I. (1993). Aggression and violence. In H. E. Adams & P. B. Sutker (Eds.), *Comprehensive handbook of psychopathology*, (2nd. ed., pp. 617-644). New York: Plenum.

Megargee, E. I. (in press). Using the Megargee MMPI-based classification system with the MMPI-2s of male prison inmates. *Psychological Assessment.*

Megargee, E. I., & Bohn, M. J., Jr. (with Meyer, J., Jr., & Sink, F.). (1979). *Classifying criminal offenders: A new system based on the MMPI.* Beverly Hills, CA: Sage.

Megargee, E. I., & Carbonell, J. L. (1985). Predicting prison adjustment with MMPI correctional scales. *Journal of Consulting and Clinical Psychology, 53*, 874-883.

Megargee, E. I., & Carbonell, J. L. (1993). *A longitudinal study of violent criminal behavior* (Final report, N.I.J. Grant No. 88-IJ-CX-0006). Tallahassee: Florida State University, Department of Psychology.

Megargee, E. I., & Carbonell, J. L. (1994, July). A longitudinal study of violent criminal behavior. Poster session presented at the Biennial World Meeting of the International Society for Research on Aggression, Delray Beach, FL.

Megargee, E. I., Cook, P. E., & Mendelsohn, G. A. (1967). Development and validation of an MMPI scale of assaultiveness in overcontrolled individuals. *Journal of Abnormal Psychology, 72*, 519-528.

Megargee, E. I., & Dorhout, B. (1976). Revision and refinement of an MMPI-based typology of youthful offenders. *FCI Research Reports, 6*(1), 1-21.

Megargee, E. I., & Dorhout, B. (1977). A new classification system for criminal offenders, III: Revision and refinement of the classificatory rules. *Criminal Justice and Behavior, 4*, 125-148.

Megargee, E. I., & Hokanson, J. E. (1975). *A program of research on antisocial behavior and violence, Phase I. Final Report. Part One. Overview of the project: Goals, procedures and results* (Final report of USPHS Grant No. 18468, [NIMH]: Center for Studies of Crime and Delinquency). Tallahassee: Florida State University, Department of Psychology.

Megargee, E. I., Hokanson, J. E., & Spielberger, C. D. (1971). The behavior research program at the Federal Correctional Institution, Tallahassee. I: Goals and initial data collection procedures. *FCI Research Reports, 3*(4), 1-48.

Megargee, E. I., & Mendelsohn, G. A. (1962). A cross-validation of 12 MMPI indices of hostility and control. *Journal of Abnormal and Social Psychology, 65*, 431-438.

Megargee, E. I., & Spielberger, C. D. (1992). Reflections on fifty years of personality assessment and future directions for the field. In E. I. Megargee & C. D. Spielberger (Eds.), *Personality assessment in America: A retrospective on the occasion of the fiftieth anniversary of the Society for Personality Assessment* (pp. 170-190). Hillsdale, NJ: Lawrence Erlbaum.

Meyer, J., Jr., & Megargee, E. I. (1972). Development of an MMPI-based typology of youthful offenders. *FCI Research Reports, 2*(4), 1-24.

Meyer, J., Jr., & Megargee, E. I. (1977). A new classification system for criminal offenders, II: Initial development of the system. *Criminal Justice and Behavior, 4*, 155-124.

Monachesi, E. D. (1948). Some personality characteristics of delinquents and non-delinquents. *Journal of Criminal Law, Criminology, and Police Science, 38*, 487-500.

Monachesi, E. D. (1950). Personality characteristics and socioeconomic status of delinquents and non-delinquents. *Journal of Criminal Law and Criminology, 40*, 570-583.

Monachesi, E. D., & Hathaway, S. R. (1969). The personality of delinquents. In J. N. Butcher (Ed.), *MMPI: Research developments and clinical applications* (pp. 207-219). New York: McGraw-Hill.

Mrad, D. F., Kabacoff, R. A., & Duckro, P. (1983). Validation of the Megargee typology in a halfway house setting. *Criminal Justice and Behavior, 10*, 252-262.

National Advisory Commission on Criminal Justice Standards and Goals. (1973). *Report on corrections.* Washington, DC: Author. Nichols, W. (1980). *The classification of law offenders with the MMPI: A methodological study* (Doctoral dissertation, University of Alabama, 1979). *Dissertation Abstracts International, 41*(1), 333B.

Panton, J. H. (1958). Predicting prison adjustment with the Minnesota Multiphasic Personality Inventory. *Journal of Clinical Psychology, 14,* 308-312.

Panton, J. H. (1959). Inmate personality differences related to recidivism, age and race as measured by the MMPI. *Journal of Correctional Psychology, 4,* 28-35.

Panton, J. H. (1960). A new MMPI scale for the identification of homosexuality. *Journal of Clinical Psychology, 16,* 17-21.

Panton, J. H. (1962a). The identification of habitual criminalism with the MMPI. *Journal of Clinical Psychology, 18,* 133-136.

Panton, J. H. (1962b). Use of the MMPI as an index to successful parole. *Journal of Criminal Law, Criminology, and Police Science, 53,* 484-488.

Panton, J. H. (1970). *Manual for a Prison Classification Inventory (PCI) for the MMPI.* Raleigh, NC: Department of Social Rehabilitation and Control.

Panton, J. H. (1979). An MMPI item content scale to measure religious identification within a state prison population. *Journal of Clinical Psychology, 35,* 588-591.

Peña, L., & Megargee, E. I. (1994, May). MMPI-A patterns among juvenile delinquents. Paper presesented at the 29th MMPI Symposium, Psychology Department, University of Minnesota, Minneapolis, MN.

Persons, R. W., & Marks, P. A. (1971). The violent 4-3 MMPI personality type. *Journal of Consulting and Clinical Psychology, 36,* 189-196.

Pope, K. S., Butcher, J. N., & Seelen, J. (1993). *The MMPI, MMPI-2, & MMPI-A in court.* Washington, DC: American Psychological Association.

Reisman, J. M. (1966). *The development of clinical psychology.* New York: Appleton-Century-Crofts.

Richardson, H., & Roebuck, J. (1965). MMPI and CPI differences between delinquents and their nondelinquent siblings. *Proceedings of the 73rd Annual Convention of the American Psychological Association* (pp. 255-256). Washington, DC: American Psychological Association.

Ross, L. (1977). The intuitive psychologist and his shortcomings: Distortions in the attribution process. In L. Berkowitz (Ed.), *Advances in experimental social psychology* (Vol. 10). New York: Academic Press.

Schultz, S. D. (1954). A differentiation of several forms of hostility by scales empirically constructed from significant items on the MMPI. *Pennsylvania State University Abstracts of Doctoral Dissertations, 17,* 717-720.

Scott, N. A., Mount, M. K., & Duffy, P. S. (1977). MMPI and demographic correlates and predictions of female prison escape. *Criminal Justice and Behavior, 4,* 285-300.

Siegel, S. M. (1956). The relationship of hostility to authoritarianism. *Journal of Abnormal and Social Psychology, 52,* 368-372.

Sines, L. R., & Silver, R. J. (1963). An index of psychopathology (Ip) derived from clinician's judgments of MMPI profiles. *Journal of Clinical Psychology, 19,* 324-326.

Sliger, G. L. (1992). *The MMPI-based classification system for adult criminal offenders: A critical review.* Unpublished manuscript, Florida State University, Department of Psychology, Tallahassee.

Smith, J., & Lanyon, R. I. (1968). Prediction of juvenile probation violators. *Journal of Consulting and Clinical Psychology, 32,* 54-58.

Steuber, H. (1975). Prediction of academic achievement with the Minnesota Multiphasic Personality Inventory (MMPI) and California Psychological Inventory (CPI) in a correctional institution. *FCI Research Reports, 5*(4), 1-32. Tallahassee, FL: Federal Correctional Institution.

Stone, F. B., & Rowley, V. N. (1963). MMPI differences between emotionally disturbed and delinquent adolescent girls. *Journal of Clinical Psychology, 19,* 227-230.

Sutker, P. B., & Moan, C. E. (1973). Prediction of socially maladaptive behavior within a state prison system. *Journal of Community Psychology, 1,* 74-78.

Timbrook, R. E., & Graham, J. R. (1994). Ethnic differences on the MMPI-2 *Psychological Assessment, 6,* 212-217.

Truxal, J. R., & Sabatino, D. A. (1972). A comparison of good and poorly adjusted institutional offenders. *Correctional Psychologist, 5,* 178-187.

Tydlaska, M., & Mengel, R. (1953). A scale for measuring work attitude for the MMPI. *Journal of Applied Psychology, 37,* 474-477.

Wattron, J. B. (1963). A prison maladjustment scale for the MMPI. *Journal of Clinical Psychology, 19,* 109-110.

Wheeler, C. A., & Megargee, E. I. (1970). Normative data for 678 federal youthful offenders on 78 MMPI scales. *FCI Research Reports, 2*(4), 1-22. Federal Correctional Institution, Tallahassee, Fl.

White, A., (1987). *The overcontrolled-undercontrolled typology and the overcontrolled-hostility scale of the MMPI: A review of the literature.* Unpublished paper, Florida State University.

Wiggins, J. (1966). Substantive dimensions of self-report in the MMPI item pool. *Psychological Monographs, 80*(22, Whole No. 630).

Wirt, R. D., & Briggs, P. F. (1959). Personality and environmental factors in the development of delinquency. *Psychological Monographs, 73*(Whole No. 485).

Zager, L. D. (1983). Response to Simmons and associates: Conclusions about the MMPI-based classification system's stability are premature. *Criminal Justice and Behavior, 10,* 310-315.

Zager, L. D. (1988). The MMPI-based criminal classification system: A review, current status, and future directions. *Criminal Justice and Behavior, 15,* 39-57.

Risk Assessment With the
MMPI-2 in Forensic Evaluations

KIRK HEILBRUN

ALFRED B. HEILBRUN, JR.

Introduction

The demand that mental health professionals assess the risk of future violent behavior is embedded in a variety of clinical-legal issues. Under various guises, it appears in legal standards governing civil commitment, bail determination, sentencing (for both adults and juveniles), hospital commitment as either incompetent to stand trial or not guilty by reason of insanity, transfers from correctional facilities to secure hospitals, release decisions from hospitals and prisons, treatment planning for high-risk populations such as spouse abusers, sexual offenders, insanity acquittees, and criminal offenders on parole or probation. Finally, as a result of *Tarasoff v. Regents of the University of California* (1976) and its progeny, the demand for prediction of future violent behavior is now embedded in legal standards governing psychotherapy in certain states.

Despite the reality that such opinions are frequently requested, the prediction of violent behavior by mental health professionals has drawn sharp criticism from a variety of quarters during the past 25 years. Concerns about inaccuracy, the failure to incorporate base rate information, the impoverished range of predictors, the insensitivity of outcome measures, and the failure to incorporate situational factors have all been cited (Cocozza & Steadman, 1976; Monahan, 1981; Monahan & Steadman, 1994).

However, such criticisms did not result in the abandonment by researchers of their attention to violent behavior and its prediction. Following Monahan's (1981) discussion of the practice of violence prediction and suggestions for its improvement, there have been two major "waves" of research. The first, called the "second generation" of violence prediction research, involved a greater focus on shorter term predictions, situational variables, and specified populations (e.g., Felson & Steadman, 1983; Hare & McPherson, 1984; Karson & Bigelow, 1987; Klassen & O'Connor, 1988a, 1988b, 1988c, 1990; Lowenstein, Binder, & McNiel, 1990; McNiel & Binder, 1986, 1989; Tardiff & Koenigsberg, 1985; see Otto, 1992, for a review).

The "third generation" of violence prediction research has been shaped by the establishment of the MacArthur Research Network on Mental Health and the Law, and its initiatives into risk assessment. Although completed empirical evidence will not be available until the completion of a 5-year outcome study, the MacArthur Network has already provided several major conceptual advances, one of which is the condensation of the various descriptions ("dangerousness assessment," "dangerousness prediction," "violence prediction") into the single phrase "risk assessment." This allowed "dangerousness" to be divided into the following component parts: (a) risk factors—the variables used to predict aggression, (b) harm—the amount and type of aggression being predicted, and (c) risk level—the probability that harm will occur (National Research Council, 1989).

Several other conceptual advances can also be attributed to the MacArthur Research Network. Aggression has been discussed as a public health issue as well as a combination of narrower personal and situational characteristics, with an analogy drawn to other kinds of health problems (e.g., cancer, heart disease) rather than exclusively to crime, with the goal of primary prevention rather than treatment or management. A more explicit use of decision theory has been advocated, expanding the classic "clinical versus statistical" debate (Meehl, 1954; Meehl & Rosen, 1955) by using not only true and false positives and negatives, but also by incorporating sensitivity (the number of true

positives divided by the sum of true positives and false negatives) and specificity (the number of true negatives divided by the sum of true negatives and
false positives) into overall considerations of accuracy. Finally, an expanded
range of predictor variables has been developed. These predictors include
psychopathy, anger, impulsiveness, delusions, hallucinations, "threat/control
override" symptoms, social support, and demographic factors (Monahan &
Steadman, 1994).

The MacArthur Network's focus has been on aggression committed by the
mentally ill. One recent study (Swanson, Holzer, Ganju, & Jono, 1990) has
indicated that categories of mental disorder including schizophrenia, mania
or bipolar disorder, major depression, substance abuse or dependence, obsessive-compulsive disorder, panic disorder, and phobia do appear to function
as risk factors for aggressive behavior. Approximately 12% of subjects diagnosed as having any of these disorders, as contrasted with the 2% of individuals without such mental disorder, responded affirmatively to at least one of
the following questions to describe behavior in the previous year:

- Did you ever hit or throw things at your wife/husband/partner?
- Have you ever spanked or hit a child (yours or anyone else's) hard enough so that
  he or she had bruises or had to stay in bed or see a doctor?
- Since age 18, have you been in more than one fight that came to swapping blows,
  other than fights with your husband/wife/partner?
- Have you ever used a weapon like a stick, knife, or gun in a fight since you were
  18?
- Have you ever gotten into physical fights while drinking? (Swanson et al., 1990).

Drug abuse raises this self-reported rate further to 19% (cannabis), 25%
(alcohol), and 35% (other drug) (Swanson et al., 1990). The presence of two
or more diagnoses approximately doubled the reported rate of aggression; the
highest reported rate was observed for substance abuse plus schizophrenia or
affective disorder.

However, to promote significant advances in knowledge about risk, programmatic research should appropriately provide information about four
classes of variable: (a) individual (demographic, personality, and neurological
characteristics), (b) historical (family, work, psychiatric, criminal, and aggression), (c) contextual (social support, physical aspects of the environment),
and (d) clinical (mental disorder, substance abuse, and global level of functioning) (Monahan & Steadman, 1994). It is useful to summarize briefly what

is presently known about these influences in the context of aggression committed by the mentally ill; more extensive reviews are available elsewhere (Krakowski, Volavka, & Brizer, 1986; Monahan, 1992; Otto, 1992; Wesseley & Taylor, 1991).

In an unselected sample comparing mentally ill subjects to those without mental illness, Link, Andrews, and Cullen (1992) compared mental patients and never-treated community residents of the Washington Heights section of New York City (total $N = 521$) on several official and self-reported measures of violent/illegal conduct (self-reported arrests, official arrests, hitting others, fighting, weapons use in fight, and ever hurting someone badly). Data were collected using the Psychiatric Epidemiology Research Interview (PERI). Mental patients demonstrated higher rates on all measures of violent/illegal behavior; these differences could not be attributed to sociodemographic and community context variables. A scale of psychotic symptoms (the false-beliefs-and-perceptions scale from the PERI, composed of 13 items such as feeling possessed by a spirit, feeling one's thoughts were not one's own, and feeling one's mind was dominated by forces beyond one's control) was the only variable that accounted for differences in levels of violent/illegal behavior between patients and never-treated community residents. Although mental patients had elevated rates of violent/illegal behavior compared to nonpatients, the differences were modest and confined to those experiencing psychotic symptoms. Overall rates of aggression were quite similar to those found by Swanson et al. (1990). Link and colleagues concluded that a history of treatment for mental disorder increased the prevalence of aggression 1.5 to 4 times over that of never-treated community residents (Link et al., 1992).

In samples that are selected prior to treatment (including civil commitment) and following discharge from hospitalization, the rates of aggression vary according to how broadly aggression is defined. When aggression is defined narrowly to include only physical acts, but not threats, the rates of aggression are lower. In one study, 3% of 2,916 individuals evaluated for treatment at a university-based psychiatric service had been physically assaultive a few days prior to evaluation (Tardiff & Koenigsberg, 1985). In two other studies, the rates of preadmission violence toward others ranged from 10% to 12% (Craig, 1982; Tardiff, 1984). These rates are consistent with findings from other studies on violence performed in the 1970s (see Otto, 1992, for a summary).

When the definition of aggression is broadened to include physical acts plus threats, the observed rates of pretreatment aggression increase. In one study,

15% of 416 persons presenting for mental health treatment in an urban psychiatric emergency room had violent ideation or violent acts in their clinical presentation (Skodol & Karasu, 1980). Other studies using this broader definition have noted somewhat higher rates of aggression, with between 20% and 36% of mentally ill individuals displaying some kind of threat or physical aggression prior to hospitalization (McNiel & Binder, 1986, 1989; Rossi et al., 1985; Tardiff & Sweillam, 1980).

Following discharge from hospitalization, between 25% and 30% of the individuals considered "potentially violent" prior to hospitalization were rearrested for violent crime or rehospitalized for a violent act during a 1-year follow-up period (Klassen & O'Connor, 1988a, 1988b, 1990). When the outcome measure is broadened to include threats (with a weapon) as well as acts, the rate is somewhat higher. Lidz, Mulvey, and Gardner (1993) conducted a study employing a 6-month follow-up period and using self report and collateral report on 357 patients (assessed by clinicians to be more likely to be violent) and matched controls (judged by clinicians to present a lower risk for violence). All patients were treated in a psychiatric emergency room in an urban setting. Some 36% of control subjects and 53% of "violence-concern" subjects were found to have committed at least one violent act during the follow-up period. The investigators found clinical judgment to contribute modestly to the accuracy of risk assessment (even controlling for demographic variables and history) for male patients, but not for female patients, due to clinicians' underestimate of the violence potential of women. The overall percentage of female subjects engaging in at least one violent act during follow-up (49%) was higher than it was for male subjects (42%) in this study.

The Nature of Risk Assessment

The empirical evidence and conceptual advances to date would suggest four major defining characteristics of risk assessment. First, it is important to specify the outcome. What is it that is being predicted? Are threats as well as physical acts of aggression included? Familiarity with the applicable legal standard and relevant case law in the specific jurisdiction are important— both may contribute to this decision.

Second, what are the base rates and risk factors for the behavior being predicted? To some extent this follows from the first step; a broader definition of aggression, including threats, yields a higher base rate.

Third, risk level is described in continuous probability rather than dichotomous terms. An individual being assessed is not considered "dangerous" or "not dangerous"; rather, the conclusion is that there is X probability that Y behaviors will occur within Z period of time.

Finally, there is a divorce from value judgments. By specifying what is being predicted, by what factors, and at what risk level, the clinician may disentangle these issues sufficiently so that there is no need to address nonscientific, value-laden questions such as "How much risk is enough?" or "What kind of harm is sufficient?"

This may present a different conceptual framework for mental health professionals accustomed to assessing "dangerousness" in the context of civil commitment. To perform risk assessment as we have described, it is necessary to incorporate existing empirical evidence on aggression of mentally ill individuals. This in turn allows the identification of base rates, and the translation of specified population characteristics into risk factors. Such risk factors may be characterized as static (unchangeable through any form of intervention) or dynamic (potentially changeable through intervention). A preliminary determination of risk level may be made by assessing whether static risk factors (e.g., age, gender, aggression history) would indicate that the individual should be considered as a lower or higher risk than the population base rate would suggest. Finally, however, each case must be individualized. What are the personal or situational characteristics that might aggravate or mitigate the risk of aggression in the immediate case? How are dynamic risk factors (e.g., substance abuse, threat/control override symptoms, anger, impulsivity, weapon access, employment, social support) being managed or treated? Answers to such questions form the substance of risk assessment for aggression. How might the MMPI-2 be used in such risk assessment?

MMPI/MMPI-2 and Aggression Risk

In this section, we will provide a brief review of risk-relevant research that has been done using the MMPI/MMPI-2. In addition, we will describe two distinct, promising research approaches that have been developed to enhance the usefulness of the MMPI in a way that would be consistent with aggression risk assessment as it has been described in this chapter. Both are approaches that could be readily adapted to MMPI-2 risk research. The first has involved the identification of an individual construct measured by the MMPI and the incorporation of it into a theory of criminal aggression. The second has involved the use of hierarchical profile interpretation, and the measurement of aggression rates for different profiles.

RELEVANT RESEARCH

Much of the research involving the MMPI and aggression has been done using a single scale, O – H, or a combination of scales, such as 4 – 3 or 4 – 9. Such research will be reviewed briefly. It should be noted, however, that these studies are typically of limited value in the applicability of their results to risk assessment, because of the methodological limitations described elsewhere in this chapter.

It was Megargee (1966) who first asserted that aggressive behavior demonstrated by overcontrolled hostile individuals was likely to be extreme. Although the O – H construct has been investigated largely with correctional populations (e.g., Blackburn, 1971, 1972; Frederiksen, 1975; Haven, 1972; Henderson, 1982, 1983; McGurk, 1978), it has also been applied to mentally disordered offenders. Blackburn (1975) cluster analyzed the results of male mentally disordered offenders ($N = 79$) and obtained four clusters that were "virtually identical" to those obtained with unselected correctional subjects. However, there was no rating of aggression obtained beyond the scales used in the cluster analysis. Lane and Spruill (1980), classifying mentally disordered offenders ($N = 110$) as overcontrolled or undercontrolled, found that more overcontrolled subjects fell into the "extremely assaultive" group, with instant offenses of murder, manslaughter, or assault with a deadly weapon. By contrast, more undercontrolled subjects fell into the "moderately assaultive" group (simple assault, battery). Thus, the O – H construct has been associated with severe but infrequent aggression, limiting its applicability to the predictive task.

The 4 – 3 code type has been described as an indicator of chronic, intense anger that is more likely to be expressed directly than is the anger that is characterized by the 3 – 4 code type (Graham, 1993). Elevated rates of aggression by individuals with 4 – 3 code types have been described by several investigators (Davis & Sines, 1971; Persons & Marks, 1971; but cf. Buck & Graham, 1978).

The 4 – 9 code type has been associated with a variety of antisocial behaviors, including aggression (Graham, 1993; Greene, 1991). A typical research paradigm has involved comparing the profiles of a "violent" group, as reflected by their legal status, with those of a control group. For example, Huesmann, Lefkowitz, and Eron (1978) reported that the sum of T scores on Scales F, 4, and 9 was significantly higher in aggressive older adolescents (juvenile delinquents) than in control (nondelinquent) subjects. Research of this kind may be useful in identifying aggression-relevant factors needing further study. However, because of the considerable overlap between groups, such findings do not translate directly into implications for prediction.

PROMISING RESEARCH APPROACHES

A theory-based, personal construct approach. The development of a theoretical model for explaining violent criminal behavior initially grew out of the dissatisfactions expressed in the 1970s with the applicability of personality measures to violence prediction. A more balanced consideration of personality attributes and situational context was encouraged by forensic scholars (e.g., Monahan, 1975; Shah, 1978) and personality generalists (e.g., Mischel, 1973; Moos, 1973) alike. From a slightly different perspective, however, Heilbrun (1979) argued that the selection of a more promising set of personality variables might improve violence prediction without introducing the uncertainties of anticipating future situations.

It was initially demonstrated that antisociality, as measured by the MMPI Scale 4, was more strongly associated with violent criminal behavior when combined with another measure—intellectual functioning (Heilbrun, 1979). It was reasoned that one source of violence resulted from the combination of a failure to inhibit criminal behavior, explicit in high Pd and antisociality, by a person showing cognitive deficits in planning, judgment, self-control, empathy, and other critical functions related to lower IQ.

Because the primary purpose of the ensuing research program was theoretical rather than applied—the goal was to generate a theory of violent criminal conduct, rather than enhance predictive accuracy—only variables retaining a conceptual relationship to the theoretical model were included. Despite this explicitly theoretical focus, however, A. B. Heilbrun demonstrated that the combination of antisociality and IQ appeared to have considerable power in explaining certain kinds of criminal violence.

The development of a "dangerousness index," with the combination of high antisociality and low IQ marking the group at highest risk, has been supported through a series of studies. Those higher on this index were more likely to have been convicted of violent (i.e., crimes against persons) than nonviolent (property) offenses (Heilbrun, 1979). Men committing more severe forms of criminal violence were higher on this index than those committing less serious violence (Heilbrun, 1990a). Individuals sentenced to death were higher than those receiving life sentences (Heilbrun, 1990b), and those displaying greater brutality in the commission of sexual offenses were higher than those showing less brutality (Heilbrun, 1994).

Although the focus of this research was primarily theoretical, this model and the studies supporting it have distinct implications for risk assessment in the context of forensic evaluations. It may be that antisociality and IQ could be treated as a single risk factor which, when arrayed in a certain combination, could be more powerful than either construct considered separately. The applicability of this model to other populations, particularly the noncriminal mentally ill, has yet to be tested—clearly, however, it should be.

An actuarial, hierarchical profile analysis approach. The second research approach using the MMPI that is particularly applicable to risk assessment is that described by Megargee and his colleagues (Megargee & Bohn, 1979). In a program of research conducted from 1970 through 1979, they administered the MMPI to 1,345 federal inmates who entered the Federal Correctional Institution in Tallahassee, Florida between 1970 and 1972. Using a hierarchical profile analysis approach (Veldman, 1967), they classified MMPI profiles into 10 distinct groups. This classification was reliable, operationally defined sufficiently well to permit computerized categorization, and was capable of distinguishing groups that differed significantly on non-MMPI variables such as lifestyles, social history, and behavior. Two types of risk-relevant outcome measures were obtained: (a) aggression while in prison, resulting in disciplinary infractions, and (b) rearrest following release. The percentages of individuals involved in violent disciplinary infractions ranged from a mean of 7.0 (Group Easy) to a mean of 18.9 (Group Jupiter), with the overall difference between groups significant ($\chi^2 = 37.3$, $df = 19$, $p < .005$). Rearrest data were cited, although unfortunately (for the purposes of this chapter) not broken down into violent and nonviolent offenses. The percentages of individuals in each group rearrested after at least 18 months in the community ranged from a mean of 37.8 (Group Easy) to a high of 64.0 (Group Foxtrot), with the overall difference between groups not statistically significant on this variable ($\chi^2 = 16.7$, $df = 19$, $p = .054$).

Research such as this can make three important contributions to risk assessment. First, the authors identify base rates of aggressive behavior in a large number of subjects. Second, the classification of individuals on one variable (MMPI profile type) can facilitate the determination of whether a given person presents a risk of aggression that is different from the overall base rate for the particular population. Third, although profile type itself does not provide the basis for individualizing risk assessment, some of the correlates of each profile may offer hypotheses about potential risk factors for aggression.

MMPI-2 Use in Risk Assessment: Implications for Practice

Psychological testing, it has been argued, may have a limited role to play in much of forensic assessment. The value of a given test should be judged both by its accuracy and its relevance to mental health constructs that relate (albeit sometimes indirectly) to the functional behavior defined by the legal test (Heilbrun, 1992). In the case of risk assessment, the MMPI-2 might be useful in describing mental and emotional functioning, response style, and/or aggression risk.

ASSESSING THE THRESHOLD ISSUE

The structure of statutes and case law relevant to forensic assessment typically includes the demand for an evaluation of mental and emotional functioning (or "threshold issue"), assessment of the functional and behavioral demands specified by the legal criterion, and a determination of the causal connection between the two (Melton, Petrila, Poythress, & Slobogin, 1987; Morse, 1978). In civil commitment proceedings, the forensic evaluation begins with an assessment of the "threshold issue": Is there a mental or emotional disorder affecting the individual's risk to self or others and need for treatment?

This is one way in which the MMPI-2 can be used in a relatively straightforward fashion. Its administration will yield actuarial data on symptoms and behavior patterns, diagnostic categories, and treatment implications (Ben-Porath, Butcher, & Graham, 1991; Butcher, 1990; Greene, 1991; Pope, Butcher, & Seelen, 1993). In addition, it could provide evidence that an individual currently does not suffer from certain kinds of severe mental disorder, and that symptoms observed at an earlier time might thus be attributable to another cause (e.g., acute drug or alcohol intoxication).

ASSESSING RESPONSE STYLE

Because another chapter in this book is devoted to the use of the MMPI-2 in detecting malingering (Berry, Chapter 4), we will say little about this particular response style. However, malingering is only one of five response styles that may be observed in the process of a forensic evaluation. Four distinct response styles have been described by Rogers (1984, 1988):

1. Malingering—a conscious fabrication or gross exaggeration of physical symptoms, psychological symptoms, or both, distinguished from factitious disorder in that the motivation for malingering goes beyond the desire to assume the patient role and is understandable in light of the individual's circumstances.
2. Defensiveness—a conscious denial or gross minimization of physical symptoms, psychological symptoms, or both, distinguished from ego defenses, which involve intrapsychic processes that distort perception.
3. Irrelevance—when one does not become engaged in the evaluation process; responses are not necessarily relevant to question content and may be random.
4. Reliability/honesty—a sincere attempt is made to be accurate in responding, with factual inaccuracies attributable to poor understanding or misperception.

A fifth response style, uncooperativeness, is seen when the individual refuses to provide information necessary for the evaluation of mental state and of the criteria associated with the particular legal issue.

The MMPI has been used to assess such response styles in a variety of studies (e.g., see Audubon & Kirwin, 1982; Greene, 1988; Grow, McVaugh, & Eno, 1980; Heilbrun, Bennett, White, & Kelly, 1990; Lanyon & Lutz, 1984; Rogers, 1984, 1988; Rogers, Dolmetsch, & Cavanaugh, 1983; Wasyliw, Grossman, Haywood, & Cavanaugh, 1988). The MMPI-2 should be equally effective in assessing response style, and can be used with increasing confidence as relevant evidence accumulates (Buigas, Nicholson, & Bagby, 1994; Pope et al., 1993; see Berry, Chapter 4, for a current summary of MMPI-2 studies).

ASSESSING THE LEGAL ISSUE: AGGRESSION RISK

The risk assessment approach described in this chapter implies five distinct, additional steps beyond assessing the "threshold issue." These may be described as follows: (a) identifying the population to which the individual belongs, and the target behavior(s) for which risk is being assessed, (b) determining the base rate of this target behavior in this population, (c) identifying both static and dynamic risk factors, and ascertaining the status of each, (d) using these risk factors, estimating whether the risk of the target behavior is above, equal to, or below the base rate identified in (b), above, and (e) describing any relevant interventions that might reduce the risk of this target behavior's occurrence. Each of these will be discussed briefly. The MMPI-2 is of very limited use in these steps of the risk assessment process.

The identification of the population might be made in any number of ways, but it is most useful to specify group membership in a way that allows maximum linkage to relevant research. Research on aggression frequently employs legal status as an independent variable, so that populations emerge according to the nature and status of ongoing litigation. Groups such as Incompetent to Stand Trial, Not Guilty by Reason of Insanity, Mentally Disordered Sex Offenders, and Corrections to Hospital Transfers have been identified among mentally disordered offenders (Monahan & Steadman, 1983). Much of the research discussed in this chapter has described individuals at various stages of the civil commitment process, particularly precommitment and postdischarge, as well as individuals who have been convicted and sentenced, but not selected according to mental disorder. Additional populations might include outpatients without ongoing legal involvement (*Tarasoff* circumstances), those threatening celebrities or public figures (Fein, Vossekuil, & Robbins, 1994), and others for whom there is reason to study aggression risk.

Defining the target behavior is largely a question of whether threats as well as physical acts should be included. If so, how serious must a threat be? Must a weapon be involved in making the threat? The rates of aggression can vary considerably, according to the breadth of this definition.

Having identified the population and defined the target behavior in a way consistent with research definitions, the clinician can then review the empirical evidence on the base rate of this target behavior in this population. As should be clear from the review of violence research presented in this chapter and elsewhere, this is a difficult task. Base rates of aggressive behavior are best described as falling within a range rather than approximating a single figure. There remain the difficulties stemming from the relatively small number of studies, using differently defined outcomes, and over varying periods of time. For the clinician, integrating these into a coherent, accurate summary can be challenging indeed. A statement such as "five studies examining the occurrence of aggression in the community following discharge from psychiatric hospitalization found that at least one aggressive act, narrowly defined, was committed by 25% to 30% of patients within 1 year of discharge, and by 40% to 50% of patients within 6 months when more broadly defined" may be the best that can be done. For some populations, there may be no published empirical research on base rates of aggression. Nonetheless, this step is important. It provides a crucial empirical connection to published research or other outcome data; the failure to consider base rate information has been described as one of the most serious errors in a predictive task (Monahan, 1981). Finally, it can be very helpful for a decision maker to receive information about whether the base rate of a given behavior is, for example, 5% to 10%, 40% to 50%, or 85% to 95%.

After the estimated base rate is described as well as possible, the next step involves individualizing the assessment of risk. If an individual is a member of a population in which 40% to 50% of those belonging commit at least one aggressive act over a 6-month period, what determines whether that individual should be considered a lower, higher, or approximately equal risk to others in this group? By identifying both static and dynamic risk factors, and determining the applicability and status of each to this individual, the clinician can make this estimate in a reasonable fashion. For example, an individual with several static risk factors associated with increased aggression risk (e.g., a lengthy aggression history, youth, and psychopathy) combined with one or more dynamic risk factors (e.g., a conflictual home situation, substance abuse, and medication noncompliance) might reasonably be judged to be at higher risk for behaving aggressively than many in this population. Conversely, the absence of such static or dynamic risk factors might suggest that the risk of future aggression is lower than the population base rate would indicate. In the face of some risk factors but not others, the clinician might best conclude that no distinction from base rate risk can be made.

The clinician performing a risk assessment might face a risk management question. Are there available interventions short of hospitalization, a decision maker might ask, that could lower aggression risk to an acceptable level? These could range from situational interventions (e.g., a change in living situation or job) to monitoring of specified behavior (e.g., taking medication, abstaining from substance use, avoiding contact with the potential victim) to therapeutic interventions to strengthen aggression-relevant deficits (e.g., anger control, impulsivity). If it appears that dynamic risk factors are (a) present,

(b) amenable to intervention that is (c) available, and can be (d) monitored to ensure compliance, then it can be helpful to provide this information for initial decision-making purposes. It can also be useful in treatment planning and release decision making, to help clinicians address the issue of risk directly and determine when planned interventions have been delivered as successfully as possible.

Finally, in addition to describing interventions that might reduce risk by mitigating the level of dynamic risk factors, the clinician can also describe the status of each intervention. Is it available? Has it been attempted? To what extent has satisfactory participation or compliance been observed? This information can help to address the risk-relevant questions of (a) *what* can be done? (b) *can* it be done? (c) *has* it been done? The final question—what difference will it make?—is more difficult to answer, unless there is a documented history of treatment of risk-relevant symptomatology.

Further Research:
Directions and Needs

The integration of the MMPI-2 into risk assessment presently shows promise but little actualization. This is perhaps understandable in light of the relatively recent conceptual shift from "dangerousness assessment" or "violence prediction" to "risk assessment." However, the risk assessment potential of an instrument such as the MMPI-2 can only be tested when proper research attention is devoted to certain areas. These will be discussed briefly.

First, it would be useful for MMPI-2 risk researchers to pay particular attention to definitions of aggression, and to legal status in defining the population. Employing definitions similar to those used by other risk researchers would facilitate comparisons between different studies. In a similar vein, the use of legal status in defining a population (particularly those who are civilly committed) would permit the comparison of MMPI-2 variables with risk factors in other studies.

One of the greatest contributions any risk researcher can make is to measure the base rates of outcome aggression prospectively, regardless of the variables being used as risk factors. MMPI research on prison and hospital samples has often employed outcome measures such as instant offense or behavior in the institution. The more meaningful outcome in a prediction context, however, is behavior that occurs *following* release. Even measures that can underestimate aggression, such as rearrest or rehospitalization, can be somewhat helpful. The best design, however, involves one in which there is ongoing contact with the individual at regular intervals and the use of collateral as well as self report. Investigators could use naturally occurring procedures, incorporating their research design into parole or conditional release, to obtain such measures on some populations. Unfortunately (for researchers), such "naturally occurring" monitoring is relatively rare for discharged civilly committed patients, so such integration can rarely be accomplished.

The third area of priority involves expanding the range of potential aggression risk factors. Either the use of single MMPI-2 scales (e.g., Psychopathic Deviate, Paranoia, Overcontrolled Hostility) or the employment of profiles might prove useful when the MMPI-2 is incorporated into a proper risk assessment design. Particularly interesting possibilities would include scales or profiles relevant to risk variables currently being investigated by the MacArthur Network: anger, impulsivity, psychopathy, hallucinations, and "threat/ control override" delusions. MMPI-2 risk researchers might also distinguish between static and dynamic risk factors, so that the latter can be incorporated into treatment planning and release decision making.

Empirical foundation for the clinician's judgment of risk "below," "at," or "above" base rate is needed. It would clearly be preferable to make such a determination on an actuarial basis, but that would require prospective risk research using appropriate designs. When this has been done, the accuracy of such judgments will undoubtedly increase.

Finally, the MMPI-2 might be employed to assess the efficacy of risk-reduction interventions, particularly when they are related to MMPI-2-generated variables. For example, how would an individual high on "threat/control override" delusions appear on Scale 6? What sort of MMPI-2 profiles would such individuals generate? If treatment is successful in reducing the intensity and inaccuracy of these perceptions, how might such success be reflected by the MMPI-2?

The recent rejuvenation of interest in and attention to risk assessment has created exciting prospects for researchers and clinicians alike. The MMPI-2 should be incorporated into risk research, if for no other reasons than its popularity in practice, actuarial nature, and ease of administration. However, if its potential contribution to risk assessment is to be fairly tested, this must be done by research incorporating the advances in both risk assessment and the MMPI/MMPI-2 that have been made in the past decade.

References

Audubon, J. J., & Kirwin, B. R. (1982). Defensiveness in the criminally insane. *Journal of Personality Assessment, 46,* 304-311.

Ben-Porath, Y. S., Butcher, J. N., & Graham, J. R. (1991). Contribution of the MMPI-2 content scales to the differential diagnosis of psychopathology. *Psychological Assessment: A Journal of Consulting and Clinical Psychology, 3,* 634-640.

Blackburn, R. (1971). Personality types among abnormal homicides. *British Journal of Criminology, 11,* 14-31.

Blackburn, R. (1972). Dimensions of hostility and aggression in abnormal offenders. *Journal of Consulting and Clinical Psychology, 38,* 20-26.

Blackburn, R. (1975). An empirical classification of psychopathic personality. *British Journal of Psychiatry, 127,* 456-460.

Buck, J. A., & Graham, J. R. (1978). The 4-3 MMPI profile type: A failure to replicate. *Journal of Consulting and Clinical Psychology, 46,* 344.

Buigas, R., Nicholson, R. A., & Bagby, R. M. (1994, March). *Assessment of malingering using the MMPI-2: Which index is best?* Paper presented at the Biennial Conference of the American Psychology-Law Society/Division 41, Santa Fe, NM.

Butcher, J. N. (1990). *Use of the MMPI-2 in treatment planning.* New York: Oxford University Press.

Cocozza, J., & Steadman, H. (1976). The failure of psychiatric predictions of dangerousness: Clear and convincing evidence. *Rutgers Law Review, 29,* 1084-1101.

Craig, T. J. (1982). An epidemiologic study of problems associated with violence among psychiatric inpatients. *American Journal of Psychiatry, 139,* 1262-1266.

Fein, R. A., Vossekuil, B., & Robbins, P. C. (1994, March). *Towards the prevention of assassination: Secret service case study research.* Paper presented at the Biennial Conference of the American Psychology-Law Society/Division 41, Santa Fe, NM.

Felson, R. B., & Steadman, H. (1983). Situational factors in disputes leading to criminal violence. *Criminology, 21,* 59-74.

Frederiksen, S. J. (1975). A comparison of selected personality and history variables in highly violent, mildly violent and nonviolent female offenders (Doctoral dissertation, University of Minnesota, 1975). *Dissertation Abstracts International, 36,* 3036B.

Graham, J. R. (1993). *MMPI-2: Assessing personality and psychopathology* (2nd ed.). New York: Oxford University Press.

Greene, R. L. (1988). Assessment of malingering and defensiveness by objective personality inventories. In R. Rogers (Ed.), *Clinical assessment of malingering and deception* (pp. 123-158). New York: Guilford.

Greene, R. L. (1991). *The MMPI-2/MMPI: An interpretive manual.* Needham Heights, MA: Allyn & Bacon.

Grow, R., McVaugh, W., & Eno, T. D. (1980). Faking and the MMPI. *Journal of Clinical Psychology, 36,* 910-917.

Hare, R. D., & McPherson, L. M. (1984). Violent and aggressive behavior by criminal psychopaths. *International Journal of Law and Psychiatry, 7,* 35-50.

Haven, H. J. (1972). Descriptive and developmental characteristics of chronically overcontrolled hostile prisoners. *FCI Research Reports, 4,* 1-40.

Heilbrun, A. B. (1979). Psychopathy and violent crime. *Journal of Consulting and Clinical Psychology, 47,* 509-516.

Heilbrun, A. B. (1990a). The measurement of criminal dangerousness as a personality construct. *Journal of Personality Assessment, 54,* 141-148.

Heilbrun, A. B. (1990b). Differentiation of death-row murderers and life-sentence murderers by antisociality and intelligence measures. *Journal of Personality Assessment, 54,* 617-627.

Heilbrun, A. B. (1994). *A new model of criminal dangerousness: Toward an understanding of violence and recidivism.* Unpublished manuscript, Emory University, Atlanta, GA.

Heilbrun, K. (1988, March). *Third party information in forensic assessments: Much needed, sometimes sought, poorly guided.* Paper presented at the Biennial Meeting of the American Psychology-Law Society/Division 41 of the American Psychological Association, Miami, FL.

Heilbrun, K., Bennett, W. S., White, A. J., & Kelly, J. (1990). An MMPI-based empirical model of malingering and deception. *Behavioral Sciences and the Law, 8,* 45-53.

Henderson, M. (1982). An empirical classification of convicted violent offenders. *British Journal of Criminology, 22,* 1-20.

Henderson, M. (1983). Self-reported assertion and aggression among violent offenders with high or low levels of overcontrolled hostility. *Personality and Individual Differences, 4,* 113-115.

Huesmann, L. R., Lefkowitz, M. M., & Eron, L. D. (1978). Sum of MMPI Scales F, 4, and 9 as a measure of aggression. *Journal of Consulting and Clinical Psychology, 41,* 425-432.

Karson, C., & Bigelow, L. B. (1987). Violent behavior in schizophrenic patients. *Journal of Nervous and Mental Disease, 175,* 161-164.

Klassen, D., & O'Connor, W. A. (1988a). Predicting violence in schizophrenic and non-schizophrenic patients: A prospective study. *Journal of Community Psychology, 16,* 217-227.

Klassen, D., & O'Connor, W. A. (1988b). A prospective study of predictors of violence in adult male mental health admissions. *Law and Human Behavior, 12,* 143-158.

Klassen, D., & O'Connor, W. A. (1988c). Crime, inpatient admissions, and violence among male mental patients. *International Journal of Law and Psychiatry, 11,* 305-312.

Klassen, D., & O'Connor, W. A. (1990). Assessing the risk of violence in released mental patients: A cross-validation study. *Psychological Assessment: A Journal of Consulting and Clinical Psychology, 1,* 75-81.

Krakowski, M., Volavka, J., & Brizer, D. (1986). Psychopathology and violence: A review of the literature. *Comprehensive Psychiatry, 27,* 131-148.

Lane, P. J., & Spruill, J. (1980). Validity of the overcontrolled-undercontrolled typology usage on criminal psychiatric patients. *Criminal Justice and Behavior, 7,* 215-228.

Lanyon, R. L., & Lutz, R. W. (1984). MMPI discrimination of defensive and nondefensive felony sex offenders. *Journal of Consulting and Clinical Psychology, 52,* 841-843.

Lidz, E. W., Mulvey, E. P., & Gardner, W. (1993). The accuracy of predictions of violence to others. *Journal of the American Medical Association, 269,* 1007-1011.

Link, B. G., Andrews, H., & Cullen, F. T. (1992). The violent and illegal behavior of mental patients reconsidered. *American Sociological Review, 57,* 275-292.

Lowenstein, M., Binder, R. L., & McNiel, D. E. (1990). The relationship between admission symptoms and hospital assaults. *Hospital and Community Psychiatry, 41,* 311-313.

McGurk, B. J. (1978). Personality types among normal homicides. *British Journal of Criminology, 18,* 146-161.

McNiel, D. E., & Binder, R. L. (1986). Violence, civil commitment, and hospitalization. *Journal of Nervous and Mental Disease, 174,* 107-111.

McNiel, D. E., & Binder, R. L. (1989). Relationship between preadmission threats and violent behavior in acute psychiatric inpatients. *Hospital and Community Psychiatry, 40,* 605-608.

Meehl, P. E. (1954). *Clinical versus statistical prediction: A theoretical analysis and a review of the evidence.* Minneapolis: University of Minnesota Press.

Meehl, P. E., & Rosen, A. (1955). Antecedent probability and the efficiency of psychometric signs, patterns or cutting scores. *Psychological Bulletin, 52,* 194-216.

Megargee, E. I. (1966). Undercontrolled and overcontrolled personality types in extreme antisocial aggression. *Psychological Monographs, 80,*(3, Whole No. 611).

Megargee, E. I., & Bohn, M. J., Jr. (with Meyer, J., Jr., & Sink, F.). (1979). *Classifying criminal offenders: A new system based on the MMPI.* Beverly Hills, CA: Sage.

Melton, G. B., Petrila, J., Poythress, N., & Slobogin, C. (1987). *Psychological evaluations for the courts: A handbook for mental health professionals and lawyers.* New York: Guilford.

Mischel, W. (1973). Toward a cognitive social learning reconceptualization of personality. *Psychological Review, 80,* 252-283.

Monahan, J. (1975). The prediction of violence. In D. Chappell & J. Monahan (Eds.), *Violence and criminal justice* (pp. 15-31). Lexington, MA: Lexington.

Monahan, J. (1981). *Predicting violent behavior: An assessment of clinical techniques.* Beverly Hills: Sage.

Monahan, J. (1992). Mental disorders and violent behavior: Attitudes and evidence. *American Psychologist, 47,* 511-521.

Monahan, J., & Steadman, H. J. (Eds.). (1983). *Mentally disordered offenders: Perspectives from law and social science.* New York: Plenum.

Monahan, J., & Steadman, H. J. (Eds.). (1994). *Violence and mental disorder: Developments in risk assessment.* Chicago: University of Chicago Press.

Moos, R. H. (1973). Conceptualization of human environments. *American Psychologist, 28,* 652-665.

Morse, S. (1978). Laws and mental health professionals: The limits of expertise. *Professional Psychology, 9,* 389-399.

National Research Council. (1989). *Improving risk communication.* Washington, DC: National Academy Press.

Otto, R. (1992). The prediction of dangerous behavior: A review and analysis of "second generation" research. *Forensic Reports, 5,* 103-134.

Pope, K. S., Butcher, J. N., & Seelen, J. (1993). *The MMPI, MMPI-2, & MMPI-A in court.* Washington, DC: American Psychological Association.

Rogers, R. (1984). Towards an empirical model of malingering and deception. *Behavioral Sciences and the Law, 2,* 93-111.

Rogers, R. (Ed.). (1988). *Clinical assessment of malingering and deception.* New York: Guilford.

Rogers, R., Dometsch, R., & Cavanaugh, J. L. (1983). Identification of random responders on MMPI protocols. *Journal of Personality Assessment, 47,* 364-368.

Rossi, A. M., Jacobs, M., Monteleone, M., Olsen, R., Surber, R. W., Winkler, E. L., & Wommack, A. (1985). Violent or fear inducing behavior associated with hospital admission. *Hospital and Community Psychiatry, 36,* 643-647.

Shah, S. A. (1978). Dangerousness: A paradigm for exploring some issues in law and psychology. *American Psychologist, 33,* 224-238.

Skodol, A. E., & Karasu, T. B. (1980). Toward hospitalization criteria for violent patients. *Comprehensive Psychiatry, 21,* 162-166.

Swanson, J., Holzer, C., Ganju, V., & Jono, R. (1990). Violence and psychiatric disorder in the community: Evidence from the Epidemiologic Catchment Area Surveys. *Hospital and Community Psychiatry, 41,* 761-770.

Tarasoff v. Regents of the University of California, 551 P.2d 334 (Cal. Supp. Ct. 1976)

Tardiff, K. (1984). Characteristics of assaultive patients in private hospitals. *American Journal of Psychiatry, 141,* 1232-1235.

Tardiff, K., & Koenigsberg, H. W. (1985). Assaultive behavior among psychiatric outpatients. *American Journal of Psychiatry, 142,* 960-963.

Tardiff, K., & Sweillam, A. (1980). Assault, suicide, and mental illness. *Archives of General Psychiatry, 37,* 164-169.

Veldman, D. J. (1967). *Fortran programming for the behavioral sciences.* New York: Holt, Rinehart & Winston.

Wasyliw, O. E., Grossman, L. S., Haywood, T. W., & Cavanaugh, J. L. (1988). The detection of malingering in criminal forensic groups: MMPI validity scales. *Journal of Personality Assessment, 52,* 321-333.

Wesseley, S., & Taylor, P. (1991). Madness and crime: Criminology vs. psychiatry. *Criminal Behavior and Mental Health, 1,* 193-228.

8

Personality Patterns of Personal Injury Litigants

The Role of Computer-Based MMPI-2 Evaluations

JAMES N. BUTCHER

M edical and legal professionals have long been aware that psychological factors influence the experience, extent, and course of pain. The importance of personality factors in the genesis or continuation of chronic pain and other somatic symptoms, especially when litigation is involved, has been observed for many years. Over a century ago Erichsen (1882) observed,

> There is, in fact, that unconscious exaggeration of symptoms, and especially of pain, which is common to all hysterical people, that simulation or nervous mimicry of real disease which has been so well described by Brodie and by Paget. This state of things will last indefinitely without any very material change. There may be daily or weekly fluctuations, but the patient neither gets materially better or worse. This state will continue, indeed, as long as the mind is impressed by the prospect of impending litigation. (p. 177)

This chapter discusses a number of key issues pertaining to the use of the MMPI-2 in forensic evaluations where the individual being assessed is claiming personal injury. Topics to be covered include the role of psychological evaluations in personal injury litigation, administration and interpretation of the MMPI-2 in such evaluations, the importance of interpreting the MMPI-2 validity scales in personal injury cases, and the use of comprehensive test interpretation strategies in these evaluations. Several cases are presented to illustrate key points, and future research directions are proposed.

Why Psychologists Have Entered
the Personal Injury Forensic Arena

Increasingly, civil court cases involve questions regarding psychological adjustment (Babitsky & Mangraviti, 1993; Conte, 1990; Eisner, 1984; Lasky, 1993; Weissman, 1985). Because of their expertise in psychopathology and personality evaluation, psychologists are being asked more frequently to serve as witnesses in court cases to provide expert opinion on such questions as: whether the basis of an individual's psychological claims is credible; whether current or past adjustment problems that a litigant might have experienced could have an impact on the current claim; whether an individual might be experiencing documentable and disabling stress-related symptoms; and whether the symptoms an individual is reporting could be attributed to lifelong, chronic maladjustment. One important reason why psychological testimony is becoming an important determinant in personal injury litigation comes from the availability of objective psychological methods of assessing individuals and problems such as the MMPI-2.

The requisite experience to qualify a psychologist as an expert in forensic personal injury litigation comes essentially through practical experience with the tests involved and the type of problem being considered (see Eisner, 1984; Goodman, 1993; Kreutzer, Harris-Marwitz, & Myers, 1990; Ogloff, this volume; Pope, Butcher, & Seelen, 1993 for discussions of the qualifications of experts). Additionally, the field of psychology has an extensive research base on which psychologists testifying in court about personal injury factors can base their opinions. The MMPI/MMPI-2 has a substantial track record of use with chronic pain and other relevant medical assessment applications that have direct bearing on forensic testimony in the area. Numerous studies concerning the use of the MMPI/MMPI-2 with medical patients support its use (Bradley, Prokop, Margolis, & Gentry, 1978; Butcher, 1985; Butcher &

Harlow, 1987; Fordyce, 1979; Henrichs, 1981; Keller & Butcher, 1991; Osborne, 1979; Roberts, 1984; Shaffer, 1981; Shaffer, Nussbaum, & Little, 1972; Sternbach & Timmermans, 1975).

The Adversarial Nature
of Forensic Assessment

In many cases, the forensic psychological practitioner has been trained in clinical or counseling psychology where most of the clients are "voluntary" and are being seen in a help-seeking situation. Psychologists who testify in court may find that clients being evaluated in forensic cases do not view the testing in the same light as patients being assessed in mental health settings. Instead, they may "act out" their motivations to appear a particular way through the tests, thereby creating a rather different interpretive task for the forensic practitioner. Moreover, the forensic arena is a different and potentially highly stressful environment as a result of the adversarial nature of the judicial system. An interpretation of a psychological test finding that is readily accepted in mental health treatment settings might be vigorously questioned in a legal hearing. The psychologist may find that a particular interpretation that seems very clear and relevant for treatment planning might be attacked as flimsy, off track, or prejudicial when examined by counsel in cross-examination.

In court situations, when the basis of an interpretation is being vigorously questioned, the psychologist needs to follow two useful practices. First, it is important that the expert be thoroughly familiar with the procedures or tests being used so that aggressive cross-examination will not disclose procedural error or faulty conclusions about the test data. Second, it is important to base one's opinions on facts, even if the facts might appear contrary to the interests of the side that has hired the expert. That is, if some aspect of the testing is weak, inconsistent, or contradictory with respect to the arguments in the case, it is important for the psychologist to acknowledge these limitations and inconsistencies and not try to cover them up.

At times, attorneys might ask a psychologist to review testing results or test a client in a personal injury case. The psychologist discovers problems or interpretations that might be potentially damaging to the attorney employing the psychologist. The attorney may then try to "mold" testimony in a more favorable direction or ask the psychologist *not* to write a report on the case.

This situation has been discussed by several authorities (Goldstein, 1986; Hoffman, 1986; Weiner, 1987).

Issues in Test Administration: The Importance of Standardized Procedures in Forensic Assessment

Standardized testing procedures need to be carefully followed in forensic assessment (see the informative discussion by Jarvis & Hamlin, 1984). However, at times forensic psychological evaluations might be conducted in an attorney's office after the client has been given meticulous preparation by the attorney as to the "things to watch out for" in the MMPI-2. Research has shown that instructional sets can play an important part in the way individuals respond to personality test items. Instructions can be used to alter honest responding (Berry, Baer, & Harris, 1991) and produce particular patterns of scores on the test. Instructions can also be used to obtain more valid test protocols (Fink & Butcher, 1972). It is imperative that psychologists be aware of the types of instructions that are provided to test takers before psychological inventories are administered. Test interpretation should be adjusted accordingly.

Problematic instructional sets can be generated by inadvertent or well-meaning deviations from standard procedures as well. For example, in several recent cases, psychologists have substantially altered standard test administration procedures to obtain personality questionnaire results from non-English-speaking subjects. In these cases, the item content of the English language version of the MMPI-2 was drastically altered by having a bilingual person translate the items simultaneously to the client rather than using an appropriately developed and validated foreign language translation of the instrument. This type of procedural alteration (perhaps acceptable in a clinical or research context) cannot be defended in forensic assessments. Personality questionnaire items cannot be adequately translated to clients in a testing session without introducing considerable distortion of item meanings. Test translation is a complex task that usually requires several translators conducting item translations or back translations. There are well-established test translation procedures that are usually followed in developing careful test translations (see Butcher, in press; Butcher & Pancheri, 1976).

Personality Profile Diversity
and Type of Litigation

No single pattern of personality test profiles has been found to exist among personal injury claimants. Rather, personality patterns of personal injury claimants differ greatly depending on a number of important factors such as the type of injury involved, legitimacy of the claim, the time at which the testing was conducted, who administered the psychological tests and where they were administered, and the amount of "prepping" or pretest briefing that might have been provided by the attorney or test administrator.

Important differences can be found in the personality profiles of personal injury litigants depending on the different circumstances in the case. For example, different attempts to present oneself in particular ways can be tied to the type of litigation motivation involved (Butcher & Harlow, 1987). There is no single pattern of MMPI-2 scores that litigants in personal injury cases produce. Rather, there are diverse patterns depending, in part, on circumstances, premorbid personality, and status of the case. All of these factors need to be weighed in reaching conclusions and making recommendations on the basis of test data. Several case examples will be provided to illustrate the need to consider both injury circumstances and test-response sets.

1. PHYSICAL INJURY—
PROLONGED VAGUE CHRONIC PAIN

Many personal injury claims result from incidents such as transportation or industrial accidents in which the individual alleges that an accident has produced prolonged intractable and disabling pain symptoms but in which actual physical findings are negligible. The MMPI-2 profiles presented in Figures 8.1 and 8.2 illustrate this situation. In their effort to look good psychologically while at the same time presenting the view that they are physically damaged, litigants may produce a noncredible MMPI-2 profile with high L scale and/or high K scale scores, often accompanied by high Hs scale scores.

The MMPI-2 profiles shown in Figures 8.1 and 8.2 illustrate this pattern of vague symptoms of chronic pain behavior. The litigant involved in this case, a food service employee, was allegedly injured on the job when she was "bumped" by a door that she had been approaching with an armload of trays. She claims to have been "slammed" against the wall, allegedly incurring an

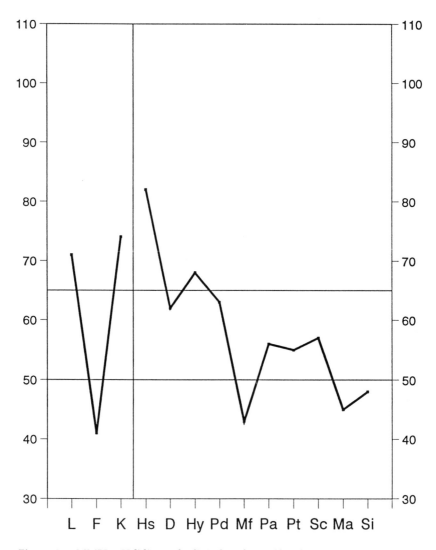

Figure 8.1. MMPI-2 Validity and Clinical Scale Profile of a 42-Year-Old Divorced Woman

injury to her back that caused her pain that had persisted for over 2 years. After the incident she worked for several days but then began to report symptoms. She went to a physician who recommended bed rest for a period

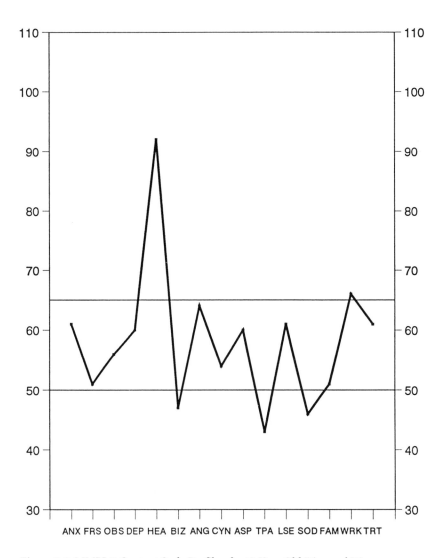

Figure 8.2. MMPI-2 Content Scale Profile of a 42-Year-Old Divorced Woman.

of time. She applied for and received worker's compensation for 6 months until the company doctor, after an examination, in which he found no organic basis to her symptoms, determined that she was able to return to work. She resumed work for a few days but stopped when her pain appeared to persist.

During her absence from work she had been referred to an outpatient chronic pain treatment program. However, she left the program after the first week, insisting that all they wanted her to do was "learn to live with pain without curing it."

Her approach to the MMPI-2 items resulted in a defensive pattern in which she presented herself as above reproach. She claimed to be a highly virtuous person who had no psychological problems and was guided by pure motives. Her approach to the test was overly moralistic. She endorsed an unlikely pattern of items suggesting high morality in an apparent manipulative effort to appear extremely honest. She presented a symptom pattern of vague physical complaints that were unlikely to be the result of an injury alone, reflected in the clinical scale pattern and the elevation on the Health Concerns (HEA) content scale. Her MMPI-2 profile reflected a noncredible picture of overly positive self presentation and an unbelievable pattern of extreme symptoms that are generally too diffuse and extensive to occur in a genuine physical disorder.

2. PSYCHOLOGICAL SYMPTOMS IN THE CONTEXT OF PHYSICAL INJURY

In this case, a 47-year-old male employee of an industrial company lost his leg in a job-related accident (see Figures 8.3 and 8.4). His legal claim involved both physical injury and psychological damages as a result of alleged emotional adjustment problems in the 2 years following the accident. His litigation centered around his claim that his loss of a limb affected his ability to do many things he previously depended on and from which he had received considerable satisfaction and self-esteem. His MMPI-2 profiles clearly indicated a pattern of psychological distress (depression) in the context of a valid test protocol. The validity scales did not suggest the presence of exaggeration or overreporting, whereas the clinical and content scale profiles revealed a credible picture of maladjustment that was consistent with the clinical picture and known history in this case.

A recent study by Flamer and Buch (1992) provided a relevant empirical basis for this type of work-related compensation claim (see Figure 8.5). Flamer and Birch studied individuals who had been seriously injured on the job by comparing their MMPI-2 profiles with those of chronic pain

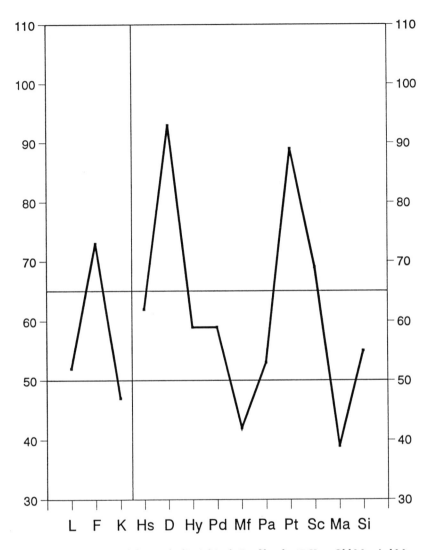

Figure 8.3. MMPI-2 Validity and Clincial Scale Profile of a 47-Year-Old Married Man

patients and with other individuals with mental health problems. Very clear differences in MMPI-2 patterns emerged. Actual work injury patients who

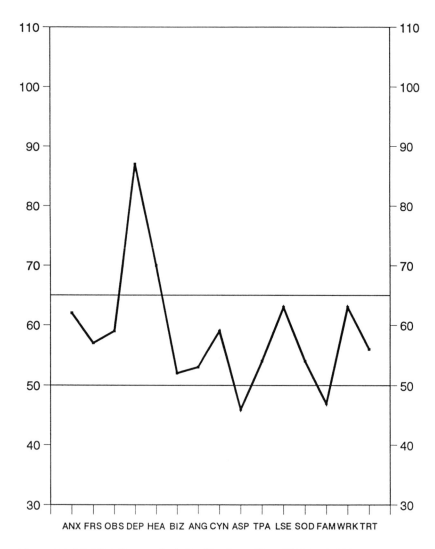

Figure 8.4. MMPI-2 Content Scale Profile of a 47-Year-Old Married Man

experienced post-traumatic stress disorder produced more genuine self presentations (i.e., the validity scales L and K were within the normal range). In

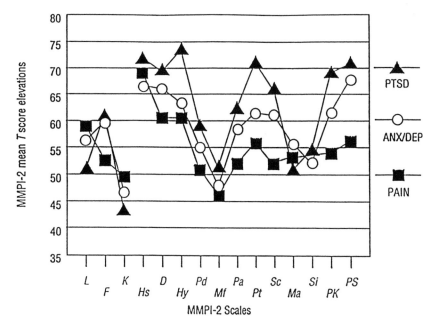

Figure 8.5. Mean MMPI-2 Validity and Clinical Scale Profiles for PTSD, Anxiety/ Depression, and Chronic Pain Samples
SOURCE: Flamer & Buch, 1992. Adapted by permission.

addition, their clinical scale pattern appeared more acutely distressed (i.e., had higher elevations on scale 7) than the psychiatric or the chronic pain patient groups.

3. PSYCHOLOGICAL DAMAGES IN A POST-TRAUMATIC STRESS DISORDER

The next case involved a lawsuit against a corporation that owned and operated a hotel chain (see Figures 8.6 and 8.7). A 32-year-old woman reported that she was raped while she was a guest at one of the hotels and reportedly had symptoms of post-traumatic stress disorder such as night terrors and depression since the rape occurred.

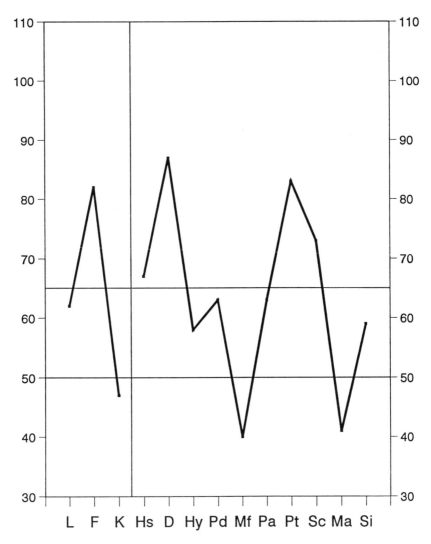

Figure 8.6. MMPI-2 Validity and Clinical Scale Profile of a 32-Year-Old Single Woman

Her MMPI-2 validity profile showed a valid self presentation. She appeared to be open and honest in her self descriptions, as reflected in the average scores on the L and K scales and a moderate elevation on the F scale. Her intense

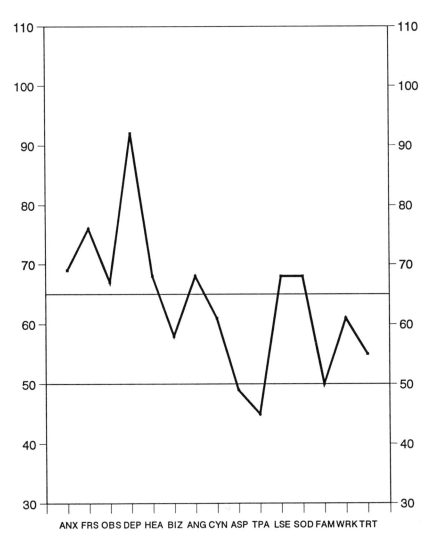

Figure 8.7. MMPI-2 Content Scale Profile of a 32-Year-Old Single Woman

anxiety and depression, as shown by the clinical and content scales, reflected considerable negative affect at this time.

Importance of the Validity
Scales in Personal Injury Cases

It is apparent from the preceding examples that the individual's motivation to be assessed and the general "mental state" that he or she hopes to present with respect to the symptom pattern can be extremely important influences on psychological tests. The client's test-taking motivation should be carefully evaluated in any forensic study because the test picture can be distorted considerably from the way the person typically is. Psychological procedures, such as the clinical interview, or psychological tests that do not have a means of appraising response "honesty" or cooperativeness, have limited utility in pretrial evaluations. On the other hand, the availability of objective standardized measures of protocol validity is one of the main strengths of the MMPI-2 in forensic psychological evaluations.

Pope et al. (1993) pointed out that there are at least four ways in which litigants in personal injury litigation respond to psychological testing that results in invalidating test results based on the MMPI-2 (or any psychological assessment procedure available today): exaggerated responding, defensive responding, inconsistent responding, and atypical profile results.

EXAGGERATED OR RARE
RESPONSES TO ITEMS IN AN EFFORT
TO SHOW SEVERE PSYCHOLOGICAL PROBLEMS

One of the most common invalidating approaches to the MMPI-2 items in personal injury cases involves extreme or exaggerated responding to present the impression of a highly disturbed psychological state. In these cases, the individual reports in an indiscriminate manner many symptoms and problems, presenting an unlikely conglomeration of mental health and physical health problems that rarely "go together" in actual disorders. The exaggerated or malingered record typically shows very high F and F(b) scale scores. Extensive research on the MMPI/MMPI-2 F scale has shown it to be an effective measure of the tendency to exaggerate or fake mental health symptoms over a wide variety of settings and conditions (see Berry, this volume; Berry et al., 1991; Schretlen, 1988 for reviews of this research). Graham, Watts, and Timbrook (1991) demonstrated that the F scale of the MMPI-2 is effective in detecting overreporting of symptoms and problems.

The intentional claim of extreme problems or exaggerated symptom checking is very different from random responding, as noted by elevated VRIN scores. The recently developed VRIN scale has proven effective in identifying random responding. Thus, a very high F scale score coupled with a relatively low VRIN scale score can be viewed as an indication of intentional exaggeration rather than random responding.

DEFENSIVE RESPONDING: PRESENTING ONESELF IN AN UNREALISTIC MANNER

A different approach to distorting the MMPI-2 pattern in personal injury litigation cases involves presenting oneself as highly virtuous, if not perfect. Some individuals who falsely claim problems in a lawsuit produce an inconsistent pattern of scores. The clinical scales suggest multiple physical complaints for which no organic explanation can be found. The validity scales suggest a person who is claiming a high degree of virtue and few or no faults of any kind. Apparently, these individuals believe that this unrealistically positive self presentation will lend credibility to the symptoms.

INCONSISTENT RESPONDING

A third pattern of MMPI-2 scores that suggests an invalid record involves the presentation of highly inconsistent information in the testing. People who endorse a large number of extreme symptoms in an unselected fashion, endorse test items randomly, or give inconsistent true or false responses produce extreme elevations on MMPI-2 symptom scales. Indexes of inconsistency on the MMPI-2, such as VRIN and TRIN, are useful in identifying such response sets.

ATYPICAL MMPI/MMPI-2 PATTERNS

Another possible indicator of malingering on the MMPI-2 involves the presence of atypical response patterns. Pope et al. (1993) described the atypical personality test pattern:

This approach is analogous to the reporting of incompatible physical symptoms such as "glove anaesthesia" which cannot be explained by actual neural connections in the hand matching the experienced pattern of the anaesthesia. Malingerers often give responses that are inconsistent with other clinical observations (McDonald, 1976). This approach with the MMPI-2 involves the use of different sources of information within the test. That is, clients may present incompatible or inexplicable symptom patterns on the test which call into question the accuracy of the profile.

In appraising this invalidating approach the interpreter matches behavior or symptoms from the client's responses to that of a modal or expected clinical pattern that is established by research on the particular sample involved or based upon the base rates of the population in question. Research has established consistent or expected behavior patterns that can be evaluated through the various scales and indexes. Hypotheses about an individual's "expected" behavior on the MMPI-2 can be matched with features of their actual behavior. For many clinical situations expected MMPI-2 performances can be found. Clients who deviate from the expected performance, particularly with respect to the validity scale pattern, would be considered as possibly malingering. (p. 110)

To determine whether MMPI-2 patterns are likely to be atypical or "expected," psychologists should refer to base rate information on the scales and code types in various assessment settings. In response to the need for information about population-specific base rates, Butcher (1993) incorporated this information into the Minnesota Report, a computer-based test interpretation program. For example, for a given profile the relative frequencies of the scale elevations, code types, or both are provided for the MMPI-2 normative sample and for various medical and other special groups. This information makes it possible for interpreters to have a clearer idea of the frequency with which a given profile is found in medical or mental health settings. Other aspects of computerized assessment are discussed next.

Computer-Based Interpretation in Personal Injury Litigation

Computer-based MMPI assessments have been available since the early 1960s and have been widely used and recommended for forensic evaluation (Ziskin, 1981). Ziskin considered it important for psychologists who testify in court to use procedures that are reliable and objective and to avoid the use of impressionistic, subjective data that could be readily challenged. Computer interpretation is widely accepted by the psychological profession as an appropriate means of evaluating test data on clients as reflected in the Guidelines for Computer-Based Assessment (American Psychological Association, 1986):

> A long history of research on statistical and clinical prediction has established that a well-designed statistical treatment of test results and ancillary information will yield more valid assessments than will an individual professional using the same information. (p. 9)

Several reasons can be found for the broad use of computer-based objective test interpretations in forensic assessment.

First, computer-assisted test interpretations are usually more thorough and better documented than those typically derived by clinical assessment procedures. Computer-based interpretation systems usually provide a more extensive and comprehensive summary of relevant test-based descriptions than the forensic psychologist has the time and background to provide in a report. Second, computer-based test interpretations eliminate subjectivity in interpretations. In interpreting the MMPI-2, a computer will usually address all of the relevant scores and indexes and not ignore "selectively" important information as sometimes happens when human beings face a complicated array of data.

Third, computer-based psychological test results can usually be obtained quite rapidly, thereby meeting the often difficult time limitations involved in preparing assessments for hectic court schedules.

Fourth, computer-based test interpretations are highly reliable, a very important requirement in forensic testimony. Computer-derived test processing always results in the same interpretive statements for a given set of test scores.

Finally, computer-based reports, particularly those based on replicated test correlates, have a high level of accuracy and external validity. In practice, however, interpretation systems vary. An important point to consider in using computer-based interpretive reports in forensic assessment is that different commercially available computer interpretation services might actually produce somewhat discrepant outputs for the same protocol. Research has shown that test interpretation services differ with respect to the amount of information and accuracy of the interpretations provided (Eyde, Kowal, & Fishburne, 1991). Practitioners using an automated interpretation system for a test should be familiar with the issues of computerized test interpretation generally and the validity research on the particular system used (see Eyde et al., 1991; Moreland, 1987).

CAREFUL USE OF COMPUTERIZED
REPORTS IN FORENSIC TESTIMONY

Essential to using an MMPI-2 computer scoring or narrative report is establishing the chain of custody for the test protocol in question so that the psychologist can document that the computer-based report is actually the report for the client in the case. The psychologist needs to be able to explain how the answer sheet was obtained and demonstrate that the computer-based results are actually those for the client in question. Pope et al. (1993) mentioned that there have been cases in which the MMPI was not allowed into evidence because the psychologist could not establish that the test interpretation was actually based on answers that the client provided.

It is important to ensure that the particular computer-based report is an appropriate interpretation of the subject's test scores. The psychologist should be able to explain how the computer report is actually appropriate for the client. Computer-based psychological tests are, for the most part, prototypes; consequently, some of the descriptions provided by the report might not be pertinent for a particular case. The psychologist may need to discuss, in cross-examination, any descriptive statements in the report that are not considered appropriate for the particular client.

As noted earlier, computer-based personality reports are generic summaries that are developed for a particular set of scores. In some reports, the prototypal information that is provided may not be relevant or appropriate for a particular case. Some correlates might not apply for all cases that have the same test pattern. It is important for the practitioner to ensure that the particular interpretation in the computer-based report is an appropriate personality description for the patient's test pattern. The closer the match between the client's scores and those of the prototype pattern on which the personality descriptions are based, the more appropriate will be the report. Any interpretations or hypotheses that are not appropriate, based on what we know about the client from other sources of information, should be ignored in the conclusions of the report (see discussion in Pope et al., 1993).

It is also important to keep in mind that computerized test reports are considered to be *raw test data,* not final psychological reports. Computer-based reports do not usually stand alone as psychological reports. The relevance and appropriateness of each interpretive statement need to be ensured so that they can be defended if challenged on cross-examination.

Future Directions for Research

Much of what we know about using the MMPI and MMPI-2 in personal injury litigation comes from the extensive research on the instrument in a variety of medical and clinical settings and practical forensic assessment rather than from rigorous research studies involving personal injury cases. These studies have involved persons being evaluated in relation to workers' compensation (Rader, 1984), disability determinations (Shaffer et al., 1972), and chronic pain and related disability (Keller & Butcher, 1991; Li, Li, & Rodriguez-de-Souza, 1991; Repko & Cooper, 1983). More specific research with a broad range of personal injury claimants would be an invaluable aid toward developing a more refined interpretation approach with the MMPI-2 in this field. The following research would expand our knowledge base for more effective test use with personal injury claimants.

1. There is a need for more information on the *impact of motivational sets on test performance.* As described earlier in this chapter, we are well aware that individuals who take the MMPI-2 in personal injury cases view the items in different ways from those taking the instrument in clinical or "help-seeking" situations. More research aimed at exploring the impact of different motivational sets on test scores would be informative, particularly studies that differentiated various motivations that could underlie the subject's schema for getting professionals involved to view his or her problems as he or she sees them. Can the MMPI-2 differentiate types of personal injury cases? Is there a "blueprint" endorsement pattern for specific motivational conditions?

2. Paralleling the needs described in the previous point, there is a substantial need *to explore further the test-based indexes that have been designed to reflect or detect the different invalidating conditions.* Much progress has been made over the past few years to obtain a clearer picture of the client's test taking attitudes with the MMPI (see, e.g., Lees-Haley, 1986). Some new scales and indexes have been developed for the MMPI-2 to provide indicators of invalidating approaches to the test items. Unfortunately, much of this research has been of "simulated faking" conditions rather than "real world" circumstances. This line of research needs to be pursued more extensively using clients under actual field conditions who have known or suspected motives to distort the item responses to create a particular impression (Butcher & Han, in press).

3. Interpretation of the MMPI and MMPI-2 in forensic cases generally follows strategies developed from research in other settings. We simply apply the behavioral correlates that have been established for particular scale elevations and profile patterns that were originally developed in other contexts assuming that these scales have the same "meaning" in all settings. There is substantial empirical support for the expectation that scale meanings generalize across settings (Butcher & Williams, 1992; Graham, 1993; Love & Peck, 1987; McCreary, Naliboff, & Cohen, 1989) and therefore are likely to apply in personal injury settings (Hersch & Alexander, 1990; Patrick, 1988). However, *a great deal more specificity with respect to how well behavioral correlates of MMPI-2 scales and indexes actually apply could be explored more fully in the settings in which the instrument is used.* Future research should be directed toward further exploring the specific behavioral relationships of pertinent MMPI-2 variables. Studies involving establishing behavioral correlates for common profile patterns (even validity scale configurations) need to be developed (see research by Trabin, Rader, & Cummings, 1987; Wilson & Walker, 1990).

4. Questions regarding the impact of litigation on the intensification, continuation of physical symptoms, or both require further study (Binder, Trimble, & McNiel, 1991; Guest & Drummond, 1992; Horlick, Cameron, Siror, Bhalerao, & Baltzan, 1984; Sprehe, 1984; Tait, Chibnall, & Richardson, 1990). As noted at the beginning of this chapter in the interesting quote from Erichsen in 1882, the actual state of court involvement seems to have a great impact on symptom expression. Many medicolegal professionals believe that the "green poultice" operates to maintain symptoms until monetary settlement is reached. Yet, this persistent impression has not been sufficiently explored in long-term follow-up. Long-term, postinjury adjustment, and postlitigation adjustment require further study to clarify the role that motivational factors play in personal injury litigation (Gallagher, Rauh, Haugh, Milhous, 1989; Moore, Armentraut, Parker, & Kivlahan, 1986; Turner, Herron, & Weiner, 1986). What do MMPI-2 profiles look like for similar injuries but in which no litigation is in process? Similarly, what is the impact of court settlement on symptom expression? Do certain profile configurations respond to change more with treatment (Kleinke & Spangler, 1988)? Long-term follow-up on cases, after they have reached settlement, could be conducted to evaluate this question. Such research could have great benefit for conducting psychological evaluations in the forensic process.

References

American Psychological Association. (1986). *American Psychological Association guidelines for computer-based tests and interpretations*. Washington, DC: Author.

American Psychological Association. (1992). *Ethical principles of psychologists and code of conduct*. Washington DC: Author.

Babitsky, S., & Mangraviti, J. (1993). *Litigating stress cases in worker's compensation*. New York: John Wiley.

Berry, D., Baer, R. A., & Harris, M. J. (1991). Detection of malingering on the MMPI: A meta-analysis. *Clinical Psychology Review, 11*, 585-598.

Binder, R. L., Trimble, M. R., & McNiel, D. E. (1991). Is money a cure? Follow-up of litigants in England. *Bulletin of the American Academy of Psychiatry and the Law, 19*, 151-160.

Bradley, L., Prokop, C. K., Margolis, R., & Gentry, W. D. (1978). Multivariate analyses of the MMPI profiles of low back pain patients. *Journal of Behavioral Medicine, 1*, 253-272.

Butcher, J. N. (1985). Assessing psychological characteristics of personal injury and worker's compensation litigants. *Clinical Psychologist, 38*, 84-87.

Butcher, J. N. (1993). *User's guide for the MMPI-2 Minnesota report: Adult clinical system*. (Rev. ed.). Minneapolis: National Computer Systems.

Butcher, J. N. (in press). *Handbook of international MMPI-2 research and clinical applications*. Minneapolis: University of Minnesota Press.

Butcher, J. N., Han, K. (in press). *Development of an MMPI-2 scale to assess the presentation of self in a superlative manner: The S scale*. In J. N. Butcher & C. D. Spielberger (Eds.), Advances in personality assessment (Vol. 10). Hillsdale, NJ: LEA Press.

Butcher, J. N., & Harlow, T. (1987). Psychological assessment in personal injury cases. In A. Hess, & I. Wiener (Eds.), *Handbook of forensic psychology* (pp. 128-154). New York: John Wiley.

Butcher, J. N., & Pancheri, P. (1976). *Handbook of cross-national MMPI research*. Minneapolis: University of Minnesota Press.

Butcher, J. N., Williams, C. L. (1992). *Essentials of MMPI-2 and MMPI-A interpretation*. Minneapolis: University of Minnesota Press.

Conte, A. (1990). *Sexual harassment in the workplace: Law and practice*. New York: John Wiley.

Eisner, D. A. (1984). Mental injury in workers' compensation: An examination of job stress. *American Journal of Forensic Psychology, 2*, 101-111.

Erichsen, J. E. (1882). *Concussion of the spine*. New York: Bermingham.

Eyde, L., Kowal, D., & Fishburne, F. J. (1991). The validity of computer based interpretations of MMPI. In T. B. Gutkin & S. L. Wise (Eds.), *The computer and the decision making process* (pp. 75-123). Hillsdale, NJ: Lawrence Erlbaum.

Fink, A., & Butcher, J. N. (1972). Reducing objections to personality inventories with special instructions. *Educational and Psychological Measurement, 27*, 631-639.

Flamer, S., & Buch, W. (1992, May). *Differential diagnosis of post traumatic stress disorder in injured workers: Evaluating the MMPI-2*. Paper presented at the 27th Annual Symposium on Recent Developments in the Use of the MMPI (MMPI-2 & MMPI-A), Minneapolis, MN.

Fordyce, W. E. (1979). Use of the MMPI in the assessment of chronic pain. In J. N. Butcher, W. G. Dahlstrom, M. D. Gynther, & S. Schofield (Eds.), *Clinical Notes on the MMPI*. Minneapolis, MN: National Computer Systems.

Gallagher, R. M., Rauh, V., Haugh, L. D., & Milhous, R. (1989). Determinants of return-to-work among low back pain patients. *Pain, 39*, 55-67.

Goldstein, R. L. (1986). Psychiatrists and personal injury litigation. *American Journal of Psychiatry, 143*, 1487-1488.

Goodman, H. (1993). *Orthopedic disability and expert opinion.* New York: John Wiley.Graham, J. R. (1993). *MMPI-2: Assessing personality and psychopathology* (2nd ed.). New York: Oxford University Press.

Graham, J., Watts, D., & Timbrook, R. (1991). Detecting fake good and fake bad MMPI-2 profiles. *Journal of Personality Assessment, 57,* 264-277.

Guest, G. H., & Drummond, P. D. (1992). Effect of compensation on emotional state and disability in chronic back pain. *Pain, 48,* 301-311.

Henrichs, T. F. (1981). Using the MMPI in medical consultation. In J. N. Butcher, W. G. Dahlstrom, M. D. Gynther, & S. Schofield (Eds.), *Clinical Notes on the MMPI.* Minneapolis, MN: National Computer Systems.

Hersch, P. D., & Alexander, R. W. (1990). MMPI profile patterns of emotional disability claimants. *Journal of Clinical Psychology, 46,* 795-799.

Hoffman, B. F. (1986). "Psychiatrists and personal injury litigation": Dr. Hoffman replies. *American Journal of Psychiatry, 143,* 1488.

Horlick, L., Cameron, R., Siror, W., Bhalerao, U., & Baltzan, R. (1984). The effects of education and group discussion in the post myocardial infarction patient. *Journal of Psychosomatic Research, 28,* 485-492.

Jarvis, P. E., & Hamlin, D. (1984). Avoiding pitfalls in compensation evaluations. *International Journal of Clinical Neuropsychology, 6,* 214-216.

Keller, L. S., & Butcher, J. N. (1991). *Use of the MMPI-2 with chronic pain patients.* Minneapolis: University of Minnesota Press.

Kleinke, C. L., & Spangler, A. S. (1988). Predicting treatment outcome of chronic back pain patients in a multidicsiplinary pain clinic: Methodological issues and treatment implications. *Pain, 33,* 41-48.

Kreutzer, J. S., Harris-Marwitz, J., & Myers, S. L. (1990). Neuropsychological issues in litigation following traumatic brain injury. Special section: Forensic-legal medical issues of neuropsychology. *Neuropsychology, 4,* 249-259.

Lasky, H. (1993). *Psychiatric claims in workers' compensation and civil litigation.* New York: John Wiley.

Lees-Haley, P. R. (1986). How to detect malingerers in the workplace. *Personnel Journal, 65,* 106-108.

Li, S. M., Li, L. M., & Rodriguez-de-Souza, L. F. (1991). Uso do MMPI a avaliacao de pacientes com sindrome de dor cronica [Use of MMPI on the assessment of the chronic pain syndrome patients]. *Arquivos de Neuro Psiquiatria, 49,* 426-429.

Love, A. W., & Peck, C. L. (1987). The MMPI and psychological factors in chronic low back pain: A review. *Pain, 28,* 1-12.

McCreary, C., Naliboff, B., & Cohen, M. (1989). A comparison of clinically and empirically derived MMPI groupings in low back pain patients. *Journal of Clinical Psychology, 45,* 560-570.

Moore, J. E., Armentrout, D. P., Parker, J. C., & Kivlahan, D. R. (1986). Empirically derived pain-patient MMPI subgroups: Prediction of treatment outcome. *Journal of Behavioral Medicine, 9,* 51-63.

Moreland, K. (1987). Computerized psychological assessment. What's available. In J. N. Butcher (Ed.), *Computerized psychological assessment* (pp. 26-49). New York: Basic Books.

Osborne, D. (1979). Use of the MMPI with medical patients. In J. N. Butcher (Ed.), *New developments in the use of the MMPI* (pp. 141-163). Minneapolis: University of Minnesota Press.

Patrick, J. (1988). Personality characteristics of work-ready workers' compensation clients. *Journal of Clinical Psychology, 44,* 1009-1012.

Pope, K. S., Butcher, J. N., & Seelen, J. (1993). *The MMPI, MMPI-2, & MMPI-A in court.* Washington, DC: American Psychological Association.

Rader, C. M. (1984). A psychological profile of industrially injured workers. *Occupational Health Nursing, 32,* 577-580.

Repko, G. R., & Cooper, R. (1983). A study of the average worker's compensation case. *Journal of Clinical Psychology, 39,* 287-295.

Roberts, A. H. (1984). *Medical applications of the MMPI: An explanatory guide for physicians.* Topics in MMPI interpretation [Workshop material]. Department of Conferences, University of Minnesota.

Schretlen, D. J. (1988). The use of psychological tests to identify malingered symptoms of mental disorder. *Clinical Psychology Review, 8,* 451-476.

Shaffer, J. W. (1981). Using the MMPI to evaluate mental impairment in disability determination. In J. N. Butcher, W. G. Dahlstrom, M. D. Gynther, & S. Schofield (Eds.), *Clinical notes on the MMPI.* Minneapolis, MN: National Computer Systems.

Shaffer, J. W., Nussbaum, K., & Little, J. M. (1972). MMPI profiles of disability insurance claimants. *American Journal of Psychiatry, 129,* 403-407.

Sprehe, D. J. (1984). Workers' compensation: A psychiatric follow-up study. *International Journal of Law and Psychiatry, 7,* 165-178.

Sternbach, R. A., & Timmermans, G. (1975). Personality changes associated with reduction of pain. *Pain, 1,* 177-181.

Tait, R. C., Chibnall, J. T., & Richardson, W. D. (1990). Litigation and employment status: Effects on patients with chronic pain. *Pain, 43,* 37-46.

Trabin, T., Rader, C., & Cummings, C. (1987). A comparison of pain management outcomes for disability compensation and non-compensation patients. *Psychology and Health, 1,* 341-351.

Turner, J. A., Herron, L., & Weiner, P. (1986). Utility of the MMPI Pain Assessment Index in predicting outcome after lumbar surgery. *Journal of Clinical Psychology, 42,* 764-769.

Weiner, I. B. (1987). Writing forensic reports. In I. B. Weiner & A. K. Hess (Eds.), *Handbook of forensic psychology* (pp. 511-528). New York: John Wiley.

Weissman, H. N. (1985). Psycholegal standards and the role of psychological assessment in personal injury litigation. *Behavioral Sciences and the Law, 3,* 135-147.

Wilson, J. P., & Walker, A. J. (1990). Toward an MMPI trauma profile *Journal of Traumatic Stress, 3,* 151-168.

Ziskin, J. (1981). The use of the MMPI in forensic settings. In J. N. Butcher, W. G. Dahlstrom, M. D. Gynther, & S. Schofield (Eds), *Clinical notes on the MMPI* (Vol. 9, pp. 1-13). Minneapolis, MN: National Computer Systems.

Use of the MMPI and the MMPI-2 in Forensic Neuropsychological Evaluations

LINDA D. NELSON

Neuropsychologists recognize that virtually any alteration of central nervous system (CNS) activity can affect an individual's personality. When the individual being examined is a litigant, then any change in personality may become a pertinent issue in his or her lawsuit. Examples of court cases in which testimony regarding personality change may be requested include accidents resulting in closed head injuries, questions of competency in the elderly, effects of solvents exposure, and some criminal acts. Each case holds in common that CNS damage is suspected. In some, direct effects of brain damage may be displayed in terms of reduced motivation, depression, anxiety, or irritability. In others, personality change is not a direct result of brain damage, but a reaction to its debilitating effects. Determining the type and degree of personality change following a known or suspected organic event thus becomes a major objective of the forensic neuropsychological exam.

As one of the most widely used, well-researched objective personality inventories, the MMPI/MMPI-2 has traditionally offered a strong empirical basis for interpretations. Of particular importance in the forensic arena is that clinical interpretations be objectively determined and empirically validated. The MMPI/MMPI-2 offers both (Pope, Butcher, & Seelen, 1993). Measurable descriptions of people's problems and symptoms can be obtained from the MMPI/MMPI-2 and systematically compared against a standardized, normative population, specific normative groups (e.g., age-based, organic) or the individual's own baseline level. Moreover, test results easily translate from clinical to lay terminology (Finn & Butcher, 1991). In short, there are many advantages to including the MMPI, and now the restandardized MMPI-2, in forensic evaluations when personality functioning is called into question. Because general comparability between the MMPI and MMPI-2 has been supported (e.g., Ben-Porath, 1990; Ben-Porath & Butcher, 1989a, 1989b; Graham, 1990), statements made here regarding the MMPI are assumed to be applicable to the restandardized version.

This chapter provides an overview regarding use of the MMPI/MMPI-2 in forensic evaluations of individuals who are known to be, or are suspected of being, neuropsychologically impaired. The empirical literature on the relation between neuropsychological impairment and scores on the MMPI/MMPI-2 is reviewed. The potential roles and limitations of the MMPI/MMPI-2 in a forensic neuropsychological test battery are discussed. Directions for further research in this area are identified.

THE ROLE OF THE
NEUROPSYCHOLOGY EXPERT

When a neuropsychologist is called into a court case as an expert witness, one of the tasks required is to help the trier of fact reach more accurate conclusions. In this role, the neuropsychology expert must be qualified before the court in the matter about which he or she will testify. To this point, the rules of jurisprudence are specific (Blau, 1993).

> An expert is one who is so qualified by study or experience that he [she] can form a definite opinion of his [her] own respecting a division of science, branch of art, or department of trade concerning which persons having no particular training or special study are incapable of forming accurate opinions or of deducing correct conclusions. (p. 3)

In *Ethical Principles of Psychologists,* the American Psychological Association (1992) supports this definition of expert witness by requiring that

Psychologists' forensic assessments, recommendations, and reports are based on
information and techniques (including personal interviews of the individual
when appropriate) sufficient to provide appropriate substantiation for their
findings. (Principle 7.02)

In rendering an opinion, the neuropsychology expert frequently addresses
questions regarding effects of brain damage—effects that often involve an
emotional component. Did the head injury produce a specific personality
change? Was the personality change a direct effect of brain damage or a
reaction to ensuing impairment? What was the individual like before the head
injury? Which personality factors represent long-standing traits, predating
the traumatic event? Which personality factors are new, supporting a change
from a prior condition?

Reasonable probability and base rates. In answering these questions, the neuropsychology expert speaks in terms of reasonable probability, rather than
conjecture or speculation (Blau, 1993, p. 3). One basis for statements of
reasonable probability stems from consideration of base rates. The clinician,
in interpreting a test or information obtained from clinical interview, must
be aware of base rates of the behavior or event with which he or she is dealing
(Meehl, 1973). According to Reber (1985), base rates represent the normal
frequency of occurrence of any response and are used as foundations against
which to evaluate effects of specific manipulations or events (e.g., head
trauma). When considering base rates as they apply to personality effects,
actual quantitative knowledge may appear to be lacking. In these cases, rather
than being unavailable, base rate information is simply underused (Faust &
Ziskin, 1988).

Accessing base rate information comes, in part, from computing data based
on cross-validational research (e.g., Miller, 1993) and estimating base rates
involves nothing more than systematic recording of specific types of information and subsequent tabulation (Meehl, 1973; Miller, 1993). The argument
raised by Faust and Ziskin (1988) makes clear that neuropsychology experts
must be ready to report base rate information, when available, and to justify
the methodology used to procure these data.

Reasonable probability and clinical experience. Research indicates that clinicians in general have trouble learning from experience (Garb, 1992). In 34
studies reviewed by Garb (1989), experienced clinicians were unable to make

more valid judgments than graduate students or less-experienced clinicians. In one example, Aronson and Akamatsu (1981) had first-year clinical psychology graduate students use MMPI results to describe symptoms and personality traits of patients. Ratings were more accurate after students completed a course on the MMPI, but did not further improve following a year-long assessment and therapy practicum. These results were then used to argue the relative ineffectiveness of clinical experience (e.g., practicum experience) on clinical judgment. The implication was that clinicians formulate opinions based on "clinical experience" no better than untrained individuals or the general lay public.

A major reason clinicians may fail to learn from experience relates to problems in processing information (Garb, 1992). When assimilating results of a neuropsychological exam, for example, neuropsychologists must take in a considerable amount of data. They then compare these data to normative standards, base rates, and to the individual's own baseline levels of functioning. In this process, inferences are made based on factors such as motivation or interest. Although difficult to measure by traditional test standards, these dynamic factors (referred to as genotypic by Meehl, 1973) may clearly affect test performance or adaptation to real life. As such, neuropsychologists assign weight to these factors in their overall interpretation of effects (or lack thereof) due to brain damage.

It is the more subjective aspect of clinical decision making that relies heavily on clinical experience, yet is most subject to challenge in the courtroom. Failure to check interpretations against available standards (e.g., actual test outcome) deprives clinical decision making of a necessary process. Further, failure to modify interpretations following such feedback can seriously lower the accuracy of judgments (Arkes, 1981; Kleinmuntz, 1984; Leary & Miller, 1986; Turk & Salovey, 1988). Neuropsychology experts recognize that clinical experience, by itself, does not result in the formation of an opinion based on reasonable probability. To make such statements, reliance on additional standards of comparison is necessary.

The Decision-Making Process

A major outcome of forensic neuropsychological examinations is the delineation of type and degree of effects (or lack thereof) due to brain damage (Guilmette, Faust, Hart, & Arkes, 1990). When cognitive effects are considered, research on brain/behavior relationships shows accuracy rates of 88%

using the Luria-Nebraska Neuropsychological Battery (Kane, Parsons, Goldstein, & Moses, 1987; Kane, Sweet, Golden, Parsons, & Moses, 1981) and from 82% to 95% for the Halstead-Reitan Battery (Kane et al., 1987; Kane et al., 1981). Interrater agreement on these batteries was supported at levels ranging from 94.3% (Halstead) to 98.6% (Luria), with an average reliability rating across the two of 83% (Diamant & Hijmen, 1981; Kane et al., 1987). The task of experienced neuropsychologists/judges in these studies was to classify individuals on the basis of test performance as brain damaged or non-brain damaged (e.g., psychiatric).

When more subtle, noncognitive (emotional) effects are considered, results tend to be less encouraging and interpretations regarding brain-behavior relationships become increasingly more complicated. As early as 1904, Adolf Meyer saw the need for caution when making judgments regarding psychiatric disability following brain damage. Sixty-four years later Lishman (1968) lamented that "current techniques for assessing brain damage—psychological, radiographic, electroencephalographic, etc.—have failed to add greatly to our knowledge, [even though] head injury material should in theory prove ideal for working towards an understanding of the connections between cerebral disorder and psychiatric disability" (p. 373). Prigatano, in 1992, asks whether we have come any further in being able to distinguish brain-behavior relationships, given improved methodology for examining emotional and motivational changes, sophisticated data analyses, and improved standardized tests, such as the MMPI/MMPI-2.

It would appear that clinicians are becoming better in the *descriptive* process, especially given the more recent rapid technological advancements in measuring neuropathological changes in the brain (e.g., Positron Emission Tomography, Functional Magnetic Resonance Imaging, Magnetic Resonance Spectroscopy). Defining exactly which cerebral mechanism accounts for which personality change in these patients, in a causal sense, poses a greater challenge (Prigatano, 1992).

The implication is that personality tests, such as the MMPI/MMPI-2, are part of the clinical decision process used to describe emotional dysfunction following brain damage. The intended outcome of this process frequently includes assessing the type and degree of emotional change (e.g., before and following a cerebral event). The decision-making process used to arrive at this outcome compares the patient or litigant's performance to published norms, base rate information, his or her own average level of performance, and premorbid levels of functioning.

In evaluating for effects of brain damage, the clinician must consider that disturbances of neural tissue may lead to immediate and permanent personality change, with the additional possibility of indirect effects on emotional and motivational responding (Prigatano, 1992). Teasing out the apparent interplay between direct organic effects and reaction to one's impairment involves a complex decision-making process. An apparent lack of emotional difficulties, for example, may reflect an organic impairment in the capacity for self insight (Prigatano & Schacter, 1991). This type of compromise is not readily indicated through personality test results alone. Rather, it is made through careful synthesis of all information presented, including that obtained based on self-report testing, family members' views of the patient, and observations of affect. Conceptualizing which affective disturbances are a direct manifestation of brain damage (e.g., limbic injury) and which are in response to environmental demands takes in multiple reporting methods (e.g., self and relative reports), direct observation of task performance, information based on clinical interview, data from cognitive indexes, and personality test results.

Mechanisms of secondary gain. Whether emotional difficulties are associated with the apparent brain damage or with mechanisms of secondary gain is another question routinely addressed in this context. Regarding the latter, Garb (1992) indicated that validity of diagnoses made by neuropsychologists depends heavily on the accurate detection of such factors as malingering or factitious disorders. Factitious disorder involves secondary gain for maintaining a "sick role" and is frequently superimposed on a severe personality disorder (Reber, 1985). This disorder may take on the appearance of memory loss, dissociative symptoms, or conversion reactions. Held in common is that symptoms from both psychiatric conditions are voluntarily produced with no more obvious aim than to reinforce the role of "patient" played by the individual.

Both malingering and factitious disorders also include symptoms that support a diagnosis of organic condition. Frequent complaints of memory problems, trouble concentrating, low energy, or visuospatial difficulties accompany neurological disorders. These complaints can easily be confused with psychogenic symptoms, such as headaches, "blackouts," and memory or sensory problems, often seen in emotional disorders (Lezak, 1983). In the forensic arena, a task of the neuropsychologist is to assess for the possibility of functional, nonorganic conditions, and to determine whether sufficient empirical evidence exists to support them. A major aspect of differential diagnosis in these cases requires distinguishing between psychogenic (functional) problems, those that have an organic base, and problems that represent a reaction to debilitating impairments caused by the organic event.

In the context of a neuropsychological exam, the MMPI/MMPI-2 may be used to help address the nature and extent of emotional and motivational changes following brain damage. According to a meta-analysis conducted by Berry, Baer, and Harris (1991), both versions of the test provide sensitive indicators of malingering and other secondary gain factors (e.g., overreporting, underreporting). In the following section, research findings related to how the MMPI/ MMPI-2 may be integrated into the neuropsychological exam process to directly examine organic and functional components of brain damage will be discussed. New approaches to elicit such information from the MMPI-2 will also be discussed as a means of better defining emotional symptoms following brain damage.

Research Findings

EARLY STUDIES USING THE MMPI

Early research using the MMPI to identify brain correlates included construction of content scales. Friedman (1950) developed one of the earliest, Parietal-frontal (Pf), followed 2 years later by the Caudality (Ca) scale (Williams, 1952). Each was designed to predict the presence/absence of brain damage, as well as discriminate anterior from posterior lesions. Results of cross-validation studies were mixed, with some investigators demonstrating the scales' ability to distinguish focal damage (Dahlstrom & Welsh, 1960; Meier, 1969), whereas others failed to uphold such support (Reitan, 1976).

Despite mixed reviews, development of MMPI content scales became an important first step toward measuring emotional effects of brain damage. Additional research using subjects classified by both caudality (anterior, posterior) and laterality (right, left hemisphere) dimensions was conducted. When MMPI correlates of localized cerebral lesions were examined, results showed evidence of emotional disturbance, but the differential findings reported earlier (e.g., Friedman, 1950) did not hold (Dikmen & Reitan, 1974). A series of five studies later conducted by Dikmen and Reitan (1977) led to the conclusion that MMPI variables may be more closely related to adaptive ability deficits than to lesion location: Patients with impaired functions were found to have more difficulty in emotional adjustment than patients who were relatively intact. Similar to Gainotti's (1972) results, Dikmen and Reitan (1977) found greater depressive reactions using the MMPI in aphasic than in nonaphasic patients with left hemisphere lesions.

Beginning in 1964, investigators (Hovey, 1964; Wiggins, 1966) began to examine MMPI items that they believed most likely represented neurologically relevant items. Hovey's five-item MMPI content scale (CNS scale) was composed of items related to health issues (e.g., No. 51: "I am in just as good physical health as most of my friends") and a score of 4 out of 5 formed the cut-off for judging "organicity." Early results were promising, leading Zimmerman (1965) to conclude that "Hovey's five MMPI items [could] identify the permanent or residual impairment due to severe brain damage" (Lezak, 1983). The scale was short lived, however, when later results were unable to discriminate organically impaired individuals from normal controls (Weingold, Dawson, & Kael, 1965) or from individuals with purely functional disorders (Maier & Abidin, 1967).

In an attempt to discriminate organic from psychiatric groups, Watson, Thomas, Anderson, and Felling (1968) took a slightly different approach. They developed rules based on the T scores from the standard scales plus the value of an "organic sign index." The organic sign index (OSI) was computed according to the formula OSI=(D + Mf + Sc) - (Pd + Ma) based on all raw scores with K-correction added. Using this formula, type of scale and degree of scale elevation were both taken into consideration. A decision was then made on each profile to call the disorder either schizophrenic or organic. Unfortunately, results only generalized to males, the sample used in the study by Watson et al. (1968). Applying these rules to females substantially lowered the accuracy of predictions (Dahlstrom, Welsh, & Dahlstrom, 1975).

The need to differentiate organic samples from schizophrenic ones came, in large part, from the degree of symptom overlap between the two conditions. Organically impaired individuals, such as those with schizophrenia, may exhibit cognitive disturbances and bizarre mentation. Percentage of codes from male Minnesota neurologic inpatients ($N = 202$), for example, showed the most frequently occurring high point to be Scales D (25.8%), Hs (19.5%), and Sc (13.7%). The highest second point in the two-point code type included Scales D (15.4%), Hs (15.2%), and Hy (15.1%). As reported by Brantner (cited in Dahlstrom et al., 1975) these Hathaway (1947) code types reflected high rates of depression and bizarre mentation among brain-impaired individuals, with characteristic patterns also including a high degree of physical symptomatology. Only physical problems (Scale Hs) and depression (Scale D) emerged as correlates of neurological disorders; these correlates were not seen to the same degree in psychiatric populations. These findings led to the conclusion by some researchers that the two areas (physical problems and depression) may provide differential rates of prediction for neurological and psychiatric conditions.

Adopting what he believed to be primary symptoms of organic involvement, Wiggins (1966) later developed the Organic Symptoms (ORG) scale. High ORG scale scores were produced by individuals who admit to headaches, nausea, dizziness, loss of mobility and coordination, loss of consciousness, poor concentration and memory, speaking and reading difficulty, poor muscular control, skin sensations, and abnormal hearing and smell.

Later research by Lachar and Alexander (1978) found elevated ORG scales in organic samples, but with a substantially different interpretation. Lachar and Alexander saw organics as admitting to a variety of sensory, motor, or general somatic concerns that may be related to psychological discomfort, general malaise, and reduced effectiveness in completing tasks. It was felt that clients who obtained high ORG scale scores may present physical symptoms that are associated with emotional conflict, such as problematic headache or back pain. The psychosomatic component of their condition thus became an aspect of test interpretation.

The difference between intepretations made by Wiggins (1966) and those of Lachar and Alexander (1978) highlighted an important issue when assessing individuals with neurological conditions. Similar ORG scale correlates could be demonstrated across studies, but marked differences in etiology (organic vs. functional) were evident. Wiggins's (1966) interpretation described high ORG scores as symptoms of an organic condition. Lachar and Alexander's (1978) interpretation focused on their reactive or functional component. The scale itself was unable to distinguish between the two etiologies (Levitt, 1989). Although it was clear that organically impaired individuals endorsed high rates of physical symptoms on the MMPI, interpreting this information as a sign of personality change was more difficult.

Shaw and Matthews (1965) recognized the challenge of distinguising functional from organic change when they constructed the Pseudo-Neurologic scale. This MMPI content scale was designed to identify patients whose neurological complaints were not supported by positive neurological findings. The scale consisted of 17 items selected primarily from Scales Hs, D, Pd, and Pt. A cutting score of 7 was established as suggestive of brain damage and

81% of the patients were successfully classified on this basis. Cross-validation studies provided mixed results, with adequate discriminant validity ($p < .01$), but high false negative rates (pseudoneurologic patients misclassified as "brain damaged") and false positive errors (Lezak, 1983).

In summarizing the literature concerning the MMPI and neuropsychological dysfunction, Farr and Martin (1988) indicated that primary efforts to distinguish brain damaged from either normal or psychiatric populations have produced mixed results. In their view, "these efforts have met with enough success to keep interest in the endeavor alive and with enough frustration to discourage primary adoption of any specific MMPI scale or index" (p. 214). The unsuccessful search for brain damage indicators using the standard clinical scales has led researchers to develop special scales, formulae, keys, and so on, as a means of more effectively distinguishing particular brain-damaged groups.

This section was not intended to provide an exhaustive review of the MMPI literature in terms of neuropsychological dysfunction. That literature has been covered extensively elsewhere (e.g., Farr & Martin, 1988; Mack, 1979). The intent was to highlight early MMPI research involving key approaches and special organicity scales that laid the groundwork for current use of the MMPI-2 in neurologic populations. The following section deals with more recent research using the MMPI-2 in this population by focusing on the methodological approaches currently in use and their application to clinical and forensic settings.

RECENT STUDIES USING THE MMPI-2

Neurocorrection. One line of research that has developed over the past 5 years builds on the earlier content scale approach. Termed *neurocorrection* by some, this method involves constructing "neurologically related" item sets derived statistically (e.g., through factor analysis, discriminative power analysis), rationally (e.g., through content validation studies), or by a combination of the two methods.

The idea in this approach is to develop a set of MMPI/MMPI-2 items that appear to be descriptive of neurologic dysfunction, then to examine the impact of this item set on obtained MMPI-2 profiles. Items that differentiate closed head injury patients from normal controls comprise the "correction factor" recommended for use in scoring the MMPI/MMPI-2.

What this method offers neuropsychologists working in clinical and foren-sic settings is a means of scoring the MMPI/MMPI-2 profile in the standard manner, then rescoring it after eliminating item responses from the neurologic symptom set. This "adjustment" effectively removes content related to physi-cal and cognitive sequelae of head injury, leaving a "purer" estimate of psychological functioning in these patients. Also, clinicians are able to deter-mine the relative impact these neurologic symptoms had on overall test performance (e.g., in terms of scale score elevations).

In a series of studies, Alfano and colleagues (Alfano, Finlayson, Stearns, & Neilson, 1990; Alfano, Finlayson, Stearns, & MacLennan, 1991; Alfano, Paniak, & Finlayson, 1992) derived what they termed a Neurobehavioral Scale. The authors began by identifying 44 MMPI items judged neurologic in content by a group of 18 medical specialists. Of the 44 items, 40 were contained on the MMPI-2. This item set was then examined in terms of frequency of item endorsement in a sample of 102 closed head injury patients. Of the 44 items, 24 were found to be endorsed in a pathological direction (i.e., endorsed by ≥ 30% of the sample). Applying principal components analysis to the 24-item set produced seven factors that accounted for 62% of the total variance.

A final set of two factors was derived, one of which was labelled the "Neurobehavioral Factor" because it consisted of complaints related to poor attention, sensory or motor dysfunction, and problems performing major life activities (adaptive functions). Twelve of the 13 items on this scale are con-tained on the MMPI-2. Like its name, the second factor, termed "Emotional-Somatic," had a psychological base. After performing the "neurocorrection approach" (i.e., removing item endorsements related to Neurobehavioral factor items) results showed a distinct alteration in the appearance of mean MMPI profile configurations in the closed head injury group. In the neuro-corrected version, elevation of the Sc scale dropped a mean of nine T-score points and Scale D dropped an average of five points.

Gass (1991) took a similar approach in constructing his MMPI-2 correction factor. Gass's sample of 75, primarily male, closed head injury patients was similar to Alfano et al.'s (1992) in terms of age and educational level. Unlike Alfano, Gass tested his subjects about 4 years after their head injury; Alfano's group was tested 2 years postinjury. Instead of content validity analyses, Gass examined discriminant validity using chi-square analyses on data from the closed head injury group and normal adults selected from the MMPI-2 standardization sample. Based on these analyses, items were found that dif-ferentiated the two groups and, like Alfano, Gass then applied principal components analysis to this item set. Twenty-three items were derived, of which eight matched items from Alfano's Neurobehavioral factor. Gass defined two factors on the basis of these results, one consisting of neurologic complaints (e.g., cognitive inefficiency, weakness, speech problems, tremor, and movement problems) and the other whose content was primarily psychiatric problems (e.g., peculiar experiences, interpersonal distrust, social discomfort). Fourteen items loaded on Gass's neurological factor; five items loaded on the emotional factor. Levels of variance from each were similar to those reported by Alfano et al. (1992).

The issue of base rates. Interestingly, results based on the neurocorrection approaches (above) are similar to those reported as base rates in non-head injured personal injury cases (Lees-Haley, 1992). Of Lees-Haley's sample, 83% reported attention problems and 53% had symptoms of numbness, both of which were defined as "neurologic" symptoms by Alfano. Subjects in Lees-Haley's study also reported that they cried easily (89%), felt like smashing things (78%), experienced dizzy spells (50%), and had headaches (91%), similar to complaints represented by Alfano's Emotional-Somatic factor. In other words, it would appear that a fairly large number of litigants with no known history of brain damage report symptoms similar to patients with known head injuries. Overlapping symptoms include cognitive (poor attention), medical (headaches, numbness), and emotional (aggressive tendencies) problems and may be cited as evidence that the patient has sustained neuropsychological impairment. As Lees-Haley pointed out, such information may also be used by the expert to form descriptive labels, such as psychiatric symptoms "due to other general [organic] medical conditions" (American Psychiatric Association, 1994), thus increasing the potential for false positive interpretations regarding the effects of "brain damage."

As research in the direction of neurocorrection using the MMPI-2 continues, the matter of base rates may pose a problem. Weiner, in Chapter 3 of this volume, addressed the need to consider the rate of false negative/positive findings and test sensitivity/specificity when questioning the relative utility of base rate information over test results. As research progresses using the neurocorrection approach, its efficiency in assessing events common to criterion (brain damaged) populations, as well as non-brain damaged populations (e.g., psychiatric, malingerers), will need to be examined directly. An important aspect of the neurocorrection method in this regard is that a combination of test items comprises each factor (neurological and emotional). As the authors have argued, this combination can effectively alter the MMPI-2 profile when results are removed and the test is rescored. Hence, singling out items from Alfano's Neurobehavioral factor or Gass's Neurologic Complaints factor and suggesting that their rates of endorsement predict no better than base rates may be premature. Nonetheless, direct study of the psychometric properties noted here is needed to adequately address the base rate problem.

Response distortion. In their meta-analytic review of 28 studies published from 1947 to 1989, Berry et al. (1991) stated that one of the most effective indicators for detection of overreporting of symptoms continues to be the F scale. Lees-Haley (1992), administering the MMPI-2 to a sample of personal injury litigants, reported that cutting scores on the F and the F – K index were lower than earlier reported, but accurately classified malingering from non-malingering subjects, nonetheless. Lees-Haley's interpretation was that litigants may potentially underreport preexisting problems (problems that pre-date injuries) and that, together with a tendency to overreport current symptoms, relatively lower F scale elevations result. Berry, in Chapter 4 of this volume, points out the importance of examining results based on the MMPI-2 Variable Response Inconsistency (VRIN) scale to help detect random responding and thus aid in identifying the source of an elevated F.

Certainly, there are a number of circumstances in which it would appear advantageous to exaggerate or even fabricate psychological symptoms. In a medicolegal context, in which possible consequences to a legal action include high monetary awards, avoidance of criminal prosecution, attainment of worker's compensation, and so forth, motivation to produce or exaggerate symptoms may be high. The impact of receiving detailed information on "closed head injury" and/or MMPI-2 validity scales on the malingering response was investigated by Lamb and colleagues (Lamb, Berry, Wetter, & Baer, 1994). In an analog design using college students, the authors found that receiving specific information on closed head injury produced multiple mean scale elevations on 7 of 10 clinical scales (not Pd, Mf, or Ma) and one validity scale (F). In contrast, the group receiving information on validity scales tended to keep the F scale relatively low. Based on overall results, the authors concluded that "coaching" may have an impact on simulation of closed head injury on the MMPI-2.

As noted earlier in this chapter, making the distinction between malingered from genuine psychological symptoms in cases in which patients with known or suspected brain damage are examined is a critical part of the decision-making process. Berry discusses this issue in Chapter 4. A cautionary note in this regard is that base rate information and sufficient cutting scores have yet to be established empirically to develop greater confidence in clinical interpretations. In their absence, the likelihood of malingering or factitious conditions represented in MMPI-2 results needs to be considered and confirmed by convergent data from other sources and methods (e.g., clinical interview information, additional, modified test procedures, behavior during testing, reports by significant others about the patient, prior history obtained through clinical record review, and so on).

Coaching. "Coaching," as an attempt to educate litigants on the content and purpose of tests such as the MMPI/MMPI-2, is an additional consideration to test interpretation. Ben-Porath (1994) pointed out the delicate balance between research using these strategies and potential misuse of this knowledge base in the public domain. The implication is that analog studies that involve coaching procedures may inadvertently guide and aid individuals who wish to distort MMPI-2 results (Ben-Porath, 1994; Berry, Lamb, Wetter, Baer, & Widiger, 1994; Pope et al., 1993). The necessity of coaching research for better understanding of malingering effects is cogently made by these authors. Alternatively, the ethical dilemma this research design presents in terms of potential misuse must be kept in mind in the context of medicolegal exams.

Neuropsychologists often face the challenge of accurately detecting intentional symptom production (e.g., malingering, factitious disorders) by litigants involved in tort action suits, criminal cases, or disability claims (e.g., review by Franzen, Iverson, & McCracken, 1990). MMPI-2 indices sensitive and, at times vulnerable, to response distortion will enhance clinical interpretations. Used together with additional screening procedures (noted earlier), MMPI-2 indices, offer neuropsychologists a means of directly evaluating the role of motivational factors in the production of poor performance. Although using the MMPI-2 to detect underreporting of premorbid functioning (pre-existing condition) is not indicated at this point, researchers (e.g., Lees-Haley, 1992) have produced encouraging, preliminary results in this regard.

FUTURE RESEARCH

As research using the MMPI-2 progresses, investigators are addressing the challenge of integrating the test into a neuropsychological context. The challenge comes, in large part, from testing a population that is often too cognitively impaired to complete lengthy personality tests, or one in which a profound indifference reaction exists that inhibits insight into their condition. The challenge also arises from a need to examine, or at best comment on, premorbid personality functioning. Here, the challenge exists because currently we have no reliable means of objectifying retrospective account. Preliminary work directly assessing premorbid personality functioning looks promising (e.g., Nelson, Mitrushina, Satz, Sowa, & Cohen, 1993; Nelson et al., 1989) and similar test methods may be useful with the MMPI-2. In cases in which known or suspected brain damage becomes the basis for a legal complaint, preexisting condition and the change in functioning based on the organic event are critical aspects for the neuropsychology expert to consider.

In addition, the issue of emotional change following brain damage often becomes critical to monitor over the course of recovery (e.g., Nelson, Cicchetti, Satz, & Sowa, 1994). Emotional effects of brain damage or reactions to debilitative impairment may occur weeks to months after the event and may alternately remit and recur throughout recovery. These effects may involve longstanding personality characteristics that predate the event and are now exacerbated by it (traits), or emotional reactions to the event and its consequences (state), or both. Investigators recognize the importance of accounting for changes in personality functioning (Putnam, Adams, & Schneider, 1992). Weiner, in Chapter 3, advocates more research designed to examine test-retest stability using the MMPI-2. This would allow for delineation of characterological, long-standing personality characteristics compared to those that arise in reaction to a given event. Edwards, Weissman, and Morrison (1993) recommended follow-up interviews to the MMPI-2 in which neurocorrected items may be discussed with patients and relatives from a temporal perspective. Butcher and Williams (1992) offer several specific suggestions on how to generate trait-based hypotheses using the MMPI-2.

New approaches. Increasingly, researchers are recognizing the shortcomings of prototypic approaches and are becoming more creative in attempts to correct them. Some (e.g., Alfano et al., 1992; Edwards et al., 1993; Gass, 1991) are devising methods of scoring and rescoring the MMPI-2 as a means of subtracting out physical, biological, and cognitive complaints common to brain damage to obtain a "purer" estimate of psychological functioning. Others (e.g., Ben-Porath, 1994; Lamb et al., 1994; Lees-Haley, 1992) are investigating malingering and devising approaches toward better understanding and measuring it using the MMPI-2.

Some investigators (e.g., Nelson et al., 1989) are currently writing personality test items so that sources close to patients/litigants, can report on their condition. Written in third person ("The patient . . . " or "My relative . . . "), items used in this approach allow for an additional perspective concerning personality functioning. In patients in which indifference may be a major symptom or in which severe cognitive difficulties, such as aphasia, render them untestable, this technique may be indicated. As noted earlier, these approaches have direct application to forensic neuropsychology in which the need is often to distinguish organic from functional components of brain damage or to monitor course of emotional recovery. Research thus far offers a novel means of accommodating the MMPI-2 to this population. Having a well-normed, well-standardized basis for determining personality functioning is imperative in this research process. The MMPI-2 offers such a basis.

General Conclusions

In this chapter, an attempt was made to focus on the decision-making process used by forensic neuropsychologists, with special attention paid to the role of the MMPI/MMPI-2 in the neuropsychological exam procedure. Although empirical support for the relevance of MMPI data to clinical interpretation was demonstrated, cautionary notes extend to several methodological limitations in these studies, such as small sample size or experimental error. Directions for further research involve creative modifications of the MMPI-2 to suit this population and additional study of subject effects.

Before an expert testifies regarding MMPI/MMPI-2 results, many factors need to be considered and anticipated. Knowledge of base rates ensures that reported changes in personality functioning do not constitute idiosyncratic phenomena. Clinical interview elicits important background information, especially regarding premorbid functioning. Predictions regarding rate of emotional recovery take into consideration type and severity of brain damage, current levels of adaptive functioning, degree of functional impairment, and personal factors, such as age and educational level of the patient. Forensic expertise requires clinical experience and an ability to systematically weigh all of these factors and compare them to available base rates, the individual's own baseline levels of functioning, and normative standard.

In recent exchanges between Adams and Putnam (1994) and Faust (1994) and in comments made by Ziskin and Faust (1991) regarding Matarazzo

(1990), disputes regarding acceptability of neuropsychologists and their methods as "experts" in forensic settings were raised. These exchanges offer contrasting arguments regarding the place of neuropsychological assessment in courtroom proceedings and illustrate the strong opposition some have to such testimony (e.g., Faust, 1994). Such views are countered by opinions that "when [neuropsychological] assessment is done well, it is patently obvious to all involved (i.e., juries, judges, and the attorneys for *both* the plaintiff and defense) that what such a psychologist-expert-witness concluded was valid (true) within the reasonable degree of certainty required" (Matarazzo, 1990, p. 1015).

Defining neuropsychological assessment "done well," from an empirical standpoint, is not an easy task. But being able to take a judge or jury through the clinical decision-making process used to derive statements of reasonable probability is imperative. This seems to be what Matarazzo is suggesting. In the context of forensic neuropsychological evaluations, the MMPI-2 offers a strong empirical base for resulting interpretations. Having such a basis supports interpretations regarding personality functioning. Using the MMPI-2 in this context requires familiarity with the literature on forensic neuropsychology. Knowing the methodological weaknesses of studies and arguments made against the MMPI-2's place in the courtroom will prepare the expert for the challenge of court testimony.

References

Adams, K., & Putnam, S. (1994). Coping with professional skeptics: Reply to Faust. *Psychological Assessment, 6,* 5-7.

Alfano, D., Finlayson, M., Stearns, G., & MacLennan, R. (1991). Dimensions of neurobehavioral dysfunction. *Neuropsychology, 5,* 35-41.

Alfano, D., Finlayson, M., Stearns, G., & Neilson, P. (1990). The MMPI and neurologic dysfunction: Profile configuration and analysis. *Clinical Neuropsychologist, 4,* 69-79.

Alfano, D., Paniak, C., & Finlayson, M. (1992, February). *A neurocorrected MMPI for closed head injury.* Paper presented at the annual meeting of the International Neuropsychological Society, San Diego, CA.

American Psychiatric Association. (1994). *Diagnostic and statistical manual of mental disorders* (4th. ed.). Washington, DC: Author.

Arkes, H. (1981). Impediments to accurate clinical judgment and possible ways to minimize their impact. *Journal of Consulting and Clinical Psychology, 49,* 323-330.

Aronson, D., & Akamatsu, T. (1981). Validation of a Q-sort task to assess MMPI skills. *Journal of Clinical Psychology, 37,* 831-836.

Ben-Porath, Y. (1990). MMPI-2 items. *MMPI-2 News and Profiles, 1,* 4-5.

Ben-Porath, Y. S. (1994). The ethical dilemma of coached malingering research. *Psychological Assessment, 6,* 14-15.

Ben-Porath, Y. S., & Butcher, J. N. (1989a). The psychometric stability of rewritten MMPI items. *Journal of Personality Assessment, 53,* 645-653.

Ben-Porath, Y. S., & Butcher, J. N. (1989b). The comparability of MMPI and MMPI-2 scales and profiles. *Psychological Assessment: A Journal of Consulting and Clinical Psychology, 1,* 345-347.

Berry, D., Baer, R. A., & Harris, M. J. (1991). Detection of malingering on the MMPI: A meta-analysis. *Clinical Psychology Review, 11,* 585-598.

Berry, D., Lamb, D., Wetter, M., Baer, R., & Widiger, T. (1994). Ethical considerations in research on coached malingering. *Psychological Assessment, 6,* 16-17.

Berry, D., Wetter, M., Baer, R., Widiger, T., Sumpter, J., Reynolds, S., & Hallam, R. (1991). Detection of random responding on the MMPI-2: Utility of F, back F, & VRIN scales. *Psychological Assessment, 3,* 418-423.

Blau, T. (1993, October). *Forensic neuropsychology: Criminal Issues* (p. 3). Paper presented at the meeting of the National Academy of Neuropsychology, Phoenix, AZ.

Butcher, J. N., Williams, C. L. (1992). *Essentials of MMPI-2 and MMPI-A interpretation.* Minneapolis: University of Minnesota Press.

Dahlstrom, W. G., & Welsh, G. S. (1960). *An MMPI handbook: A guide to use in clinical practice and research.* Minneapolis: University of Minnesota Press.

Dahlstrom, W., Welsh, G., & Dahlstrom, L. (1975). *An MMPI handbook: Volume 1: Clinical interpretation, 1.* Minneapolis: University of Minnesota Press.

Diamant, J., & Hijmen, R. (1981). Comparison of test results obtained with two neuropsychological test batteries. *Journal of Clinical Psychology, 37,* 355-358.

Dikmen, S., & Reitan, R. (1974). MMPI correlates of localized cerebral lesions. *Perceptual and Motor Skills, 39,* 831-840.

Dikmen, S., & Reitan, R. (1977). MMPI correlates of adaptive ability deficits in patients with brain lesions. *Journal of Nervous and Mental Disease, 165,* 247-254.

Edwards, D., Weissman, H., & Morrison, T. (1993, October). *"Neuro-corrected items" on the MMPI-2: Endorsement rates in a psychiatric sample.* Paper presented at the annual meeting of the National Academy of Neuropsychology, Phoenix, AZ.

Farr, S., & Martin, P. (1988). Neuropsychological dysfunction. In R. Greene (Ed.), *The MMPI: Use with specific populations* (pp. 214-245). Philadelphia: Grune & Stratton.

Faust, D. (1994). Comment on Putnam, Adams, and Schneider, "One-day test-retest reliability of neuropsychological tests in a personal injury case." *Psychological Assessment, 6,* 3-4.

Faust, D., & Ziskin, J. (1988). The expert witness in psychology and psychiatry. *Science, 241,* 31-35.

Finn, S., & Butcher, J. (1991). Clinical objective personality assessment. In M. Hersen, A. Kazdin, & A. Bellack (Eds.), *The clinical psychology handbook* (2nd ed., pp. 362-373). New York: Pergamon.

Franzen, M., Iverson, G., & McCracken, L. (1990). The detection of malingering in neuropsychological assessment. *Neuropsychology Review, 1,* 247-279.

Friedman, S. (1950). *Psychometric effects of frontal and parietal lobe brain damage.* Unpublished doctoral dissertation, University of Minnesota, Minneapolis.

Gainotti, G. (1972). Emotional behavior and hemispheric side of the lesion. *Cortex, 8,* 41-55.

Garb, H. (1989). Clinical judgment, clinical training, and professional experience. *Psychological Bulletin, 105,* 387-396.

Garb, H. (1992). The trained psychologist as expert witness. *Clinical Psychology Review, 12,* 451-467.

Gass, C. (1991). Emotional variables and neuropsychological test performance. *Journal of Clinical Psychology, 47,* 100-104.

Graham, J. (1990). Congruence between the MMPI and MMPI-2 code types. *MMPI-2 News and Profiles, 1,* 1-2.

Guilmette, T., Faust, D., Hart, K., & Arkes, H. (1990). A national survey of psychologists who offer neuropsychological services. *Archives of Clinical Neuropsychology, 5,* 373-392.

Hathaway, S. (1947). A coding system for MMPI profiles. *Journal of Consulting Psychology, 11,* 334-337.

Hovey, H. (1964). Brain lesions and five MMPI items. *Journal of Consulting Psychology, 28,* 78-79.

Kane, R., Parsons, O., Goldstein, G., & Moses, J. (1987). Diagnostic accuracy of the Halstead-Reitan and Luria-Nebraska neuropsychological batteries: Performance of clinical raters. *Journal of Consulting and Clinical Psychology, 55,* 783-784.

Kane, R., Sweet, J., Golden, C., Parsons, O., & Moses, J. (1981). Comparative diagnostic accuracy of the Halstead-Reitan and standardized Luria-Nebraska neuropsychological batteries in a mixed psychiatric and brain-damaged population. *Journal of Consulting and Clinical Psychology, 49,* 484-485.

Kleinmuntz, B. (1984). The scientific study of clinical judgment in psychology and medicine. *Clinical Psychology Review, 4,* 111-126.

Lachar, D., & Alexander, P. (1978). Veridicality of self-report: Replicated correlates of the Wiggins MMPI Content Scales. *Journal of Consulting and Clinical Psychology, 46,* 1349-1356.

Lamb, D., Berry, D., Wetter, M., & Baer, R. (1994). Effects of two types of information on malingering of closed-head injury of the MMPI-2: An analog investigation. *Pyschological Assessment, 6,* 8-13.

Leary, M., & Miller, R. (1986). *Social psychology and dysfunctional behavior: Origins, diagnosis, and treatment.* New York: Springer-Verlag.

Lees-Haley, P. (1992c). Neuropsychological complaint base rates of personal injury claimants. *Forensic Reports, 5,* 385-391.

Levitt, E. (1989). *The clinical application of MMPI special scales.* Hillsdale, NJ: Lawrence Erlbaum.

Lezak, M. (1983). *Neuropsychological assessment* (2nd ed.). New York: Oxford.

Lishman, W. (1968). Brain damage in relation to psychiatric disability after head injury. *British Journal of Psychiatry, 114,* 373-410.

Mack, J. (1979). The MMPI and neurological dysfunction. In C. S. Newmark (Ed.), *MMPI: Clinical and research trends* (pp. 53-79). New York: Praeger.

Maier, L., & Abidin, R. (1967). Validation attempt of Hovey's five-item MMPI index for central nervous system disorders. *Journal of Consulting Psychology, 31,* 542.

Matarazzo, J. (1990). Psychological assessment versus psychological testing. *American Psychologist, 45,* 999-1016.

Meehl, P. E. (1973). Antecedent probability and the efficiency of psychometric signs, patterns or cutting scores. In P. Meehl (Ed.), *Psychodiagnosis: Selected papers* (pp. 32-62). Minneapolis: University of Minnesota Press.

Meier, M. (1969). The regional localization hypothesis and personality changes associated with focal cerebral lesions and ablations. In J. N. Butcher (Ed.), *MMPI: Research developments and clinical applications* (pp. 243-261). New York: McGraw-Hill.

Meyer, A. (1904). Anatomical facts and clinical varieties of traumatic insanity. *American Journal of Insanity, 60,* 373-441.

Miller, W. (1993, October). *Oft neglected issues in forensic neuropsychology.* Symposium conducted at the meeting of the National Academy of Neuropsychology, Phoenix, AZ.

Nelson, L., Cicchetti, D., & Satz, P. (1994). Emotional sequelae of stroke: A longitudinal perspective. *Journal of Clinical and Experimental Neuropsychology, 16,* 796-806.

Nelson, L., Mitrushina, M., D., Satz, P., Sowa, M., & Cohen, S. (1993). Cross-validation of the *Neuropsychology Behavior and Affect Profile* in stroke patients. *Psychological Assessment, 5,* 374-376.

Nelson, L., Satz, P., Mitrushina, M., Van Gorp, W., Cicchetti, D., Lewis, R., & Van Lancker, D. (1989). Development and validation of the Neuropsychology Behavior and Affect Profile. *Psychological Assessment: A Journal of Consulting and Clinical Psychology, 1,* 266-272.

Pope, K. S., Butcher, J. N., & Seelen, J. (1993). *The MMPI, MMPI-2, & MMPI-A in court.* Washington, DC: American Psychological Association.

Prigatano, G. (1992). Personality disturbances associated with traumatic brain injury. *Journal of Consulting and Clinical Psychology, 60,* 360-368.

Prigatano, G., & Schacter, D. (Eds.) (1991). *Awareness of deficit after brain injury: Theoretical and clinical implications.* New York: Oxford University Press.

Putnam, S., Adams, K., & Schneider, A. (1992). One-day test-retest reliability of neuropsychological tests in a personal injury case. *Psychological Assessment, 4,* 312-316.

Reber, A. (1985). *Dictionary of psychology.* Middlesex, UK: Penguin.

Reitan, R. (1976). Neurological and physiological bases of psychopathology. *Annual Review of Psychology, 27,* 189-216.

Shaw, D., & Matthews, C. (1965). Differential MMPI performance of brain-damaged versus pseudo-neurologic groups. *Journal of Clinical Psychology, 21,* 405-408.

Turk, D., & Salovey, P. (Eds.) (1988). *Reasoning, inference, and judgment in clinical psychology.* New York: Free Press.

Watson, C., Thomas, R., Anderson, D., & Felling, J. (1968). Differentiation of organics from schizophrenics at two chronicity levels by use of the Halstead-Reitan organic test battery. *Journal of Consulting and Clinical Psychology, 32,* 679-684.

Weingold, H., Dawson, J., & Kael, H. (1965). Further examination of Hovey's "Index" for identification of brain lesions: Validation study. *Psychological Reports, 16,* 1098.

Wiggins, J. (1966). Substantive dimensions of self-report in the MMPI item pool. *Psychological Monographs, 80*(22, Whole No. 630).

Williams, H. (1952). The development of a caudality scale for the MMPI. *Journal of Clinical Psychology, 8,* 293-297.

Zimmerman, I. (1965). Residual effects of brain damage and five MMPI items. *Journal of Consulting Psychology, 29,* 394.

Ziskin, J., & Faust, D. (1991). Reply to Matarazzo. *American Psychologist, 46,* 881-882.

10

Use of the MMPI-2/MMPI-A in Child Custody Evaluations

RANDY K. OTTO

ROBERT P. COLLINS

In this chapter the utility of the MMPI-2/MMPI-A with respect to child custody evaluations is examined.[1] This chapter is not intended to provide the reader with a template for conducting child custody evaluations (for such direction, see Grisso, 1986; Melton, Petrila, Poythress, & Slobogin, 1987; Weithorn, 1987), but rather, to identify how the MMPI-2/MMPI-A may be incorporated into the child custody evaluation process, a process that is necessarily multisource and multimethod (Committee on Professional Practice and Standards, 1994; Grisso, 1986; Melton et al., 1987; Weissman, 1991; Weithorn & Grisso, 1987). After a brief overview of the significance of this area, the legal parameters of child custody decision making and the courts' treatment of the MMPI/MMPI-2 with respect to child custody evaluations are reviewed. Next, current child custody evaluation practices and criticisms of these practices are presented. This is followed by a review of MMPI research that is potentially relevant to parenting and child custody decision making and evaluations. Recommendations for how the MMPI-2/MMPI-A may be used in the custody evaluation process are followed by recommendations for further research in this area. Finally, a case study that depicts the potential utility of the MMPI-2 in child custody evaluations is presented.

Child Custody Decision Making and Child Custody Evaluations

There is perhaps no area of forensic evaluation in which emotions run as high as they do in child custody. When parents dispute the custody and placement of their children (either in the midst of a divorce or subsequent to a divorce and initial custody arrangement) the legal decision maker (i.e., presiding judge) sometimes seeks input from psychologists and other mental health professionals, with the hope of gaining information that will prove helpful in reaching a decision that is in the "best interests of the child/children" (Grisso, 1986; Rohman, Sales, & Lou, 1987; Wyer, Gaylord, & Grove, 1987). However, the frequency with which mental health professionals are asked to conduct such evaluations is probably lower than thought by many mental health professionals.

Melton et al. (1987) estimated that 90% of custody decisions are made by divorcing parents without the formal evaluation or input of mental health professionals. McIntosh and Prinz (1993) reported that in only 14% of the 603 divorce cases that they reviewed was custody of the children an issue. Agreements about custody were presumably reached by the divorcing parents in the large majority of cases. Approaching the issue from a somewhat different perspective, Melton, Weithorn, and Slobogin (1985) surveyed Virginia judges and reported that three quarters indicated that clinical testimony or reports were offered in less than 25% of the child custody cases they heard. Thus, mental health professionals, contrary to public or professional opinion, may conduct child custody evaluations and offer expert testimony based on such evaluations in a small minority of the total number of divorce cases. But with the divorce rate approaching 50% in the United States (U.S. Department of Commerce, 1993), the number of such evaluations conducted annually still remains significant.

Legal Parameters of Child Custody Decision Making and Implications for Use of the MMPI-2/MMPI-A in Child Custody Evaluations

A brief review of legal standards for adjudication of child custody in the case of divorce will shed some light on the courts' interest in the opinions of mental health professionals when considering the placement of children. This review will also serve to demonstrate how the MMPI-2/MMPI-A may prove helpful in conducting child custody evaluations.

RELEVANT LEGAL TESTS AND LEGAL ISSUES

The Uniform Marriage and Divorce Act (UMDA; 1979) has served as a model for marriage and divorce laws in many states (Grisso, 1986; Rohman et al., 1987; Wyer et al., 1987). With respect to matters of child custody, Section 402 of the UMDA directs:

> The court shall determine custody in accordance with the best interests of the child. The court shall consider all relevant factors including:
> 1. the wishes of the child's parent or parents as to his custody;
> 2. the wishes of the child as to his custodian;
> 3. the interaction and interrelationship of the child with his parent or parents, his siblings, and other persons who may significantly affect the child's best interests;
> 4. the child's adjustment to his home, school, and community; and
> 5. the mental and physical health of all individuals involved.

Michigan's child custody statute (Child Custody Act of 1970) has also served as a model for a number of states' codes (Grisso, 1986). The Michigan standard directs that custody decisions are to be made "in the best interests of the child" and are to be based on the following:

> 1. The love, affection, and other emotional ties existing between the parties involved and the child
> 2. The capacity and disposition of the parties involved to give the child love, affection, and guidance and continuation of educating and raising of the child in its religion or creed, if any

3. The capacity and disposition of the parties involved to provide the child with food, clothing, medical care, or other remedial care recognized and permitted under the laws of this state in lieu of medical care, and other material needs

4. The length of time the child has lived in a stable, satisfactory environment and desirability of maintaining continuity

5. The permanence, as a family unit, of the existing or proposed custodial home

6. The moral fitness of the parties involved

7. The mental and physical health of the parties involved

8. The home, school, and community record of the child

9. The reasonable preference of the child, if the court deems the child to be of sufficient age to express preference

10. The willingness and ability of each of the parents to facilitate and encourage a close and continuing parent-child relationship between the child and the other parent

11. Any other factor considered by the court to be relevant to a particular child custody dispute

Use of the MMPI-2/MMPI-A in child custody evaluations is indicated to the degree that the instruments assist the mental health professional in forming an expert opinion[2] about any of the factors identified by the UMDA or similar state child custody statutes. Strictly speaking, psychologists and other mental health professionals who cannot or do not make clear how the MMPI-2/MMPI-A aids them in forming expert opinions about the legally relevant issues identified in state statutes risk having testimony or reports based (in full or in part) on these instruments ruled inadmissible.[3]

THE COURTS' ACCEPTANCE
OF THE MMPI-2/MMPI-A IN THE
CONTEXT OF CHILD CUSTODY EVALUATIONS

Given their widespread acceptance among psychologists and other mental health professionals, it is not surprising that expert opinions based (in full or in part) on the Minnesota instruments are readily admitted by the courts (Ogloff, this volume; Pope, Butcher, & Seelen, 1993). Expert opinions related to child custody and parental rights based, in part, on results of the MMPI/ MMPI-2, have been admitted in a large number of cases, only a sample of which is presented (*Ayers v. Ayers,* 1993; *Bjerke v. Wilcox,* 1987; *Bunch v. Bunch,* 1985; *Cronier v. Cronier,* 1989; *Fitzgerald v. Brown,* 1993; *Gilbertson v. Gilbert-*

son, 1992; *Goote v. Lightner*, 1990; *Hreha v. Hreha*, 1986; *In Re D.H.*, 1986; *In Re Willis*, 1992; *Isom v. Isom*, 1989; *JEP v. JCP*, 1988; *Multnomah County v. Grannis*, 1984; *Novotny v. Novotny*, 1986; *Scott v. Prince George County*, 1988; *Utz v. Kienzle*, 1991; *Weece v. Cottle*, 1986). As a result of this apparent acceptance by the courts, and the courts' casual scrutiny of expert testimony offered by mental health professionals generally (see Note 3), mental health professionals who incorporate the MMPI-2/MMPI-A into their custody evaluation process are unlikely to have their opinions challenged and barred simply on the basis of use of the instrument(s).

Current Clinical Practice With Respect to Child Custody Evaluations

Despite widespread acceptance by the courts, the child custody evaluations conducted by mental health professionals, and the expert evidence offered by them in custody proceedings, have been criticized by mental health and legal commentators alike. Criticisms of clinical practice are presumably based on commentators' anecdotal impressions of custody evaluations because there has not been one published study in which investigators examined and described a randomly selected sample of child custody evaluations prepared for, or testimony offered to, the courts (see Heilbrun, 1992, for discussion of this issue more generally).

Questioning how much mental health professionals have to offer the courts in many custody cases, Melton et al. (1987) concluded, "there is virtually no scientific basis for provision of opinions about the kinds of questions that the courts must decide in divorce cases when children are involved . . . there is probably no forensic question on which overreaching by mental health professionals has been so common and so egregious" (p. 330). More specifically, the misuse of standard, psychological measures for purposes of child custody decision making has also been cited by authorities. Grisso, 1984 (cited in Melton et al., 1987) stated,

> Mental health professionals do not have reason to be proud of their performance in this area of forensic assessment. Too often we still evaluate the parent but not the child, a practice that makes no sense when the child's own, individual needs are the basis for the legal decision. Too often we continue to rely on assessment

instruments and methods that were designed to address *clinical* questions, questions of psychiatric diagnosis, when clinical questions bear only secondarily upon the real issues in many child custody cases. Psychiatric interviews, Rorschachs, and MMPIs might have a role to play in child custody assessments. But these tools were not designed to assess parents' relationships to children, nor to assess parents' child-rearing attitudes and capacities, and *these* are often the central questions in child custody cases. (p. 330, emphasis in original)

Similarly, Melton et al. (1987) concluded, "(child custody) opinions have often been based on clinical data that are, on their face, irrelevant to the legal questions in dispute" (p. 330). Others, too, have questioned whether mental health professionals have anything to offer legal decision makers in these cases and criticized the product delivered to legal decision makers who are seeking input when making decisions about child custody (Brodzinsky, 1993; Keith-Spiegel & Koocher, 1985; Okpaku, 1976).

Practitioners conducting child custody evaluations report using a variety of standard clinical instruments, almost all of which were not designed for purposes of assessing parenting capacities or decision making with respect to child custody. Keilin and Bloom (1986) surveyed 190 mental health professionals who conducted child custody evaluations, 79% of whom were doctoral-level psychologists. Three quarters of the respondents reported that they conducted psychological testing with both the parents and children in custody cases. The MMPI was the test most frequently used by those evaluators who included testing in their evaluation of parents—71% of the respondents reported using the MMPI in an average of 89% of the evaluations they conducted. The next most frequently used test with adults (the Rorschach Inkblot Technique) was used by only 42% of the respondents. Of course, it is difficult to determine whether these techniques are used appropriately or not without an evaluation of the reports that are completed and testimony that is offered by child custody evaluators (see above). But the concerns of Grisso (1984, 1986) and Melton et al. (1987) do hold some merit and they, in conjunction with ethical and practice standards (American Educational Research Association et al., 1985; American Psychological Association, 1992; Committee on Ethical Guidelines for Forensic Psychologists, 1991), require that psychologists present a reasoned and defensible rationale for using the MMPI-2/MMPI-A (and any other assessment technique, whether or not specifically developed for purposes of child custody decision making) in the context of child custody evaluations.

MMPI/MMPI-2/MMPI-A Research
on Child Custody, Divorce, and Parenting

Despite the wealth of research regarding the utility of the MMPI/MMPI-2/ MMPI-A in terms of diagnosis and assessment of psychopathology, the description of behavior patterns and personality, and treatment planning, there is a relative paucity of research related to the MMPI/MMPI-2/MMPI-A and its specific application in child custody proceedings. Those areas of research broadly relevant to child custody, marital distress, and parenting issues are reviewed.

MMPI/MMPI-2[4] PROFILES AND PARTICIPATION IN CHILD CUSTODY EVALUATIONS

As part of a custody evaluation process, Ollendick and Otto (1984) administered the MMPI to 38 sets of divorcing parents who were ordered to a community mental health center by a family court for child custody evaluations. The mean scores of four groups (mothers receiving custody, mothers not receiving custody, fathers receiving custody, fathers not receiving custody) are reported in Table 10.1. Parents awarded custody by the court obtained lower scores on Scales F, 2, 4, 5, 6, 9, and the MacAndrew Alcoholism Scale (MacAndrew, 1965), and higher scores on the K scale. However, the analyses used (multiple ANOVAs) resulted in an inflated alpha rate and the group mean differences were generally very small (i.e., all differences were within six T-score points or less with the exception of Scale 4). Apparently using the same sample, Ollendick (1984) reported similar findings for another alcohol scale (DeGroot & Adamson, 1973).

Because the MMPIs were administered as part of the custody evaluation process, the examiners' clinical opinions were presumably shaped, in part, by the test profiles, and the judges' decisions were in turn affected by the examiners' opinions. Therefore, little can be concluded about the ability to predict judges' opinions or decisions by way of the MMPI/MMPI-2 profile.

Within the past 3 years a new child custody evaluation instrument has been introduced that incorporates administration of the MMPI-2. The Ackerman-Schoendorf Scales for Parent Evaluation of Custody (ASPECT; Ackerman & Schoendorf, 1992) is a rating instrument designed to assess parent fitness in custody evaluations. The ASPECT incorporates the examiner's observations

Table 10.1 Group Mean MMPI Profiles of Parents Receiving and Not Receiving Custody

							MMPI Scales							
	L	F	K	1(Hs)	2(D)	3(Hy)	4(Pd)	5(Mf)	6(Pa)	7(Pt)	8(Sc)	9(Ma)	0(Si)	MAC
Fathers (n = 38)	53	52	61	51	54	59	60	59	57	55	55	59	48	22
Receiving custody (n = 15)	54	50	63	50	53	58	54	58	54	55	53	55	49	21
Not receiving custody (n = 23)	52	53	59	51	55	59	64	59	59	55	57	61	48	23
Mothers (n = 38)	53	51	61	49	50	56	63	46	58	57	52	53	49	21
Receiving custody (n = 23)	53	50	63	49	49	57	62	46	57	57	52	53	47	20
Not receiving custody (n = 15)	53	52	57	48	51	54	64	46	60	57	52	54	52	22
p values														
Custody	.357	.039*	.044*	.861	.197	.886	.040*	.036*	.030*	.527	.114	.046*	.407	.001**
Sex	.714	.446	.801	.126	.015*	.076	.263	.001**	.598	.005**	.069	.011*	.830	.027*

SOURCE: Adapted from Ollendick and Otto (1984); $Journal of Psychology, 117$, 227-232. Reprinted with permission of the Helen Dwight Reid Educational Foundation. Published by Heldref Publications, 1319 Eighteenth St., N. W., Washington, D. C. 20036-1802. Copyright © 1994.
NOTE: MacAndrew scale shows raw scores. MMPI clinical and validity scales show T scores.
*$p < .05$; **$p < .001$.

and interviews of the parents and children, the Parent Questionnaire developed specifically for the ASPECT, and the results of a variety of psychological instruments including the MMPI (or MMPI-2), the Rorschach Inkblot Technique, Wechsler Adult Intelligence Scale-Revised (WAIS-R), an age appropriate intelligence test for children, either the Wide Range Achievement Test-Revised (WRAT-R) or the Norris Educational Achievement Test (NEAT), the Draw-A-Family Test, and either the Thematic Apperception Test (TAT) or the Children's Apperception Test (CAT). Questions in the ASPECT were developed based on a review of the psychological and legal literatures. Sources included expert opinion, parenting studies, and surveys of mental health professionals and judges involved in custody cases. The ASPECT yields an overall summary index of parenting effectiveness for each parent—the "Parent Custody Index" (PCI).

The ASPECT is comprised of three subscales: the Observational Scale, the Social Scale, and the Cognitive-Emotional Scale. The Observational Scale reportedly assesses the "self-presentation and appearance of the parent" (Ackerman & Schoendorf, 1992, p. 2). This scale has nine items that direct the examiner to assess factors such as the parents' hygiene and grooming, the parents' attitude toward the evaluation process, the appropriateness of the interactions between the parents and the child, and the parents' "maturity and insight." This information is attained through observation of the parent and child and from items on the ASPECT's Parent Questionnaire.

The Social Scale reportedly assesses the "social environment provided by the parent" (Ackerman & Schoendorf, 1992, p. 32). This scale requires the examiner to draw conclusions about the parents' involvement with the child based on items from the ASPECT's Parent Questionnaire, observation of the parent and child, an interview with the child, and the TAT or the CAT. Items are also included that are devoted to possible sexual or physical abuse, the parents' arrest record, and potential for or history of alcohol abuse.

The Cognitive-Emotional Scale reportedly assesses cognitive and affective capacities for parenting by assessing such factors as psychological adjustment, psychopathology, ego strength, social judgment, and cognitive capacity. This index incorporates information from a number of psychological tests, including the MMPI (or MMPI-2), Rorschach, appropriate intelligence tests for both the parent and child, and the WRAT-R.

The MMPI/MMPI-2 plays a moderate role in the ASPECT evaluation. Seven of the 19 items in the Cognitive-Emotional scale use the results of an MMPI/MMPI-2 administration (6 of the 7 items are compatible with the MMPI-2).

These items include information drawn from two validity scales (L and K), elevations of the clinical scales as a general measure of psychopathology, the Ego Strength scale, the Control scale, and the MacAndrew Alcoholism scale.

The ASPECT standardization sample included 100 pairs of parents seeking custody evaluations (Ackerman & Schoendorf, 1992). The normative sample was not representative of the United States population—the ASPECT sample was reported as 96.9% White, 2.6% Black, and .5% Hispanic. Parents' ages ranged from 24 to 57 years, with a mean of 34.4 years; children's ages ranged from 4 months to 17 years, with a mean of 2.28 years. The socioeconomic status level of the subjects, assessed only through the highest education level attained, was also unrepresentative of the U.S. population with only 6% of the sample having less than a high school education. The authors suggest that this discrepancy may be due to a higher level of sophistication of individuals who use the legal system to resolve their custody disputes. Examiners participating in the standardization procedure were psychologists in private practice; no other information about selection criteria for, or demographic data of, the examiners was provided.

The reliability of the ASPECT was assessed by measures of internal consistency and interrater reliability. The internal consistency, calculated with alpha coefficients, was adequate for both the PCI and the Social subscale (.76 and .72, respectively) but low for the Observational and Cognitive-Emotional subscales (.50 for both). The authors suggest that the low internal consistency of the Observational and Cognitive-Emotional subscales reflects the heterogeneity of the components of the underlying constructs. The authors caution against interpreting the scores of these two subscales and conducting profile analysis due to the low internal consistency of these subscales. Interrater reliability scores are high, ranging from .96 for the PCI to .92 for the Observational subscale. No statistical analysis of the underlying factors of ASPECT or its subscales is reported in the manual. The corrected item-to-total correlations are generally small for all three subscales with two items below .05, suggesting a heterogenous set of items.

The authors' presentation of validity data on the ASPECT is confusing and incomplete. The authors report that predictive validity was assessed by comparing recommendations made on the basis of the ASPECT with the parents in the normative study to their judges' final custody decisions. Although the test manual is unclear, apparently, in 59 of the 100 sample cases, results of the ASPECT were conclusive enough to recommend custody for one parent or the other and this recommendation was offered to the court. The authors report that the ASPECT correctly "predicted" the judges' custody decisions in about 75% of the cases (Ackerman & Schoendorf, 1992, p. 53). This, of course, is not true predictive validity because the results of the ASPECT presumably formed the basis of the examining psychologists' opinions that were presented to the court. The authors also report findings for a sample of 12 families in which ASPECT results were apparently not presented to the court. The judges reached a decision regarding custody that was identical to that suggested by the ASPECT in 75% ($n = 8$) of these cases (pp. 53-54).

Other than an informal assessment of the face validity/content validity of the items by the authors, no attempt to determine whether this instrument actually assesses some parental fitness criteria is provided. Although the ASPECT represents an interesting attempt to identify and assess constructs relevant to the custody decision-making process, virtually no validity data are available. Additionally, there is no report of an attempt to follow the families and assess the outcome of decisions based on results of the ASPECT. Agreement between custody recommendations based on the ASPECT and judges' opinions is not particularly convincing, particularly when the judges' decisions are presumably based, in part, on results of the ASPECT. As the authors note, further research with the ASPECT is needed so that its efficacy in describing the relative strengths and weaknesses of parents can be determined.

MMPI/MMPI-2 AND MARITAL DISTRESS

Some investigators have administered the MMPI to couples who were in the process of divorce, recently divorced, or receiving marital counseling. The reported results are consistent and not surprising, and suggest that the MMPI/MMPI-2 is sensitive to marital distress. But the applicability of these findings to child custody evaluations and decision making is, at best, strained.

Hackney and Ribordy (1980) found that group mean MMPI profiles of persons reporting marital difficulties and couples who were in the process of divorce were higher than the profiles of persons who reported being in good marriages or who were divorced. Ollendick, Otto, and Heider (1983) reported similar findings upon comparing the group mean profiles of couples receiving marital therapy and couples seeking therapy for their children. Similar findings were reported by Snyder and Regts (1990).

Scale 4 (Pd) is typically one of the most elevated scales among men and women receiving marital counseling, reporting marital problems, or undergoing divorce (Arnold, 1970, cited in Hjemboe, Almagor, & Butcher, 1992;

Cookerly, 1974; Hackney & Ribordy, 1980; Hjemboe & Butcher, 1991; Ollendick et al., 1983; Snyder & Regts, 1990). Of course, given the variety of issues tapped by Scale 4, identification of individuals as having marital difficulties or experiencing marital distress simply on the basis of such an elevation results in significant misclassification (Hjemboe et al., 1992; Hjemboe & Butcher, 1991).

Hjemboe et al. (1992) developed a Marital Distress Scale (MDS) for the MMPI-2, which consists of those items that showed the greatest correlation with the Spanier Dyadic Adjustment Scale. Preliminary research suggests that this scale has shown some ability to identify individuals who are experiencing some kind of marital distress (Hjemboe et al., 1992).

MMPI/MMPI-2 PROFILES, PARENTING BEHAVIORS, AND BEHAVIORS RELEVANT TO PARENTING AND CHILD CUSTODY

Little research has been published that addresses directly the utility of the MMPI/MMPI-2 in assessing parenting behaviors. Using PsychLit to access the MMPI literature, relevant search parameters, such as parent, mother, father, child, parenting, personality, assessment, parent-child relationship, as well as combinations of the aforementioned parameters, yielded few directly relevant studies on the MMPI/MMPI-2 and parenting.

In one of the more relevant studies, Mrazek, Klinnert, Mrazek, and Macey (1991), in an investigation on the parental influences of early asthma onset, suggested that standardized instruments such as the MMPI should assess some aspects of the personality and adjustment of parents that relate to parenting. In this study the MMPI was used in validating newly developed global scales designed to assess aspects of parental difficulties. Results showed that mothers assessed as having parental difficulties were more likely to have elevated scores on scales F, 2, and 4, lower scores on the K scale, and elevated scores on the Dependency and Ego Strength scales. All of the scores of the mothers with parental difficulties fell within the normal range, however, which suggests that these results would be of marginal clinical utility in most custody assessments.

Heinicke, Diskin, Ramsey-Klee, and Oates (1986) used the Warmth scale of the MMPI in assessing prebirth maternal characteristics. Results suggest a positive relationship between maternal warmth as measured by the MMPI/MMPI-2 and both parental responsiveness to infant needs and child's aggression modulation at a 2-year follow-up.

Some investigators have examined the relationship between the personality characteristics of parents as assessed by the MMPI and the behavior and adjustment of their children. A number of these studies examined the parental MMPI profiles of children with emotional or behavioral problems (Archer, Sutker, White, & Orvin, 1978; Dean & Jacobson, 1982; Frick, Lahey, Hartdagen, & Hynd, 1989; Lahey, Russo, Walker, & Piacentini, 1989; Smith, Burleigh, Sewell, & Krisack, 1984). Results of these investigations suggest a complex and inconsistent association between MMPI profiles of parents and their children's behavior or pathology, with the general exception of pervasive antisocial patterns. No one profile representing specific parental characteristic has been consistently associated with particular childhood psychopathology (Archer et al., 1978).

Investigators have also examined the MMPI/MMPI-2 profiles of parents who are at risk for, accused of, or admitted to sexual or physical abuse of their children (Chaffin, 1992; Egeland, Erickson, Butcher, & Ben-Porath, 1991; Erickson, Walbek, & Seely, 1987; Friedrich, 1991; Hamilton, Stiles, Melowsky, & Beal, 1987; Kirkland & Bauer, 1982; Paulson, Abdelmonen, Thomason, & Chaleff, 1974; Paulson, Schwemer, & Bendel, 1976; Plotkin, Twentyman, & Perri, 1982; Scott & Stone, 1986; Wright, 1976). Results consistent with those above have been reported; there is no clear, identifiable profile that identifies a parent as an abuser or that is associated with abuse (Paulson et al., 1974).

The above review indicates that there is relatively little research examining the relationship between MMPI/MMPI-2 scales or profiles and behaviors specific or directly relevant to parenting or children's behaviors. The research to date has not proved promising with respect to drawing relationships between specific profiles or scale elevations and behaviors relevant to parenting. Therefore, as is later described in more detail, psychologists must use caution when using the MMPI-2 to identify behavioral styles or ways of interacting and drawing conclusions about their effects on children.

Recommendations for the Use of the
MMPI-2/MMPI-A in Child Custody Evaluations

Given the rationale and basis for the Minnesota instruments, a strong case can be made for including them in some child custody evaluations.[5] The Minnesota instruments can be used to assess the emotional functioning and adjustment of the parents, other persons who may significantly affect the child (e.g., stepparents, live-in relatives, or others), and (adolescent) children. The MMPI-2/MMPI-A will also prove of some relevance to child custody evaluations to the degree that they offer a description of, and inform the court about, the parents' (or other potential caretakers') and (adolescent) child's traits and behavior. Finally, the MMPI/MMPI-2 also may prove to be of some value with respect to assessing the overall test-taking set that parents, other potential caretakers, and (adolescent) children have adopted with respect to the evaluation process. To the degree that minimization or denial of problems and shortcomings is a potential concern in child custody evaluations, the Minnesota tests' validity scales may also prove of some value.

THE MMPI-2/MMPI-A AND THE ASSESSMENT OF PSYCHOPATHOLOGY AND MENTAL DISORDERS

The utility of the Minnesota instruments with respect to appraising a person's symptom patterns, emotional difficulties, and psychopathology is well established (e.g., Archer, 1992; Butcher, 1990; Graham, 1993; Greene, 1980). A review of the UMDA and Michigan statutes indicates that the emotional adjustment/mental health of the parents (or other caretakers) and the children are specific issues that the court will consider when making decisions about child custody.[6] In agreement with these statutes, judges, when making child custody decisions, are reasonably concerned about the physical and emotional health of the potential custodial parents. For example, Lowery (1981) surveyed Kentucky family court judges and hearing officers and found that the factor that they weighted most heavily with respect to determining a child's placement when custody was disputed was the "mental stability" of each parent. Clearly then, clinical inquiries designed to establish the absence or presence of significant mental disorders/emotional difficulties are appropriate, particularly in those cases in which there is a specific allegation of such difficulties occurring at the time of the evaluation or in the past. The Minnesota instruments can be used to identify possible problems or difficulties relevant to parenting behavior that can be investigated or verified through third-party accounts. Similarly, the Minnesota instruments can be used to verify, discount, or further describe relevant problems or difficulties that are suggested by other sources.

The potential role of emotional adjustment and psychopathology must be put in perspective, of course. The Draft Guidelines for Child Custody Evaluations in Divorce Proceedings (Committee on Professional Practice and Standards, 1994) note that while questions of psychopathology are relevant to such a determination, they are not the primary focus (p. 678). Particular psychopathology or symptomatology is only relevant to the degree that it potentially affects that parent and his or her interactions with the child. With respect to assessment of parents or other potential caretakers, the MMPI-2 can prove valuable in the context of a child custody evaluation to the degree that it helps

1. establish and/or corroborate the absence of alleged or suspected mental disorder or emotional difficulties, or
2. establish and/or corroborate the presence of mental disorders and emotional difficulties, describe the extent and effect of such disorders and difficulties on legally relevant issues before the court, and suggest a prognosis given involvement or lack of involvement in treatment.

A multisource, multimethod approach suggests that careful clinical interview and examination, structured psychological testing, and contact with knowledgeable third parties (e.g., past or current treatment providers) are all techniques that should be used by the evaluator in addressing this issue.

The court, in determining child custody, is also concerned about the medical, mental health, emotional, and other needs of the child (children) involved. Clearly, clinical inquiries designed to establish the absence or presence of significant mental disorders/emotional difficulties with the child, and identify particular needs the child may have as a result of any existing difficulties are appropriate, particularly when there is a specific allegation that such difficulties are present at the time of the evaluation or have occurred at some time in the past.

With respect to the assessment of adolescent children who are the subject of child custody disputes, the MMPI-A can prove valuable to the degree that it helps

1. establish and/or corroborate the absence of alleged or suspected mental disorder or emotional difficulties, or
2. establish and/or corroborate the presence of mental disorders or emotional difficulties, and identifies treatment, environmental, and other kinds of needs that the adolescent has as a result of these difficulties.

A multisource, multimethod approach suggests that careful clinical interview and examination, structured psychological testing, and contact with knowledgable third parties (e.g., past or current treatment providers) are all techniques that should be used by the evaluator when addressing this issue.

THE MMPI-2/MMPI-A AND THE ASSESSMENT
OF BEHAVIOR PATTERNS AND PERSONALITY STYLES

The utility of the Minnesota instruments with respect to appraising a person's behavior patterns, personality style, and typical ways of responding to events is well established (e.g., Archer, 1992; Butcher, 1990; Graham, 1993; Greene, 1980). A review of the UMDA and the Michigan Statute indicates that the court may also be interested in information that the evaluator may provide about the parents' general demeanor and patterns of responding and relating to others.[7] The Minnesota instruments can be used to identify relevant behaviors that can be investigated or verified through third-party accounts. Similarly, the Minnesota instruments can be used to verify, discount, or further describe relevant behaviors that are suggested by other sources.

Given the nature of the MMPI-2, this line of inquiry will largely be focused on negative attributes that parents or other caretakers could have, that might negatively affect their ability to establish a positive relationship with, or positive environment for, the child or children. Relative strengths that parents may have with respect to interacting with their children will largely go untapped via use of the MMPI-2. However, because MMPI-2 profiles can provide information about parents' behavior patterns, personality traits, and ways of interacting with others, and how these patterns may affect ways in which parents interact with their children, use of the MMPI-2 in this manner can be considered.

Examiners using the MMPI-2 in this way will have to make one or more inferences to draw a connection between the parent's behavioral style or personality type and behaviors directly relevant to the custody question. Because use of the MMPI/MMPI-2 in this manner presents the greatest potential for misuse of the instrument, and is probably the practice that forms the basis for much of the criticism leveled by mental health and legal commentators, examiners should make clear to the legal decision maker the inferences that they make when extrapolating from personality traits or behavioral styles suggested by the MMPI-2. When offering descriptions of the parents or potential caretakers in this way, the psychologist should be careful not to make assumptions about how particular behavior patterns, personality styles, or ways of responding may affect a child's development. Although a psychologist's impressions about a parent's behavior patterns or personality style can be informed by results of the MMPI-2 and constitute expert testimony in which the court is interested, the psychologist should not begin to offer conjecture to the court about how such styles might positively or negatively affect the child, in the absence of any data supporting such claims.[8] Opinions regarding mental disorder, emotional adjustment, and resulting treatment and environmental needs that are derived from the MMPI-2 and MMPI-A, must be differentiated from opinions that may be offered regarding such things as behavioral strengths and assets that may affect parenting behavior, which may in turn affect the child.

THE MMPI-2/MMPI-A AND
ASSESSMENT OF TEST-TAKING SETS

One of the reasons that the Minnesota tests have enjoyed such widespread use, particularly in forensic settings, is that they include scales designed to assess the test-taking set of the examinee and evaluate the validity of the test profile (Ziskin, 1981). Compared to therapeutic evaluation and practice, issues such as truthfulness and candor are of special concern in forensic evaluation in which examinees often have a considerable investment in a particular outcome (Heilbrun, 1992; Melton et al., 1987; Rogers, 1988). The utility of the Minnesota instruments' validity indices in terms of identifying examinees who are exaggerating, minimizing, and responding in an honest and straightforward manner is well established (Berry, this volume; Greene, 1988; Ziskin, 1981). Because examiners completing child custody evaluations must draw some conclusions about the truthfulness or candor of the various examinees,[9] they can consider making inferences about the examinees' self-report during the examination process based, in part, on the validity scale configuration obtained on the MMPI-2/MMPI-A profile.[10] Examiners are encouraged to use the multisource, multimethod approach when drawing conclusions regarding veracity and candor, paying particular attention to the technique of third-party contacts (Heilbrun, 1988; Melton et al., 1987).

CASE EXAMPLE

To demonstrate how the MMPI-2 may prove useful in child custody evaluations, excerpts from an evaluation conducted by the senior author are presented for review. Identifying and background information irrelevant to the case is omitted or is changed to protect the anonymity of the examinees. Because of space constraints, the complete evaluation is not included. It is again emphasized that child custody evaluations must be multisource and multimethod in nature.

Background information. Gary and Judith H. were referred for a psychological evaluation to assist the court with respect to determining custody of their 7-year-old son, Matthew. At the time of the evaluation Matthew was living with his mother, although he had been spending half of each week with each parent until approximately 6 months prior to the evaluation. Both parents sought primary residence and sole parental responsibility for Matthew.

Both parents agreed that Matthew had displayed numerous and significant behavioral and emotional difficulties since the age of 5 including encopresis, physical aggression toward classmates, tantrums at home and school, and academic underachievement. Accounts of behavioral, emotional, and academic difficulties at school were confirmed by Matthew's teachers. Although Mr. H. appreciated the significance of Matthew's problems, Ms. H. appeared to downplay and minimize their severity. Mr. H. described various strategies and behavioral programs that he had developed and implemented in response to these behaviors. Ms. H. was unable to identify any such strategies and expressed concern that her ex-husband was too strict with Matthew. Mr. H. believed that his ex-wife's failure to respond to Matthew's problems was problematic. Mr. H. also expressed concern that his wife, who had experienced a depressive episode after the birth of Matthew, might be experiencing a recurrence of depression and not following through with Matthew as she otherwise might. Mr. H. saw his wife's failure to maintain regular contact with Matthew's schoolteacher, as had been requested by the teacher, as problematic (this request and Ms. H.'s failure to follow through were verified by Matthew's teacher). Ms. H. admitted to experiencing a period of depression after Matthew's birth but denied experiencing periods of depression prior to or subsequent to that episode.

In response to Matthew's problems, Mr. and Ms. H. entered treatment with three different psychologists in the span of 12 months. Treatment with the first psychologist was terminated early because of Mr. H.'s discomfort with the psychologist. Treatment with the second psychologist was discontinued by Ms. H. who disagreed with his approach to treatment. Mr. and Ms. H. finally

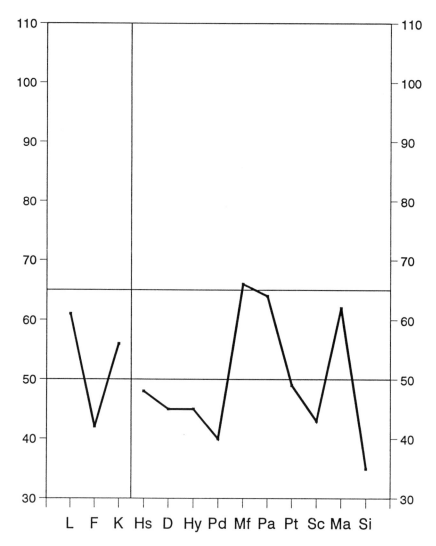

Figure 10.1. MMPI-2 Validity and Clinical Scale Profile of Mr. H., a 28-Year-Old Divorced Man

agreed to see a third psychologist, by whom they were being treated when the custody evaluation was initiated. However, treatment was discontinued by the third psychologist because Ms. H. missed and failed to cancel a number of scheduled appointments. This psychologist described Ms. H. as "unable to follow through."

Major issues in the custody decision were the special needs that Matthew had as a result of his behavioral difficulties, how much each parent appreciated these needs, and the parents' ability and willingness to follow through with psychological treatment, school contact, and a home structure designed to respond to these needs.

Mr. H.'s MMPI-2 Profile and Interpretation[11]

Profile Validity: The client has presented himself in a somewhat defensive manner, claiming more personal virtue than people generally do (see Figure 10.1). This self-view might reflect membership in a subcultural group that values strong moral character. However, this pattern is also found among individuals who consciously distort their answers to project a favorable self-image or who have unrealistically positive views of their own virtue. Although the MMPI-2 profile is a valid one and the individual's profile provides a reasonably good appraisal of the client's personality, it should be kept in mind that the individual has attempted to present an overly virtuous image and that the profile may underestimate problems. Individuals who present themselves in this manner tend to have little insight into their psychological state.

Symptomatic Patterns: Individuals with this MMPI-2 pattern are not admitting to many psychological symptoms or problems. His profile is within the normal range, suggesting that he considers his present adjustment to be adequate. He has, however, reported some personality characteristics, such as being overly sensitive, hyperactive, and overideational, which may cause him problems at times. He has diverse interests that include aesthetic and cultural activities. He is usually somewhat passive and compliant in interpersonal relationships, is generally self-controlled, and dislikes confrontation. He may have difficulty expressing anger directly and may resort to indirect means. In addition, the following description is suggested by the content of this client's responses. The client does not appear to be an overly anxious person prone to developing unrealistic fears. Any fears he reports are more likely to be viewed by him as reality-based rather than internally generated. He considers himself in good health and does not complain of somatic difficulties.

Interpersonal Relations: Individuals with this profile tend to be somewhat rigid and controlling in interpersonal situations. Quite outgoing and sociable,

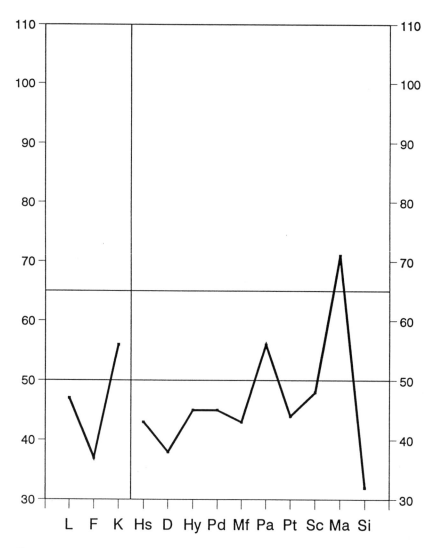

Figure 10.2. MMPI-2 Validity and Clinical Scale Profile of Mrs. H., a 26-Year-Old Divorced Woman

he has a strong need to be around others. He is gregarious and enjoys interpersonal attention.

Behavioral Stability: This MMPI-2 profile type reflects some persistent personality features. The relative elevation of the highest scales in his clinical profile shows very high profile definition. His peak scores on this testing are likely to be very prominent in his profile pattern if he is retested at a later date. Social introversion-extraversion tends to be a very stable personality characteristic over time. The client's typically outgoing and sociable behavior is likely to remain similar if he is retested at a later time.

Ms. H.'s MMPI-2 Profile and Interpretation[12]

Profile Validity: Although this client approached the MMPI-2 in a somewhat defensive manner, her defensiveness probably was not much different from most parents taking the test in such circumstances (see Figure 10.2). The resulting MMPI-2 profile is valid and probably a good indication of her present level of personality functioning. This may be viewed as a positive indication of her involvement with the evaluation. She has not indicated the highest level of education she has attained on the answer form. The Minnesota Report has been processed as though she has completed a 12-year high school education (the examinee completed 13 years of education). If the education level is actually different from high school then the Minnesota Report, particularly interpretations related to educational background such as those based on the Mf scale, should be carefully evaluated and modified accordingly.

Symptomatic Patterns: The client is probably experiencing some psychological difficulties. She appears to be hyperactive, tending to drive herself excessively and overextend herself. Often she has unrealistic plans and agitated behavior, and is unable to complete things she begins because she despises details and tends to be disorganized. Such clients appear overly self-confident and narcissistic, and when things do not go their way they become frustrated, irritable, and moody. In addition, she is easily bored and will act out impulsively, sometimes showing poor judgment and behaving in ways that create difficulties for herself or others. Overuse of addictive substances might result in problems for her. In addition, the following description is suggested by the content of this client's responses. She seems to be highly manipulative and self-indulgent. The client does not appear to be an overly anxious person prone to developing unrealistic fears. Any fears she reports are more likely to be viewed by her as reality-based rather than internally generated. She appears to be happy with life and feels positive about the future. Her response content reflects a high degree of self-confidence and the ability to deal with life tasks. The content of the items she endorsed suggests that she views herself as very responsible and tries to live up to her obligations. She is independent, poised, and feels able to cope well with life. She reports no significant sex-role conflicts. She considers herself in good health and does not complain of somatic difficulties.

Interpersonal Relations: She is likely to be quite manipulative and has rather superficial relationships. Her tendency to use others results in difficult interpersonal problems. She might be experiencing strained interpersonal relationships owing to her poor judgment and acting-out behavior. She may need a lot of interpersonal stimulation; she tends to become easily bored and irritated with others. Many women with this profile have had problems related to their sexual behavior. Quite outgoing and sociable, she has a strong need to be around others. She is gregarious and enjoys interpersonal attention. The content of this client's MMPI-2 responses suggests the following additional information concerning her interpersonal relations. She seems to be fun-loving and may give the appearance of being "the life of the party" at times. She enjoys being with others and has no problems interacting in group situations.

Behavioral Stability: Individuals with this profile are often emotionally labile and may have high moods for no apparent reason and downswings that serve as marked contrasts. The relative elevation of the highest scales in her clinical profile shows very high profile definition. Her peak scores on this testing are likely to be very prominent in her profile pattern if she is retested at a later date. Social introversion-extraversion tends to be a very stable personality characteristic over time. The client's typically outgoing and sociable behavior is likely to remain similar if she is retested at a later time.

Discussion. The case above demonstrates how the MMPI-2 can be of assistance when included as part of a child custody evaluation. First, the MMPI-2 offers an objective, empirically based assessment of the emotional functioning and psychopathology of Mr. and Ms. H. This is of particular importance in this case given Ms. H.'s history of depression and her ex-husband's allegations of depression at the current time. Ms. H.'s claim that she was not experiencing any symptoms of depression is supported by the results of the MMPI-2.[13]

The MMPI-2 also proved of some value in assessing Mr. and Ms. H.'s behavior patterns and personality styles. Matthew was exhibiting significant behavioral problems that were affecting his adjustment at school and home. All three psychologists who attempted to treat the family agreed that psychotherapeutic intervention, and consistency and structure on the part of Matthew's parents, were necessary. Ms. H.'s MMPI-2 profile added support to impressions offered by two psychologists and Mr. H. regarding Ms. H.'s ability to organize and prioritize things, "follow through," and meet various responsibilities. Ms. H.'s MMPI-2 profile also portrayed her as highly focused on her own needs, which might also partly explain her difficulty in meeting some of Matthew's important needs at the time of the evaluation.

Finally, the MMPI-2 proved of some utility in assessing the "test-taking sets" with which Mr. and Ms. H. approached the evaluation process. Validity indices of the MMPI-2 portrayed Mr. H. as responding somewhat defensively to the inventory and presenting himself in a positive light, suggesting that extra care should be taken in evaluating his accounts of himself, Matthew, and his ex-wife. To the contrary, validity indices of Ms. H.'s MMPI-2 profile portrayed her as responding to the inventory in a less defensive manner, suggesting that her accounts might be more candid and less vulnerable to distortion.

Research Directions

Although the research literature is growing, there remains much to learn about divorce, child custody decision making, different child custody arrangements, and the effects these events have on the parents and children involved. Research incorporating the use of the MMPI-2/MMPI-A can help illuminate a number of important areas.

Although many writers agree that the divorce and custody decision-making process is a stressful and challenging one for both children and parents, our understanding about the exact nature and extent of these effects, and who and how many people suffer negative (or positive) effects related to separation and divorce is incomplete. Research incorporating the MMPI-2/MMPI-A could prove of some assistance in documenting the effects of divorce on parents and adolescent children alike. Administration of the MMPI-2 and MMPI-A to relevant parties (i.e., separating and divorcing parents and their adolescent children) at multiple points in time both prior and subsequent to the divorce would provide valuable information (see Felner & Terre, 1987, and Rohman et al., 1987, for a review of this developing literature).

Such research would provide mental health professionals with additional information about the effects of divorce on adjustment and psychological functioning. This information could prove helpful in two ways. First, with respect to interventions with these families, such information would help mental health professionals differentiate "normal" responses from more problematic ones that are more likely to require intervention. Such information would also prove helpful if communicated to attorneys, who may act as gatekeepers and mental health referral sources with respect to the mental health needs of divorcing families.

Second, with respect to custody decision making, a better understanding of the effects of divorce and custody decision making on parents and children will help child custody evaluators better evaluate the relevant parties, and assist them in distinguishing situational reactions related to the divorce (the "symptoms" of which would hopefully dissipate over time) from preexisting and subsequently developing conditions that may have implications for custody decision making.

Although research focusing on the relationship between MMPI-2 and behaviors specifically relevant to parenting will also prove interesting, it is less likely to have implications for evaluation practice. It will be difficult to identify relationships between particular MMPI-2 scales or profiles and parenting behaviors that will be strong enough to have predictive ability that is of much clinical utility.

Summary

The MMPI/MMPI-2 is the psychological assessment instrument most frequently used in child custody evaluations today. A review of the legal underpinnings of the child custody decision-making process provides ample support for the circumscribed use of the MMPI-2 and MMPI-A in such evaluations. There is a clear research base that documents the ability of the MMPI-2 and MMPI-A to identify and describe the emotional adjustment of parents and adolescent children who are involved in the divorce and custody decision-making process. Similarly, the research literature documenting the Minnesota instruments' ability to assess the test-taking sets of examinees is well established and this, too, may prove helpful to the psychologist conducting child custody evaluations.

There is relatively little literature, however, examining the relationship between particular MMPI/MMPI-2 profiles or scale elevations and specific parenting behaviors or styles, or particular behavioral outcomes of children. Use of the Minnesota instruments in this manner presents the greatest potential for error. It is therefore incumbent on evaluators who use the MMPI-2 to predict or describe parenting styles or behaviors, or to predict how a child may be affected by particular behavior patterns that are suggested by the parent's MMPI-2 profile, to identify the rationale and support for this approach, and identify any inferences that are made as past of this process.

MMPI-2/MMPI-A research examining the effects of divorce on adults and adolescent children should provide valuable information about the effects of divorce on families and the utility of the MMPI-2 and MMPI-A in making decisions about the custody and living arrangements of children.

Notes

1. The focus of this chapter is on child custody evaluations and decision making in the context of divorce. Depending on differences and similarities in the law, the analyses presented here may or may not be applicable to other, related areas such as child guardianship proceedings, neglect and abuse proceedings, and termination of parental rights proceedings. For a discussion of how these laws may differ, see Mnookin (1975).

2. Admissibility of expert testimony in child custody cases (and all other cases) is determined by evidentiary rules adopted by the jurisdiction in which the action is tried. A full discussion of the nature of expert opinions and the admissibility of expert testimony is beyond the scope of this chapter. For a general discussion on mental health expert testimony and admissibility see Ogloff (this volume), Heilbrun (1992), and Pope et al. (1993).

3. The importance of the mental health professional justifying use of the test for the court by drawing a connection between the psychological construct being assessed or measured and the legally relevant behavior (i.e., establishing "relevancy") cannot be underestimated (see Heilbrun, 1992, for a discussion of this issue and that of the role of psychological testing in forensic assessment more generally). This being said, however, it is important to note that a perception of many mental health professionals who testify is that the courts are not nearly strict enough in terms of requiring mental health professionals to make the relevancy of their assessments clear. Psychologists and other mental health professionals who include the MMPI-2 or MMPI-A (or any other assessment instrument or technique) as part of their custody evaluation process must be familiar with applicable research and be able to demonstrate empirical support for drawing conclusions relevant to custody decision making via use of the instruments.

4. The validity and clinical scales of the MMPI-2 are regarded as nearly identical to the original MMPI in terms of reliability, validity, and item content allowing for comparable

interpretations of high point scores, profile codes, and profile types (Graham, 1993; Graham, Timbrook, Ben-Porath, & Butcher, 1991; Pope et al., 1993).

5. It is emphasized that the Minnesota instruments should be considered as instruments to be used as part of a much broader inquiry made by the mental health professional, focused on a variety of issues deemed relevant by the courts and legislature (see the UMDA and Michigan statute for custody decision making on pp. 197-198). Child custody evaluations must be multi-source and multimethod given the numerous and varied issues with which the court is concerned.

6. The UMDA directs, in part, that "The court shall consider all relevant factors including . . . the mental and physical health of all parties involved." The Michigan statute directs that custody decisions are to be based, in part, on "the mental health and physical health of the competing parties." Even those commentators (e.g., Mnookin, 1975, p. 282; Okpaku, 1976, p. 1118) who have described the intricacies of child custody decision making and pointed out the limitations of what mental health professionals have to offer in these matters differentiate assessment of parents' mental states relevant to psychopathology from other types of inquiries or assessments made by mental health professionals.

7. Section 402 of the UMDA directs, in part, "The court shall consider all relevant factors including . . . the interaction and interrelationship of the child with his parent or parents, his siblings, and other persons who may significantly affect the child's best interests." The Michigan statute directs that custody decisions are to be based, in part on "the love, affection, and other emotional ties existing between the competing parties and the child" and "the capacity and disposition of competing parties to give the child love, affection and guidance and continuation of educating and raising the child in its religion or creed, if any." These abilities or capacities, although admittedly vague, may be affected by behavioral styles and patterns of responding that are tapped and measured by the MMPI/MMPI-2.

8. In the absence of empirical data, psychologists are discouraged from offering opinions about the relationship between certain behavioral styles or personality types, parenting behaviors, and their effects on children based on their "clinical experience," given the multitude of problems that can occur when impressions and perceived relationships are based on something other than empirical investigation. For a discussion of this issue, and other errors in clinical decision making that can occur in forensic contexts, see Borum, Otto, and Golding (1993).

9. In his guidelines for using psychological testing in forensic assessments, Heilbrun (1992) recommends that "Response style should be explicitly assessed using approaches sensitive to distortion, and the results of psychological testing interpreted within the context of the individual's response style" (p. 267).

10. It is reasonable to infer that there is a relationship between how the examinee responds to the MMPI-2 and how the examinee responds to questions posed by the psychologist conducting the child custody evaluation. Of course, the nature of this inference must be made clear to the legal decision maker.

11. This edited interpretation is extracted from the *Minnesota Report: Adult Clinical System Interpretive Report* by James N. Butcher. It is reprinted with permission of the Regents of the University of Minnesota and National Computer Systems.

12. This edited interpretation is extracted from the *Minnesota Report: Adult Clinical System Interpretive Report* by James N. Butcher. It is reprinted with permission of the Regents of the University of Minnesota and National Computer Systems.

13. Some readers might question whether there is a history of bipolar affective disorder or cyclothymia given Ms. H's history and the MMPI-2 profile. This hypothesis was not supported based on reports offered by Mr. H., Ms. H., and Ms. H.'s mother.

References

Ackerman, M. J., & Schoendorf, K. (1992). *ASPECT: Ackerman-Schoendorf scales for parent evaluation of custody.* Los Angeles, CA: Western Psychological Services.

American Educational Research Association, American Psychological Association, and National Council on Measurement in Education. (1985). *Standards for educational and psychological testing.* Washington, DC; American Psychological Association.

American Psychological Association. (1992). Ethical principles of psychologists and code of conduct. *American Psychologist, 47,* 1597-1611.

Archer, R. P. (1992). *MMPI-A: Assessing adolescent psychopathology.* Hillsdale, NJ: Lawrence Erlbaum.

Archer, R. P., Sutker, P. B., White, J. L., & Orvin, G. H. (1978). Personality relationships among parents and adolescent offspring in inpatient treatment. *Psychological Reports, 42,* 207-214.

Ayers v. Ayers, (Oh. Ct. App., 1993).

Bjerke v. Wilcox, 401 N.W.2d 97 (Min. Ct. App. 1987).

Borum, R., Otto, R. K., & Golding, S. (1993). Improving clinical judgment and decision making in forensic evaluation. *Journal of Psychiatry and Law, 21,* 35-76.

Brodzinsky, D. M. (1993). On the use and misuse of psychological testing in child custody evaluations. *Professional Psychology: Research and Practice, 24,* 213-219.

Bunch v. Bunch, 469 So.2d 1191 (Lou. Ct. App. 3rd Cir. 1985).

Butcher, J. N. (1990). *Use of the MMPI-2 in treatment planning.* New York: Oxford University Press.

Chaffin, M. (1992). Factors associated with treatment completion and progress among intrafamilial sexual abusers. *Child Abuse & Neglect, 16,* 251-264.

Child Custody Act of 1970. (1992). Michigan Comp. Laws, Chapter 722-23.

Committee on Ethical Guidelines for Forensic Psychologists. (1991). Specialty guidelines for forensic psychologists. *Law and Human Behavior, 15,* 655-665.

Committee on Professional Practice and Standards, American Psychological Association. (1994). Guidelines for child custody evaluations in divorce proceedings. *American Psychologist, 49,* 677-680.

Cookerly, J. R. (1974). The reduction of psychopathology as measured by the MMPI clinical scales in three forms of marriage counseling. *Journal of Marriage and the Family, 36,* 332.

Cronier v. Cronier, 540 So.2d 1160 (Lou. Ct. App. 1st Cir. 1989).

Dean, R. S., & Jacobson, B. P. (1982). MMPI characteristics of parents of emotionally disturbed and learning-disabled children. *Journal of Consulting and Clinical Psychology, 50,* 775-777.

DeGroot, G. W., & Adamson, J. D. (1973). Responses of psychiatric inpatients to the MacAndrew Alcoholism Scale. *Quarterly Journal of Studies of Alcohol, 34,* 1133-1139.

Egeland, B., Erickson, M. F., Butcher, J. N., & Ben-Porath, Y. S. (1991). MMPI-2 profiles of women at risk for child abuse. *Journal of Personality Assessment, 57,* 254-263.

Erickson, W. D., Walbek, N. H., & Seely, R. K. (1987). The life histories and psychological profiles of 59 incestuous stepfathers. *Bulletin of the American Academy of Psychiatry and the Law, 15,* 349-357.

Felner, R. D., & Terre, L. (1987). Child custody dispositions and children's adaptation following divorce. In L. A. Weithorn (Ed.), *Psychology and child custody determinations: Knowledge, roles and expertise* (pp. 106-156). Lincoln: University of Nebraska Press.

Fitzgerald v. Brown, 857 P.2d 708 (Mont. Sup. Ct. 1993).

Frick, P. J., Lahey, B. B., Hartdagen, S., & Hynd, G. W. (1989). Conduct problems in boys: Relations to maternal personality, marital satisfaction, and socioeconomic status. *Journal of Clinical Child Psychology, 18,* 114-120.

Friedrich, W. N. (1991). Mothers of sexually abused children: An MMPI study. *Journal of Clinical Psychology, 47,* 778-783.

Gilbertson v. Gilbertson, 1192 Minn. App. 1058 (Minn. Ct. App. 1992).

Goote v. Lightner, 224 Cal.App.3d 587. 274 Cal.Rptr. 697, Cal. Ct. App., 4th App. Dist., Div. 1 (1990).

Graham, J. R. (1993). *MMPI-2: Assessing personality and psychopathology* (2nd ed.). New York: Oxford University Press.

Graham, J. R., Ben-Porath, Y. S., & Ott, E. K. (1994, May). *Correlates of MMPI-2 scales in outpatient mental health center patients.* Paper presented at the 29th Annual Symposium on Recent Developments in the Use of the MMPI (MMPI-2 and MMPI-A), Minneapolis, MN.

Graham, J. R., Timbrook, R. E., Ben-Porath, Y. S., & Butcher, J. N. (1991). Congruence between MMPI and MMPI-2: Separating fact from artifact. *Journal of Personality Assessment, 57,* 205-215.

Greene, R. (1980). *The MMPI: An interpretive manual.* New York: Grune & Stratton.

Greene, R. L. (1988). Assessment of malingering and defensiveness by objective personality inventories. In R. Rogers (Ed.), *Clinical assessment of malingering and deception* (pp. 123-158). New York: Guilford.

Greene, R. L. (1991). *The MMPI-2/MMPI: An interpretive manual.* Needham Heights, MA: Allyn & Bacon.

Grisso, T. (1984, June). *Forensic assessment in juvenile and family cases: The state of the art.* Keynote address at the meeting of the Summer Institute on Mental Health Law, University of Nebraska, Lincoln.

Grisso, T. (1986). *Evaluating competencies: Forensic assessments and instruments.* New York: Plenum.

Gynther, M. D., Altman, H., & Sletten, I. W. (1973). Replicated correlates of MMPI two-point types: The Missouri actuarial system. *Journal of Clinical Psychology, 29*(Suppl. 39), 263-289.

Hackney, G. R., & Ribordy, S. C. (1980). An empirical investigation of emotional reactions to divorce. *Journal of Clinical Psychology, 36,* 105-110.

Hamilton, A., Stiles, W. B., Melowsky, F., & Beal, D. G. (1987). A multilevel comparison of child abusers with nonabusers. *Journal of Family Violence, 2,* 215-225.

Heilbrun, K. (1988, March). *Third party information in forensic assessments: Much needed, sometimes sought, poorly guided.* Paper presented at the Biennial Meeting of the American Psychology-Law Society/Division 41 of the American Psychological Association, Miami, FL.

Heilbrun, K. (1992). The role of psychological testing in forensic assessment. *Law and Human Behavior, 16,* 257-272.

Heinicke, C. M., Diskin, S. D., Ramsey-Klee, D. M., & Oates, D. S. (1986). Pre- and post-antecedents of 2-year-old attention, capacity for relationships, and verbal expressiveness. *Developmental Psychology, 22,* 777-787.

Hjemboe, S., Almagor, M., & Butcher, J. N. (1992). Empirical assessment of marital distress: The Marital Distress Scale (MDS) for the MMPI-2. In J. N. Butcher & C. D. Spielberger (Eds.), *Advances in personality assessment: Vol. 9* (pp. 141-152). Hillsdale, NJ: Lawrence Erlbaum.

Hjemboe, S., & Butcher, J. N. (1991). Couples in marital distress: A study of personality factors as measured by the MMPI-2. *Journal of Personality Assessment, 57,* 216-237.

Hreha v. Hreha, 392 N.W.2d 914 (Minn. Ct. App. 1986).

In Re DH, 342 S.E.2d 367 (Ga. Ct. App. 1986).

In Re Willis, 599 N.E.2d 179 (Ill. App. Ct. 3rd Dist. 1992).

Isom v. Isom, 538 N.E.2d 261 (Ind. Ct. App. 3rd Dist. 1989).

JEP v. JCP, 432 N.W.2d 483 (Minn. Ct. App. 1988).

Keilin, W. G., & Bloom, L. J. (1986). Child custody evaluation practices: A survey of experienced professionals. *Professional Psychology: Research and Practice, 17,* 338-346.

Keith-Spiegel, P., & Koocher, G. P. (1985). *Ethics in psychology: Professional standards and cases.* Hillsdale, NJ: Lawrence Erlbaum.

Kirkland, K. D., & Bauer, C. A. (1982). MMPI traits of incestuous fathers. *Journal of Clinical Psychology, 38,* 645-649.

Lahey, B. B., Russo, M. F., Walker, J. L., & Piacentini, J. C. (1989). Personality characteristics of the mothers of children with disruptive behavior disorders. *Journal of Consulting and Clinical Psychology, 57,* 512-515.

Lowery, C. R. (1981). Child custody decisions in divorce proceedings: A survey of judges. *Professional Psychology: Research and Practice, 12,* 492-498.

McIntosh, J. A., & Prinz, R. J. (1993). The incidence of alleged sexual abuse in 603 family court cases. *Law and Human Behavior, 17,* 95-101.

Melton, G. B., Petrila, J., Poythress, N., & Slobogin, C. (1987). *Psychological evaluations for the courts: A handbook for mental health professionals and lawyers.* New York: Guilford.

Melton, G. B., Weithorn, L. A., & Slobogin, C. (1985). *Community mental health centers and the courts: An evaluation of community-based forensic services.* Lincoln: University of Nebraska Press.

Mnookin, R. H. (1975). Child custody adjudication: Judicial functions in the face of indeterminacy. *Law and Contemporary Problems, 39,* 226-293.

Mrazek, D. A., Klinnert, M. D., Mrazek, P., & Macey, T. (1991). Early asthma onset: Consideration of parenting issues. *Journal of the American Academy of Child Adolescent Psychiatry, 30,* 277-282.

Multnomah County v. Grannis, 680 P.2d 660 (Ore. Ct. App. 1984).

Novotny v. Novotny, 394 N.W.2d 256 (Minn. Ct. App. 1986).

Okpaku, S. R. (1976). Psychology: Impediment or aid in child custody cases? *Rutgers Law Review, 29,* 1117-1153.

Ollendick, D. G. (1984). Scores on three MMPI alcohol scales of parents who receive child custody. *Psychological Reports, 55,* 337-338.

Ollendick, D. G., & Otto, B. J. (1984). MMPI characteristics of parents referred for child-custody studies. *Journal of Psychology, 117,* 227-232.

Ollendick, D. G., Otto, B. J., & Heider, S. M. (1983). Marital MMPI characteristics: A test of Arnold's signs. *Journal of Clinical Psychology, 39,* 240-245.

Paulson, M. J., Abdelmonen, A. A., Thomason, M. L., & Chaleff, A. (1974). The MMPI: A descriptive measure of psychopathology in abusive parents. *Journal of Clinical Psychology, 30,* 387-390.

Paulson, M. J., Schwemer, G. T., & Bendel, R. B. (1976). Clinical application of the Pd, Ma, and (OH) experimental MMPI scales to further understanding of abusive parents. *Journal of Clinical Psychology, 32,* 558-564.

Plotkin, R. C., Twentyman, C. T., & Perri, M. G. (1982). The utility of a measure of aggression in differentiating abusing parents from other parents who are experiencing familial disturbance. *Journal of Clinical Psychology, 38,* 607-610.

Pope, K. S., Butcher, J. N., & Seelen, J. (1993). *The MMPI, MMPI-2, & MMPI-A in court.* Washington, DC: American Psychological Association.

Rogers, R. (1988). Introduction (to the text). In R. Rogers (Ed.), *Clinical assessment of malingering and deception* (pp. 1-9). New York: Guilford.

Rohman, L. R., Sales, B. D., & Lou, M. (1987). The best interests of the child in custody disputes. In L. A. Weithorn (Ed.), *Psychology and child custody determinations: Knowledge, roles and expertise* (pp. 59-105). Lincoln: University of Nebraska Press.

Scott, R. L., & Stone, D. A. (1986). MMPI profile constellations in incest families. *Journal of Consulting and Clinical Psychology, 54,* 364-368.

Scott v. Prince George County, 545 A.2d 81 (Mar. Ct. Spec. App. of 1988).

Smith, P. E., Burleigh, R. L., Sewell, W. R., & Krisack, J. (1984). Correlations between the Minnesota Multiphasic Personality Inventory profiles of emotionally disturbed adolescents and their mothers. *Adolescence, 19,* 31-38.

Snyder D. K., & Regts, J. M. (1990). Personality correlates of marital dissatisfaction: A comparison of psychiatric, maritally distressed, and non-clinic samples. *Journal of Sex and Marital Therapy, 16,* 34-43.

Uniform Marriage and Divorce Act. (1979). *Uniform Laws Annotated,* 9A.

U.S. Department of Commerce, Bureau of the Census. (1993). *Statistical abstract of the United States.* Washington, DC: Author.

Utz v. Kienzle, 574 So.2d 1288 (Lou. Ct. App. 3rd. Cir. 1991).

Weece v. Cottle, 352 S.E.2d 131 (W. Va. Sup. Ct. 1986).

Weissman, H. N. (1991). Child custody evaluations: Fair and unfair professional practices. *Behavioral Sciences and the Law, 9,* 469-476.

Weithorn, L. A. (Ed.). (1987). *Psychology and child custody determinations: Knowledge, roles, and expertise.* Lincoln: University of Nebraska Press.

Weithorn, L. A., & Grisso, T. (1987). Psychological evaluations in divorce custody: Problems, principles, and procedures. In L. A. Weithorn (Ed.), *Psychology and child custody determinations: Knowledge, roles and expertise* (pp. 157-181). Lincoln: University of Nebraska Press.

Wright, L. (1976). The "sick but slick" syndrome as a personality component of parents of battered children. *Journal of Clinical Psychology, 32,* 41-45.

Wyer, M. M., Gaylord, S. J., & Grove, E. T. (1987). The legal context of child custody evaluations. In L. A. Weithorn (Ed.), *Psychology and child custody determinations: Knowledge, roles and expertise* (pp. 3-22). Lincoln: University of Nebraska Press.

Ziskin, J. (1981). The use of the MMPI in forensic settings. In J. N. Butcher, W. G. Dahlstrom, M. D. Gynther, & S. Schofield (Eds), *Clinical notes on the MMPI* (Vol. 9, pp. 1-13). Minneapolis, MN: National Computer Systems.

Forensic Applications of the MMPI-2

Current Status and Future Directions

JOHN R. GRAHAM

YOSSEF S. BEN-PORATH

KATHLEEN P. STAFFORD

The purposes of this final chapter are to reach some conclusions about the current status and the use of the MMPI-2 in forensic evaluations and to suggest some directions for future research in this area. The chapter is based, to a large extent, on earlier chapters in this volume and on discussions that took place at the Kent Psychology Forum in April 1994. However, the opinions expressed here are those of this chapter's authors and are not necessarily endorsed by all Forum participants.

Background

The MMPI was the most widely used psychological test in the world (Graham, 1993). All indicators to date suggest that the MMPI-2 has been widely adopted by psychologists (Webb, Levitt, & Rajdev, 1993) and probably will enjoy even more popularity than the original MMPI. Although the MMPI was originally developed to assist in the assignment of psychiatric diagnoses to inpatients, the purposes for which it came to be used were diverse. The instrument was routinely used in outpatient mental health settings and in a variety of medical settings. Screening of applicants for sensitive jobs (e.g., police officers, firefighters, airline pilots) has often involved the MMPI. In the past decade or so, as the role of psychologists in the forensic arena has expanded dramatically, the MMPI has been used as part of psychological assessments triggered by a variety of legal issues including sanity, competency, and child custody.

As the MMPI has been used for purposes different from those for which it was developed, responsible professionals have raised questions about the appropriateness of such use. The basic question that has been raised over and over again is whether the MMPI (and now MMPI-2) has validity for the various specific purposes for which it has come to be used. The answer in most cases has been yes. The scales of the MMPI/MMPI-2 have similar behavioral correlates in psychiatric inpatient (Gynther, Altman, & Sletten, 1973), mental health outpatient (Graham, Ben-Porath, & Ott, 1994), medical (Henrichs, 1981), and employment (Butcher, 1979) settings. Although data concerning correlates in forensic settings are limited, they suggest that the MMPI/MMPI-2 assesses similar characteristics in these settings as in others in which the instrument has been researched (Pope, Butcher, & Seelen, 1993).

Research Concerning Validity of the MMPI/MMPI-2 in Forensic Settings

There are several reasons why we have limited research data concerning the validity of the MMPI/MMPI-2 in forensic settings. First, the use of the instruments in forensic settings has occurred far more recently than in other kinds of settings. Thus, there has been less time for a meaningful database to be accumulated. Second, in most forensic settings it is difficult to obtain appropriate criterion information against which the MMPI/MMPI-2 can be evaluated. The test results often influence conclusions and decisions that are reached about individuals in these settings. Therefore, there is a serious contamination of test and criterion variables. For example, suppose that we want to evaluate the extent to which the MMPI-2 scales are valid for assessing defendants' competency to stand trial. The MMPI-2 would be administered to defendants as a part of a pretrial evaluation. Reports would be written to the court concerning competency. These reports would be based, at least in part, on MMPI-2 results. The reports would be evaluated by the court and decisions would be reached about competency. Even if there were significant correlations between MMPI-2 scores and the eventual decision of the court concerning competency (e.g., Nicholson & Kugler, 1991), it could very well be that the correlations do not reflect actual relationships between MMPI-2 scores and competency. Rather, it could be that what is being reflected here is a relationship between the reports that were based in part on MMPI-2 results and the court's decisions that were based in part on the reports. It is quite possible that neither the MMPI-2 scores nor the court's decision reflect the actual competencies of the defendants assessed. Even for the more limited task of predicting the courts' decisions regarding competency, this design would be inappropriate because of the contamination of the independent and dependent variables.

A third factor is that it is very difficult to obtain follow-up information in forensic settings. For example, suppose that we are interested in conducting research to determine the extent to which the MMPI-2 is able to assess the risk that persons will engage in dangerous behavior in the future. We would assess persons using the MMPI-2 at a particular point in time, perhaps following an arrest for violence or at the time of a hearing to determine whether civil commitment is indicated. How are we to follow these persons and determine if the predictions based on the MMPI-2 turn out to be accurate? A very common approach is to search arrest records and determine which persons subsequently were arrested for charges involving dangerousness. This approach clearly has limitations. What about the persons who engage in dangerous behaviors but are not arrested? Or those who leave the jurisdiction in which the research is being conducted?

Another example of the difficulty in obtaining appropriate follow-up data involves the use of the MMPI-2 in custody evaluations. Suppose that we are conducting a study in which the MMPI-2 is administered to parents who are involved in disputed custody. There may be some MMPI-2 results that suggest to us that some parents will behave in ways that will not be in the best interests of their children. Yet, how are we to determine if our predictions are accurate? The most appropriate way to do so would be to follow the parents over an extended period of time, regularly assessing their behaviors in relation to their children. Moreover, we would have to ignore the MMPI-2 results in making a recommendation to the court or risk, once again, contaminating our independent and dependent variables. Clearly, such procedures are not very practical.

In spite of these problems in conducting research concerning the validity of the MMPI/MMPI-2 in forensic settings, there are some relevant data available in the literature. Previous chapters have reviewed some of these data in detail. We will mention several examples of the kinds of data that are available.

Heilburn and Heilbrun (this volume) reported that most studies involving the prediction of aggression or violence from the MMPI have used single scales, most often the Overcontrolled-Hostility (O–H) scale (Megargee, Cook, & Mendelsohn, 1967). There also have been attempts to relate aggression, violence, or both to specific MMPI code types (e.g., 34/43, 49/94). Although some studies of single scales and code types have identified significant relationships with aggression/violence, the strength of the relationships has not been strong enough to support the use of the scales or code types for prediction in individual cases. Heilbrun (1994) has found that a dangerousness index involving Scale 4 of the MMPI and a measure of intellectual functioning has considerable power in explaining certain kinds of criminal violence. The MMPI typology developed by Megargee and Bohn (1979) has been helpful in identifying persons in correctional settings who are prone to violent behavior while incarcerated.

Rogers and McKee (this volume) reviewed five studies in which MMPI scores of defendants judged to be sane were compared with scores of defendants judged to be insane. In general, there were very few differences between groups. This is not a surprising finding, given that the MMPI assesses current emotional status and the determination of criminal responsibility is based primarily on status at an earlier time when a specific act was committed. Rogers and McKee also reviewed some recent data suggesting that scores on Scale 4 and on the Antisocial Practices content scale of the MMPI-2 may offer corroborative data concerning antisocial characteristics of criminal defendants.

Otto and Collins (this volume) indicated that very few studies have examined the relationship between MMPI scores and parenting abilities of persons involved in child custody determinations. Although parents who were awarded custody by the courts had lower MMPI scores, differences between parents who did and did not receive custody were rather small. Because the courts had knowledge of MMPI results when making the custody determinations, there was a confound between MMPI scores and the custody determination. Further, there were no follow-up data concerning the quality of parenting of those parents who were awarded custody.

Clearly, there are only limited data available concerning the relationships between MMPI performance and legal issues such as criminal responsibility, risk assessment, or child custody. Even fewer MMPI-2 studies are available.

Current Status

In spite of the limitations just identified, the MMPI (and now MMPI-2) is widely used by psychologists conducting forensic evaluations of various kinds (Lees-Haley, 1992). Courts have been overwhelmingly accepting of expert testimony based on MMPI/MMPI-2 results (Ogloff, this volume). In fact, courts probably have not been critical enough in asking for evidence concerning the validity of the MMPI/MMPI-2 for the specific purposes for which the test is used in forensic settings. Based on the existing research literature, earlier chapters in this volume, and the discussions that took place at the 1994 Kent Psychology Forum, some conclusions can be reached concerning the extent to which the MMPI-2 is relevant to forensic issues. It seems clear to us that the MMPI-2 can make important contributions to the assessment of many forensic issues. However, it is equally clear that many clinicians are using the test in ways that cannot be justified from the existing research literature. Therefore, it is important to try to specify the purposes for which the MMPI-2 should and should not be used in forensic evaluations.

DETECTING RESPONSE BIAS

The MMPI-2 has demonstrated utility in detecting response bias. In almost all forensic evaluations, the persons being evaluated have potential motivation to distort their responses. A defendant who has entered a plea of not guilty by reason of insanity may very well believe that it is in her or his best interest to answer the MMPI-2 items as if she or he is more emotionally disturbed than she or he really is. Parents involved in child custody evaluations understandably might want to present an overly positive picture of themselves when completing the MMPI-2. Other persons, because of limited reading ability, inability to follow instructions, or uncooperativeness, may respond to items without giving appropriate consideration to their content. Obviously, these various response sets have significant implications for the interpretations that should be made of the resulting test scores.

As indicted by Berry (this volume), there is a substantial research base indicating that the validity scales of the MMPI have been able to identify invalidating response biases. Recent data suggest that the validity scales of the MMPI-2 perform similarly to those of the original MMPI in identifying these biases (Graham, Watts, & Timbrook, 1991). The Variable Response Inconsistency (VRIN) scale accurately detects persons who have responded randomly to MMPI-2 items. The Infrequency (F) and Back F (Fb) scales are very useful in identifying persons who malinger symptoms of psychopathology when responding to the MMPI-2 items. Although the detection of underreporting of symptoms (defensiveness) is less readily detected by the MMPI-2 validity scales, there is ample evidence that the L and K scales can be used for this purpose.

In spite of considerable evidence suggesting that the MMPI-2 validity scales are useful in detecting response bias, several caveats concerning their use in forensic settings are in order. First, most of the research concerning cutting scores and classification rates has not been conducted with forensic subjects. It may very well be that optimal cutting scores in forensic settings will differ somewhat from those in mental health settings. Second, there is mounting evidence that test subjects can be "coached" to present themselves as having emotional problems that they do not really have and to avoid detection of the response distortion. Berry (this volume) indicated that giving subjects information about the specific disorders that they are trying to malinger has little effect on the extent to which the malingering can be detected by the validity scales of the MMPI-2. However, giving test subjects specific information about the MMPI-2 validity scales increases the likelihood that they will be able to malinger various kinds of psychopathology without being detected by the validity scales.

Assessing Clinical Condition

In most instances in which the MMPI-2 is used in relation to specific legal issues, the presence or absence of serious psychopathology is a very important factor. For example, "mental disease or defect" is a key component of the criteria for insanity. In most states, the "mental health" of parents is a factor considered in determining custody of children.

The original MMPI was designed specifically to assess various aspects of psychopathology, and there is a considerable research base suggesting that scores on the MMPI and the MMPI-2 are related to emotional status. Assuming that persons have approached the testing in a valid manner, scores on MMPI-2 scales that are markedly above those of the normative samples suggest the existence of serious psychological or emotional problems. Although most of the research concerning the relationships between MMPI/MMPI-2 scores and symptoms and emotional problems has been conducted in traditional mental health settings, there is good reason to believe that similar relationships exist in forensic settings (Ben-Porath, Shondrick, & Stafford, 1995). For example, persons with very high scores on scale 2 (Depression) are likely to be manifesting symptoms of clinical depression, whether they are being assessed in a mental health center or in a court clinic. Persons with very high scores on Scale 8 (Schizophrenia) and the Bizarre Mentation content scale are likely to show signs of disturbed thinking regardless of the setting in which they are assessed.

The substance abuse scales of the MMPI-2 (MacAndrew Alcoholism Scale, Revised; Addiction Acknowledgment Scale; Addiction Potential Scale) offer important information about the likelihood that persons being evaluated abuse alcohol, other substances, or both. The optimal cutting scores to be used to classify accurately abusers and nonabusers are likely to vary from setting to setting, and it is not yet clear just what scores will be most useful in forensic settings. Scores on these scales should not be used alone to determine if someone is a substance abuser. Rather, they represent one important source of information to be used along with other information such as interview, history, and drug screens.

The MMPI-2 is best at identifying *current* emotional status. It is less useful in understanding emotional status at some time in the past or in predicting future emotional status. However, evidence that significant psychopathology is present or absent at the time of a forensic evaluation is one important kind of information that can be helpful in establishing past psychopathology or predicting future psychopathology. For example, clear evidence of psychotic processes at the present time increases our confidence that a person who is claiming such problems at an earlier time should be believed. Similarly, evidence that a person has a serious substance abuse problem at the present time increases our concern about such problems in the future.

Weiner (this volume) pointed out that extrapolations from present MMPI-2 scores to past or future behaviors are appropriate to the extent that MMPI-2 scores are temporally stable. The MMPI has generally been accepted as having good temporal stability. Spiro, Bosse, Butcher, Levenson, and Aldwin (1993) reported 5-year stability coefficients for MMPI-2 scales ranging from .55 (scale 6) to .85 (scale 0).

Because many interpretations of MMPI-2 scales involve consideration of code types, it is important to know to what extent code types remain stable over time. Data for the MMPI have suggested that code types remain relatively stable over time if the code types are well defined (at least 5 T-score points between the lowest scale in the code type and the next highest scale in the profile) and if the scores on scales in the code types are significantly elevated ($T>70$). Although no data have yet been published concerning the stability of MMPI-2 code types, there is reason to believe that the MMPI-2 code types will be similar in stability to those of the original MMPI. Spiro et al. (in press) found that the men in their study maintained the same relative rank order on the clinical scales over a 5-year period.

Clearly, there is enough evidence to conclude that the stability of MMPI-2 scores and configurations of scores is high enough to permit some extrapolations from present scores to past or future behaviors. As is the case with all psychological tests, we should have more confidence in shorter term predictions than in longer term ones.

As was reported in several of the chapters of this volume, there is little support for the notion that there are demonstrated patterns of scores (i.e., profiles) for persons who are or are not likely to engage in particular behaviors that are relevant to many forensic evaluations. For example, there is not a typical profile for persons who are likely to commit such crimes as murder or child sexual abuse. Nor is there a typical profile for persons who are likely to be exceptionally good (or bad) parents. Ogloff (this volume) pointed out that the courts generally have rejected this notion that there are typical MMPI/MMPI-2 patterns associated with specific behaviors relevant to forensic issues.

SPECIFIC LEGAL ISSUES

Previous chapters in this volume have analyzed the extent to which the MMPI-2 is useful in assessing specific legal issues. The general conclusion that can be reached from these chapters is that the MMPI-2 is relevant to some aspects of most issues that clinicians are likely to be asked to address from forensic evaluations. However, the instrument is more relevant to some issues than to others.

Heilbrun and Heilbrun (this volume) concluded that, although there is not a typical MMPI-2 profile associated with dangerous or violent behavior,

MMPI-2 scores can add to our understanding and prediction of such behaviors. MMPI-2 scores (particularly Scale 4) are likely to be most useful in this regard when they are considered along with other information such as intelligence level and history of violent behavior.

Rogers and McKee (this volume) pointed out that psychological tests are of limited utility in assessing criminal responsibility, because we are trying to address past mental status from present test results. However, they view the test as useful in identifying response sets in defendants who are participating in insanity evaluations. Scale 4 is a useful source of collaborative data considering antisocial characteristics, which are to be considered in all insanity evaluations. Finally, descriptors based on individual scale elevations and on code types are helpful in developing an overall understanding of defendants' personality characteristics, many of which may be relevant to determining sanity versus insanity.

Otto and Collins (this volume) reached somewhat similar conclusions concerning the use of the MMPI-2 in child custody evaluations. The validity scales of the MMPI-2 are useful in identifying persons who approach the evaluation in other than candid, straightforward ways. Most domestic relations or family courts place considerable weight on the mental health of parents (and other potential custodians) in determining custody. The MMPI-2 is especially appropriate for assessing current emotional status. There is not a single or typical MMPI-2 profile that is associated with effective or ineffective parenting. However, the MMPI-2 assesses characteristics that certainly could be related to parenting skills and deficits. For example, it would be reasonable to infer that a person with very elevated scores on Scales 9 and 4 would be less likely to provide structure and limit setting, or to place the needs of a child before his or her own, than would a person with elevated scores on Scales 2 and 7. The extent to which these characteristics are relevant to decisions about custody is, of course, ultimately a legal decision to be made by the court.

Nelson (this volume) concluded that the MMPI-2 should not be used to determine the presence or absence of brain damage. Early efforts to use the MMPI in this manner were singularly unsuccessful. However, the MMPI-2 can be used to assess the direct emotional effects of brain damage and emotional effects that result from trying to cope with limitations imposed by brain damage. Differentiating between direct and indirect emotional effects often is a difficult task. The MMPI-2 will be most helpful in neuropsychological assessments when it is used along with other data (e.g., neuropsychological test scores, history, observation, medical tests).

Megargee and Carbonell (this volume) described ways in which the MMPI-2 can be used effectively in assessing correctional subjects. Individual scales and code types have not been very effective in predicting relevant behaviors of prisoners. However, more configural typologies were developed for the MMPI that were predictive of behaviors such as violent behavior in prison and recidivism. Preliminary work has indicated that a similar typology for the MMPI-2 is likely to be equally effective. One of the clear advantages of using the typology rather than variables such as offense is that the typology is sensitive to changes in the individual that occur over time.

Butcher (this volume) saw the MMPI-2 as useful with persons who are being assessed in relation to personal injury litigation. As with other applications, the validity scales are useful in identifying persons who are malingering or otherwise approaching the assessment in less than an honest and straightforward manner. Butcher concluded that there is not a typical profile of persons evaluated as part of personal injury litigation. However, skilled interpretations of MMPI-2 scores can yield information concerning the extent to which reported distress and maladjustment are believable. Butcher recommended the use of computerized interpretations because they are more reliable, more thorough, and less subjective than standard clinician-generated interpretations. However, it is necessary for clinicians to use other sources of information to determine the extent to which computerized interpretations are appropriate for the particular clients with whom they are being used.

In summary, the MMPI-2 has utility for a variety of forensic assessment issues. It is especially useful in assessing test-taking attitudes and current clinical condition of test subjects. However, MMPI-2 scores and configurations of scores also can be used to generate inferences about personality characteristics and behaviors that may have considerable relevance to legal issues under consideration.

Future Research Directions

There is generally good agreement that the MMPI-2 is a reliable instrument that has validity for a variety of purposes in mental health settings (Archer, 1992; Nichols, 1992). There is a substantial research base suggesting that the validity scales of the MMPI-2 are useful in detecting deviant response sets among test subjects. Likewise, there is strong evidence that accurate inferences about clinical condition and personality characteristics can be made from individual scales and code types.

Given that the MMPI and MMPI-2 permit accurate inferences in some other settings as well (e.g., medical, employment), it seems reasonable to expect that the instrument also can be used to generate accurate inferences in forensic settings. However, the instrument's validity for addressing some specific legal issues in forensic settings has not been as adequately established.

Therefore, the most pressing research need is to demonstrate that the MMPI-2 can be used as effectively in forensic settings as in mental health settings. Perhaps the most basic research would be to determine the extratest correlates of elevated scores on individual scales and of code types based on the scales. It will be important to establish the extent to which descriptors identified in mental health settings should be applied in forensic settings. For example, should forensic subjects who have very elevated Scale 2 scores be described as being clinically depressed, a description that we probably would apply to mental health center patients with such scores? Such research also should establish the levels of scores on each scale at which certain inferences are appropriate. For example, should clinical depression be inferred for forensic subjects who have Scale 2 T scores above 65, or is some other cutoff score more appropriate? When studying code types, it will be important to determine if descriptors apply to code types regardless of how well defined they are. Based on research in mental health settings, we would expect that more reliable correlates will be identified when the code types are well defined (i.e., when the lowest scale in the code type is at least 5 T-score points higher than the next highest scale in the profile). Identifying and using appropriate and reliable extratest measures will be very important. Structured interview data and behavioral observations should be examined.

In addition to determining the extent to which behavioral correlates can be generalized from mental health to forensic settings, it will be important to determine if there are unique correlates within forensic settings and the extent to which correlates can be generalized across subgroups within forensic settings. For example, are the correlates of scales and code types the same for male and female forensic subjects and for those from minority and majority groups? Are the correlates of a particular scale (e.g., Scale 4) the same for criminal defendants as for parents involved in domestic relations evaluations?

Recent research (e.g., Ben-Porath, Butcher, & Graham, 1991) has indicated that the content scales of the MMPI-2 add significantly to the clinical scales for some purposes. It will be important to determine if the content scales are also useful in forensic evaluations. For example, does the Antisocial Practices content scale of the MMPI-2 add to scale 4 in identifying antisocial characteristics of forensic subjects?

Knowing that a particular score or configuration of scores is very common or very rare in a particular setting can be of considerable use to clinicians who are interpreting MMPI-2 results. Such information is now routinely available to clinicians who use computerized MMPI-2 interpretations in mental health and medical settings. We know very little about the frequencies of scores and code types in forensic settings. The systematic accumulation and reporting of such frequency data in forensic settings would be most helpful.

It has been suggested by some that we need specific MMPI-2 norms for forensic settings. They maintain that, because some MMPI-2 scales tend to be more elevated in forensic settings than in others, it is not appropriate to use the same norms in interpreting test results in the forensic settings. Obviously, the extent to which forensic norms would lead to more or less accurate inferences about forensic subjects is an empirical matter that should be addressed. However, based on previous experiences with specific norms, it seems unlikely that such norms will be needed in forensic settings. When Dahlstrom, Lachar, and Dahlstrom (1986) conducted a comprehensive investigation of specific versus general norms for African American psychiatric patients, they concluded that specific norms were not indicated. In fact, they demonstrated that using specific African American norms led to underestimates of the psychiatric problems of the African American patients. Whether a similar result would be found for forensic subjects remains to be determined. The most direct way to assess the need for specific forensic norms would be to collect MMPI-2 data and reliable extratest data from a large number of forensic subjects. Raw scores could be converted to T scores based on the standard MMPI-2 norms and on norms derived specifically from forensic data. A comparison could then be made between the accuracy with which the extratest measures could be predicted with the two sets of scores.

To date there have been few investigations of the extent to which MMPI or MMPI-2 validity scales can detect overreporting or underreporting of symptoms and problems in forensic settings. Based on research in other settings, it seems likely that overreporting can be detected accurately using the F scale. Underreporting is likely to be more difficult to detect. Studies assessing both kinds of response distortion in forensic settings are needed. It will be especially important to design and conduct studies using forensic defendants and litigants rather than college students or other groups who are instructed to distort in some particular way when responding to test items. A very real challenge is to design studies in which the actual motivation to distort is known and not assumed.

In some settings (e.g., domestic relations or family courts) response distortions are so common that they become the norm. For example, parents who are seeking custody of their children almost always try to present overly positive impressions of themselves, resulting in a defensive pattern on the validity scales. It would be important to know when the test distortion exceeds what is normative for the setting, thereby suggesting that the MMPI-2 scores should be interpreted differently from those of most subjects in that setting.

In other chapters in this volume, authors suggested research directions specific to particular forensic applications of the MMPI-2. Weiner (this volume) encouraged more research concerning the extent to which MMPI-2 interpretations can be generalized to women and to members of ethnic minority groups. He also stressed the importance of studying the long-term stability of MMPI-2 scores and code types. Although we agree with Weiner that such research would be informative, we are not as convinced as he is that temporal stability is necessary to extrapolate from present scores to past or future behaviors. If we can establish a strong current relationship between MMPI-2 scores and a behavior pattern that tends to be quite stable (e.g., schizophrenia), we can then have confidence that persons who are exhibiting the behavior pattern now are also likely to display the behavior pattern in the future and probably displayed it in the past as well.

Several chapter authors advocated the use of MMPI-2 data along with other sources of information. We believe that research should be conducted to determine the extent to which adding MMPI-2 data to other information, such as observation of parent-child interactions, prior criminal behavior, treatment records, or current knowledge of court procedures, increases the accuracy of our inferences. However, we are cognizant of past research findings suggesting that more is not always better (e.g., Garb, 1984). Clinicians may feel more confident of their inferences if they are based on multiple data sources, but without research evidence indicating that more data increase accuracy, we should not assume that to be the case.

Otto and Collins (this volume) indicated that there is little information concerning relationships between MMPI-2 scores and specific parenting skills or deficits. They recommended that research be conducted to try to establish these links. We agree that this kind of research is very important, but we suspect that limitations of the MMPI-2 item pool may preclude finding many strong links between tests scores and specific parenting characteristics. Otto and Collins also stressed the importance of studying the effects of divorce on parents and children. Certainly, the MMPI-2 could be used as one measure of emotional distress. Such studies would be helpful because they would permit us to understand the extent to which parents obtain deviant MMPI-2 scores because of the process in which they are involved rather than because of some long-standing emotional problems.

Determining the kinds of research to be done concerning forensic applications of the MMPI-2 is relatively easy. In most cases the data that are needed but missing are obvious. How to conduct this research is a more difficult issue. To conduct the kinds of research that are suggested in this volume will require access to forensic subjects at various stages of the legal process. They will have to be evaluated prior to and following various legal proceedings. In many cases the research process could actively interfere with the legal process, and in other cases the legal process can interfere with the research. Eliciting cooperation of courts, attorneys, plaintiffs, and defendants will be necessary. To do so we will have to convince these parties that the research that we are proposing will have some substantial long-term benefits.

It also is clear that most of the research that needs to be conducted will require larger samples of particular kinds of forensic subjects than can be collected in most single settings. Collaborative research involving multiple forensic sites will be needed.

Research funding is another very real problem for those of us who do MMPI-2 research of any kind. Because the MMPI-2 is an owned instrument, federal and state agencies are not interested in supporting applied MMPI-2 research. However, it may be possible to request funding for projects that are not specifically MMPI-2-oriented but in which MMPI-2 data will be collected. For example, domestic violence is a social problem of considerable magnitude in the United States. Recent events have called national attention to the importance of predicting and preventing domestic violence. We expect that agencies would be interested in sponsoring research concerning the prediction of such violence, and the MMPI-2 could be one of the instruments used in such research.

Training

Because most forensic applications of the MMPI-2 involve members of both the mental health and legal professions, both professions should be considered in the development of training resources. The most basic issue is how to ensure that persons who will be involved in using the MMPI-2 in forensic settings have the training necessary to understand the strengths and weaknesses of the instrument so that they will use it appropriately and effectively.

PSYCHOLOGISTS

Given the litigious nature of contemporary society, it is likely that most psychologists involved in service delivery, and some who are not, will find themselves involved in situations in which they are using the MMPI-2 to address psycholegal issues. It is important that these psychologists have adequate training to permit them to use the MMPI-2 effectively. They need to know the purposes for which the test should and should not be used, the research base underlying forensic applications of the MMPI-2, and the strengths and weaknesses of the instrument. Although courts have not been very critical in asking for evidence that the MMPI-2 is valid for the purposes for which it is being used (Ogloff, this volume), it is essential that the psychologists using the test are well informed about such matters so that they can present information effectively without overstating the validity and generalizability of their MMPI-2 interpretations.

The Ethical Principles of Psychologists and Code of Conduct (American Psychological Association [APA], 1992) and the Specialty Guidelines for Forensic Psychologists (American Psychology-Law Society, 1991) both state clearly that psychologists should limit their activities to those for which they are properly trained and experienced. The important question is what constitutes proper training. Although most graduate training programs in clinical psychology include instruction concerning the MMPI-2 in their curricula (Moreland & Dahlstrom, 1983), typically the instrument is covered along with others in a single quarter- or semester-long course. It seems likely that this approach to training does not permit enough time to address specifically forensic applications of the MMPI-2. Forensic psychology courses are not required in most training programs, and when they are, general issues (e.g., insanity, competency) are addressed, and it is not likely that the applicability of the MMPI-2 receives major attention.

What then do we see as desirable training for psychologists who are likely to find themselves in situations in which they will be using the MMPI-2 to address psycholegal issues? Given the popularity of the MMPI-2 in general clinical and forensic practice, we believe that graduate training programs should include a semester-long course (or its equivalent) devoted to the MMPI-2. In addition to addressing issues such as reliability and validity of the test, the course should include a significant component devoted to forensic applications. The students should also have some practical experiences concerning the application of the MMPI-2 to forensic issues. These experiences could involve supervised forensic assessments or a laboratory component in which they can become familiar with the use of the MMPI-2 in relation to forensic issues. Failure to provide graduate students with minimal preparation for using the MMPI-2 in general clinical and forensic practice is a disservice to future practitioners who will need the information that such a course would provide.

Students who aspire to more extensive forensic practice, of course, should have even more MMPI-2 training specific to that goal. In addition to the course described above, they should have supervised experience in conducting forensic assessments. They also should choose internships that emphasize forensic activities and conduct thesis and dissertation research on forensic topics. Given the other requirements of clinical training programs, it seems likely that specialized training in forensic psychology will have to take place at a postdoctoral level. However, there are several graduate training programs in the United States and Canada that offer doctoral-level training with specializations in forensic psychology. There also are some programs in which students earn degrees in both psychology and law.[1] Finally, psychologists who aspire to full-time forensic practice should strongly consider pursuing postdoctoral specialty certification from the American Board of Professional Psychology, which awards the Diploma in Forensic Psychology.

Realizing that most clinicians who use the MMPI-2 in forensic settings have not and will not receive even the minimal training described above, how might they prepare themselves for using the MMPI-2 for such applications? Several continuing education programs are currently available for this purpose. Workshops conducted by APA continuing education sponsors, such as the MMPI-2 Workshops & Symposia at the University of Minnesota or the American Academy of Forensic Psychology, often include applied training in forensic applications of the MMPI-2.

OTHER PROFESSIONS

Psychologists are not the only professionals who use and deal with the MMPI-2 in relation to legal issues. Psychiatrists, counselors, and social workers often use MMPI-2 data in reaching opinions about persons involved in legal matters. Lawyers, judges, referees, and other legal professionals also deal with MMPI-2 data. These professionals need MMPI-2 training if they are to understand MMPI-2-based opinions in legal matters.

Although members of these other professions sometimes attend MMPI-2 workshops and research presentations, typically they will not be attracted to continuing education programs in which the focus is specifically on a particular psychological test. It is more likely that they would be interested in some MMPI-2 training if it were integrated into programs addressing more general legal issues. For example, a legal workshop concerning child custody could include a component concerning the use of the MMPI-2 for assessment of parents involved in such proceedings. Or a workshop concerning expert witnesses could have a component dealing with expert testimony based on MMPI-2 data. Psychologists should take the initiative to try to have such components included in workshops offered by other professional groups, such as bar associations, state and national judicial colleges, the National Organization of Forensic Social Workers, the American Academy of Psychiatry and the Law, and the National Council of Juvenile and Family Court Judges.

Another effective way of communicating information concerning forensic applications of the MMPI-2 would be to prepare review articles for legal journals. Legal professionals are much more likely to read such articles than those appearing in psychology journals. It might also be quite helpful to the legal profession to have available some generic legal briefs concerning the application of the MMPI-2 to various psycholegal issues. Such briefs could be prepared in advance and be easily accessible when they are relevant to a particular legal case.

General Conclusions

Although some professionals use the MMPI-2 inappropriately in relation to legal issues, the instrument can be used with confidence to address relevant aspects of forensic evaluations. First, the MMPI-2 is probably the most effective tool available to assess response sets or distortions. In situations in which persons are very likely to have strong motivation to distort the manner in which they present themselves, having a way to assess the honesty and accuracy of their self-descriptions can be extremely valuable. Second, the MMPI was designed to assess clinical condition, and the MMPI-2 is well suited for this purpose as well. MMPI-2 data can add significantly to our understanding of the emotional status of persons involved in legal matters. Third, MMPI-2 data can be used to generate descriptions and hypotheses about behaviors and characteristics that can have a direct bearing on a particular legal issue.

Although there is a significant research base underlying the interpretations of MMPI-2 data, most of the research has been conducted in mental health or medical settings rather than in forensic ones. More research is needed to determine to what extent findings from the mental health settings can be generalized to forensic settings. In addition, it will be important to determine more exactly the utility of the MMPI-2 in addressing particular legal issues (e.g., insanity, competence, custody).

Although most psychologists receive some graduate training concerning the MMPI-2, the training often is inadequate and not specifically relevant to forensic applications of the instrument. Graduate training programs should recognize that most psychologists, whether or not they choose to specialize in forensic psychology, will find themselves in circumstances in which they will use the MMPI-2 to address forensic issues. Greater emphasis on forensic applications of the MMPI-2 in graduate training programs is indicated. Because other professionals also deal with MMPI-2 data and/or testimony, psychologists should make efforts to ensure that these professionals are informed about appropriate and inappropriate uses of the MMPI-2 in relation to forensic issues.

In his critical review of the MMPI-2 in the *Eleventh Mental Measurements Yearbook,* Archer (1992) concluded that "the psychodiagnostician selecting a structured inventory for the first time will find no competing assessment device for abnormal psychology has stronger credentials for clinical description and prediction" (p. 567). Based on the information presented in this volume and discussions that took place at the Sixth Annual Kent Psychology Forum in 1994, we believe that a similar statement could be made concerning the use of the MMPI-2 in forensic assessment. Although there are limitations to the use of the MMPI-2 for such purposes and more research is needed to determine more exactly how the MMPI-2 relates to specific forensic issues, the MMPI-2 is clearly the most useful personality test available for the assessment of persons in forensic settings.

Note

1. For more information concerning forensic psychology and joint psychology/law training programs, contact the Training and Careers Committee of the American Psychology-Law Society.

References

American Psychological Association. (1992). *Ethical principles of psychologists and code of conduct.* Washington DC: Author.

American Psychology-Law Society. (1991). Speciality guidelines for forensic psychologists. *Law and Human Behavior, 15,* 655-665.

Archer, R. P. (1992). Minnesota Multiphasic Personality Inventory-2. In J. J. Kramer & J. C. Conoley (Eds.). *Eleventh mental measurements yearbook* (pp. 558-562). Lincoln, NE: Buros Institute of Mental Measurements.

Ben-Porath, Y. S., Butcher, J. N., & Graham, J. R. (1991). Contribution of the MMPI-2 content scales to the differential diagnosis pf psychopathology. *Psychological Assessment: A Journal of Consulting and Clinical Psychology, 1,* 345-347.

Ben-Porath, Y. S., Shrondrick, D. D., & Stafford, K. P. (1995). MMPI-2 and race in a forensic diagnostic center. *Criminal Justice and Behavior, 22,* 19-32.

Butcher, J. N. (1979). Use of the MMPI in personel selection. In J. N. Butcher (Ed.), *New developments in the use of the MMPI-2* (pp. 165-201). Minneapolis: University of Minnesota Press.

Dahlstrom, W. G., Lachar, D., & Dahlstrom, L. E. (1986). *MMPI patterns of American minorities.* Minneapolis: University of Minnesota Press.

Garb, H. N. (1984). The incremental validity of information used in personality assessment. *Clinical Psychology Review, 4,* 641-655.

Graham, J., Watts, D., & Timbrook, R. (1991). Detecting fake good and fake bad MMPI-2 profiles. *Journal of Personality Assessment, 57,* 264-277.

Graham, J. R. (1993). *MMPI-2: Assessing personality and psychopathology* (2nd ed.). New York: Oxford University Press.

Heilbrun, A. B. (1994). *A new model of criminal dangerousness: Toward an understanding of violence and recidivism.* Unpublished manuscript, Emory University, Atlanta, GA.

Henrichs, T. F. (1981). Using the MMPI in medical consultation. In J. N. Butcher, W. G. Dahlstrom, M. D. Gynther, & S. Schofield (Eds.), *Clinical Notes on the MMPI.* Minneapolis, MN: National Computer Systems.

Lees-Haley, P. (1992b). Psychodiagnostic test usage by forensic psychologists. *American Journal of Forensic Psychology, 10,* 25-30.

Megargee, E. I., & Bohn, M. J., Jr. (with Meyer, J., Jr., & Sink, F.). (1979). *Classifying criminal offenders: A new system based on the MMPI.* Beverly Hills, CA: Sage.

Megargee, E. I., Cook, P. E., & Mendelsohn, G. A. (1967). Development and validation of an MMPI scale of assaultiveness in overcontrolled individuals. *Journal of Abnormal Psychology, 72,* 519-528.

Moreland, K. L., & Dahlstrom, W. G. (1983). A survey of MMPI teaching in APA-approved clinical training programs. *Journal of Personality Assessment, 47,* 115-119.

Nichols, D. S. (1992). Minnesota Multiphasic Personality Inventory-2. In J. J. Kramer & J. C. Conoley (Eds.), *Eleventh mental measurements yearbook* (pp. 562-565). Lincoln, NE: Buros Mental Measurement Institute.

Nicholson, R. A., & Kugler, K. E. (1991). Competent and incompetent criminal defendants: A quantitative review of comparative research. *Psychological Bulletin, 111,* 355-370.

Pope, K. S., Butcher, J. N., & Seelen, J. (1993). *The MMPI, MMPI-2, & MMPI-A in court.* Washington, DC: American Psychological Association.

Spiro, A., Bosse, R., Butcher, J. N., Levenson, M. R., & Aldwin, C. M. (1993, August). *Personality change over five years: The MMPI-2 in older men.* Paper presented at the 101st Annual Convention of the American Psychological Association, Toronto, Ontario, Canada.

Webb, J. T., Levitt, E. E., & Rajdev, R. (1993, March). *After three years: A comparison of the clinical use of the MMPI and MMPI-2.* Paper presented at the 53rd Annual Meeting of the Society for Personality Assessment, San Francisco, CA.

Index

About the Editors

Yossef S. Ben-Porath is Associate Professor of Psychology at Kent State University. His research interests involve assessment and forensic psychology. He has published books on the MMPI-2 and MMPI-A and is coeditor of a recently published Sage book on memory and testimony in the child witness.

John R. Graham, Professor and Chair of Psychology at Kent State University, is a world-renowned authority on the Minnesota Multiphasic Personality Inventory (MMPI). He is the author of the internationally acclaimed book, *MMPI-2: Assessing Personality and Psychopathology.*

Gordon C. N. Hall is Associate Professor of Psychology at Kent State University. His research interests are in sexual aggression and in ethnic minority issues. He recently edited *Sexual Aggression: Issues in Etiology, Assessment, and Treatment.* He is President of the Society for the Psychological Study of Ethnic Minority Issues, Division 45 of the American Psychological Association.

Richard D. Hirschman is Professor of Psychology and former Director of Clinical Training in the Department of Psychology at Kent State University. His training is in clinical and community psychology and psychophysiology, and he has published numerous articles in these areas. Currently, his primary research is on sexual aggression.

Maria S. Zaragoza is Associate Professor of Psychology at Kent State University. Since 1985, she has been a major contributor to research on the suggestibility of eyewitness memory in both children and adults, as evidenced by her publication in edited volumes and leading journals in the field. Her research on suggestibility is funded by grants from the National Institute of Mental Health.

About the Contributors

David T. R. Berry, PhD, is Associate Professor in the Department of Psychology at the University of Kentucky, where he is currently the director of the clinical training program. His research interests include detection of invalid response sets in psychological and neuropsychological testing. He has an active private practice in forensic clinical neuropsychology.

James N. Butcher, PhD, is currently Professor in the Department of Psychology at the University of Minnesota. He received an MA in experimental psychology in 1962 and a PhD in clinical psychology in 1964 from the University of North Carolina at Chapel Hill. He is a member of the University of Minnesota Press's MMPI Consultative Committee. He is currently the editor of *Psychological Assessment* and serves as consulting editor for numerous other journals in psychology and psychiatry. He is a Fellow of the American Psychological Association and the Society for Personality Assessment. He is the author of numerous articles and 34 books, many on the MMPI/MMPI-2, including (with C. L. Williams) *MMPI-2 and MMPI-A: Essentials of Clinical Interpretation* (1992) and (with K. S. Pope and J. Seelen) *MMPI/MMPI-2/MMPI-A in Court: Assessment, Testimony, and Cross-Examination for Expert Witnesses and Attorneys* (1993).

Robert Collins is a graduate student in the doctoral program in clinical psychology at the University of South Florida. His interests include psychological assessment and behavioral medicine.

Joyce L. Carbonell is an Associate Professor in the Department of Psychology at Florida State University. She received her doctoral degree in clinical psychology from Bowling Green State University and completed an internship at Baylor College of Medicine. She previously served as the Director of the Florida State University Psychology Clinic and is currently director of the Florida State University Crisis Management Unit. She has been the principal and co-principal investigator on numerous grants and has been the recipient of several university teaching awards. She has conducted research concerning factors associated with adjustment to prison, prediction of dangerous behavior, and longitudinal studies of criminal and violent behavior.

Alfred B. Heilbrun, Jr. is currently Professor Emeritus in the Department of Psychology, Emory University, having previously served as Emory's Director of Clinical Training in psychology. He has conducted programmatic research in the areas of counseling readiness, psychological assessment, sex role stereotypes, eating and substance use disorders, schizophrenia, and dangerousness in criminal offenders. He is a Fellow of the American Psychological Association and a Diplomate in Clinical and Forensic Psychology, American Board of Professional Psychology.

Kirk Heilbrun is currently Professor and Codirector in the Law and Psychology Program, Department of Psychology, Medical College of Pennsylvania, Hahnemann University. His research and practice interests include forensic mental health assessment, aggression risk assessment, and the treatment of mentally disordered offenders. He is a Fellow of the American Psychological Association and a Diplomate in Clinical and Forensic Psychology, American Board of Professional Psychology.

Geoffrey R. McKee, PhD ABPP, is Chief Psychologist at the William S. Hall Psychiatric Institute and Associate Professor of Psychiatry at the University of South Carolina School of Medicine.

Edwin I. Megargee, PhD, CCHP, is Professor of Psychology at Florida State University. He earned his BA *magna cum laude* from Amherst College and his PhD from the University of California at Berkeley. The author of over 100 books, chapters, and journal articles on correctional assessment, he has consulted with numerous criminal justice agencies in the United States and Great Britain, including the Federal Bureau of Prisons and the United States Secret

Service. He was awarded the Second Annual Award for Significant Research on the MMPI from the University of Minnesota in 1987 and has received lifetime achievement awards from the American Association of Correctional Psychologists (1985) and the National Commission on Correctional Health Care (1994).

Linda D. Nelson is Associate Professor in the Department of Psychiatry at the University of California, Irvine, where much of her clinical work and teaching is currently in the areas of forensic neuropsychology and clinincal neuropsychological assessment. She received her doctoral degree in clinical psychology from Ohio State University, where she worked in the areas of test construction/validation and personality assessment. Following her doctoral training, she went on to complete a 2-year postdoctoral fellowship in neuropsychology at the University of California, Los Angeles. Dr. Nelson has published extensively on use of personality tests, including the MMPI/MMPI-2, in clinical and neurological populations. She also has expertise in the field of test development and test validation. Among her many accomplishments is a test, which is one of the first to effectively measure personality change in severe brain-damaged individuals.

James R. P. Ogloff, JD, PhD, received his PhD in psychology and his JD from the University of Nebraska-Lincoln. He is a registered psychologist in British Columbia. He has worked in the areas of forensic psychology; experimental/social psychology; law, ethics, and issues of professional responsibility; and the development of training in law and psychology. Dr. Ogloff is Associate Professor and Associate Chair in the Department of Psychology at Simon Faser University, and Associate Member of the School of Criminology. He also holds an appointment as Adjunct Professor of Law at the University of British Columbia. He coordinates the graduate program in law and psychology. He serves as a director of the Canadian Psychological Association and is Chair of the Committee of Ethics. He currently serves on the editorial boards of four journals.

Randy Otto, PhD, is Assistant Professor in the Department of Mental Health Law & Policy, Florida Mental Health Institute, University of South Florida and Adjunct Assistant Professor at Stetson University College of Law. Dr. Otto is a licensed psychologist and Diplomate in Forensic Psychology, American Board of Professional Psychology. Before joining the University of South

Florida faculty, he was a Postdoctoral Fellow in the Law/Psychology Program at the University of Nebraska. His research and clinical interests include forensic assessment and the quality of testimony and reports provided to the legal system, risk assessment, and clinical judgment and decision making.

Richard Rogers, PhD, ABPP, is Professor of Psychology and Director of Clincial Training at the University of North Texas. He is the recipient of the Distinguished Contributions to Forensic Psychology Award from the American Academy of Forensic Psychology, the Guttmacher Award from the American Psychiatric Association, and the Amicus Award from the American Academy of Psychiatry and Law.

Kathleen P. Stafford, PhD, is a clinical psychologist with the Diplomate in Forensic Psychology from the American Board of Professional Psychology. She has faculty appointments in the Department of Psychology at Kent State University and Northeastern Ohio Universities College of Medicine. She is president of the American Academy of Forensic Psychology and Chair of the Educational Outreach Committee for the American Psychology-Law Society (APA Division 41). She directs the Court Psycho-Diagnostic Clinic in Akron, Ohio and maintains a private consulting practice in forensic psychology.

Irving B. Weiner, PhD, is Clinical Professor of Psychiatry and Behavioral Medicine at the University of South Florida in Tampa, where he is currently in the private practice of clinical and forensic psychology. He is an American Board of Professional Psychology Diplomate in Clinical Psychology and a Fellow of the American Psychological Association. For many years he has been concerned, both as a scholar and a practitioner, with psychodiagnostic assessment and forensic issues. He served as the editor of the *Journal of Personality Assessment* from 1985 to 1993 and since 1990 has been the editor of *Rorschachiana: Yearbook of the International Rorschach Society.* His books include *Psychodiagnosis in Schizophrenia* (1966), *Rorschach Handbook of Clinical and Research Applications* (1971), *Clinical Methods* (1976, 1983), *Rorschach Assessment of Children and Adolescents* (1982, 1995), and *Handbook of Forensic Psychology* (1987).